D0544970

Developing Professional Practice 14–19

The Corey Centre
Canterbury College
New Dover Road
Canterbury, Kent CT1 3AJ

CLASS No. 374.1102.DEV

BOOK No. 153329

LOAN PERIOD 3W

SHELF Main Collection

Canterbury College

153329

Developing Professional Practice series

The *Developing Professional Practice* series provides a thoroughly comprehensive and cutting edge guide to developing the necessary knowledge, skills and understanding for working within the 0–7, 7–14 or 14–19 age ranges. Each of the three titles offers a genuinely accessible and engaging introduction to supporting the education of babies to young adults. Discussion of current developments in theory, policy and research is combined with guidance on the practicalities of working with each age group. Numerous examples of real practice are included throughout each text.

The *Developing Professional Practice* titles each provide a complete resource for developing professional understanding and practice that will be invaluable for all those involved with the education of children from birth to 19 years.

Titles in the series:

Blandford and Knowles, *Developing Professional Practice 0–7*

Wilson and Kendall-Seatter, *Developing Professional Practice 7–14*

Armitage, Donovan, Flanagan and Poma, *Developing Professional Practice 14–19*

Developing Professional Practice 14–19

Andy Armitage, Gina Donovan, Karen Flanagan and Sabrina Poma

Canterbury Christ Church University and Kent County Council

Longman
is an imprint of

Harlow, England • London • New York • Boston • San Francisco • Toronto • Sydney • Singapore • Hong Kong
Tokyo • Seoul • Taipei • New Delhi • Cape Town • Madrid • Mexico City • Amsterdam • Munich • Paris • Milan

Pearson Education Limited
Edinburgh Gate
Harlow
Essex CM20 2JE
England

and Associated Companies throughout the world

Visit us on the World Wide Web at:
www.pearsoned.co.uk

First published 2011

© Pearson Education Limited 2011

The rights of Andy Armitage, Gina Donovan, Karen Flanagan and Sabrina Poma to be
identified as authors of this Work have been asserted by them in accordance with the
Copyright, Designs and Patents Act 1988.

All rights reserved. No part of this publication may be reproduced, stored in a retrieval system,
or transmitted in any form or by any means, electronic, mechanical, photocopying, recording or
otherwise, without either the prior written permission of the publisher or a licence permitting
restricted copying in the United Kingdom issued by the Copyright Licensing Agency Ltd, Saffron
House, 6–10 Kirby Street, London EC1N 8TS.

All trademarks used therein are the property of their respective owners. The use of any
trademark in this text does not vest in the author or publisher any trademark ownership rights
in such trademarks, nor does the use of such trademarks imply any affiliation with or
endorsement of this book by such owners.

Pearson Education is not responsible for the content of third part internet sites.

ISBN 978-1-4058-4116-0

British Library Cataloguing-in-Publication Data
A catalogue record for this book is available from the British Library

Library of Congress Cataloguing-in-Publication Data
A catalog record for this book is available from the Library of Congress

Developing professional practice, 14-19 / Andy Armitage . . . [et al.].
    p.   cm.
  ISBN 978-1-4058-4116-0 (pbk.)
  1. High school teachers--Training of--Great Britain.   2. Teachers--Professional
relationships--Great Britain.   3. Effective teaching--Great Britain.   I. Armitage,
Andy, 1950-
  LB1777.4.G72D48 2011
  373.1102--dc22
                                                              2010052053

10 9 8 7 6 5 4 3 2 1
14 13 12 11

Typeset in 9.75/12pt Giovanni Book by 35
Printed by Ashford Colour Press Ltd., Gosport

Brief Contents

Supporting resources

Visit **www.pearsoned.co.uk/14-19** to find valuable online resources

Companion Website for students
- Interactive chapter tutorials
- Podcast interviews with students and practitioners
- Self-study questions to test and extend your knowledge
- Extra case studies
- Online glossary defining key terms

For instructors
- Downloadable PowerPoint slides for use in presentations

For more information please contact your local Pearson Education sales representative or visit **www.pearsoned.co.uk/14-19**

Contents

Guided Tour

CHAPTER 11 Reflecting on Learning

In this chapter, you will:
• Understand the debate about the effectiveness of reflective practice as a tool for teacher development
• Become familiar with the key principles of learning from experience
• Be acquainted with the views of two key theorists, Schön and Brookfield
• Examine the qualities of effective reflective practice
• Consider the process of recording reflection

Pearson Education Ltd/Jon Wedgwood

Each chapter begins with a list of **Learning objectives**, providing a quick overview of what will be covered and clearly setting out the key learning goals.

Case Study boxes present vignettes that give an insight into real practice. The short questions posed in the **What Do You Think?** boxes provide regular opportunities to stop and reflect on what you've learnt.

---

30   CHAPTER 2 COMMUNITIES OF LEARNERS

CASE STUDY

Peer learning in 14–19 education context: the 'study buddy' scheme at Lewisham College of Further Education

Since the early 2000s, Lewisham College, in South London, has established a learning support 'study buddy' scheme. The aim of this learning support is to use students to help others within the same or a lower-level class. The scheme has evolved from one-to-one support to group peer learning. The College wanted to establish a 'community' where individual skills, experiences and learning issues could be shared and complemented. The teaching/learning support offered is not dissimilar to 'classroom assistant' work except that helpers are identified within the same or upper level of studies. They have therefore first-hand experience of the subject and learning process. In some areas such as Construction, study buddies offer more practical teaching and learning and fully support the tutor. Study buddies are initially trained and have regular feedback sessions with the support team. 'Helped' students also participate in the evaluation process where an individual study buddy's contribution is identified and discussed.

Mutual benefits for both study buddy and student include:
• the improvement of communication skills
• gaining confidence in the subject matter
• greater understanding of the learning process.

The scheme 'regenerates' every year; in time, 'helped' students are encouraged to become 'helpers' or study buddies themselves. This cycle contributes to the creation of a community of learners.

Informal learning

WHAT DO YOU THINK?

What would you say counts as formal and informal learning?

In an education system which relies entirely on accumulation of credentials, it may be difficult to consider the contribution of informal learning. However, the place for informal learning for 14–19 learners is not to be neglected. From previous examples seen in this chapter there is strong evidence that effective learning can occur outside the classroom. There is also no doubt that learning does not need to be contained within a 'scheme' or 'programme' and happens as a result of life events or professional practice. This experience gained is unfortunately left invalidated and mostly unused by the educational system. It is fair to say that, in educational settings, little is made of the very valuable lessons that life offers.

Currently, the recognition of prior learning is mostly limited to an APL (Accreditation of Prior Learning) system. It means that previously acquired qualifications are used as

---

DEVELOPMENT THEORIES   53

Theories of development traditionally focused on birth through childhood, and expected milestones were fairly rigorously applied in order to make comparative judgements. It is now recognised that while general models or patterns can be applied, individuals develop at differing rates and at differing times. Young people therefore should be seen as individuals who will develop in different ways and in different time spans. Thomas Keenan, a development psychologist, proposed the principle of **multidirectionality** (2002), and maintains there is no single 'normal' path for development, and particularly in adulthood some aspects of cognitive development improve as others decline or mature at a different rate. This has particular implications during adolescence. Research suggests intellectual capacity and ability matures before psychosocial development during adolescence. Key areas that make life difficult for teenagers, and indeed those around them, are:

• Poor impulse control
• Reduced ability to delay gratification, and
• Vulnerability to peer pressure.

RESEARCH FOCUS

The MacArthur Foundation Research Network on Adolescent Development and Juvenile Justice in the USA has conducted research that suggests that adolescents should be dealt with differently in the juvenile system (www.fairsentencingforyouth.org). They do not see this as an excuse for criminal activity, but feel that the legal system should recognise the impact that differing intellectual and psychosocial development can have on the decision-making process, particularly that of culpability – that is, the blameworthiness of an individual. In 2005 a landmark ruling outlawed the death penalty for offenders who were younger than 18 when they committed their crimes.

The idea of mitigating circumstances when meting out punishment is not new. If we apply the logic behind this research to school and educational setting in the UK, this could have an impact on the type of punishment young people receive in relation to their acts. This poses some interesting questions as to whether the punishment is disproportionate to the 'crime'. In particular, it raises questions about the disproportionate impact of exclusion and future life chances. What do you think? Should the immaturity of decision-making processes, the susceptibility to peer pressure and a reduced ability to delay gratification be taken into consideration when dealing with unwanted adolescent behaviour?

Theories of development and learning are of enormous importance and use to educators and in particular for their training. The current focus of initial teacher training on the practical skills required for classroom teaching has reduced the light that subjects such as sociology, psychology and philosophy can throw on teaching and

Research focus explores classic and contemporary research studies, and examines their applications in the classroom.

The **Activity** feature includes questions and activities that encourage you to interrogate core issues, and reflect on their influence on your attitudes and your practice.

THE CONCEPT OF 'ADOLESCENCE' **57**

The term 'teenager', referring to a separate and defined stage, emerged in the 1940s as a result of the recognition of a consumer market (Hine 1999). Thomas Hine explores the concept of adolescence as a period that has led to the justification of the delay of maturity and of deferred 'adult' responsibility. This is made worse by the lengthening of dependency, particularly that of economic dependency.

It is clear that the period between childhood and adulthood has lengthened from that of milestones or other rites of passage that denoted the end of childhood, for example recognition of sexual maturity with a girl's first menarche, or recognition of adult status when stepping over the threshold after marriage. This process is complicated by the acceptance of 'adulthood' as a term, without formal examination or clarification over what this means. When are you an adult? You can have sex at 17, die for your country at 17 but not buy cigarettes or alcohol.

Thomas Hine in his book *The Rise and Fall of the American Teenager* (1999) felt that many young people are resistant to the idea of responsibility and feel that they 'deserve' a period of freedom. Consider the increase in the idea of a gap year, for example, before settling down into the weightiness of responsibility.

ACTIVITY

How do today's teenage years differ from your own?

- Describe the differences and illustrate these with examples – e.g. young people's socialising especially with the use and access to technology.
- What are the similarities – for example, arguing over curfew times?
- What do you think are the major challenges for young people?
- Do you think 'adulthood' can be specified by age or by the completion of 'tasks' – for example, marriage, or being financially and emotionally independent? Or can adulthood be attained after a prolonged period of 'maturity'? Is it a state of being?

Notions of responsibility are a central theme in our society, especially with regards to individuals devolving 'blame' and judging the worthiness, or not, of others to 'deserve' help. Craig Newnes and Nick Radcliffe in their compelling book *Making and Breaking Children's Lives* (2005) make a strong case for the way children, particularly those who are the responsibility of us all as corporate parents, are 'hurt in modern society', as the importance of psychosocial aspects of development is minimised in the rush to prescribe drugs and medically diagnose and label young people. A clear example of the 'nonsense' of responsibility is illustrated by Newnes and Radcliffe in their opening chapter – 'children and adolescents are urged to be more responsible despite the remarkable complexity of the strictly legal interpretation of the expression: a child can be found guilty of murder aged 10, but cannot drive until they are 17' (2005: 33). The recognition of societal and cultural influence is particularly important when we consider that achievement gaps between socio-economic groups, while relatively minor as children start school, have tripled by the time these children reach 10 years old.

---

60 CHAPTER 4 DEVELOPMENT AND LEARNING

stimulated and channelled into positive activity, especially as they mature and develop their cognitive and psychosocial skills.

Development tasks and challenges of the adolescent

The main challenges of adolescence are those of adapting to change, including that of:

- biological maturity
- the development of personal identity
- the establishment of intimate sexual relationships
- working towards independence and autonomy.

These challenges and changes can be frightening for individuals and can be somewhat paradoxical as they strive for personal identity and individuation as well as express a need to be accepted, included and 'normal'. The development of abstract thought can lead to personal questioning such as 'Who am I?', 'Am I valued?', 'Am I clever?' and 'Am I normal?' Reassurance in these areas is important for the development of self-esteem. Body image is increasingly becoming an issue for young people. For girls, in particular, who naturally develop body fat as part of puberty, self-esteem can be linked to body image. While girls are more likely to suffer from a range of eating disorders, this is no longer a solely female issue, especially with the existence of the 'ideal body size and shapes' that are so strongly featured in the media. The need to be liked and 'normal' means that peers begin to have far more influence than families or teachers.

IN PRACTICE

Paul is 15 years old. He was until recently a quiet member of the class. Lately he has been arguing with his teacher and not getting on with his work. He constantly talks to his friends during sessions, refuses to take out his earphones and is becoming increasingly rude to his teacher, especially when he asks him to focus, or to stop talking. Quite a lot of his comments are tactless, which makes his teacher feel increasingly upset and a little angry, especially as many of Paul's friends seem to find these comments funny.

Paul's teacher is not sure what to do and does not understand why Paul is acting this way – especially as he has taught Paul since he was 11 and, as he points out, 'he hasn't changed'.

Discuss this scenario with an experienced teacher or your mentor and together:

- Identify three possible reasons that may have contributed to the change in Paul's behaviour and attitude
- Identify two strategies the teacher could try to reduce these behaviours.

The following table outlines the main developmental tasks for the adolescent.

The **In Practice** feature helps you to make direct connections between the chapter content and your own classroom experience.

---

254 CHAPTER 14 INCLUDING ALL LEARNERS FOR INDEPENDENT LEARNING

directed at listening to individuals nor to taking account of public wishes or needs but at polling and marketing, spinning and selling in a kind of democratised consumerism where we can choose how best to position ourselves as producers and products in competitive markets.

In this chapter it is important to understand that inclusion relates to the high profile of the individual's needs and wishes in our society and the widespread notion that we have many rights. Alongside this come responsibilities, and the 14–19 phase teacher supporting learners with decisions about their futures is working in a challenging context. Inclusion is now central to educational principle and practice (The National Curriculum Inclusion Statement, DfEE/QCA 1999) and it is valuable to give critical consideration as to how we view the implications of this in our work as teachers.

DISCUSSION POINT

What can **inclusion** achieve?

Inclusion requires that schools and teachers establish ways of working that actively secure the fullest participation of all learners – both in curricular and social terms. It is incumbent upon institutional and individual attitudes to change, rather than an expectation that a pupil who is at risk of marginalisation because of issues of 'race', religion, gender or sexual orientation will be moulded to 'fit' pre-existing conditions and arrangements within a school.

Commentary

The concept and practice of educational inclusion has become the prevailing initiative in education systems throughout Western Europe. It has been driven by a commitment to the rights of all learners to secure those opportunities to enable them to function as equal participants in twenty-first-century society.

Inclusive practice in education has been influenced by far wider and international notions of human rights. In the past few years increasing importance has been placed on inclusive principles by national and local governments. A significant number of academics, administrators, politicians, parents and practitioners have come to regard the approach as the single most effective means of combating discriminatory attitudes, creating welcoming communities and building an inclusive society (Multiverse 2009).

Do you agree with the final statement? You may wish to research alternative views on effective approaches: for example, the view that questions attempt to include or fit the excluded groups and individuals within the existing structures which originally excluded them. Instead consider the case for changing the society and its structures more radically.

For a range of views, read Edwards and Armstrong (2001), Labonte (2004) and Jupp (1992).

Discussion Point boxes tackle the more divisive topics, encouraging you to examine both sides of the argument and helping you to form your own point of view.

Guided Tour continued

The emphasis on applied learning in the diplomas raises two important issues in relation to student learning styles. Firstly, many of the aspects of the broader notion of applied learning as described above by Harkin would be best suited to an andragogical approach to learning in its emphasis on self-directedness, experience as a prime focus for learning and real-life situations as desirable learning contexts. Secondly, will the emphasis on the active, experiential dimension of applied learning lead to those with certain learning profiles, Kolb's divergers and accommodators, finding this approach to learning more preferable and disenfranchise the convergers and assimilators who would be less suited to it?

SUMMARY

It is easy to understand the attraction of the notion of individual learning styles to teachers, trainers and institutions faced with the challenge of meeting the learning needs of a range of individual learners. It is very tempting to believe that the administration of a particular learning style inventory to students will produce clear individual profiles which can then be used to determine teaching strategies to be used with them. However, some studies have called into question the value of such measures. By considering a range of learning style models, the question has been posed as to whether it is possible to group together a consistent series of features of an individual's learning such that we can call it a 'style'. The instruments which claim to measure learning style have been examined and their claim to be able to do so, and do so consistently, scrutinised. Finally, the implications of andragogy, pedagogy, deep and surface learning and applied learning for teachers of 14–19-year-olds have been considered.

Find out more

Two reports for the Learning and Skills Research Centre by Frank Coffield and colleagues have been influential in shaping the views of practitioners about the value of the use of learning styles, learning models, inventories and questionnaires with students:

Coffield, F., Moseley, D., Hall, E. and Ecclestone, K. (2004) *Should We be Using Learning Styles: what research has to say to practice and Learning Styles and Pedagogy in Post 16 Learning: a systematic and critical review*. London: Learning and Skills Research Centre. Available at: www.lsrc.ac.uk/.

In spite of a highly critical analysis of 13 key learning style models in the second report, the authors come

to some very positive recommendations about the potential of using investigating learning styles:

A reliable and valid instrument which measures learning styles and approaches could be used as a tool to encourage self-development, not only by diagnosing how people learn, but by showing them how to enhance their learning.

We wish to recommend that consideration be given to developing for schools, colleges, universities and firms new programmes of study focused on human learning and how it can be fostered.

The tutors/trainers who involve their students/ staff in dialogue need to be knowledgeable about the strengths and limitations of the model they

---

End of chapter **Summary** boxes pull together the key topics covered in the chapter, to help consolidate your understanding.

The **Find out more** feature directs you to related additional reading and websites.

Introduction

Why 14–19?

This book is the third in a series aimed at developing professional understanding and practice for those involved with the education of children and young people from birth to 19 years. The current text focuses on the education of the 14–19 age group, partly because major education reforms throughout the decade have been concentrated on this age group but also because, with increasing numbers of 14–16-year-olds participating in learning in FE colleges and with schools involved in considerable curriculum change at Key Stage 4 onwards, the age group represents an increasingly identifiable educational phase with its own aims and purposes: a phase in which the major qualifications for progress to work and higher education are taken, a phase during which young people undertake the transition to adulthood. It is written at a time when there are unprecedented developments related to this phase. The introduction of new vocational, occupationally specific qualifications and pre-vocational or general vocational qualifications such as the diplomas, populating a Qualifications and Credit Framework (QCF) creating and accrediting these qualifications, together with the introduction and enhancement of existing academic qualifications, is reshaping the curriculum landscape. New bodies are becoming responsible, on both a local and national basis, for the funding of provision in the sector: the Young People's Learning Agency funds 16–19 education and all the academies' provision, while the Skills Funding Agency is responsible for funding the education and training of adults 20+. Institutions in the sector are collaborating in the delivery of programmes such as the diplomas, FE colleges working with schools, adult and community learning services and work-based learning providers. Students are therefore learning and teachers teaching in a wider, more diversified set of contexts in the sector than before. Teachers are being required to play a much wider set of roles than previously because of these varied contexts and changing curriculum.

The book is aimed at all of those teaching and training young people in this age group. You may be following a course of initial teacher training either pre-service or in-service, such as the PGCE (11–18, 14–19, Post-Compulsory), Preparing to Teach in the Lifelong Learning Sector (PTLLS), Certificate in Teaching in the Lifelong Learning Sector (CTLLS) or Diploma in Teaching in the Lifelong Learning Sector (DTLLS). You may be pursuing a formal programme of continuing professional development such as a BA, MA or MTL, or be involved in shorter, more informal professional development activity. Those seeking Associate Teacher Learning and Skills (ATLS) or Qualified Teacher Learning and Skills (QTLS) status, for those with an associate or full teacher role respectively, are required by the Institute for Learning to undertake continuing professional development to maintain their licence to practise and the text could provide support through that process.

The structure of this book

The book is divided into four themed parts.

Part 1, Influences on Teaching and Learning, sets 14–19 teaching in context by exploring the range of key factors which impact on learning and teaching. The part begins with a chapter which considers the contexts of teaching and learning in the 14–19 phase and considers that it could be described as a 'hybrid' phase across established institutions such as secondary schools, academies and FE colleges offering various 14–19 educational programmes and qualifications. The chapter considers this diversity of routes and qualifications on offer which appears as fragmented and disjointed but wonders whether the multiplicity of routes available is a potential strength of the UK educational system. Chapter 2 goes on to consider that it has been recognised that some learners would benefit from a different system in which learning can be accomplished through a variety of contexts, especially through the Diploma, leading to opportunities to develop a more social approach to learning in this phase. The chapter considers how conceiving of groups of 14–19 learners and their teachers as learning communities might enhance the experience of both. Chapter 3 examines why values are important aspects of the practitioner's professional identity, as well as the wider political and societal values which underpin teaching and learning and the organisations in which they are carried out. Chapter 4 considers aspects of development related to the 14–19 phase with a particular focus on adolescence. It considers what it describes as the key challenges of adolescence – biological maturity, development of personal identity, establishment of intimate sexual relationships and the development of independence and autonomy – and examines how they might impact on teaching and learning, particularly with regard to students' relationships with their peers and their teachers. Chapter 5 looks at the increasing emphasis on the individual learner through the promotion of personalised and applied learning.

Part 2, Teaching for Learning, considers the knowledge and understanding required of teachers of the 14–19 age group and the ways in which they need to apply this to a range of aspects of learning. Chapter 6 considers the nature of subject knowledge in the sector, the particular characteristics of specialisms, evaluates models of professional development and considers the professionalisation of the sector and the role of professional standards. Chapter 7 examines the diversity of learning environments and associated technologies, a diversity, it is argued, which is both

enriching and challenging depending on the outlook, expertise, resources and commitment of those involved. There is far wider recognition today, it is claimed, than in previous years, of the need to make learning relevant and to acknowledge that it can and does take place across a wider range of formal and informal environments. Chapter 8 offers a critical analysis of key learning style models, the major features of andragogy and pedagogy, the notions of deep and surface learning and the place of applied learning in the vocational diplomas. Chapter 9 examines behaviour management, in particular the identification of difficult or unwanted behaviour, teachers' own responses to behaviours, and explores practical strategies for promoting positive behaviours. Chapter 10 considers the importance of assessment *for* learning as opposed to *of* learning, the impact of assessment on learning, motivation and achievement, the importance of effective feedback on learning, the principles, methods and types of assessment and the impact of curriculum change on assessment.

Part 3, Enhancing Teaching for Learning, builds on the previous section by examining five aspects of professional practice seen as key for those working in the sector. Chapter 11 focuses on the importance of reflecting on learning as an activity in the development both of the student and of the practitioner. Chapter 12 looks at the role of research in professional contexts and the links with practice, arguing that research and enquiry are key tools of professional development. Chapter 13 considers the different levels of collaboration individuals and organisations are increasingly engaged in across and beyond their institutions. Chapter 14 examines inclusion and its importance in the 14–19 transformation agenda. Chapter 15 looks at the teacher's repertoire, particularly the teaching methods, teaching styles and range of key teaching roles which that repertoire is composed of.

Part 4, Learning Futures, considers current and future developments in the phase. Chapter 16 builds on Chapter 7, Environments for Learning, and asks whether learning technology enables us to address the opportunities and threats currently visible in the educational landscape and perhaps those as yet indistinct. Can learning technologies be categorised as somehow distinct from other aspects of teaching and learning without distorting our understanding of their place? Chapter 17 builds on Chapter 13, Collaborating to Promote Learning, in considering the current and likely future emphasis on partnership working, and investigating why partnership and collaboration are excellent in theory but that bringing about the best in the shared delivery of education and training has always been a challenge. Chapter 18 considers the international dimensions of 14–19 education both locally in the four nations and globally, focusing on both similar and contrasting features. Chapter 19 highlights those aspects of the teacher's role which are likely to be most affected in changing learning institutions: the requirement to personalise learning, the need to understand the features of assessment for learning, in particular the relationship between learning approaches and assessment strategies, a capacity to teach generic skills, an awareness of how information, advice and guidance might be given to students, the need to consider the challenges of working in collaboration and an awareness and understanding of the importance of reflective practice. Finally, Chapter 20 recognises that all teaching roles involve both leadership and management and considers the relationship between these two notions, aspects of good practice in management and leadership, the relationship of managerialism to professionalism, the importance of emotional competences and intelligence in working with other people and the importance of effective curriculum management to 14–19 delivery.

Acknowledgements

The authors would like to thank: Richard Archibald who provided the case study 'Study buddy' for Lewisham College in Chapter 2; Alison Cogger and Simon Cleary for the pen portrait in Chapter 6; Melanie Sibley for help with the case study in Chapter 12; Barbara Adewumi for the Individual Development Planner and Reflective Journal in Chapter 19; and the following reviewers.

Dylan Gwyer-Roberts, Bath Spa University
Alan Harding, University of Southampton
Professor Janet Hoskyns, Birmingham City University
Terry Hudson, Teach First Yorkshire and Sheffield Hallam University
Dr Liz Keeley-Browne, Oxford Brookes University
Dr Robert Lawy, University of Exeter
Charlotte Meierdirk, University of Portsmouth
Lynn Senior, University of Derby.

Publisher's acknowledgements

We are grateful to the following for permission to reproduce copyright material:

Picture Credits

The publisher would like to thank the following for their kind permission to reproduce their photographs:

(Key: b-bottom; c-centre; l-left; r-right; t-top)

Alamy Images: 367bc/18.2, Alamy Images 56bl/4.1; **Education Photos:** 149bc/8.2, 386tc/19.1; **Getty Images:** 26tc/2.2; **Pearson Education Ltd:** 1128/5.1, Ben Nicholson 37tr/3.2, Gareth Boden 98tc/6.1, Ian Wedgewood 1tc, 37tl/3.1, 47bc/3.3, 123tc/7.1, 202tc/11.2, 274bc/15.1, 287tc/15.2, 417tc/20.2, 337a, 338bc/17.1, Imagestate 359tc/18.1, Jules Selmes 142tc/8.1, Ken Wilson-Max 302bc/16.1, 504a, Lord and Leverett 232tc/13.1, 344tc/17.2, MindStudio 83tc/5.2, 133/7.3, 210tc/12.1, 391tc/19.2, 171309bc/10.1, Naki Kouyioumtzis 111tc/6.2, Photodisc 263tc/14.1, Rob Judges 8bc/1.1, 21bc/2.1, 238tl/13.2, Sophie Bluy 169, Studio 8 15tc/1.2, 75tc/5.1, 126tc/7.2, 216bc/12.2, Trevor Clifford 195tc/11.1, Tudor Photography 403tc/20.1

Cover images: *Front:* **Getty Images**

All other images © Pearson Education

Every effort has been made to trace the copyright holders and we apologise in advance for any unintentional omissions. We would be pleased to insert the appropriate acknowledgement in any subsequent edition of this publication.

Cartoons

Cartoon 9.2 from Ref: grin644, http://www.cartoonstock.com/cartoonview.asp?catref=grin644, CartoonStock.com, reproduced with permission.

Figures

Figure 4.1 from *Indicators of Social and Family Functioning*, Department of Family and Community Services, Canberra (Zubrick, S. R., Williams, A. A. and Silburn, S. R. 2000) Copyright Commonwealth of Australia reproduced by permission; Figures 6.1 and 15.4 adapted and reprinted from *Implementing mentoring schemes, chapter 1: Mentoring – Introduction and definitions* (Klasen, N. and Clutterbuck, D. 2001), p. 17, Copyright 2001, with permission from Elsevier.

Tables

Table 4.1 adapted from article published in *Forfar and Arneil's Textbook of Paediatrics* 6th ed., Churchill

Livingstone (McIntosh, N., Helms, P. and Smyth, R. (eds) 2003) 1757–68, Copyright Elsevier 2003, reproduced with permission; Table 4.2 adapted from *Psychology* 5th ed., Pearson Education (Lefton, L. 1994), pp. 4–6 © 1994 Allyn & Bacon. Reproduced by permission of Pearson Education, Inc. Table on pages 409–14 from Website for the Consortium for Research on Emotional Intelligence in Organizations, www.elconsortium.org/reports/emotional_competence_framework.html, reproduced with permission.

Text

Extract on page 100 from 'You wouldn't expect a maths teacher to teach plastering . . .', *Embedding literacy, language and numeracy in post-16 vocational programmes – the impact on learning and achievement*, pp. 30–32 (Casey, H., Cara, O., Eldred, J., Grief, S., Hodge, R., Ivanic, R. 2006), London: National Research and Development Centre for Adult Literacy and Numeracy, Crown copyright material is reproduced under the terms of the Click-Use Licence; Extract on pages 112–13 from 'CPD for teachers in post-compulsory education', *CPD for Teachers in Post-Compulsory Education, Occasional Paper No. 18*, pp. 8–9 (Hafez, R. *et al.* 2008), Universities Council for the Education of Teachers, reproduced with permission; Extract on pages 282–83 from *The diploma and its pedagogy*, Qualifications and Curriculum Development Agency (QCDA 2008), reproduced with permission; Extract on pages 376–77 from Office of the United Nations High Commissioner for Human Rights, http://www2.ohchr.org/english/law/crc.htm, reproduced with permission; Extract on pages 381–82 adapted from DCSF (since changed to Department of Education), The five components of personalised learning available at http://nationalstrategies. standards.dcsf.gov.uk/node/83149?uc=force_uj, Crown Copyright material is reproduced under the terms of the Click-Use Licence; Extract on pages 387–88 from *What's 'key'/'core' about literacy in FE? Authorising resonance between everyday literacy practices and formal learning*, Paper presented at the British Educational Research Association Annual Conference, 6–9 September, University of Warwick (Smith, J. and Mannion, G. 2006), This work formed part of an ESRC funded research project entitled 'Literacies for learning in further education'. See www.lancs.ac.uk/lflte, reproduced with permission from the authors; Extract on pages 415–16 from *Manual of good practice from 14–19 pathfinders* (Department for Education and Skills 2005), Crown Copyright material is reproduced under the terms of the Click-Use Licence.

In some instances we have been unable to trace the owners of copyright material, and we would appreciate any information that would enable us to do so.

List of Abbreviations

ACL	Adult and Community Learning
AEN	Additional Educational Need
AfL	Assessment for Learning
ARG	Assessment Reform Group
ASDAN	Award Scheme Development and Accreditation Network
ASET	Accreditation Syndicate for Education & Training (National Awarding Body for vocational learning)
ATLS	Associate Teacher Learning and Skills
AVCE	Advanced Vocational Certificate of Education
Becta	British Educational Communication Technology Agency
BIS	Department for Business, Innovation and Skills
BTEC	Business and Technology Education Council
CETT	Centre for Excellence in Teacher Training
CoVE	Centre of Vocational Excellence
CPPD	Continuing Personal and Professional Development
CTLLS	Certificate in Teaching in the Lifelong Learning Sector
DCSF	Department for School, Children and Families
DES	Department of Education and Science (1964–July 1992)
DfE	Department for Education (July 1992–July 1995)
DfE	Department for Education (May 2010–)
DfEE	Department for Education and Employment (July 1995–June 2001)
DfES	Department for Education and Skills (June 2001–June 2007) – split into two departments the DIUS (Department for Business, Innovation, Universities and Skills, targeted adult education) and the DCSF
DIUS	Department for Innovation Universities and Skills
DTLLS	Diploma in Teaching in the Lifelong Learning Sector
EBP	Education Business Partnership
ECM	Every Child Matters
ESOL	English as a second or other language
FE	Further Education
FENTO	Further Education National Training Organisation
FSM	Free school meals
GCSE	General Certificate of Secondary Education
GNVQ	General National Vocational Qualification
GTC	General Teaching Council
HE	Higher Education

HEI	Higher Education Institution
HLTA	Higher Level Teaching Assistant
IAG	Information Advice and Guidance
ICT	Information and Communication Technologies
IEP	Individual Educational Plan
IfL	Institute for Learning
IFP	Increased Flexibility Programme
IiP	Investors in People
ILP	Individual Learning Plan
ILT	Information Learning Technology
ITE	Initial Teacher Education
JISC	Joint Information Systems Committee
KS4	Key Stage 4
LA	Local Authority
LAA	Local Area Agreement
LEA	Local Education Authority
LLDD	Learners with learning disabilities and/or difficulties
LLN	Literacy, Language and Numeracy
LLUK	Lifelong Learning UK
LSDA	Learning and Skills Development Agency
LSIS	Learning and Skills Improvement Agency
LSN	Learning and Skills Network
MBTI	Myers–Briggs Type Indicator
NAB	National Awarding Body
NALDIC	National Association for Language Development in the Curriculum
NEET	Not in education, employment or training
NFER	National Foundation for Educational Research
NQF	National Qualifications Framework
NVQ	National Vocational Qualification
Ofsted	Office for Standards in Education
PLTS	Diploma Personal Learning and Thinking Skills
PRU	Pupil Referral Units, known as short-term schools from September 2010
PSA	Public Service Agreement (target)
PSHE	Personal, Social, Health and Economic education
PTLLS	Preparing to Teach in the Lifelong Learning Sector
QCDA	Qualifications and Curriculum Development Authority
QIA	Quality Improvement Agency
QTLS	Qualified Teacher Learning and Skills
QTS	Qualified Teacher Status
RJ	Restorative Justice
RPA	Raising of the [compulsory] Participation Age – to 17 in 2013 and 18 in 2015
SA	School Action
SA+	School Action Plus

SATs	Standard Attainment Tests
SEN	Special Educational Needs
SENCO	Special Educational Needs Coordinator
SLC	Subject Learning Coach
SRE	Sex and Relationship Education
SVUK	Standards Verification UK
TA	Teaching Assistant, also known as Classroom Assistant
TDA	Training and Development Agency for Schools
UCAS	Universities and Colleges Admission Service
VLE	Virtual learning environment
WBL	Work-based learning

Developing Professional Practice 14–19 is a comprehensive guide to 14–19 education. It puts what is a complex area into context by helpfully outlining the history and development of the sector whilst keeping learning at the centre of the book. Armitage *et al*. successfully balance detailed information with suggestions for wider reading (including relevant websites) and issues for discussion. This is a thought-provoking and practical in depth guide with accessible case studies and stimulating activities that add topical interest for anyone involved and connected with this sector.

Alaster Scott Douglas, Roehampton University

It is with great pleasure that I am able to endorse this excellent text. It is a rich resource for developing a well-informed and critical approach to the subject of Professional Practice.

The layout of the text is open and accessible, with great opportunities for students to actively respond to the literature and an extensive array of concepts and theories. The opportunities to look closely at the research focus and case study is very useful and the sections on 'discussion' and 'what do you think?' could be easily transferred to the VLE forum to provoke digital dialogues.

Finally, the range and depth of the content is impressive, and well juxtaposed to encourage a critical engagement with the material. I will certainly add this book to my library and recommend it to students on the PGCE and other postgraduate courses in Education. This is a welcome resource for both teachers and learners.

Dr Yvonne Hill, Keele University

This is a very impressive text. It covers a wide range of key issues and offers a well considered balance between theoretical underpinning and application in the classroom and beyond. Though covering a great deal of relevant research this is far from being a 'dry' read. The authors write in a flowing style that engages the reader whilst offering challenge. I will be recommending this book to anyone who is concerned about learners and is aspiring to be a more effective teacher – and certainly for anyone who is carrying out educational study at Master level and beyond.

Terry Hudson, Teach First Yorkshire and Humber and Sheffield Hallam University

Armitage *et al*. have pulled off a real coup in this text, managing to capture the complexity of professional activity in changing times. The book covers a wide range of areas in a comprehensive way and will not only be useful as a text for new teachers, but for those in practice across a range of sectors and disciplines.

Dr Liz Keeley-Browne, Oxford Brookes University

Developing Professional Practice 14–19 is one of the most up to date books on the market reviewing 14–19 education. 14–19 education is rapidly changing and this book is a must for educators and student teachers in this area. The book contains a diverse range of chapters that both inform and provide challenging questions for the reader. An accessible and informative read.

Charlotte Meierdirk, University of Portsmouth

Pearson Education Ltd./Ian Wedgewood

PART 1 Influences on Teaching and Learning

This part sets 14–19 teaching in context by exploring the range of key factors which impact on learning and teaching.

- The part begins with a chapter which considers the contexts of teaching and learning in the 14–19 phase and considers that it could be described as a 'hybrid' phase across established institutions such as secondary schools, academies and FE colleges offering various 14–19 educational programmes and qualifications. The chapter considers this diversity of routes and qualifications on offer which appears as fragmented and disjointed but wonders whether the multiplicity of routes available is a potential strength of the UK educational system.

- Chapter 2 goes on to consider that it has been recognised that some learners would benefit from a different system in which learning can be accomplished through a variety of contexts, especially through the Diploma, leading to opportunities to develop a more social approach to learning in this phase. The chapter considers how conceiving of groups of 14–19 learners and their teachers as learning communities might enhance the experience of both.

- Chapter 3 examines why values are important aspects of the practitioner's professional identity, as well as the wider political and societal values which underpin teaching and learning and the organisations in which they are carried out.

- Chapter 4 considers aspects of development related to the 14–19 phase with a particular focus on adolescence. It considers what it describes as the key challenges of adolescence – biological maturity, development of personal identity, establishment of intimate sexual relationships and the development of independence and autonomy – and examines how they might impact on teaching and learning, particularly with regard to students' relationships with their peers and their teachers.

- Chapter 5 looks at the increasing emphasis on the individual learner through the promotion of personalised and applied learning.

CHAPTER 1

Contexts of Learning

By the end of this chapter you will be able to:

- Explain the 14–19 learning context in England
- Discuss the main aspects of the 14–19 policy and education context
- Consider the need for reform within the 14–19 English education sector

Pearson Education Ltd./Ian Wedgewood

Introduction

This section will focus on the 14–19 learning context in England. It will explore the reform which has shaped 14–19 education (see Table 1.1: The 14–19 eduction policy timeline). We suggest you read this chapter in conjunction with Chapter 17, Extending Partnerships, in Part 4, Learning Futures, which examines collaboration between institutions and agencies within 14–19 education. This section intends to present and explain the 14–19 learning context and examine, in particular, the 14–19 Diploma and its place within the existing 14–19 framework. Finally, alternatives to the existing 14–19 framework will be introduced.

Defining the 14–19 education phase

The present 14–19 education phase is a product of the 14–19 agenda set out by the 14–19 White Paper *Education and Skills* (DfES 2005) focusing on the learning needs of 14–19-year-olds. It aims at bridging the gap between compulsory and post compulsory education. Within the secondary sector, 14–16 consists of Key Stage 4 (KS4) with years 10 and 11. At KS4 learners are expected to take their GCSEs in compulsory subjects such as English, Maths, ICT, Physical Education and Citizenship, and optional subjects such as Modern Languages or Humanities. Post compulsory education stretches from 16+ but there is also a well-defined 16–19 phase in which students undertake academic or vocational studies and training from foundation to level 3. Some qualifications such as A levels sit within the two sectors: schools' sixth forms on the one hand and Further Education (FE) colleges and sixth-form colleges on the other.

At present the 14–19 phase could be described as a 'hybrid' between the compulsory or secondary and the post compulsory sector, also known as further education or learning and skills sector. The diversity of routes and qualifications on offer within this phase could be interpreted as one of the strengths of the English education system. However, there are still issues concerning the effectiveness of the present 14–19 education programme. The divide between both vocational and academic learning is very much alive. Recent proposals such as the 14–19 Diploma were meant to alleviate concerns and gaps in 14–19 education but so far, its validity to do so is being questioned.

Background to the 14–19 reform

Although the idea of a 14–19 phase has been explored since the 1980s (Hodgson and Spours 2008), the debate seemed to have come to a head when in 2004, after a range of Green and White Papers (see Table 1.1), Mike Tomlinson, New Labour's education adviser, embarked on a mission to examine the secondary educational system and, in particular, the qualification framework, which was dominated by GCSEs at KS4 and A levels at level 3.

Table 1.1 The 14–19 education policy timeline

Date	Initiative/event	Aims/summary in relation to 14–19 context
1997	Dearing Report	To reduce the academic and vocational divide at 16–19 education. To establish a half-way AS level to A levels. To align GNVQs with A levels, to create an AS in key skills (communication, application of number and ICT) and to consider the Diploma route and a common grading system across all qualifications
1997	Kennedy Report *Learning Works*	To increase participation in further education (FE). Identified FE is at the core of a national strategy to widen educational participation
1997	Green Paper *Qualifying for Success*	To review the 16–19 qualification system, in particular A levels and GNVQs. The consultation paper put forward the notion of unitisations of advanced qualifications to include in a broad learning programme
2000	Learning and Skills Act	To create academies partly privately and state-funded but independent from LEAs – later renamed as Academies
2000	Curriculum 2000	Reform of the level 3 provision by implementing *Qualifying for Success* – AS and A2 modular programmes and key skills are introduced, GNVQ is replaced by AVCE qualifications
2002	Green Paper *14–19 Education: extending opportunities, raising standards*	To set up proposals for a more coherent 14–19 phase. To extend the 16–19 reform to the 14–19 phase. To make the secondary system qualification more flexible and to consider a broader curriculum
2003	Green Paper *Every Child Matters*	To protect and support children and young people 0–19 to 'be healthy stay safe, enjoy and achieve, make a positive contribution and achieve economic well-being'
2003	White Paper *14–19: Opportunity and Excellence*	To develop cooperation between schools and colleges and improve vocational education and training offer
2004	Tomlinson Report *14–19 Curriculum and Qualifications Reform*	To improve 14–19 education by introducing a unified framework
2005	White Paper *Education and Skills*	To introduce 14–19 curriculum and assessment reform
2008	Curriculum 2008	To refine A-levels' modular system from 6 to 4 modules, to introduce a grade A* and the standalone extended project
2008	Education and Skills Act	To raise participation in learning to 17 by 2013 and 18 by 2015 – does not replace school-leaving age (SLA) – to enable young learners to stay in either full-time, part-time or work-based learning education
2010	First teaching of functional skills	Integration of English, Maths and ICT from entry to level 2
June 2010	End of Diploma entitlement announced	To remove compulsory Diploma offer in schools, FE and sixth-form colleges. The development of the Extended Diploma is stopped

In 2000, the A-level examination became a modular qualification. The 'Curriculum 2000' reform split the A level into Advanced Subsidiary (AS) and A2 levels. AS levels could be taken separately or as part of a two-year programme leading to the full A-level qualification. A new UCAS tariff system was also introduced to replace grades. In theory it meant that entry to higher education would be based on the overall points gained and not just individual grades. Students were also given the opportunity to sit their exams on a more regular basis and to decide whether to 'cash in' their grades or not. This change proved popular with students who saw an opportunity to diversify their studies, while being able to improve on their grades. But overall, this strategy was less well received by A-level teachers who, at times, saw their role reduced to mere exam preparation facilitators. As for higher education institutions, although they recognised the new points system, most still valued the quality of the subject matter and the length of studies rather than the quantity of points accumulated over two years. The standards crisis following exam results in 2002 and 2003 confirmed the fragile status of the new A-levels system.

In addition, 'satellite' qualifications such as GNVQs and NVQs remained marginal qualifications for 14–19-year-old learners (Lumby and Foskett 2005) despite a rebranding as Advanced Vocational Certificate of Education (AVCE). Further efforts to improve the vocational area were made by introducing Key Skills to the AVCE curriculum and the Modern Apprenticeship scheme for level 3 learning.

The main concern was that the 14–19 educational provision was not meeting learners' needs and not equipping them with necessary skills, including basic skills, to progress to adult life and for the world of work. It is also estimated that Britain loses more post-16 learners than any other developing country (OECD 2004 in Hodgson and Spours 2006: 327). In addition, the confusion concerning the organisation of the post compulsory education system contributes to low retention and disengagement.

Mike Tomlinson, former chief inspector of schools, was given the task of looking into 14–19 education. Tomlinson's initial investigation claimed that some learners were underachieving and unchallenged by the curriculum. The validity of vocational routes and their currency in the workplace were also identified as problematic. Finally, it was felt that the teaching and learning were 'burdened' by assessment (DfES 2004). In his final report, published late 2004, Tomlinson recommended a new 14–19 framework by replacing the qualification and learning system. This development would reconcile academic and vocational studies in a learning programme (see Table 1.2, overleaf) including a core literacy, ICT, numeracy, an extended project, common skills and a recognition of wider activities.

The report did not discard the existing NVQs, GCSEs and A levels but suggested they became a 'component' of the new learning and qualification framework. The new framework would have been composed of ladders of learning with a 'pick and mix' approach. This may have promoted a cross-subject culture where academic learners have the opportunity to study a vocational subject and vice versa.

Ideologically, this might have encouraged learners to cross the existing academic/vocational divide. The proposals also suggested giving more curriculum freedom to teachers by using more internal methods of assessment and therefore reducing the control exercised by external qualification bodies.

Overall the report was well received within the different educational settings, but for some it also suggested a progressive absorption of academic qualifications such as A levels within a Diploma framework, which was politically problematic. Academic and in particular A-level qualifications have always been supported by the Conservatives and the middle-class electorate and, with elections looming, the New Labour government could not afford to make such a drastic change to the education system. Consequently, the government's response did not show much support for the proposal. On publication, the prime minister personally confirmed that GCSEs and A levels would be maintained. But, while the government's reaction marked the end of an attempt to streamline the 14–19 qualification framework, it did not entirely eradicate the concept of a Diploma or the need for a 14–19 reform.

The 14–19 reform

> We want an excellent system of 14–19 education; a system where all young people have opportunities to learn in ways which motivate and engage them and through hard work position themselves for success in life.
>
> *Department of Children, Schools and Families (DCSF 2008a)*

Despite the fact that the Tomlinson Report was not accepted in its entirety by the New Labour government, it nevertheless initiated the 14–19 reform. The 14–19 reform is 'based primarily around the ideas of coherent provision leading to "seamless" progression' from level 1 to level 3 (Hodgson and Spours 2006). The 14–19 education concepts were firmly rooted within the New Labour 14–19 agenda to increase post-16 education and training participation by raising the participation age to 18 and reforming the curriculum (DCSF 2008b).

In 2005, the *14–19 Education and Skills* White Paper proposed a 'radical reform of the system of 14–19 education' (DfES 2005:1) via the implementation of learning around core functional skills but still alongside existing GCSEs and A levels. The then 'specialised' Diploma was to provide the needed vocational and academic bridge. The 14–19 policy is regarded as key to finally attending to the economic needs of a future workforce and social issues that seem to develop around the 14–19 age range (Sims and McMeeking 2004). It is aimed at addressing the weaknesses of the current system and preventing learners from disengaging from learning by Key Stage 4.

Interestingly, the DCSF also recognised that the lack of interest in education applies equally in academic and vocational areas of learning, which would leave some teenagers little options and chances of a future in a society where qualifications act as currency. The assumption is that a new curriculum offer which would involve more practical learning activities and collaborative institutional arrangements will convince learners to 'stay on' and consider wider educational paths for their futures. There is a strong argument that learning in various contexts is enriching and provides various perspectives on the subject matter (see Chapter 2 for examples). What is obvious is that the 14–19 agenda has become instrumental to upgrading the skills of the future workforce.

WHAT DO YOU THINK?

- At what age or in which grade is it reasonable to start thinking about a future career?
- Should 14–19 education be directly linked to future employment?

There is a long-standing argument regarding the link between employability and education. Some educationalists feel that choosing a career path at the age of 14 is perhaps too early and that students may not have the maturity needed to make such a decision. Others, however, including policy makers, think it is an appropriate time to engage in a lifelong learning commitment, which includes participating in the UK's economic growth.

In practice, learning as part of the 14–19 reform is to take place on full- or part-time education or work-based learning and learning programmes. The framework includes a combination of old and new qualifications and initiatives such as the 14–19 Diploma. It should, in theory, be interlocked and possibly integrated in a unified framework in the future (Sims and McKeeming 2004). In this system (see Table 1.2), a variety of options operate either independently, e.g. the international baccalaureate (IB) or within some main qualifications such as functional skills with GCSEs, extended project with A levels or the 14–19 Diploma. It should be noted that most state secondary schools follow the 'standard' GCSE and A-levels route while grammar and private institutions have also adopted the international baccalaureate and the Cambridge Pre-U which aim to identify the best students at level 3 for university entry.

Photo 1.1
How major a role should education play in preparing and training students for the world of work?

Source: Pearson Education Ltd. Rob Judges

Table 1.2 The 14–19 qualification framework

Level	Existing qualifications
Entry 1,2,3	Entry-level certificates Skills for Life
1	GCSEs grades D–G Skills for Life and Key skills (functional skills) Foundation Diploma BTEC Introductory and OCR Nationals NVQs
2	GCSEs grades A*–C BTEC and OCR Nationals Higher Diploma NVQs Skills for Life and Key skills (functional skills)
3	AS/A2 levels GCE in applied subjects OCR Nationals Progression and Advanced Diploma Key skills BTEC Diplomas, Certificates NVQs Extended project Cambridge Pre-U International baccalaureate

The 14–19 vocational pathways

The 14–19 education phase is more often associated with standard academic studies but vocational educational pathways such as work-based learning (**WBL**) still concern a significant number of 14–19 learners.

To begin with let us state a few facts:

- WBL's learning programmes include **apprenticeships, entry to employment** (E2E) (pre or entry to employment for school leavers focusing on individual, basic skills and vocational learning) and NVQs.
- There are 180,000 16–18-year-old apprentices.
- 130,000 employers are involved in the Apprenticeship scheme.
- They have a 63 per cent completion rate.

- A target of 240,000 for the 16–18 apprentices by 2013.
- A target of 400,000 by 2020 and 190,000 successful completions.
- WBL 16–18 participation has dropped from 11.3% in 1994 to 7.5% in 2005.

It seems logical that 14–19 work-based learning be driven by economic pressure. The Leitch report (2006), reviewing skills needed in the UK to compete on a global market, underlined concerns vis-à-vis the future of the British economy. Leitch also suggested that this problem could be remedied by solid vocational training. WBL is perhaps better known for its NVQ qualification and Apprenticeship schemes. The Apprenticeship scheme is not a qualification in itself but a collection of training and learning that may include qualifications such as NVQs. Unfortunately present and future schemes entirely rely on the availability of apprenticeship places, existing training within companies and courses in local FE colleges. In the past few years, places have substantially been reduced, due perhaps to the traditional vocational occupations' limited appeal to school leavers but also because of a reduction of involvement from employers. According to employers, the present scheme is expensive, lacks credibility and there is a shortage of appropriate candidates. There are also concerns surrounding the mixed quality of teaching providers whether 'in house', private contractors or in FE provision. But the work-based learning route is still recognised as the most coherent route to access the world of work post general education.

RESEARCH FOCUS: NUFFIELD REVIEW ON APPRENTICESHIP 2008

The Nuffield Foundation is a charitable trust aiming at improving social well-being and in particular education. The 14–19 Education and Training Review was set up to examine the 14–19 education phase between 2003 and 2009. The 14–19 review team was led by university professors but also involved professionals involved in various aspects of 14–19 education.

As part of the 14–19 review, The Nuffield Foundation commissioned two pieces of research on work-based learning.

Key findings:

- The Apprenticeship targets are seen as 'ambitious'
- The participation has lowered since 1994
- Apprenticeship places are mainly offered in traditional sectors (engineering, construction, catering, etc.)
- Apprenticeships will be in competition with new 'flagship government policies' such as the 14–19 Diploma
- Schools may not promote the vocational route for retention purposes
- The rationale for HE pathway progression is unclear
- The female and ethnic minorities participation is low
- Financial incentives may not convince employers to offer places

Recommendations:

- Clearer guidance towards WBL routes is needed
- A 'cross cutting theme' on the world of work should be set up in schools
- The involvement of Black and Minority Ethnic (BME) employers is necessary to increase ethnic minorities participation
- More clarity is needed over the progression between WBL and the Diploma
- Apprenticeships should not be led by 'college based' programmes
- Flexibility is key to attract employers to the scheme.

Nuffield Review of 14–19 Education and Training (2008a) *Issues Paper 3: Apprenticeship I, Prospects for growth* and Nuffield Review of 14–19 Eduction & Training (2008b) *Issues Paper 4: Apprenticeship II, A high quality pathway for young people?* Both available on line at **www.nuffield14-19review.org.uk**.

The 14–19 Diploma

The 14–19 Diploma is a qualification aimed at learners from 14 to 19 years old. Its aim is to integrate theoretical and practical learning in a seamless progression from foundation to higher education. The structure (see Figure 1.1, overleaf) follows a developmental pattern of skills and learning as well as practical experience across 17 learning lines (see Table 1.3). The use of 'learning lines', for example, 'Society, Health and Development' instead of subjects such as 'Sociology' is pertinent here as it denotes a desire to move away from pure and perhaps narrow subject basis to a more holistic view of learning (see Table 1.4, overleaf). The 14–19 Diploma emphasises the application of learnt knowledge while tackling 'soft' and 'key' skills and allowing for progression between levels.

The Diploma intends to offer progression between learning lines, from the vocational to the academic, e.g. Construction to Science at various levels. This flexibility is a 'selling point' for the qualification (for an applied example see Chapter 2) and therefore more motivating for the 'alternative' learner for whom the standard vocational or academic system is not working.

Table 1.3 The 14–19 Diploma learning lines and implementation dates

2008: Construction and the Built Environment, Engineering, Society, Health and Development, IT, Creative and Media

2009: Land-based and Environmental studies, Manufacturing, Hair and Beauty, Business Administration and Finance, Hospitality and Catering

2010: Public Services, Sport and Leisure, Retail, Travel and Tourism

2011: Humanities, Languages, Science (These have now been cancelled.)

Table 1.4 Diploma levels and currency

Level	Diploma title	Equivalence	Length of course
1	Foundation	5 GCSE (D–G)	2 years
2	Higher	7 GCSE (A*–C)	2 years
3	Progression	2 A2 + 1 AS	
	Advanced	3 A2 + 1 AS	
		300 UCAS points + 120 UCAS Additional and Specialist learning	2 years

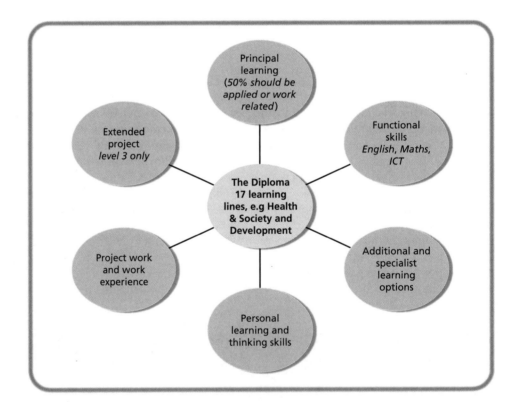

Figure 1.1
The 14–19
Diploma
structure

In practice, the 14–19 Diploma is to be delivered as a collaborative exercise. One of the challenges but also opportunities for the 14–19 Diploma lies within the fact that the delivery is to be shared among educational institutions. As a result of these partnerships, 14–19 learners on the Diploma may have to attend more than one institution to cover all areas of the course. For most schools, the lack of experience and facilities to deliver the vocational units is central to the adoption of a collaborative model.

The case study example below indicates a possible scheme of subject delivery within a partnership. It seems obvious that each institution utilises its expertise resourcefully and in accordance with its institutional specialism, e.g. for a more vocational Diploma a FE college is more likely to have the staff, premises and equipment than a school, while the Higher Education Institutions can provide much more advanced knowledge and skills.

CASE STUDY

This case study is an example of a possible application of the Diploma within an extensive partnership. Look, in particular, at the range of institutions involved in such a scheme.

Curriculum delivery exemplar for an Engineering Diploma (Advanced level) delivered in South County Consortium

Institutions	New Diploma delivery
2 Schools and 1 Academy (River Comprehensive, Downs High and Channel Community College)	**Functional skills:** Science and Maths English: e.g. *using specialised vocabulary, expressing ideas and company communication* **Extended project:** based on individual interest, e.g. *use of solar energy in car manufacturing*
2 FE colleges (Mid County College and North Region College)	**Principal learning:** *The engineered world, discovering engineering technology, engineering the future* **Functional skills:** ICT – *use of 3D* **Personal learning:** *problem-solving and team work*
2 local Employer and Specialist Professional body (Tokonda cars, SunMech, Crystals Engineering)	**Work experience and Project:** Undertaken in design offices and factory – designated professional mentor for chosen project
2 Higher Education (Ashland University and East County College of HE and FE)	**Additional and specialist learning:** 'Robotics' and Telecommunications **Extended project:** e.g. *Engineering and the environment*

WHAT DO YOU THINK?

What are the strengths attached to such content and model of delivery?

Initially there are evident educational strengths attached to this mode of delivery. The shared and localised knowledge enables the learning to occur within specific areas of expertise. Ideologically, the 14–19 Diploma presents itself as holistic, inclusive and flexible. It is designed to bridge the gap between academic and vocational studies and can be accessed at any age between 14 and 19. It also aims at preparing learners for the world of work.

As a curriculum, it offers a variety of topics and assessments such as reflective diaries, observation records, risk-assessment reports, case studies results, presentation and summative external assessment. It also has the scope to include other qualifications such as GCSEs or A levels. Pedagogically, the learning is to be practical and in the context of the subject studied. As a qualification, the 14–19 Diploma is equivalent to levels 1, 2 and 3 and can be undertaken in parallel with other qualifications (see Table 1.4).

WHAT DO YOU THINK?

Go to the following websites and find out all you can about the Diploma and its framework:

www.education.gov.uk

www.diplomainfo.org.uk/AQA-City-and-guilds-diplomas.asp

From your findings and what you have read so far, can you think of any weaknesses for the Diploma?

You may have listed some of the following points:

- Is it really bridging the academic and vocational divide?
- The design is too complex.
- The content is unrealistic for lower-level abilities.
- Has it got currency for HE and the world of work?
- It's neither vocational nor academic.
- Travelling between institutions is problematic in both busy city and rural areas.
- There is a shortage of adequate work experience opportunities.
- Synchronicity of teaching and learning may be difficult to achieve across a partnership.
- Staff expertise is 'patchy' as it is a new qualification.
- Collaboration may be difficult between institutions, especially in a market-led educational environment.
- There is a significant staff pay parity issue between secondary teachers and FE lecturers who will have to work on the same course but on different salaries.
- New government = change of direction. What role will the Diploma play in the new government's plans for education?

Until recently, the 14–19 Diploma has acted as a flagship for the 14–19 reform. Despite many criticisms, which will be discussed below, the overall approach focusing on the variety of topics and assessment methods and the notion of learning in context

Source: Pearson Education Ltd. Studio 8

Photo 1.2
Does the diploma risk increasing the academic and vocational as well as the social divide – is it a credible alternative route to Higher Education, for example?

makes this qualification attractive to learners and some educationalists. It can also work in conjunction with GCSE and A levels, which reinforces the notion of flexibility of learning.

Some criticisms of the 14–19 Diploma

Although there are some undeniable advantages to the 14–19 Diploma, as we have seen above, the implementation of the New Diploma raises issues in particular concerning partnerships (see Chapter 17). As the teaching and learning of the Diploma is to be disseminated across a range of 'partners' such as schools, colleges and businesses, this arrangement may be regarded as too complex.

The fact that the Diploma is only one of many qualifications on offer in the 14–19 framework is also problematic. In this competitive qualification market, currency vis-à-vis HE progression or employment is crucial. Already, the Cambridge Pre-U and the International Baccalaureate are acknowledged as the 'jewels' of the level-3 educational crown. The Pre-U was partly designed in anticipation of the 2013 A-level review (which could have seen the scrapping of the A level in favour of the Diploma) and has become a serious contender to A levels by recruiting from private schools. As a result the A level is now left to 'the masses' (Allen and Ainley 2007) although it is still considered the 'preferred route for the most able students and their parents' (Hodgson and Spours 2007: 664). Consequently the 14–19 Diploma may end up near the bottom of the preferred qualifications list. There is also a risk that the 14–19 Diploma may be seen as a replacement of the late GNVQ, which was used for years to bridge the gap between vocational and academic learning but overall never achieved any real credibility from either side (Allen and Ainley 2007). The Diploma also has a major rival in the form of the BTEC qualification. The BTEC is overall well integrated within the framework and has enjoyed steady support by institutions, teachers, students, HEIs and employers alike and it seems unlikely that it will be replaced by the Diploma, given its present success. The Diploma still has a lot to prove as progression towards higher education or the world of work. It is likely that the 14–19 Diploma will find a 'niche market' within the 14–19 framework but the entitlement forcing every school to offer access to every Diploma line was removed in June 2010, undermining previous efforts to support the qualification.

The future of 14–19 education?

There is a general consensus among educationalists that England would benefit from a more homogenous and egalitarian 14–19 education system. The baccalaureate framework used by Continental countries and Wales has often been cited as a solution to the challenging and imbalanced English 14–19 phase. As discussed above, education within a market-led educational system can only lead to a system where some qualifications have a higher status than others. This issue is of importance when you consider the notion of equality and parity among learners.

The proposed approach is to adopt a 14–19 framework with common aims, values and purposes (Nuffield Review 2008c). Breadth would also be increased by the introduction of general education as opposed to single-subject qualifications. The model also diverges from the existing product and outcome focus towards a more process-based curriculum model. The focus on pedagogy rather than qualification outcomes (Nuffield Review 2008d) would be central to this approach. A topic or theme approach to learning is said to be beneficial for young learners who need relevance to their own context (Nuffield 2008b). For example, the theme 'understanding British cultural identity' may contain elements of history and literature but also incorporates sociological elements regarding the impact and outcomes of colonisation and notions of diversity within the UK. In this framework, the role of the teacher would be seen as crucial to the development of the curriculum but also to the implementation of progressive assessment strategies. It is suggested that a greater emphasis on the formative and more varied methods of assessment may be key for better learning.

However, there have been calls for a more defined framework of an English baccalaureate, which recognises not only the above learning approach but also the role of both vocational and general education for the 14–19 phase. While these proposals may echo the 14–19 Diploma model, they also differ essentially as far as currency is concerned. The English baccalaureate would become universal and replace the present 14–19 education model. In theory, this signifies an end to the present hierarchical qualification system. In practice, there is a concern that a 'sub-Baccalaureate system' may emerge with the dominance of more academic lines of learning. The French Baccalaureate is renowned for privileging its science branch over the literature or business areas of learning. Nevertheless, the English Baccalaureate may be an option to unify the fragmented and unequal current 14–19 education framework.

ACTIVITY: SWOT (STRENGTHS, WEAKNESSES, OPPORTUNITIES AND THREATS) ANALYSIS

A SWOT analysis is an exercise enabling you to reflect on a particular issue from various perspectives.

Whether you work or are training in a school/FE or sixth-form college/academy or in the work place, consider working across 14–19 education:

- Draw a list of strengths and weaknesses of the existing 14–19 educational phase.
- What are the opportunities for your own professional development and practice in relation to the 14–19 framework?
- Consider factors which may threaten these opportunities.

Exemplar

Strength	Weakness	Opportunities	Threats
Variety of 14–19 qualifications	This diversity makes the framework confusing	I only teach on GCSEs and could develop my practice by teaching on the Diploma – it would give me another pedagogical perspective	My school may not adopt the Diploma – it looks time-consuming

SUMMARY

In this chapter we have established that the 14–19 learning context is a diverse and 'confusing landscape' (Hodgson and Spours 2006), set within the 14–19 education policy context. The emergence of the 14–19 Diploma has perhaps increased this confusion by adding, yet again, another 'middle of the road' qualification.

So far, 14–19 policies have failed to bring any significant change to 14–19 education and qualification landscape. The diversity of the present system can be justified on the grounds that it offers a variety of qualifications and therefore a choice for learners but it only reinforces the incoherence of the 14–19 framework. Reforming 14–19 education has proven to be a challenge which is unlikely to be resolved without a firm commitment to establish a common learning framework.

Find out more

This chapter has raised a range of issues regarding the implications of the 14–19 reform. In addition, some educationalists have also voiced further recommendations and concerns regarding the 14–19 education phase (full details of publications to be found in the Bibliography):

- Is the 14–19 education phase coherent? **(Hodgson and Spours, 2006; Sims & McMeeking, 2004)**
- Does more diversity of contexts of learning/institutions mean automatically more participation at 14–19? **(Hodgson and Spours, 2006)**
- Will new collaboration on the 14–19 Diploma increase or decrease competition among institutions? **(Nuffield Review, Issues Paper 10, 2008c)**
- Will the new 14–19 curricula increase educational inequalities? **(Hodgson and Spours, 2006)**
- Will the best schools and independent colleges retain highly academic curricula while 'average' schools are left with the teaching of the Diploma? **(Allen and Ainley, 2007)**
- Will the academic versus vocational divide be further increased? **(Lumby and Foskett, 2005; Hodgson and Spours, 2007; Allen and Ainley, 2007)**

- Will FE teachers have the same working conditions as school teachers if they are expected to teach across the 14–19 phase? **(Hodgson and Spours, 2006)**
- How will teachers be trained to teach the Diploma? **(www.dcsf.gov.uk, Jephcote and Abbott, 2005)**
- Should there be a unified 14–19 PGCE training and qualification for all? **(Donovan, 2005; Thompson and Robinson, 2008; Fisher and Webb, 2006)**
- Does the 14–19 educational phase means one set of educational values? **(Nuffield Review, Issues Paper 6, 2008b)**
- Shouldn't the government have adopted the initial Tomlinson's suggestions of a full reform of 14–19? **(Hodgson and Spours, 2007; Nuffield Review, Issues Paper 10, 2008c; Jephcote and Abbott, 2005)**
- Will the 14–19 agenda resolve the vocational work-based learning and training issues in England? **(Keep, 2005)**
- An English Baccalaureate? **(Hodgson and Spours, 2003 and 2007)**

Bibliography

Allen, M. and Ainley, P. (2007) *Education make you fick, innit?* London: Tufnell Press.

Briggs, A. (2008) Modeling complexity, making sense of leadership issues in 14–19 education, *Management in Education*, 22(2): 17–23.

DCSF (2007) *Building on the Best*, Final report and implementation plan of the review of 14–19 work-related learning, 14–19 Education and Skills, available online at: **www.dcsf.gov.uk/14-19/documents/14-19workrelatedlearning_web.pdf**

DCSF (2008a) *Diploma Communications*, **http://www.dcsf.gov.uk/14-19**

DCSF (2008b) *Raising Expectations: supporting all young people to participate until 18*, Nottingham: DCSF Publications.

DfES (2004) *14–19 Curriculum and Qualifications Reform*. Final report on the working group 14–19 Reform, Nottingham: DfES.

DfES (2005) *Education and Skills* White Paper, TSO: available online at: **www.dcsf.gov.uk/14-19/documents/14-19whitepapersum.pdf**

DfES (2006) *14–19 – Partnership Guidance*, available online at: **www.dcsf.gov.uk/14-19/documents/Partnership%20Guidance.pdf**

DfES (2007) *National Statistics*, GCE/VCE, A/AS and equivalent examinations results in England, 2005/2006, SFR 02/2007 Report, **Dfes.gsi.gov.uk**.

DFES (2008) *What are Academies?* **www.standards.dfes.gov.uk/academies/what_are_academies?/**

DIUS (2007a) *World Class Skills: Implementing the Leitch Review of Skills in England*, available online at: **http://www.dius.gov.uk/publications/worldclassskills.pdf**

Donovan, G. (2005) *Teaching 14–19: everything you need to know about teaching and learning across the phases*, London: David Fulton Publishers.

Foster (2005) *Realising the Potential – a review of the future role of further education colleges*, available online at: **http://www.dfes.gov.uk/furthereducation**

Fisher, R. and Webb, K. (2006) Subject specialist pedagogy and initial teacher training for the learning and skills sector in England: the context, a response and some critical issues, *The Journal of Further and Higher Education*, 30(4): 337–49.

Hodgson, A. and Spours, K. (2003) *Beyond 'A' Levels, Curriculum 2000 and the Reform of 14–19 Qualifications*. London: Kogan Page.

Hodgson, A. and Spours, K. (2006) The organisation of 14–19 education and training in England: beyond weakly collaborative arrangement, *Journal of Education and Work*, 19(4): 325–42.

Hodgson, A. and Spours, K. (2007) Specialised diplomas: transforming the 14–19 landscape in England?, *Journal of Education Policy*, 22(6): 657–73.

Hodgson, A. and Spours, K. (2008) *Education & Training 14–19: Curriculum, Qualifications & Organization*, London: Sage.

Jephcote, M. and Abbott, I. (2005) Tinkering and tailoring: the reform of 14–19 education in England, *Journal of Vocational Education and Training*, 57(2): 181–202.

Keep, E. (2005) Reflections on the curious absence of employers, labour incentives and labour market regulation in English 14–19 policy: fist signs of a change in direction? *Journal of Education Policy*, 20(5): 533–53.

Leitch, S. (2006) *Review of Skills, Prosperity for All in the Global Economy: world class skills*, Norwich: HMSO.

Lumby, J. and Foskett, N. (2005) *14–19 Education: Policy, Leadership & Learning*, London: Sage.

Nuffield Review of 14–19 Education & Training (2008a) Issues Paper 3: *Apprenticeship I, Prospects for Growth* and Issues Paper 4: *Apprenticeship II, A High Quality Pathway for Young People?* available online at **www.nuffield14-19review.org.uk**

Nuffield Review of 14–19 Education & Training (2008b) Issues Paper 6: *Aims and Values*, available online at **www.nuffield14-19review.org.uk**

Nuffield Review of 14–19 Education & Training (2008c) Issues Paper 10: *General Education in the 14–19 Phase*, available online at **www.nuffield14-19review.org.uk**

Nuffield Review of 14–19 Education & Training (2008d) Issues Paper 7: *The Whole Curriculum 14–19*, available on line at **www.nuffield14-19review.org.uk**

QCA (2004) 14–19 Learning, **http://www.qca.org.uk/ 14-19/11-16-schools/index_s6-0-collaboration.htm**

Sims, D. and McMeeking, S. (2004) *Mapping the 14–19 Learning Landscape*, LGA Research report 10/04, Berkshire: NFER, **http://www.teachernet.gov.uk/ teachingandlearning/14to19/strategyandimplications**

Thompson, R. and Robinson, D. (2008) Changing step or marking time? Teacher education reforms for the learning and skills sector in England, *Journal of Further and Higher Education*, 32(2): 161–73.

CHAPTER 2

Communities of Learners

In this chapter you will:

- Reflect upon the concept of a 'communities of learners' within the 14–19 education phase
- Examine current schemes following a 'communities of learners' approach
- Consider opportunities to foster the 'communities of learners' concept within the 14–19 education phase

Pearson Education Ltd./Ian Wedgewood

Introduction

In Chapter 1 we explored the 14–19 education contexts and concluded that the 14–19 education phase displayed different aims and values borrowed from the secondary and the post compulsory sectors. In this chapter we hope to introduce the concept of 'communities of learners', which revolves around the notion that learning is shared among various stakeholders, for instance schools involving learners, parents and the wider community with the teaching and learning. We will explore how the 14–19 education could provide the ideal grounds for the nurturing of the communities of learners concept while reserving judgement upon the feasibility of its application within such a complex context.

Community of learners or community of practice?

The rise of individualistic values has meant that learning is now seen as an individual journey taking place within an institutionalised system bearing little relation to our lives (Wenger 1998). The concept of a community of learners, which originated in the United States, is closely related to **social learning theories** and the assumption that learning occurs in various settings, formal or informal, in collaboration with others and/or within a group.

Central to a community of learners is the sharing of common values and an active engagement to learn together and from others' experiences. This 'mutual recognition' of

Source: Pearson Education Ltd. Rob Judges

Photo 2.1
The mutual recognition of others' experience and knowledge is crucial to the idea of a community of learning

experience, knowledge and/or skills initiates a 'shared practice' (in our case the teaching and learning) with its own repertoire. The 'community' is not confined to experts but invites novices and 'masters' to complement each others' knowledge and experiences and as a result create a 'practice' (Wenger 1998). In education you could assume that the novice is characterised by the learner and the master by the teacher. However, as the concept allows for the sharing of practice, it recognises that learners can also be masters in their own rights and teachers may become novices or partners, depending on the topic or level of learning.

IN PRACTICE

Eva is a History teacher within an academy in Kent. She has introduced the concept of historical perspectives to her level 2 Humanities students. The previous week she had asked her students to identify one specific family event for them to investigate from various family members' perspectives. This week she is asking each student to share their findings with the rest of the class. As learners will be discussing their family history, they will not only be taking ownership of their learning and building on their current knowledge but also become 'masters' of their subject matter. Equally, students, the students' families and Eva become 'partners' in the learning, thus beginning to create a community of learners.

In addition, the process is not an exclusive relationship, as communities can interact with others and individuals can belong to various communities. For example, Eva could belong to a community within her own department, her academy community as well as the community of teachers teaching History but also the wider community of teachers and so on . . .

The difficulty with concepts such as communities of practice and communities of learners is that it echoes the chicken and egg quandary. What comes first? You could argue that within education, the teachers' community of practice creates the community of learners. On the other hand, it is the community of learners which creates the learning leading to the teacher's practice. What is clear is that learning is seen as a mutual, homogenous and reflexive concept.

WHAT DO YOU THINK?

- How many communities do you think you belong to?
- What is your place within these communities? Are you a 'novice' or 'master'?
- Do your 'communities' have specific practices?

If learning is central to our social world, then it also involves the shaping of the whole person and the construction of his/her identity as well as the perpetuation of the actual community. Within a community of practice, learning is not seen as 'a condition for membership, but is itself an evolving form of membership' (Lave and Wenger 1991: 53). Learning is therefore created by all the agents involved in the community.

In most Western societies, learning is regarded as a practice mostly reserved to educational and/or formal institutions. But the learning is constructed by a multitude of participants. In the 14–19 education phase learners, parents, teachers, institutions such as schools, academies and colleges, and support agencies such as Connexions, can be considered members of a community of learners.

Issues with the application of the concept of community of learners

It may be rather difficult for most teachers/trainers to think of learners as belonging to a community. Recent educational reforms and initiatives have encouraged institutions to look at learning within a 'personalised' framework such as **individual learning plan**, **tutorial**, **differentiation**, and **record of achievement**, etc. It is also safe to say that education has become a product and currency for future employment whereby a learner (or 'client' as some FE colleges may call them) can gain credentials via undertaking a specific course. The content of learning is set up as a commodity by various exam boards and a syllabus can be chosen off the shelves by individual institutions. It is then delivered to learners and assessed individually by an exam and/or a portfolio system. Effectively, a community of learners may happen as a result of certain teaching practices but is not officially recognised as the driving force behind learning. Rhetoric regarding the concept of community of learners is often heard but in practice its application is rare. The choice of educational ideology and curriculum models and methods of delivery for the current pre and post compulsory phases are mainly driven by an accumulation of credentials culture.

So, as the community of learning concept requires the acceptance that learning is shared and is to take place in any social situation, whether formal or informal:

- How does this impact on the learning situated in institutionalised settings such as schools?
- Can our learners belong to such communities in the present formal educational system?
- How can our learners be part of and construct their own learning if their learning is dictated and packaged?

Learning in a community is about learning from each other's experience, as a group as well as sharing own knowledge and understanding. The current educational agenda is not particularly sympathetic to this holistic view of learning. The 14–19 focus on future employment could further reduce learning to a mere acquisition of skills and generic skills. It is therefore critical for young learners to make educational and career decisions about their future on their learning experience and not just on exam results.

The 14–19 community of learners

At the heart of the 14–19 education reform are concerns that many young learners have been unable to gain appropriate skills and knowledge to pursue their education and/or engage with learning altogether. It is believed that this disengagement appears around Key Stage 4 and that the school system and formal approaches to education are partly responsible for this lack of interest in learning (Lumby and Foskett 2005). Undeniably, the current secondary programmes leading to GCSEs carry a 'burden of assessment' (DfES 2004) characterised by frequent examinations. This puts great pressure on teachers to focus on the product rather than the process and consequently prevents them from implementing a more inclusive model of learning. It has been recognised that some learners would benefit from a different approach where learning can be accomplished through a variety of contexts and learning models. The 14–19 education phase may be able to offer an alternative learning path. Learning beyond the boundaries of institution and formal class learning may help to build a stronger relationship between learners and learning.

At first, the connection between the 14–19 agenda and 'communities of learners' is not particularly obvious but the variety of learning and contexts of the 14–19 curriculum and, in particular, the Diploma could lead to an opportunity to develop a more social learning approach for this phase.

In Chapter 1 we discussed the fact that learning in context can encourage learners to stay in education after the age of 16. It is also true that many young people cannot cope with the rigidity of an academic curriculum and exams and need alternative learning strategies.

DISCUSSION POINT

From what you have read in Chapter 1 and the information below, which characteristics of the Diploma could be associated with the concept of 'communities of learners'?

For example, the 14–19 Diploma in Society, Health and Development is offered at level 1, 2 and 3 and covers three main areas of learning:

Principal learning:
- Knowledge, understanding and skills related to the sector
- Each level contains between 6 and 9 individual units, e.g. partnership working or growth, development and healthy living
- Delivery is applied and experiential learning, e.g. case studies

Generic learning:
- Functional skills (English, ICT and Maths)
- Personal learning and thinking skills

- A project (including the extended project)
- Work experience (10 days (level 1 and 2) to 20 days (level 3)

Additional and specialist learning:
- Inclusion of other related qualifications, e.g. GCSEs, A levels, NVQs, etc.

Assessment
- Internal, e.g. reflective diaries, observation records, risk assessment reports, case studies results/presentation and summative external assessment

Adapted from Edexcel guidance units for the Diploma in SHD (**www.edexcel.com**)

The approach to learning in the above Diploma is particularly relevant to the construction of a community of learners. One of the Diploma's requirements is the use of applied and experiential learning (minimum 50% of the course) and the inclusion of case studies. For each unit there is a central point of learning and a consolidation activity. Although widely used in Higher Education Health studies and in professional environments, the use of case study activities has been widely neglected in schools and colleges. However, on the Diploma, learners are introduced to collaborative work where the topic is introduced and developed via the case study. The case study is then to be resolved through communication outside the educational context. The collaborative factor is therefore essential and learners are expected to work as a group and take ownership of the case study. They also need to investigate the issue by talking to the sector's practitioners, e.g. social workers, nurses. As part of their course, learners will also be expected to apply their knowledge gained in practice through work experience. Theoretically, the 14–19 Diploma presents an excellent opportunity to diverge from set classroom and teacher-centred teaching. By seeking understanding of their subject beyond the classroom environment, learners would become agents of their own learning and construct a learning community where novices and experts seek and share knowledge, experiences and skills.

The 14–19 Diploma has the potential to break some of the barriers between learning and learners by adopting a more participative approach to learning. However, as previously stated, the current education system (secondary and tertiary) operates in competitive settings and concentrates a great deal on the delivery of syllabi to meet national performance targets. Consequently, the introduction of a full community-based learning environment where the ownership of learning is transferred to its learners is problematic. On a practical level, the 'seamless' education that the Diploma is meant to offer is likely to be tested by the lack of facilities and cohesion between staff delivering the units in various institutions. Finally, the constant reminder of the link between education and the economy in the 14–19 education phase is also a major obstacle to the achievement of a more democratic and progressive way of learning.

Photo 2.2
A student on a work experience placement. How might 14–19 learners benefit from learning that takes place outside the classroom

Source: Getty Images

Fostering a community of learners' scheme

In the 1990s, the US educationalists Ann Brown and Joseph Campione (1996) developed the 'Fostering a community of learners' (FCL) programme, a pedagogical approach focusing on deep reflective processes and the sharing of learning and knowledge. This constructivist model of teaching is based on the principle that knowledge is built upon existing knowledge and consists of empowering learners with their learning. The use of research techniques and peer learning of their subject's 'big idea' originally identified by the teacher are key to this approach. The 'big idea' refers to the notion of a central theme connecting to other themes. This means that subjects are not studied in block but in relation to other subjects or topics.

IN PRACTICE

After her introductory session on 'Historical perspectives', Eva, the Humanities teacher, realised she could link the concept to a 'big idea'. She has only been teaching on this flexible level-2 programme for the past two years and felt her students were disengaging with the module. They did not understand how it all 'fitted in'. Eva then started planning for greater connection between sections of her Humanities module around the 'big idea': London 2012. She had realised that it would enable her to explore issues of history, identity, ethnicity, geography, cultures and languages as well as engaging her students with an exciting sporting event. Working in groups, students were given specific areas to investigate and reported their findings on a regular basis to other groups. They would be expected to present their project in year 2 of the course to the rest of the school.

The principles of a FCL project are 'democratic, student centred, and inquiry based instruction' (Mintrop 2004: 141). In practice, FCL is to encourage students to take a real responsibility for their subject and gain expertise via jigsaw group research and reciprocal teaching or teaching each other. The idea that students can embody the role of the teacher is particularly significant to the concept of FCL.

It is the overall contribution by each member that constitutes the learning. Learners are encouraged to make sense of their learning in a variety of domains (Schoenfeld 2004). The notion of 'sense-making' is crucial to the learning process as it allows individual learners to link their learning to the real world.

Here is a summary of a typical FCL approach to learning (based on Rico and Shulman 2004) for a Science class in the United States.

The learning context	Secondary education
The discipline	Science
The unit	Endangered species
The Big Idea	Interdependence of ecosystem
The jigsaw research groups	Individual species' characteristics, reproduction, camouflage, habitat, etc.
Method	Groups' reciprocal teaching Teacher as a facilitator
The consequential task	Creating a document gathering all findings and conclusions made as a result of reciprocal teaching 'conversations'

WHAT DO YOU THINK?

Can you identify some issues linked to the FCL approach to teaching and learning?

RESEARCH FOCUS

Multiple Learning Communities: students, teachers, instructional designers, and researchers by A. Shoenfeld, Professor of Education, University of California, Berkeley, 2004.

In this research Shoenfeld reviews and continues the discussion of action research type investigations undertaken by secondary schools' practitioners in the USA into the implementation of FCL in four disciplines (Social studies, English language Arts, Science, and Mathematics).

Shoenfeld identified a number of problematic issues in relation to the actual implementation of a FCL approach in the classroom:

- The identification of the big idea
- Students' grasp of this concept and approach to teaching
- The crossing of boundaries between subject specialism
- Time and resources needed to develop a FCL unit
- Staff development and training of teachers.

In conclusion Shoenfeld found that practising the full FCL reform was difficult and that a hybrid was more likely to emerge.

ACTIVITY: FOSTERING A COMMUNITY OF LEARNERS IN YOUR OWN PROFESSIONAL CONTEXT

Fill in the following table starting with your 'big idea'. This could be linked to your subject specialism or a course you teach on.

The learning context
The discipline
The unit
The Big Idea
The jigsaw research groups
Method
The consequential task

It is worth adding that the FCL model may be a challenge to implement within the English education system. Most of the qualifications designed by examination boards leave little room for creativity. Our History teacher, Eva, is lucky to be working on a flexible level-2 programme where she has more control over topics and teaching pedagogy. Nevertheless, the 'hybrid' concept identified by Shoenfeld means that there is still a possibility to adapt the fostering of a community of learners model to teaching and learning in the 14–19 education phase.

Peer learning

To a certain extent the US FLC approach is close to the concept of **peer learning** found within the UK education system. Peer learning is: 'the acquisition of knowledge and skill through active helping and supporting among status equals or matched companions' (Topping 2005: 631). In practice, peer learning is learning from and with a colleague or other learner within the same group or subject area: for example, two students on an A-level Sociology course revising for their exam and exchanging ideas about their understanding of research methods. Peer learning is not a uniform scheme in schools and colleges and varies from 'peer tutoring, peer learning to collaborative learning'. In some institutions it is fully integrated in the day-to-day teaching while in others it is an 'added value' option offered to students to support their studies.

In fact, there is a risk that peer learning may be used as learning 'support'. This differs from some of the original characteristics of a community of learners based on sharing of expertise from novices to experts. Indeed, there are often assumptions that peer learning is a one-way process whereby the 'teaching' is undertaken by better students stigmatising the weaker student (Topping 2005: 631). In order to be valid, the concept of community of learners must rest on mutual learning.

WHAT DO YOU THINK?

- How much of peer learning is happening in your classroom?
- Could you establish a peer learning scheme for some of your students?
- How would you do this?

Peer learning schemes are found to be most effective when mutually designed and directed by teachers and students (Ashwin 2002). Research shows clearly that peer learning can make a difference to retention or results and academic achievement (Topping 2005). It can also help towards the construction of a community, transforming the 'helped' or novice into a 'helper' or master for the next generation of learners.

CASE STUDY

Peer learning in 14–19 education context: the 'study buddy' scheme at Lewisham College of Further Education

Since the early 2000s, Lewisham College, in South London, has established a learning support 'study buddy' scheme. The aim of this learning support is to use students to help others within the same or a lower-level class. The scheme has evolved from one-to-one support to group peer learning. The College wanted to establish a 'community' where individual skills, experiences and learning issues could be shared and complemented. The teaching/learning support offered is not dissimilar to 'classroom assistant' work except that helpers are identified within the same or upper level of studies. They have therefore first-hand experience of the subject and learning process. In some areas such as Construction, study buddies offer more practical teaching and learning and fully support the tutor. Study buddies are initially trained and have regular feedback sessions with the support team. 'Helped' students also participate in the evaluation process where an individual study buddy's contribution is identified and discussed.

Mutual benefits for both study buddy and student include:

- the improvement of communication skills
- gaining confidence in the subject matter
- greater understanding of the learning process.

The scheme 'regenerates' every year; in time, 'helped' students are encouraged to become 'helpers' or study buddies themselves. This cycle contributes to the creation of a community of learners.

Informal learning

WHAT DO YOU THINK?

What would you say counts as formal and informal learning?

In an education system which relies entirely on accumulation of credentials, it may be difficult to consider the contribution of informal learning. However, the place for informal learning for 14–19 learners is not to be neglected. From previous examples seen in this chapter there is strong evidence that effective learning can occur outside the classroom. There is also no doubt that learning does not need to be contained within a 'scheme' or 'programme' and happens as a result of life events or professional practice. This experience gained is unfortunately left invalidated and mostly unused by the educational system. It is fair to say that, in educational settings, little is made of the very valuable lessons that life offers.

Currently, the recognition of prior learning is mostly limited to an APL (Accreditation of Prior Learning) system. It means that previously acquired qualifications are used as currency to count towards an equivalent or higher-level course. The practice of APL is common in adult and higher education. On the other hand, the APEL (Accreditation of Prior Experiential Learning) considers an individual's learning journey through his/her professional experience.

Again, this scheme tends to be implemented only in a mature-adult learning environment where the actual learning is tested via the submission of evidence of learning such as portfolios and/or written work. A typical 14–19 learner, however, is unlikely to have gained such work experience and the use of their 'family' or 'community' learning is seen as purely anecdotal.

Nevertheless, there are ways of recording informal learning within 14–19 education such as the use of reflection of one's learning or the writing of a work experience report. Perhaps the Diploma, which recognises the 'out of classroom' learning and the level-3 extended project, presents an opportunity to incorporate more of their experience and tacit personal knowledge and beliefs into the 'formal' learning environment.

It is unlikely that a full recognition of informal learning will take place within 14–19 education; however, there are strategies that can be applied within the present curriculum to promote alternative methods of teaching in line with or diverting from the community of learners' model of learning.

Strategies to foster community of learners within own professional practice

So, in practice how could you foster a community of learners? There are several ways the concept of 'communities of learners' can be introduced within our day-to-day teaching.

The following points summarise some strategies which may help you engage with such a scheme.

Characteristics of a 'community of learners'	Examples of strategies to foster the communities of learners concept
Having a common identity	Reinforce the notion of 'we are working together' by frequently encouraging students to contribute to planning and allowing for frequent feedback
Building on previous learning and experience	Ask students to relate to own learning and personal experience in classroom conversations or essays. Make it formal within the instructions
Learning from various teachers/'masters' and areas of expertise	Invite speakers from other institutions or organisations to enrich what you are teaching, e.g. Union representative or local MP for Politics session
Learning from peers	Plan individual or group presentations on a regular basis

◐

Characteristics of a 'community of learners'	Examples of strategies to foster the communities of learners concept
Learning in context	Give clear examples of how the theory/issue applies in students' life: e.g. for English functional skills asking students to refer to the type of language used around them
Learning in a less formal environment	Take the students out of the institution whenever possible. Trips to museums, events and abroad encourage students to apply understanding of their subject and to use generic skills in a different context
Structuring challenging learning	Devise problem-based learning to be undertaken in groups
Mentoring	Discuss with students and colleagues if you can organise a group of strong or confident students who would be happy to support weaker/less confident students
Fostering independence	Include project/research work within your teaching

ACTIVITY

- Give precise examples on how you could apply the above strategies within your own practice.
- Do you have you own ideas on how to foster a community of learners within your institution?

SUMMARY

In 14–19 education, the concept of communities of learners is complex as far as its application is concerned. The 'race' for credentials at levels 2 and 3 signifies that most of the learning is restricted to a set curriculum and in the classroom. The rare opportunities to expand learning are often left to interpretation and not fully exploited. In addition, the training of teachers in England does not cater for a more 'organic' way of developing teaching and learning. Qualified professionals are not encouraged to deviate from any practice that may not meet prescribed teaching standards. If teachers could engage with curriculum design, they may be able to review current practices and focus on a more holistic way of learning, bringing a sense of community among learners. Rethinking the structure, purpose and values of a 14–19 education is therefore needed for the concept of 'communities of learners' to reach its full potential.

Find out more

Etienne Wenger (1998) *Communities of Practice, Learning, Meaning, and Identity*, **Cambridge: Cambridge University Press.**
This is a challenging but essential read if you intend to take the concept of 'communities of learners' further. The book offers a different perspective on social learning theories and introduces the concept of community of practice.

Jean Lave and Etienne Wenger (1991) *Situated Learning: Legitimate peripheral participation*, **Cambridge: University of Cambridge Press.**
Claimed by many as a 'breakthrough' text. In this book Lave and Wenger discuss learners as part of the community of practice. They explore the relations between the learners, learning and its community.

Barbara Larrivee (2008) *Authentic Classroom Management: creating a community of learners*, **3rd edn, Boston: Allyn & Bacon.**
This book focuses on the concept of 'communities of learners' in relation to classroom management. The text demonstrates how the creation of such a community can be beneficial to learners' behaviours and therefore learning. The book offers conceptual and concrete examples of practice. Although US-based, the strategies mentioned are also applicable to the UK context.

Bibliography

Ashwin, P. (2002) Implementing peer learning across organizations: the development of model, *Mentoring & Tutoring*, 10(3): 221–31.

Avis, J., Bathmaker, A. M. and Parsons, J. (2002) Community of practice and the construction of learners in post compulsory education and training, *Journal of Vocational Education and Training*, 54(1): 27–50.

Brown, A. L. and Campione, J. C. (1996) Psychological theory and the design of innovative learning environments: on procedures, principles, and systems, in L. Schauble and R. Glaser (eds), *Innovations in Learning: new environments for education*, Mahwah, NJ: Erlbaum.

Coffield, F. (2008) *Just Suppose Teaching and Learning Became the First Priority* . . . London: LSN.

DfES (2004) *14–19 Curriculum and Qualifications Reform*. Final report on the working group 14–19 Reform, Nottingham: DfES.

Guidance and units – Edexcel Diplomas levels 1–3, in Lave, J. and Wenger, E. (1991) *Situated Learning: legitimate Peripheral Participation*, Cambridge: Cambridge University Press.

Lumby, J. and Foskett, N. (2005) 14–19 *Education: Policy, Leadership & Learning*, London: Sage.

Mintrop, H. (2004) Fostering constructivist communities of learners in the amalgamated multi-discipline of social studies, *Journal of Curriculum Studies*, 36(2): 141–58.

Rico, Stephanie A. and Shulman, Judith H. (2004) Invertebrates and organ systems: science instruction and 'Fostering a community of learners', *Journal of Curriculum Studies*, 36(2): multiple 159–81.

Shoenfeld, Alan H. (2004) Learning communities: students, teachers, instructional designers, and researchers, *Journal of Curriculum Studies*, 36(2): 237–55.

Topping, Keith J. (2005) Trends in peer learning, *Educational Psychology*, 25(6): 631–45.

Wenger, E. (1998) *Communities of Practice: learning, meaning and identity*, Cambridge: Cambridge University Press.

Working group on 14–19 Reform (2004) *14–19 Curriculum and qualifications reform*, final reports, Tomlinson Report.

Values to Promote Learning

In this chapter you will:

- Consider what is meant by 'values'
- Identify your own values
- Reflect on your own experiences and the impact this has had on your own values
- Explore personal values which may conflict with that of your organisation or government policy
- Explore and consider a range of value systems including differing ideologies and differing cultures
- Consider ways of implementing values in your own practice

Pearson Education Ltd./Ian Wedgewood

Introduction

This chapter will attempt to define what is meant by values and consider a range of interpretations. It will also identify why values are important aspects of the practitioner's professional identity. It will explore the notion that values are not fixed but, instead, are dependent on culture, time, background and experiences. You will explore values and engage in an activity that will allow you to reflect on the nature of your own and wider values, and the impact these have on the world around you, the education system and the curriculum. You will also be able to explore the impact education has on shaping an individual and moulding them to the ideals of the society they are born into, as well as the idea that education can indeed 'compensate for society' (Bernstein 1970): that is, does education compensate, or balance inherent or societal inequalities? Are there universal values? You will also consider how your own experiences have shaped your identity and 'value system' and the impact that these may have on conflicting values from your pupils, the ethos of the school or education environment within which you have to work and the code of professional conduct of the Institute for Learning (IfL – the professional body for teachers, working in the lifelong learning and skills sector, in England).

What are values?

A value is simply the 'worth' or importance of something. When we refer to moral values and principles, we assign an **intrinsic** worth to these, as opposed to the monetary cost assigned to merchandise or goods. The difference in the nature of these values leads to conflict within education systems. This dichotomy is clearly illustrated between the drive to make places of education commercially viable *businesses*, alongside ideals of an education system that can indeed compensate for a society that is inherently unequal, one that levels out the playing field and at the same time produces young adults of high moral fibre. Oscar Wilde captured the intrinsic nature of value as opposed to its monetary worth by referring to the role of a jewellery valuer who 'know[s] the prices of everything and the values of nothing' (Wilde, quoted in Honderich 1995: 895).

In order for 'something' to be *valued*, be it material or more ethereal in nature, a **sentient** being has to attach value, hence the subjective nature of value(s).

As human beings we live and judge others by our own values all the time. However, we do not often stand back and reflect on the curious nature of values, how these are formed, or even articulate what these values are. Often these feelings are rooted in **moral judgements**. A moral judgment relates to that which you *ought* to do – or not do, rather than what necessarily *is*, a **judgement** of what is right or wrong based on your own feelings or conscience, as opposed to the law. These are frequently highly **emotive**. Our own 'moral compass' defines personal principles and has a considerable influence on our personal choices, preferences and judgements, and also as an inhibitory factor in curbing base impulses.

The **subjective** (the personal opinions or beliefs of an individual formed through own experiences) nature of a value is important. In order for something to be of value, it must, in itself, be valued by *somebody*, and thus have meaning for an individual. If all values were *sui generis* in nature – that is, unique to the individual – it is difficult to see how we could avoid perpetual conflict in the absence of any universally accepted principles or codes: for example, that it is wrong to murder. When viewed in this way, the words of the 17th century English philosopher, Thomas Hobbes (1588–1679), in his Magnum Opus *Leviathan* (1651), that life is 'nasty, brutish and short', take on a frightening reality. It is ironic that an existence of many unique values could lead to as much chaos and destruction as a world or society without *any* universal values.

WHAT DO YOU THINK?

Consider the following paragraph by Hobbes.

Whatsoever therefore is consequent to a time of war, where every man is enemy to every man, the same consequent to the time wherein men live without other security than what their own strength and their own invention shall furnish them withal. In such condition there is no place for industry, because the fruit thereof is uncertain: and consequently no culture of the earth; no navigation, nor use of the commodities that may be imported by sea; no commodious building; no instruments of moving and removing such things as require much force; no knowledge of the face of the earth; no account of time; no arts; no letters; no society; and which is worst of all, continual fear, and danger of violent death; and the life of man, solitary, poor, nasty, brutish, and short.

Hobbes (1651)

While it may be initially appealing to lead an egotistical life – free to act at will and without restraint:

- What would human society be like without any personal or societal values or morals?
- How would *you* act in a world without moral constraint?
- How do you think *others* would act towards you?
- How would *teachers* act?
- How would *pupils* act?
- Would there be an education system?

Why are values important within education?

That education is perceived as a good is generally accepted, so why do we value education – do we value it in its own right or because of the function it serves? What then is the *purpose* of education? Is it to simply impart information? If so, what type of

Source: Pearson Education Ltd. Ian Wedgewood

Source: Pearson Education Ltd. Ben Nicholson

Photo 3.1 and 3.2 Should the 14–19 phase of education be mostly academic or vocational, or a mixture of both? What is important?

information is considered important; who decides upon the content of the curriculum and how it is to be delivered? This has particular relevance when you think about the ongoing debate regarding the 'academic and vocational divide'. The former is often assigned a higher value with its focus on knowledge, reflection and scholarly activity, the latter of skill, dexterity, application and practicality. Both forms of education are of equal value and required in the world of work. This may be a reflection of an outdated view of education as a system of a selective, esoteric, arts-based schooling.

Are formal education systems structurally organised to reproduce existing inequalities in society? Paul Willis, a cultural theorist, believed that the education system was inherently flawed and biased towards more favourable outcomes for those from the middle classes. His classic text *Learning to Labour* (1977), explored how working-class pupils went on to gain working-class jobs through a system of education which produced malleable and obedient workers who are 'ready for the world of work'. The issue of whether or how we can instil in or teach 'values' to young people is not new, nor is the notion of preparing young people, *through schooling*, for a place in society. The foreword of *The Handbook of Suggestions for Teachers* produced by the Board of Education, a forerunner of the Ministry of Education, (1937, reprinted 1950) explains that 'the general introduction deals with the school child, his reaction to his surroundings as a complete personality, and his preparation through his school life for full membership of a modern community' (p. 4), going on to assert that the 'emphasis in recent years has been on the wider aim of an all round training of character' (p. 9).

This idea of schooling young people for a place in society has remained constant, although more recent emphases on this in government reports (for example, *21st Century Skills* (2003), the Foster Report *Realising the Potential: a review of the future role of FE colleges* (2005) and the Leitch Report *Prosperity for All in the Global Economy – world class skills* (2006)) which argue for this in terms of raising skills, the economic benefit to society and preparation for the world of work, as opposed to the development of moral character. This change, in particular of the language associated with education, was highlighted in the Nuffield 14–19 review (issue paper no. 6: *Aims and Values*) which asks 'what kind of society is being nurtured by this investment and whose interests are being served?' (2008: 2).

This suggests that as well as questioning the purpose of education, one should also examine and explore the curriculum itself, and, perhaps even more importantly, the question, 'Who benefits from it?'

> ## WHAT DO YOU THINK?
>
> - Who benefits from education?
> - What are these benefits? List a minimum of three.
> - Are these benefits equally distributed and accessible by every person aged 14–19 in society?

If education is a good in itself then surely all should benefit equally and all should receive the same education and opportunities. In the English system, for example, we still have the obvious division between private and public education, the grammar system, faith schools and more recently the government's encouragement of businesses to sponsor or manage academies. One of the first acts of the Minister for Education, Michael Gove, under the Conservative Liberal Democrat coalition in May 2010, was to invite all secondary schools, except Pupil Referral Units (PRUs) to apply for Academy status. Professor Richard Pring warns that there is the 'risk of damaging the values that define an educated and humane society'. He points out that 'the pursuit of economic prosperity could be at the expense of social values, such as greater community cohesion, or personal fulfilment and growth . . . The language employed 'suggests the management of business rather than the very different task of promoting the welfare of young people' and 'if one speaks the language of management, one is in danger of treating young people and their teachers as objects to be managed'. (Nuffield Review 2008: 4). He further illustrated this point by reminding the reader of an extract from Professor Larry Cuban's text, *The Blackboard and the Bottom Line: why schools can't be businesses*, (2004) which refers to a businessman who told an audience of teachers, 'if I ran a business the way your people operate your schools, I wouldn't be in business very long'. When he was cross-examined by a teacher, he declared he collected his blueberries and sent back those that did not meet the 'high quality' he insisted on. To this, the teacher replied 'we can never send back our blueberries. We take them rich, poor, gifted, exceptional, abused, frightened, confident, homeless, rude and brilliant. We take them with Attention Deficit Disorder, Junior Rheumatoid arthritis, and English as their second language. We take them all, every one. And that . . . is why it is *not* a business, it is a school'.

ACTIVITY

Your task is to design an education system that all 14–19-year-olds would have to attend, from behind a 'veil of ignorance' (Rawls 1971). This means you do not know what your position will be in this society, including that of your wealth, health, race and class. Therefore, one of your primary concerns should be that of optimising your own and future generations' educational opportunities no matter what the circumstances of your birth. For example, if you did not know whether you were going to be wealthy or poor, to optimise your own chances you may decide that all education, including resources, should be free. This is, in effect, a clean slate on which to design and implement a system that reflects your own values.

- Who would be educated?
- Would you impose a national curriculum – if so, what subjects would be covered and why?
- What choices would be available to accommodate the diverse range of learners?
- What will be the purpose of this education system – would it be to produce individuals who have occupational skills (remember these skills can change) or to promote personal growth and development?
- How would learners be assessed?
- How would achievement be recognised?

This activity will help you to recognise your own personal beliefs regarding the value of education and its purpose.

Education to 'compensate for society', or a system to reproduce existing inequalities?

The reforms of the education system reflected in the 1944 Education Act were heralded as having the potential to end the class-based education system, with the introduction of a new era of education based on meritocracy, i.e. effort and ability as opposed to class and wealth. The class system within education remains remarkably resilient. As A. H. Halsey, a British sociologist, has stated: 'The essential fact of 20th-century educational history is that egalitarian policies have failed' (*The Spectator* 2008). In terms of educational reform, it is not always clear whether it is the reforms that have addressed past inequalities, such as the attainment gap between males and females, or whether it is a change in social attitudes that have made a difference. Social mobility, which means an individual's chances of furthering themselves beyond the position they were born into, remains an issue, and while qualifications are significant for mobility, they are not the key determinant. Class background seems to be a more powerful determinant and so is the inequality of original position' (Alexiadou et al. 2002). Further, 'parental social class clearly continues to be strongly associated with educational attainment' (Buxten et al. 2004: 21). Other policies such as those developed from the Kennedy Report *Learning Matters* (1997) hoped to address issues of participation in further education in an attempt to widen access. Opportunities to succeed were a central tenet and a matter of equity for each and every young person. Prior to this, the Warnock Report of 1978 addressed the need for support for children with special educational needs and recognised that mainstream schooling could and should support a large number of these young people.

IN PRACTICE

The following is the opening paragraph of the Warnock Report, and, as Blamires notes on the TTRB SEN website, it is interesting, especially when you consider that this report was written over three decades ago:

> It is imperative that every teacher should appreciate that up to one child in five is likely to require some form of special educational help at some time during his school career and that this may be provided not only in separate schools or classes but also, with suitable support, in the regular classes of ordinary schools. The procedures which we have proposed for identifying, assessing and meeting the needs of children who require special educational provision will demand insight on the part of all teachers into the special needs which many children have. They must also be aware of the importance of working closely with parents and with other professionals and non-professionals concerned with helping those children who have special needs. The positive attitudes required of teachers in recognising and securing help for children with special educational needs, and the necessary skills, must be acquired in the course of training.

Either:

- Identify one pupil who you teach who has special educational needs

Or:

- Use a hypothetical example of a pupil who has dyslexia

And then:

- Identify three practical strategies you can implement in everyday teaching contexts to support that learner
- Identify three wider professionals to whom you could refer that pupil for additional support.

While many reforms, papers and initiatives use value-laden language, such as 'fulfilling potential' and 'individualised learning', the focus in the lifelong learning sector and at Key Stage 4 remains on a set of narrowly defined skills, reducing the learner and educator to component parts of a system in which individual learner progress is disregarded unless it can be audited, counted and officially accredited.

WHAT DO YOU THINK?

- What is more important – accredited outcomes (qualifications) or the learning journey?

Education can thus be seen as a vehicle for change: the answer or solution to a litany of societal problems. There has been much attention focused on the decline of juvenile and adolescent behaviour. As humans we naturally seek to try to explain behaviours – it should be remembered that the focus of the media is on *bad behaviours* as opposed to *good behaviours*. If, as we considered at the start of the chapter, values are subjective and are able to be changed through experience, the development of knowledge, and that the actions of others can have an impact on these, then educational institutions would seem an obvious place within which young people can be influenced. Young people spend the equivalent of a quarter of each working day (Monday–Friday) within educational institutions. The difficulty with this idea is the identification of 'which values should be transmitted'. The imposition of one set of values is important with regard to the **discourse** of inclusion, given the diverse nature of learners and their backgrounds and the friction of an imposed *national* curriculum and *national* system of training. While some theorists have argued for a coherent (school-based) framework for the development of what has been termed as 'character' or 'moral' education (McKown 1935; Brooks and Goble 1997 in Arthur 2003) and others have argued for the need for an individual school-based approach (DeRoche and Williams 2001 in Arthur 2003), the complex nature of character necessarily leads to a lack of consensus as to which values should in themselves be valued and which should not.

Consider the value associated with an autonomous, critical and enquiring learner. Many educators would consider these to be positive traits. However, in many cases, young people who learn to question can themselves be damned for this during adolescence, when it can be seen to be rude, disruptive or disrespectful. Instilling such values can of course form part of the teacher's own personal agenda or 'hidden' (covert) curriculum beyond that of the codified or public curricula (Keddie 1973). This raises the question of 'who' decides which values are to be valued and why? Marxists would argue that educational institutions are merely vehicles for reproducing the dominant **hegemony** of those who hold power. This could be illustrated with the continued high status of vocational professions such as lawyers or doctors, as compared to the lower status associated with vocations such as plastering, hair and beauty.

IN PRACTICE

Part A

Either conduct an audit of your own resources for one particular course or topic, or download a range of examples from a teaching website such as the TDA (Teacher Development Agency). Examine these from a 'values' point of view.

1. Do they promote stereotypical attitudes – do they perpetuate stereotypical roles or family systems, for example?
2. Are they gender-biased – if your specialism is a traditionally female or male oriented field of work, do your resources continue to reflect this?
3. Do they promote multiculturalism – do your resources reflect and contain a range of examples from different faiths or ethnic origins?

IN PRACTICE *CONTINUED*

Part B

Produce an activity that, as well as meeting the outcomes of the set task, also addresses values. This could for example be a discussion to meet literacy outcomes appropriate for its set audience, while the topic of discussion could raise awareness of the increase in sexually transmitted diseases and promote sexually responsible behaviour. Case studies are a useful way of allowing young people to explore choices and decisions – what would they have done – why? This allows young people to explore their own values as well as the values of others.

If values are integral to our 'selves', that is, they are what define us as individuals, or provide us with our identity in terms of the society and world in which we live, it is perhaps surprising that many of us accept these, not as considered and *chosen* values but as those which have been handed down to us by our forbears and the society we have grown up in.

When reflecting on values it is important to distinguish between those which are chosen and those which we have 'inherited'. Many advocates of reflective practice such as Donald Schön and Stephen Brookfield argue that we must critically explore and reflect on our own personal values as well as those which we inherit. The act of 'critical reflection urges us to create conditions under which each person is respected, valued, and heard' (Brookfield 1995: 27).

Own value system

As practitioners, we are also persons with our own set of values. We bring these values to the classroom, as do our students. Personal values are often deep-seated and can lead to conflict, which can easily escalate in each individual, be they tutor or student. Both can feel so strongly they are right, that neither can back down, or one of them will feel that the other has behaved in an unreasonable way, that an injustice has been committed. Such values may underpin disputes over apparently minor matters such as student clothing and self-presentation. The teacher prohibiting the wearing of headgear in the classroom may be unaware of the needs of the autistic student who cannot make eye contact, or those who are lacking in confidence; it may be that for some the wearing of baseball caps is a means of 'hiding' their 'selves' from the outside world.

IN PRACTICE

Consider a situation where you have been involved in a conflict that has revolved around your own or a student's values. For example, being on time may be of importance to you. You may associate this with enthusiasm and respect. However, you have a student who is constantly late, who makes no apologies for this and appears not to care. From the student's point of view, they do not understand why you get so 'moody' about this – it's 'only 5 minutes', they 'don't miss anything', so 'what's the problem'?

Where do you go from here?

- If you cannot think of a personal example ask your peers, or consider the above scenario.
  - Describe what happened from the student's viewpoint.
  - How do you think the student felt?
  - In light of these reflections what would you do differently next time?

Societal and wider values

When considering societal values it is easy to presume those values which we consider important have always been thus. Many of these values are enshrined in law, for example the Disability Discrimination Act 1995, and many are considered to be rights, such as the right to life, or the right to education. While as rational beings we are aware that the law is subject to change, how often do we reflect on these changes and consider how these changes come about? Do attitudes or changes in values lead to changes in the law, or do changes in the law lead to attitudinal change? What is the momentum that leads to these changes?

We live in a society where, on the surface at least, women have the same legal rights as men and sexism is outlawed. Shulamith Firestone, a radical feminist, who wrote the influential text *The Dialectic of Sex: the case for feminist revolution* (1979), argued that instead of promoting equal rights, this in fact only served to drive sexist attitudes underground to the extent that they were 'invisible'. For Firestone, tinkering with reform, no matter how radical, will never be enough to ensure absolute gender equality. Indeed, the only way in which women may be equal to men is through the abolition of biological differences. She advocated the use of *in vitro* fertilisation, cybernetics and the mechanical or artificial womb. While this may seem extreme, and, on the surface at least, women may now appear to 'have it all', it could be argued that in fact women 'do it all', and in many cases 'do it all' for less than their male counterparts. In the same way, many argue for wholesale change within the design of the 14–19 education system rather than this continued tinkering, which only serves to mask continued inequalities.

Values are often associated and developed over time among kinship, class or community groups. Thus values can be unique to the individual, associated with an organisation or enshrined in mission statements, for example.

ACTIVITY

- What is the mission statement of your local FE college or school?
- Can you identify the values of that educational organisation that are considered the most important?
- Do you agree?

Values can also be part of a community or group culture or ethos. At a national level they can be enshrined in law, or at an international level enshrined in treaties, or conventions and rights. That every culture, society and community, no matter the size, wealth, influence, power or stage of development, has values is without doubt. It is the nature of these values and what is deemed to be of value, or otherwise, that differs.

If we consider wider values, such as those found at a national or international level, we must once again consider the roots of these and how have they developed. Why were they developed? How 'wide' are they? The Universal Declaration of Human Rights (1948) is arguably a set of world values. The key point to note when considering wider values is that these too are subject to change and are fluid in nature. The European Convention on Human Rights (1950), for example, is a **'living instrument'**. In legal terms, this allows for differing interpretation and application to recognise change in attitude and social mores, so while homosexuality was still criminalised at the time of codification, the criminalisation of homosexuality is now considered to be a violation of human rights.

It is important to remember not only that societal and legal values *change,* but also that people like you are responsible for these changes; change comes about through individual challenge and questioning, which in turn gather momentum and turn into larger scale lobbying.

This implies that, as individuals, *we can and do make a difference.*

ACTIVITY

Consider one attitude of modern society that has led to change in the law, e.g. the use of children as factory workers, entitlement to free education, apartheid, the welfare system, the right to vote for *all* men and/or women, or the decriminalisation of suicide, for example.

a) Identify the relevant act or law that codified these changes in societal attitudes
b) Identify three benefits to the individual or society
c) Identify your own value position with regards to these changes.

Professional values

The issue of professional values is as complex as that of personal or societal values – who defines these, for example? When should a professional be bound by these regulations: within the workplace only, or at all times? It could be argued that with professional status and recognition, tutors should be responsible for upholding moral and ethical values within their professional and personal lives. Individual values and behaviours are often prescribed and expected to be adhered to. Many of us will have experienced codes of behaviour with our employment and in many other forms, such as student learning contracts. Codes of professional behaviour are designed to prescribe and monitor the behaviour of recognised professionals. Significantly, these values have been codified and made explicit, as opposed to societal values and norms which are rarely codified or made explicit. Young people are often expected to assimilate behaviours and values through the mimicking of behaviour and social learning; perhaps it is therefore unsurprising that so many differences and interpretations of social mores and values exist.

The codification of expected behaviours and values does make it easier for them to be understood or followed. The Institute for Learning (IfL) is the 'professional body for teachers, trainers, tutors and student teachers in the learning and skills sector' and, under the 2007 government reforms of teacher training and the further education workforce, provides the vehicle through which tutors register and become licensed practitioners. In April 2008, the IfL published its code of professional practice which 'outlines the behaviours expected of members – for the benefit of learners, employers, the profession and the wider community' (IfL 2008). Note the reference here to behaviour outside of the specific working context within the 'wider community'. There are seven behaviours which must be maintained: 'professional integrity; respect; reasonable care; professional practice; criminal offence disclosure; responsibility during institute investigations [and finally] responsibility (to act at all times in accordance to the Institute's conditions of membership)' (IfL 2008). It is perhaps an indication of the current climate within the teaching profession that the emphasis of these 'behaviours' is on control, regulations and legislative requirements, illustrated by its web page statement: 'the Code applies to all members of the Institute and will be enforced to protect the interests of learners and the wider public' (**www.ifl.ac.uk/membership/professional-standards/code-of-professional-practice**). While 'values' are referred to under behaviour 1.1 'that members shall meet their professional responsibilities consistent with the Institute's Professional values' (IfL 2008), these have not been codified. The standards for practitioners in the lifelong learning sector clearly articulates a set of professional values.

Teachers in the secondary sector who have QTS status are covered by their own *Code Of Conduct And Practice For Registered Teachers* regulated by the General Teaching Council for England (GTCE). Their standards were revised in 2008, and the code of practice revised in 2009. The driving force behind the 2008 revisions to the standards were changes in the educational landscape, such as the *Every Child Matters* agenda, the 14–19 reforms and the personalised learning agenda. There are eight principles of conduct and practice for registered teachers.

ACTIVITY

Part A

- List a minimum of four of your own personal professional values.
- Rank these in order of importance.

Part B

- Compare these to the relevant professional values for your setting – what are the similarities and/or differences?
- Identify one value you would be happy to relinquish from either list and explain why.
- Identify one additional value that you do not feel is adequately covered in the list and justify its inclusion.

Professional values lifelong learning sector	Professional values secondary sector
1. AS 1 All learners, their progress and development, their learning goals and aspirations and the experience they bring to their learning.	1. Put the well-being, development and progress of children and young people first
2. AS 2 Learning, its potential to benefit people emotionally, intellectually, socially and economically, and its contribution to community sustainability.	2. Take responsibility for maintaining the quality of their teaching practice
3. AS 3 Equality, diversity and inclusion in relation to learners, the workforce and the community.	3. Help children and young people to become confident and successful learners
4. AS 4 Reflection and evaluation of their own practice and their continuing professional development as teachers.	4. Demonstrate respect for diversity and promote equality
5. AS 5 Collaboration with other individuals, groups and/or organisations with a legitimate interest in the progress and development of learners.	5. Strive to establish productive partnerships with parents and carers
	6. Work as part of a whole-school team
	7. Cooperate with other professional colleagues
	8. Demonstrate honesty and integrity and uphold public trust and confidence in the teaching profession

Values for learning

What are values for learning? Given the diverse, individual, societal or cultural aspect of values it is difficult to define what values for learning mean, as they may well suggest different things to different individuals. One definition of values for learning is an environment and attitude from pupils and teachers that is conducive to the exploration and assimilation of new ideas and concepts, that allows for personal growth and the ability to challenge these ideas, while being able to listen to the views and perspectives of others. When considering values for learning, it is important to remember that most learners value education differently at different times during their education journey. For example, a learner may not value or see any purpose in education while at secondary school. However, as a mature student enrolled on an access course, that learner's views might have undergone a marked change. It is also important to remember that while some learners may recognise the value of education per se, it does not follow that they will display positive or even appropriate behaviours for learning within the classroom setting.

Attitudes towards education are further complicated and influenced by family, peer and/or social viewpoints and the perceived relevance of education to the individual. Some families may value education and encourage their children to engage, others will see it as a waste of time. 'Parents teachers and peers were three of the most significant influences upon young people's attitudes towards education' (Craddock et al. 2007: 1). Many pupils do not value the curriculum on offer and do not see its relevance. The nature of students' engagement with the curriculum is of particular importance, given the recent government policy with regard to the Raising of the Participation Age (RPA), from 16 to 17 in 2013 and 18 in 2015. For those who are disengaged from the curriculum, or do not see the value of education, this could prove counter-productive in terms of negative attitudes and behaviours. Wolf suggests that 'the most likely effect of corralling unwilling learners is that they will reduce opportunities for others' (2008: 14).

Source: Pearson Education Ltd. Ian Wedgewood

Photo 3.3
Positive pupil/teacher relationships make teaching and learning more enjoyable and effective.

Relationships between students and teachers also have an impact not only on the way in which young people behave within the classroom, but also on the young person's view of at least that part of the curriculum offer. Relationships with tutors therefore can impact on the options students take at 14, 16 and later, and their enjoyment or otherwise of a particular subject.

Motivation is of course key to learning and thus to promoting positive learning values. Given the influence that peers and teachers can exert over individuals, it is within this sphere perhaps that teachers should focus their energies in terms of promoting positive learning values. This can be achieved in a variety of ways, for example:

- By creating positive student/tutor relationships
- By designing engaging resources
- By demonstrating positive values, and acting as a role model
- By reminding students of the personal benefits of learning in terms of achievement, as a means to an end and, of course, employment and earning opportunities
- By creating stimulating and active working environments
- By actively seeking students' views and feedback about the types of learning activities they enjoy and learn most from
- By using the students' imagination, interests and creativity to learning opportunities and assessment tasks for their peers.

IN PRACTICE

Many practitioners focus on a small percentage of learners who display negative attitudes (and often behaviours) towards learning. This can lead to a somewhat warped perception of a group or indeed an individual.

Either

Consider one of your teaching groups and:

1. Identify five positive learning values that are displayed by individuals within this group (engagement, time on task or listening, for example)
2. Identify *one* of these above values that is of most importance to you
3. Over a period of two weeks, focus your session evaluations on identifying how often, by whom and how this value is demonstrated in behavioural (observable) terms and when this behaviour occurs
4. Analyse your findings in order to promote your understanding of when and why this behaviour occurs (for example, increased learner engagement may be related to the nature of the task or your teaching methods)
5. Produce an action plan that promotes this learner value within your lesson/session plans
6. After six weeks repeat steps 3 and 4 in order to make a comparison.

Or

Reflect on your own experiences of being taught and:

- Identify when you felt valued by a teacher – how did this make you feel; what impact did this have on your attitude to work?
- Identify *how* the teacher made you feel valued – was this by a look? words? a nod of the head?
- Ensure you model this behaviour in your own teaching environments.

SUMMARY

As you will have realised from this chapter, values are not easily defined, nor indeed fixed. We rarely interrogate our own values, but frequently judge the values of others. Values can be subjective and unique to an individual, community, group, culture, nation or can be universal, such as the Declaration of Human Rights. Values are fluid and subject to change over time and in differing contexts. Some values are codified. However, these are generally to ensure compliance, and provide regulation and the means to enforce or punish through disciplinary procedures.

Using education as a means of mass socialisation and a vehicle to instil values and social norms is not new, nor is the debate over which types of education should be more highly valued. Educational values are contradictory in nature, as they strive to achieve social justice and compensate for social inequality as well as deliver educational knowledge and skills.

And finally, never forget the positive influence that you, as an individual *and* a practitioner can have on individuals and therefore in the long term on society. Teachers can and do make a difference.

Find out more

The Nuffield Foundation is a charitable trust set up in 1943 by William Morris (Lord Nuffield). The foundation aims to 'advance social well being'. It is not funded by the government, but by the returns on its own investments. The Nuffield review of education 14–19 was a six-year independent review of 14–19 education and training, which concluded in 2009 and can be found online at **www.nuffield14-19review.org.uk/files/news58-2.pdf**

The full version of the Warnock Report 1978 is available online: **http://sen.ttrb.ac.uk/viewArticle2.aspx?contentId**

=13852. This is the Teacher Training Resource Bank for teachers working with Pupils who have Special Education Needs. (ttrb SEN)

The Code of Conduct and Practice for registered teachers can be found at: **www.gtce.org.uk/documents/ publicationpdfs/code_of_conduct_1009.pdf**

The overarching professional standards for teachers, tutors and trainers in the lifelong learning sector can be found at: **www.lluk.org/documents/ professional_standards_for_itts_020107.pdf**

Bibliography

Alexiadou, N. (2002) Social exclusion, and educational opportunity: the case of English education policies within a European context. Paper presented at the European Conference on Educational Research, University of Lisbon, 11–14 September 2002.

Arthur, J. (2003) *Education with Character; the moral economy of schooling*, Routledge: London.

Bernstein, B. (1970) Education cannot compensate for society, *New Society*, 387: 344–7.

Brookfield, S. D. (1995) *Becoming a Critically Reflective Teacher*, San Francisco, CA.: Jossey Bass.

Board of Education (1937, reprinted 1950) *The handbook of Suggestions for Teachers*, HMSO: London.

Buxton, J., Clarke, L., Grundy, E. and Marshall, C. (2004) ONS Longitudinal Study *Social Class, Own Social Class, Educational Attainment and Timing of First Birth: results*, London: Centre for Longitudinal Studies. Available at: **www.statistics.gov.uk/articles/population_trends/ PT121_BuxtonClarkeGrundy.pdf** [accessed 12.08.08].

Craddock, C., Dodgson, R., Lowrey, J., Lowther, H. and Simpson, G. (2007) *Young People's Attitudes to Education* III. Northumbria University Centre for Policy research. Available at: **www.viewnortheast.co.uk/ document.asp?id=680&pageno=2&extlink=546** [accessed 12.08.08].

Cuban, L. (2004) *The Blackboard and the Bottom Line: why schools can't be businesses*. Cambridge MA and London: Harvard University Press.

Firestone, S. (1979) *The Dialectic of Sex: the case for feminist revolution*, London: The Women's Press.

Gillard, D. (2006) *The Hadow Reports: an introduction*, at: **www.dg.dial.pipex.com/articles/educ27.shtml** [accessed 24.07.08].

Hobbes, T. (1651, English edn) *Leviathan*, available at: **oregonstate.edu/instruct/phl302/texts/hobbes/ leviathan-c.html** [accessed 18/08/08].

Honderich, T. (1995) *The Oxford Companion to Philosophy*, Oxford: Oxford University Press.

Institute for Learning (2008) *Promote: the code of professional practice*, at: **www.ifl.ac.uk**

Keddie, N. (1973) *Tinker, Taylor: the myth of cultural deprivation*, edited by M. Young, Harmondsworth: Penguin.

LLUK (2007) *The New Overarching Professional Standards for tutors, teachers and trainers in the lifelong learning sector*. Available at: **www.lluk.org/ documents/professional_standards_for_itts_020107.pdf** [accessed 15.08.08].

McKeown, H. C. (1935) *Character Education*, New York: McGraw Hill Book Co.

NFER (2008) *The Effects of the School Environment on young people's attitudes towards education and learning*. Available at **www.nfer.ac.uk/nfer/ research/projects/building-schools-future/ building-school-future_home.cfm**

Nuffield Review of Education and Training, England and Wales (2008) Issue Paper No. 6 *Aims and Values*. Available at: **www.nuffield14-19review.org.uk/files/ documents179-1.pdf** [accessed 16.07.08].

Rawls, J. (1971) *A Theory of Justice*, Cambridge MA: Belknap, Harvard University Press.

The Spectator (2008) 'Social mobility disappeared with grammar schools' (*The Times*). Stephen Pollard, 24.08.08. Available at: **www.spectator.co.uk/coffeehouse/ 794476stephenpollard-social-mobility-disappeared- with-grammar-schools-the-times.thtml**

Standards Verification United Kingdom (2007) *New Overarching Professional Standards for* teachers, tutors and trainers in the lifelong learning sector. Available at: **www.standardsverificationuk.org/ documents/professional_standards_for_itts_020107.pdf** [accessed 12.08.08].

Willis, P. (1977) *Learning to Labour: how working class kids get working class jobs*, New York: Columbia University Press.

Wolf, A. (2008) *Diminished Returns: how raising the leaving age to 18 will harm young people and the economy*, Policy Exchange. Available at: **www.policyexchange.org.uk/publication.cqi?id=65**

CHAPTER 4

Development and Learning

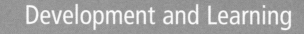

In this chapter you will:

- Consider aspects of cognitive, social and physical development
- Increase your understanding of the concept of 'adolescence' and adolescent development
- Consider theories of brain development
- Examine the implications of development issues for your teaching

Pearson Education Ltd./Ian Wedgewood

Introduction

The area of development is of interest to all – ask any new parent and they will be able to tell you where and at what age their child first smiled, articulated a word or walked. All of these are developmental milestones. Development relates to the normal changes that occur to an individual throughout their lifetime. Much development is related to maturation – the changes that occur naturally over time, in particular physical changes. While every individual experiences developmental changes, it should be remembered that people develop at different rates and the impact this has on an individual can vary enormously. Not all development is linear; changes rarely happen overnight and people may regress.

Much of this chapter explores the natural changes that occur during adolescence and the impact this has on the individual – in their behaviour and attitudes, skills and abilities. It therefore asks whether there should be a distinct training programme for teachers who teach adolescents. If so, what age range should this cover, as people develop at different rates, and levels of maturity can be vastly different in pupils of the same age. This is particularly the case with gender: for example, girls tend to experience puberty roughly two years earlier than boys. The differences in gender tend to be more marked during early adolescence as boys 'catch up' with the girls during mid and late adolescence. You will explore the relatively new concept of adolescence as a distinct phase, which marks the period of time between childhood and adulthood and consider popular theories of development and the challenges faced by adolescents, including physical and social development with a particular focus on the emerging and unique identity of the individual. You will also explore the area of brain development – an area that is attracting increased attention as researchers recognise the continued ability of the brain to develop and change beyond adolescence. The chapter finishes by exploring how the information could be useful in teaching settings.

Development theories

Development theories apply to the expected, ordered and significant changes that occur during an individual's lifetime. In general, these theories are concerned with understanding the spectrum of 'normal' development by recognising changes as milestones, for example from crawling to walking. Knowledge about these changes and how they affect the way individuals and groups behave, and common patterns of behaviour, particularly those associated with adolescence, allow the teacher to anticipate and thus plan how to respond in an objective and constructive manner, rather than through emotional or 'gut' responses. Development can be seen as:

- Physical – changes to the body
- Personal – changes to personality
- Social and emotional – changes in relationships and emotional capacity, such as the ability to relate to others
- Cognitive – changes to the way you think.

Theories of development traditionally focused on birth through childhood, and expected milestones were fairly rigorously applied in order to make comparative judgements. It is now recognised that while general models or patterns can be applied, individuals develop at differing rates and at differing times. Young people therefore should be seen as individuals who will develop in different ways and in different time spans. Thomas Keenan, a development psychologist, proposed the principle of **multidirectionality** (2002), and maintains there is no single 'normal' path for development, and particularly in adulthood some aspects of cognitive development improve as others decline or mature at a different rate. This has particular implications during adolescence. Research suggests intellectual capacity and ability matures before psychosocial development during adolescence. Key areas that make life difficult for teenagers, and indeed those around them, are:

- Poor impulse control
- Reduced ability to delay gratification, and
- Vulnerability to peer pressure.

RESEARCH FOCUS

The MacArthur Foundation Research Network on Adolescent Development and Juvenile Justice in the USA has conducted research that suggests that adolescents should be dealt with differently in the juvenile system (**www.fairsentencingforyouth.org**). They do not see this as an excuse for criminal activity, but feel that the legal system should recognise the impact that differing intellectual and psychosocial development can have on the decision-making process, particularly that of culpability – that is, the blameworthiness of an individual. In 2005 a landmark ruling outlawed the death penalty for offenders who were younger than 18 when they committed their crimes.

The idea of mitigating circumstances when meting out punishment is not new. If we apply the logic behind this research to school and educational setting in the UK, this could have an impact on the type of punishment young people receive in relation to their acts. This poses some interesting questions as to whether the punishment is disproportionate to the 'crime'. In particular, it raises questions about the disproportionate impact of exclusion and future life chances. What do you think? Should the immaturity of decision-making processes, the susceptibility to peer pressure and a reduced ability to delay gratification be taken into consideration when dealing with unwanted adolescent behaviour?

Theories of development and learning are of enormous importance and use to educators and in particular for their training. The current focus of initial teacher training on the practical skills required for classroom teaching has reduced the light that subjects such as sociology, psychology and philosophy can throw on teaching and learning. This has had an impact on the training of new teachers in two ways – firstly, the academic dimension of teacher training has been devalued and there is a perception among many trainees that it is either too hard or, sadly, of no relevance. Secondly, while it can be argued that the basics and practical side of teaching should be of primary importance during the early stages of teacher training, it is the underpinning knowledge of theory that will enable practitioners to develop and refine their teaching skills. If we liken a teacher's development to those of **stages** found in many psychological theories such as those espoused by Sigmund Freud, Erik Erikson and Jean Piaget, who have influenced much of contemporary thought on psychological development, it makes sense that as with any other craft, higher levels of mastery and understanding should follow on from the rudimentary stage. Underpinning theories can also help us to understand why certain strategies are encouraged as good practice, rather than being perceived as adopted pragmatically to satisfy external audit.

In psychological terms, '**staging**' refers to different developmental phases. Three of the most influential of these are Jean Piaget (1896–1980), a biologist whose theories, rooted in the observation of children, have been highly influential in the areas of child development, particularly that of maturation. His stages of cognitive development related to the theory that children could only complete certain tasks at certain stages of development and not before. These theories have in part influenced the national curriculum in terms of scheduling.

Erik Erikson (1902–94) was a developmental psychologist and a psychoanalyst. He is associated with the term 'identity crisis', which plays a crucial role within his psychosocial theory of development.

Sigmund Freud (1856–1939) was a neurologist and a founding father of psychoanalysis. His psychosexual theory of development is also divided into clearly defined periods of development, or stages.

Theories of staging are of particular importance when we consider the ages at which young people go through educational selection procedures, such as that at 11+ and at the age of 14 when young people are now required to make future career choices, particularly when one considers the nature of the choices students are making at an age when developmentally they may not have the criticality or higher-level reasoning skills required to make informed judgements. Career choices could be made on the basis of what their peers are doing, or where they gain immediate gratification such as monetary gain.

This has implications for the times at which young people are asked to make decisions as well as the training of teachers for this age range. Gina Donovan (2005) suggests that 'in order to preserve high quality learning experiences for the 14–19 phase, there is a pressing need to develop the role of the specialised teacher as manager and monitor of students' progress' (Donovan 2005: 42). The difference between teacher training for different educational phases, for example between secondary and post compulsory, is increasingly becoming blurred. It is important therefore that providers for both phases should be willing to learn from each other's professional experience and knowledge. Certainly, greater emphasis within teacher training for those who teach 14–19 should be on understanding development and the multiple changes that can occur during adolescence.

DISCUSSION POINT

Do you think that there should be distinct training programmes for teachers of 14–19-year-olds?

- What should be included in this curriculum?
- Justify your selection.
- Are there gaps in your own knowledge regarding 14–19 education? Identify these and produce an action plan for your own continued professional development needs.

The concept of 'adolescence'

Many of us refer to adolescence without fully exploring the changes that occur in adolescence or how and why these occur. The term 'adolescence' is relatively new historically and marks a clear period of time between childhood and adulthood. Historically in many societies the period from which an individual was recognised as an adult as distinct from a child was marked by rituals or rites of passage. It certainly was not associated with a distinct and *prolonged* phase of development, although it is clear that biological and developmental change would have been recognised as they are clearly evident. The prolonged or elongation of childhood has had an impact on the way societies view adolescence and, in particular, the period before which an individual is recognised as an adult. The focus of this series, for example, is on 14–19 education – this is in itself a fairly recent concept, and while policy makers and teachers use this term widely and accept this new 'phase', it remains clear that there is no coherent phase or system for the education of 14–19-year-olds, or even where they should be educated – school, the workplace, private providers, college?

So what is 'adolescence'? The term adolescence comes from the Latin *adolescere* – 'to grow into maturity'. The World Health Organisation defines adolescents as those who are between the ages of 10 and 19 (whereas 'youths' are aged between 15 and 24 and 'young people' are aged between 10 and 24!). In general the term 'adolescence' refers to the transition from childhood to adulthood, from immaturity to maturity, usually marked by the onset of puberty at around the age of 11 for girls and 13 for boys. The onset of puberty is, however, happening earlier, probably as a result of better nutrition. This of course raises questions in relation to legally defined periods of 'adulthood' and the contradiction in terms of what adulthood implies, such as the ability to make rational choices, or to be able to participate in adult acts. For example, the smoking age has recently been raised to 18 – the age at which young people can vote and get married without their parents' consent. However, sexual relationships are legally sanctioned from the age of 16 and young people can fight and die for their country at the age of 17 (in England). One definition of adulthood is the ability to make informed decisions and choices and certainly, in the medical field, Gillick's Law acknowledges the right of a young person who is deemed to be competent under the age of 16 to give consent to medical treatment *without* their parent/guardian's consent. The question of informed consent (informed in this case relates to the young person's full understanding of the issue, their ability to consider the implications of any choices they make, without external pressure), should be considered carefully in light of neuroscientific findings which demonstrate that the part of the brain that allows us to make informed and considered decisions is not fully matured until the early 20s, and myelination ('the process by which neural fibres are coated with a fatty sheath called myelin which makes message transfer more efficient' (Woolfolk et al. 2008: 719)) continues into the third decade of life. The increase of effective neuronal connectivity, through cognitive stimulus, in other words *learning*, is also shown to be effective in delaying or reducing the onset of memory problems such as those associated with Alzheimer's disease late in life.

When asked to consider adolescence in historical terms, one tends to think of children who were socialised through imitation of parents early into preparation for the world of work. This was limiting in terms of social mobility or improving upon the position of your birth and stereotypically gender-biased. Children were also employed at a very young age, for example as sweeps (poignantly described in Charles Kingsley's novel *The Water Babies* (1863)), or within factories (during the industrial revolution). In spite of the lack of literature pertaining to 'adolescence' as a distinct period, it is hard to imagine that 'adolescence' was not recognised as a transitional period in some form or other, given the obvious physical changes associated with puberty and the marked difference between childhood and adulthood.

Photo 4.1
Adolescence is often a troubling and confusing time; mixed laws and messages often add to identity uncertainty

Source: Alamy Images

The term 'teenager', referring to a separate and defined stage, emerged in the 1940s as a result of the recognition of a consumer market (Hine 1999). Thomas Hine explores the concept of adolescence as a period that has led to the justification of the delay of maturity and of deferred 'adult' responsibility. This is made worse by the lengthening of dependency, particularly that of economic dependency.

It is clear that the period between childhood and adulthood has lengthened from that of milestones or other rites of passage that denoted the end of childhood, for example recognition of sexual maturity with a girl's first menarche, or recognition of adult status when stepping over the threshold after marriage. This process is complicated by the acceptance of 'adulthood' as a term, without formal examination or clarification over what this means. When are you an adult? You can have sex at 16, die for your country at 17 but not buy cigarettes or alcohol.

Thomas Hine in his book *The Rise and Fall of the American Teenager* (1999) felt that many young people are resistant to the idea of responsibility and feel that they 'deserve' a period of freedom. Consider the increase in the idea of a gap year, for example, before settling down into the weightiness of responsibility.

ACTIVITY

How do today's teenage years differ from your own?

- Describe the differences and illustrate these with examples – e.g. young people's socialising especially with the use and access to technology.

- What are the similarities – for example, arguing over curfew times!

- What do you think are the major challenges for young people?

- Do you think 'adulthood' can be specified by age or by the completion of 'tasks' – for example, marriage, or being financially and emotionally independent? Or can adulthood be attained after a prolonged period of 'maturity'? Is it a state of being?

Notions of responsibility are a central theme in our society, especially with regards to individuals devolving 'blame' and judging the worthiness, or not, of others to 'deserve' help. Craig Newnes and Nick Radcliffe in their compelling book *Making and Breaking Children's Lives* (2005) make a strong case for the way children, particularly those who are the responsibility of us all as corporate parents, are 'hurt in modern society', as the importance of psychosocial aspects of development is minimised in the rush to prescribe drugs and medically diagnose and label young people. A clear example of the 'nonsense' of responsibility is illustrated by Newnes and Radcliffe in their opening chapter – 'children and adolescents are urged to be more responsible despite the remarkable complexity of the strictly legal interpretation of the expression: a child can be found guilty of murder aged 10, but cannot drive until they are 17' (2005: 33). The recognition of societal and cultural influence is particularly important when we consider that achievement gaps between socio-economic groups, while relatively minor as children start school, have tripled by the time these children reach 10 years old.

Adolescent development

Adolescence is a period of immense change intellectually, physically and emotionally. Adolescence is usually divided into three phases or stages of development – early adolescence (approx. 10–13), middle adolescence (approx. 13–16) and late adolescence (approx. 16–20). However, as with all developmental changes it is important to remember that these changes will occur at different rates and times for individuals. Gender also has an impact and females tend to mature faster than males. It is also important to remember that individuals could mature early physically, for example with the onset of puberty, but be late developers emotionally or cognitively. Many young boys mature physically at a much faster rate than they do emotionally. It is important for teachers to remind themselves that while they may physically look older, they are not yet adults. Progression from one stage to the next is thus variable, as is development within each of the following areas.

Adolescent development can be divided into three broad areas:

- Physical
  - rapid weight and height growth
  - puberty – development of hormones and secondary sex characteristics (for example, facial hair in males)
  - brain development – particularly those affecting emotional, physical and mental proficiency

- Cognitive: development of
  - reasoning
  - abstract thinking (the ability to interpret images or ideas in a different way to that which is merely presented literally). Abstract thinking is normally contrasted with concrete thinking in which an individual is able to ascribe literal meaning only to an image or idea
  - meta-cognition (the ability to think about thinking)

- Psychosocial
  - establishing an identity – including that of sexuality
  - working towards and gaining independence
  - the ability to develop close relationships and intimacy.

Traditionally theorists have focused on these as three distinct areas. In the field of medicine and the context of disease or illnesses, George Engel's (1977) **biopsychosocial** approach is now increasingly dominant: that is, an approach that recognises the impact and effect of the social and psychological as well as the biological on health. This approach critiqued the narrowly defined biomedical model that reduced human patients to 'objects' and ignored their subjective experiences. The impact of this model can be seen with the integration of a range of health-care professions from differing disciplines and an increased recognition of the range of factors that can lead to ill health.

Urie Bronfenbrenner, a Russian American psychologist (1989), developed a **bioecological** model of human development which recognises a many layered approach to development and the impact of the biological as well as a range of social contexts and

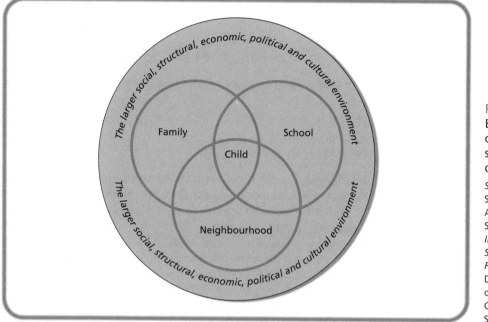

**Figure 4.1
Ecological
contexts
shaping child
development**

Source: Zubrick,
S. R., Williams,
A. A. and Silburn,
S. R. (2000).
*Indicators of
Social and Family
Functioning,*
Department
of Family and
Community
Services, Canberra

levels on development. Both these models recognise that development cannot be viewed in simple isolation of any one type of factor, such as the biological or social.

Bronfenbrenner's model also illustrated the *bi-directional* influences that occur within differing systems and levels: thus the teacher can have an impact on the parent and vice versa, and the young person can have an impact on the teacher as well as the teacher having an impact on the young person.

Understanding a range of behaviours that fall into the 'normal' spectrum

Understanding what is within the range of normal adolescent behaviour is important to the teacher. For example, many adolescents will use early to mid adolescence to test boundaries and rules, for example those connected with wearing uniform or about timings. It is important therefore to ensure boundaries are made clear and consistent. Mid to older adolescents are developing their own moral, value or belief system. Often during mid adolescence, this is fixed with no blurred boundaries. This can of course lead to conflict within the classroom, with diverging values between peers and students and teachers. Disaffected adolescents often have a heightened sense of right and wrong which can lead to a real sense of injustice and unfairness especially within disciplinary processes. Many students will also begin to challenge their teachers in terms of teacher knowledge and the selection, delivery and appropriateness of materials. Often this can be mistaken for rebelliousness rather than normal adolescent behaviour.

While the media may paint a picture of angst, alienation and antisocial behaviour in relation to young people, it is important to remember that the vast majority of 14–19-year-olds are lively, engaging and with enquiring minds that can be motivated, stimulated and channelled into positive activity, especially as they mature and develop their cognitive and psychosocial skills.

Development tasks and challenges of the adolescent

The main challenges of adolescence are those of adapting to change, including that of:

- biological maturity
- the development of personal identity
- the establishment of intimate sexual relationships
- working towards independence and autonomy.

These challenges and changes can be frightening for individuals and can be somewhat paradoxical as they strive for personal identity and individuation as well as express a need to be accepted, included and 'normal'. The development of abstract thought can lead to personal questioning such as 'Who am I?', 'Am I valued?', 'Am I clever?' and 'Am I normal?' Reassurance in these areas is important for the development of self-esteem. Body image is increasingly becoming an issue for young people. For girls, in particular, who naturally develop body fat as part of puberty, self-esteem can be linked to body image. While girls are more likely to suffer from a range of eating disorders, this is no longer a solely female issue, especially with the existence of the 'ideal body size and shapes' that are so strongly featured in the media. The need to be liked and 'normal' means that peers begin to have far more influence than families or teachers.

IN PRACTICE

Paul is 15 years old. He was until recently a quiet member of the class. Lately he has been arguing with his teacher and not getting on with his work. He constantly talks to his friends during sessions, refuses to take out his earphones and is becoming increasingly rude to his teacher, especially when he asks him to focus, or to stop talking. Quite a lot of his comments are tactless, which makes his teacher feel increasing upset and a little angry, especially as many of Paul's friends seem to find these comments funny.

Paul's teacher is not sure what to do and does not understand why Paul is acting this way – especially as he has taught Paul since he was 11 and, as he points out, 'he hasn't changed'.

Discuss this scenario with an experienced teacher or your mentor and together:

- Identify three possible reasons that may have contributed to the change in Paul's behaviour and attitude
- Identify two strategies the teacher could try to reduce these behaviours.

The following table outlines the main developmental tasks for the adolescent.

Table 4.1

	Biological	Psychological	Social
Early adolescence	Early puberty (girls: breast bud and pubic hair development, start of growth spurt; boys: testicular enlargement, start of genital growth)	Concrete thinking but early moral concepts; progression of sexual identity development (sexual orientation); possible homosexual peer interest; reassessment of body image	Emotional separation from parents; start of strong peer identification; early exploratory behaviours (smoking, violence)
Mid adolescence	Girls: mid-late puberty and end of growth spurt; menarche; development of female body shape with fat deposition Boys: mid-puberty, spermarche and nocturnal emissions; voice breaks; start of growth spurt	Abstract thinking, but self still seen as 'bullet proof' [i.e. nothing can harm them]; growing verbal abilities; identification of law with morality; start of fervent ideology (religious, political)	Emotional separation from parents; strong peer identification; increased health risk (smoking, alcohol, etc); heterosexual peer interest; early vocational plans
Late adolescence	Boys: end of puberty; continued increase in muscle bulk and body hair	Complex abstract thinking; identification of difference between law and morality; increased impulse control; further development of personal identity; further development or rejection of religious and political ideology	Development of social autonomy; intimate relationships; development of vocational capability and financial independence

Adapted from McIntosh, N., Helms, P. and Smyth, R. (eds) 2003 *Forfar and Arneil's Textbook of Paediatrics*. 6th edn, Edinburgh: Churchill Livingstone, 1757–68.

Source: Viner, R. and Christie, D. (2005) ABC of adolescence, *British Medical Journal*.

Moves towards autonomy

Piaget (1965) and Erikson (1959) argued that an emotional separation from family is required in order for identity to form. Freud (1905) also argued that emotional detachment from parental authority was required during adolescence, although he argued this was in order to further the development of society (individuals can only become original thinkers and thus develop new ideas that enable a society to progress once they become independent) and also to renounce incestuous feelings. While this fight against imposed authority in order to establish own identity takes place primarily within the family, it is clear that these theories can have an impact in terms of teachers' understanding of *why* adolescents begin to question authority, particularly if this is perceived to be illegitimate. Understanding that this is a normal process towards adult-hood and autonomy for teenagers can help the teacher to view these sometimes fraught

Table 4.2 Erikson's stages of psychosocial development 4–6

Stages	Approx. age	Important event	Description
4. Industry versus inferiority	6–12 years	School	The child must deal with demands to learn new skills or risk a sense of inferiority, failure and incompetence
5. Identity versus role confusion	Adolescence	Peer relationships	The teenager must achieve identity in occupation, gender roles, politics and religion
6. Intimacy versus isolation	Young adulthood	Love relationships	The young adult must develop intimate relationships or suffer feelings of isolation

Source: Lefton, L. (1994) *Psychology* 5th edn, Pearson Education, in Woolfolk et al. (2008) *Psychology in Education*, Pearson.

interactions, not as personal attacks on their authority or knowledge but as part of the challenge teenagers face on their journey towards adulthood.

Erikson views adolescence as a time of turmoil and stress for the individual (this often affects those closest to the individual, for example family and educational settings). Like Piaget he sees development through stages – Erikson defined these as the 'eight stages of man'. These development stages occur throughout an individual's life. Those most relating to adolescents are stages 5 and 6; stage 4 has been included in Table 4.2 to give some idea of the transition between these stages.

The table highlights the developmental crisis of each stage where a positive or unhealthy outcome for the individual is possible. Outcomes at each stage have an impact on the way individuals perceive themselves and society, as social and cultural developmental experiences impact on the individual, illustrating Erikson's acceptance of the impact of a range of influences. Thus during the industry versus inferiority stage, individuals must 'master new skills and work towards new goals, whilst being compared to others and risking failure' (Woolfolk et al. 2008: 88). Failure at this stage can have a significant impact on later achievement and impact on an individual's willingness to attempt new tasks. While it is common to talk about stages and relate these to developmental milestones in terms of achievement, and this is certainly the current language of performance indicators within school settings, it is important to remember that Erikson was a humanitarian as well as a psychoanalyst and his experiences took him beyond the narrow confines of the clinical setting. He was clear that these stages did not start and end in linear fashion but overlapped and developed organically. At each stage, the opposing outcomes or dispositions need to be balanced in order to successfully pass through each stage: for example at stage 6, intimacy (the ability to maintain healthy relationships) versus isolation needs to be balanced between the extremes of exclusivity and promiscuity. He was also hopeful that at every stage, just as one could 'fall from grace', so could a person who has been unsuccessful turn this around and succeed. The ability to be able to redeem oneself is perhaps one of the most compelling aspects of Erikson's theory, and perhaps could be used as a timely reminder to society, that our systems could and perhaps should be based on the opportunity for every individual to make 'good'.

Identity

Adolescence is central to the construction of identity and involves the many developmental changes occurring during this stage, especially the expansion of cognitive processes that allow the individual to consciously explore questions about who they are and who they are going to be as an adult. 'Identity refers to the organisation of the individual's drives, abilities, beliefs, and history into a constant image of self. It involves deliberate choices and decisions particularly about work, values, ideologies and commitments to people and ideas' (Marcia 1987, Penuel and Wertsch 1995 in Woolfolk et al. 2008: 89). Past developmental experiences will have an impact on the development of identity. If these aspects of identity are not assimilated, role confusion will follow. Ethnic identity can be particularly problematic for young people who are caught between two or more cultures, as they have even more conflicting values and roles to experiment with and choose from. As a teacher it is particularly important to model pro-social behaviour to teenagers and act as positive role models during this phase.

In terms of identity, it is crucial that adolescents are given opportunities to explore and experiment and thus make choices and commitments. James Marcia (1966), a Canadian psychologist, identified four identity statuses (the status or condition of a person in relation to their circumstances):

- Identity diffusion – no exploration, actions, or conclusions in terms of who they are or what they want to become – not only do these pupils not know what they want to do, but also they have little interest in the process.

- Identity foreclosure – have committed themselves but with no personal exploration, rather they are following the wishes of others: for example, their families have always been doctors and therefore that is what they will become.

- Moratorium – have explored options but with no commitment – this is common with the elongation of childhood and can be considered healthy.

- Identity achievement – exploration of options undertaken and commitment made (this can change later): for example, they have made an informed decision about career paths.

Identity diffusion and foreclosure may lead to difficulty within the classroom in terms of withdrawn or rebellious behaviour for the former and dogmatic or defensive behaviour for the latter.

IN PRACTICE

Either:

- Ask your pupils to identify role models that are important to them and why. Develop this further in terms of your own subject specialism by highlighting role models that are not particularly well known: for example, female playwrights such as Aphra Behn. ▶

IN PRACTICE *CONTINUED*

Or:

• Many young people remain 'stuck' in the stage of identity diffusion or foreclosure. Identify ways in which you and the wider network of professionals available within your own educational setting or within your local community could help these young people to think about their future choices.

Cognitive development

For Piaget, adolescence was the period from 12 to adulthood, the 'formal operational' stage of cognitive development, when individuals are able to move from concrete to abstract thought. This stage also reflects a decrease in narcissism or egocentricism by about the age of 15–16. However, prior to this decrease, many young people feel extremely self-conscious, and do indeed feel that the world is watching them and judging them and, further, that their experiences are unique only to them (may lead to feelings of abnormality). Many young people may also feel they are 'bullet-proof' which can lead to, and explain, some risk-taking behaviours. While experimentation and risk-taking is normal adolescent behaviour (Roth and Brooks-Gunn 2000), many of these risks, if habitualised, can lead to problems – for example, relating to drug and alcohol dependency.

The move to the formal operational stage of cognitive development is crucial as it supports the capacity for abstract thinking, allowing young people to create hypothetical situations and solutions, to evaluate, to think about cause and effect, and the consequences of their actions for *themselves* and *others*. It allows them to self-reflect and set goals. It also helps them to recognise and manage their own emotions as well as the emotions of others, to demonstrate self-restraint, or to manage conflict in a more constructive manner.

IN PRACTICE

Either:

Devise a learning activity that encourages your students to reflect on choices and decisions. Appropriate 'circle time' is an excellent way to pose hypothetical situations and a means of encouraging students to explore and reflect upon their own and others' choices. Case studies can also be extremely useful for this type of activity as they offer in-depth information about a single 'case' or example. They are also 'safe' as students do not have to disclose own choices – right or wrong – and provide the information needed for them to make informed choices objectively. In *trusted and secure* peer groups you could extend this activity by asking individuals to imagine what other members of the group would do in the same situation, or, asking them what they think an older or younger person would do. Alternatively, students enjoy discussions around 'what they ought not to do in the same situation' – this allows the teacher to facilitate discussions involving risk behaviour. Extend these activities by asking students what they would do in the same situations to ensure a positive outcome as well as a negative outcome. Discuss the consequences of these differing outcomes.

Or:

Many schools operate restorative justice systems. The aims of restorative justice in schools was to 'reduce offending, bullying and victimisation, and to improve attendance. Restorative justice enables offenders and victims to communicate and agree on how the harm caused by offending behaviour is to be repaired' (Youth Justice Board. *Restorative Justice in schools*: p. 4) available at: **www.yjb.gov.uk/Publications/Resources/Downloads/RJ%20in%20Schools.pdf**.

The following is a case example cited within the report.

> *[A] student was withdrawn from school by his mother after he had been repeatedly bullied. It emerged that the bullied student often provoked the bully by acting in a silly manner.*
>
> *As a result of the conference, the bully agreed to stop her aggression, and the bullied student agreed to stop his provocative behaviour.*

- Identify a situation you, a friend or a colleague have experienced where restorative justice could have helped. Who would have benefited from this intervention and how?

Brain development

We have explored the importance of cognitive development, but this cannot be viewed in isolation and without a wider understanding of the physical development of the brain. During gestation, the brain grows at an enormous rate and at birth the baby is born with a brain already 80 per cent of its adult size (the brain is the only organ that is not fully formed at birth). The brain is enormously complex and its raw material consists of the nerve cell or neuron. The neuron cells send out branches or fibres which then connect or are 'wired' to other neuron cells, connections which are known as synapses. 'Neuronal pathways connect different parts of the brain that govern everything we do from breathing to thinking' (Shore 1977). By about the age of three an infant will normally have around a thousand trillion synapses, about half those of an adult. Growth is the process of creating, strengthening or discarding these synapses or 'pathways'. This process is fundamental for development. The brain 'prunes' synapses that are not subject to stimulation and thus 'use'. Pruning discards those connections that are not used, which allows the remaining connections to strengthen and increase their efficiency. This is where the term 'use it or lose it' has a very real physical meaning and refers to the 'plasticity' of the brain: that is, the way the brain is able to change and adapt according to environmental demands and stimuli. A lack of stimulation during the early years can lead to long-term physical, cognitive and mental or emotional health issues, regardless of whether the brain is genetically normal at birth. Awareness of the plasticity of the brain is important to consider when teaching or working with 14–19-year-olds, especially given recent research by Oxford University (2009) that shows the learning of new skills can improve connectivity in the brain and lead to an increase in white matter. 'We tend to think of the brain as being static, or even beginning to degenerate, once we reach adulthood,' says Dr Heidi Johansen-Berg of the Department of Clinical Neurology, University of Oxford, who led the work. 'In fact we find the structure of the brain is ripe for change. We've shown that it is possible for the brain to condition its own wiring system to operate more efficiently' ('Juggling enhances connections in the brain', 12 October 2009 press release available at www.ox.ac.uk/media/news_stories/2009/091012_2.html).

Until recently much attention has been paid to early developmental opportunities (three and under) as *the* 'critical period' within development. This has become known as the 'zero to three' debate. There are opponents of the 'zero to three' debate such as John Bruer (1999), an American philosopher, who has argued in his book *The Myth of the First Three Years*, that, particularly in America, policies have been implemented without any deep understanding of the neuroscience findings that demonstrate growth and plasticity of the brain beyond the initial period of 0–3 years. Helene Guldberg, writing in *The Guardian* (2004) also urges caution against '**infant determinism**', while accepting that extreme neglect does have a considerable impact on development so that 'extreme conditions of emotional deprivation may be so exceptional that they tell us absolutely nothing about the situations where there is engagement between the adult and child'. Therefore, Jesuit notions of 'give me the child until he is seven and I will give you the man', have been disavowed.

While stimulation is of course crucial to development, young people are capable of learning, adapting and changing; many are remarkably resilient, and neglect would have to be extreme to deprive a child of all stimuli. A second wave of pruning occurs around the onset of puberty following growth in grey matter – responsible for process and storage of information. This second stage of pruning continues into the early 20s and is particularly associated with the prefrontal cortex – associated with problem-solving, emotions, responses, higher-order thinking skills such as abstract thought, reasoning and meta-cognition, and impulse control. Myelination is also associated with pruning – the increase of a fatty white matter which coats the axons of nerve cells and increases the efficiency accuracy of communication between the brain's circuitry. This is important as this process continues beyond adolescence. Use of MRI scans such as those used in a longitudinal study by Dr Jay Giedd et al. (1999) have demonstrated that this area of the brain is a 'work in progress' during the adolescent stage. These technological advances in our understanding of brain development have been used in some court cases in America to reduce personal culpability under the age of 18 as outlined at the beginning of this chapter. Thus the area of the brain (the prefrontal cortex) associated with adult behaviours – decision-making, reasoning, the ability to control impulses, to regulate emotions, making informed judgements, to be able to consider the consequences of actions, the ability to adapt behaviour according to context, and so on – is not only the *last* area of the brain to develop and mature, but also undergoes its *greatest* changes, not by the age of 12, but during adolescence and into the early 20s. The plasticity of the brain at this stage implies that the potential to learn during this stage is extremely high. However, it is also a time when young people are more likely to indulge in risk-taking behaviours.

IN PRACTICE

Dr. Giedd (Head of Brain Imaging, National Institute of Mental Health, Washington, USA) comments: 'You are hardwiring your brain in adolescence. Do you want to hard wire it for sports and playing music and doing mathematics – or, for lying on the couch in front of the television?' (ACT for Youth 2002)

The above quotation implies that adolescence is a time of immense opportunity in terms of learning positive or negative behaviours.

In what ways might an explanation of brain development be used to motivate young adults? How could you incorporate this into your own teaching practice?

Implications of understanding developmental processes for teaching

Lack of maturity of thought processes, coupled with a still developing brain, mean that many young people make decisions based on gut reactions (through the amygdala) rather than logical reasoning (through the pre-frontal cortex) and are more likely to make meaning of learning through concrete and authentic experiences. It is estimated that 99% of sensory input is filtered out so, in order to promote attention, information should be meaningful to the individual and/or create an emotional response. 'Traditional teaching methods such as the lecture or "skills and drills" workshop [provide] little opportunity for students to contribute or exchange views and little possibility to choose topics or learn in different ways' (Harkin et al. 2001: 35).

Learning contexts that are productive and promote brain development and growth are experiences that are active, meaningful and make use of social interaction.

Rote learning may therefore be 'remembered' but it may have no meaning for the individual and certainly no opportunities to build and extend this knowledge to the world around them and their relationships. This is what Gibbs (1992) refers to as **surface learning**. In contrast, **deep learning** is meaningful to the individual, and allows the individual to question, to experience, to reflect, to challenge and be challenged and of course to develop their psychosocial skills. In essence, surface learning reproduces 'information' in isolation, whereas when deep learning occurs, the learner is able to understand the topic and extend this knowledge – to make personal meaning, develop critical arguments for and against and to relate this knowledge to other areas of knowledge.

SUMMARY

You have explored a number of theories and considered the physical, social, psychological and cognitive aspects of development within this chapter. You have also explored concepts of adolescence and the difficulties of a clear definition of this term and thus the expectations of *normalised* behaviour for young people who all experience adolescence in different ways and at different times.

Do these theories help us with teaching, or help us to understand adolescent behaviour? Do they provide insight into instructional techniques or approaches? Do they help us to interact or communicate more effectively? In short, is information on development useful merely as background knowledge, or can it help to transform our teaching approaches? Will you use the information to 'explain' behaviours in a deterministic way, thus reducing your own responsibility for classroom stimulation and management, or will you use this knowledge to develop your teaching skills and to promote learning opportunities for your students?

This chapter has explored the extremely complex and intricate nature of adolescent development, the elongation of adolescence, various theories of adolescence and their challenges. In terms of brain development, the emergence of scientific evidence from MRI scanning and longitudinal studies has had a clear impact not only as science in itself, and for those interested in developmental psychology, but also in terms of our understanding of 'adolescence'.

Find out more

Restorative Justice (RJ) approaches in schools are becoming increasingly popular and used as a means of reducing school exclusions and a means of mediation. RJ can be used as an 'alternative approach to behaviour and relationship management in schools. The idea is based on ancient tribal practices as a form of repairing harm caused by inappropriate behaviours that damage the communities that we live in, by bringing together those involved to discuss and talk through the issues that lead to their conflict' (**www.teachingexpertise.com/articles/ restorative-justice-696**). Copies of research findings in relation to RJ can be found on the Youth Justice Board website at: **www.yjb.gov.uk/Publications/ scripts/prodview.asp?idproduct=208**.

A book that explores the importance of loving relationships and the development of the brain is *What's Love Got to Do with It?* It is written by Sue Gerhardt and was first published in 2004 by Brunner-Routledge. If parents to be were provided with reading lists, we would insist on this being a core text.

For a comparison of the size of a brain in normal three-year-olds compared to those who have experienced extreme neglect, as well as the importance of relationships and social interaction on development of the brain, see: **www.se-rj.com.br/TEXTOS-INGLES/ 0043BrainGlobalneglet.doc**.

A psychology text that relates theory to educational practice is *Psychology in Education* by Anita Woolfolk, Malcolm Hughes and Vivienne Walkup, published by Pearson Education Limited in 2008 – a necessity for any trainee or experienced teacher interested in developing their understanding of psychological theory to improve their practice.

Bibliography

ACT for Youth (2002) *Research Facts and Findings: adolescent brain development.* Available at **www.actforyouth.net/documents/may02factsheetadolbraindev.pdf** [accessed 26.08.08].

Bronfenbrenner, U. (1989) Ecological systems theory, in R. Vasta (ed.) *Annals of Child Development*, 9 Vol. 6. 187–249. Boston MA: JAI Press.

Bruer, J. (1999) *The Myth of the First Three Years: A New Understanding of Early Brain Development and Lifelong Learning*, New York: The Free Press.

Donovan, G. (2005) *Teaching 14–19: everything you need to know about teaching and learning across the phases*, London: David Fulton Publishers.

Engel, G. (1977) The need for a new medical model: a challenge for biomedicine, *Science* 196: 129–36.

Gibbs, G. (1992) *Improving the Quality of Student Learning*, Technical and Educational Services, Bristol.

Giedd, J. N., Blumenthal, J. and Jeffries, N. (1999) Brain development during childhood and adolescence: a longitudinal MRI study, *Nature Neuroscience*, 2(10): 861–3.

Guldberg, H. (2004) 'The determinist myth', *The Guardian* 03.11.2004 available at: **www.guardian.co.uk/education/2004/nov/03/research.highereducation** [accessed 26.08.08].

Harkin, J., Turner, G. and Dawn, T. (2001) *Teaching Young Adults*, London: RoutledgeFalmer.

Hine, T. (1999) *The Rise and Fall of the American Teenager*, New York: HarperCollins.

Illeris, K. (2007) *How We Learn: learning and non-learning in school and beyond.* Oxon: Routledge.

Keenan, T. (2002) *An Introduction to Child Development*, London: Sage.

Marcia, J. E. (1966) Development and validation of ego identity statuses, *Journal of Personality and Social Psychology*, 3: 551–8.

Newnes, C. and Radcliffe, N. (2005) *Making and Breaking Children's Lives*, Ross on Wye: PCCS Books.

Roth, J. and Brooks-Gunn, J. (2000) What do adolescents need for healthy development? Implications for youth policy, Social Policy Report. *Society for Research in Child Development.*

Shore, R. (1997) *Rethinking the Brain*, New York: Families and Work Institute.

Steinberg, L. and Silverberg, S. B. (1986) The vicissitudes of autonomy in early adolescence, *Child Development*, 57: 841–51.

Viner, R. and Christie, D. (2005) ABC of adolescence, *British Medical Journal*. Available at **www.bmj.com/cgi/content/full/330/7486/301** [accessed 14.08.08].

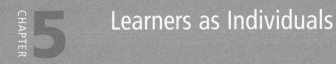

In this chapter you will:

- Consider the definitions of the learner as an individual
- Review some competing demands influencing current views of what individuals should learn
- Examine the impact of reforms on approaches to individualised/personalised learning
- Find the voice of some individual learners
- Explore the challenges of changing attitudes to equality and diversity for individuals
- Consider the implications of new approaches within your teaching
- Review potential developments

Pearson Education Ltd./Ian Wedgewood

Introduction

Who are individual learners? At any age pupils and students are of course individuals. What aspects of this individuality are important for teachers dealing with each person in a learning setting? At 14–19 the individuals we teach will be both adult and child in transition. The individual learner is the person with whom the teacher establishes a secure relationship based on trust which both supports and allows the individual to develop. The individual learner in this phase will be establishing an identity and claiming more autonomy as they continue to learn how to learn. They have to make choices which will affect them throughout life, and their success and failure, as we all know, can have a profound impact upon them. Teachers working in this phase as in others will know that the opportunity to expand the horizons of young people is very important to enable real choice and to make learning exciting and rewarding for the adult throughout life.

In this chapter we must also acknowledge that in the 14–19 phase we are dealing with a range of views and approaches to teaching and learning which stem from various philosophical, political, religious and other strongly held beliefs. For several decades now legislation has moved the British educational system towards a market-led model which claims to serve the needs of many efficiently, and has given pupils, students and parents an identity not unlike that of the individual consumer of services.

Increasingly the learner as individual has been given a centre stage position in certain areas like teaching standards, school, college and marketing material, while often contradictory messages are presented in other settings. Learners are potential assets: workers-in-waiting to be exploited in a global arena of competitive wealth creation. As such it can seem as if they must be shaped, and even in childhood they may be perceived and characterised as a resource for employers. We frequently ask what skills are being prioritised rather than how contented and fulfilled they are.

Private finance may flow into new academies in a very public way and the motives for costly, high-profile, corporate involvement are those very explicit, overlapping business and political agendas rather than pure altruism. No apology is made for this attitude but rather an assumption of a shared belief in a common greater good in which the individual learns to accept the dominance of the market to shape their future for maximum economic benefit.

The tension between these positions can polarise views quite artificially and shift the debate away from a professional practice focus. It is not necessarily helpful to separate preparation for future employment from individual learning to learn as for wider personal benefit. These goals are far from mutually exclusive. As John Lea et al. (2003: 82) point out,

> If we are all individuals with our own learning styles, does that mean that we all need an individual learning programme? If that is the case, then what is the value of learning as a social activity? Would people gain more from learning alone in their own way?

Learning styles are discussed in much greater detail in Chapter 8, but in the face of increasingly complex factors for teachers to consider and choices for learners to

Photo 5.1
A young learner
being supported
to follow an
individual plan

Source: Pearson Education Ltd. Studio 8

navigate, it is worth maintaining a balanced view, of the kind always applicable in the learning and skills sector:

> The diversity of learners in the post-compulsory sector of education is as wide as the types of courses and programmes on which they enrol. Faced with such diversity, and the pressures on tutors to respond to every individual's learning needs, it is not surprising that we sometimes lose sight of the similarities between learners and their common goals.
>
> *(Lea et al. 2003: 89)*

Teachers will understand better than many that care for the common good of the group and of the individual can be complementary rather than mutually exclusive.

Learners as individuals in a reformed 14–19 phase

The focus of reforms towards individual learning is given an urgency and drive for very practical reasons. New Labour's initial and continuing focus on education as a route to deeper and more lasting solutions does place particular pressures on the system and its professionals to produce answers to some of the most troublesome aspects of the UK experience. The present serious economic crisis only adds to the need to ensure that the significant investment of time, planning and painfully negotiated compromises which have resulted in reform implementation across so many areas has been good value.

The Nuffield Review of *14–19 Education and Training* highlights some of the long-term issues that the reforms and, in particular, the new qualifications and approaches are designed to address. It is clear that the interest in learners as individuals is informed by a real sense that re-engagement, stimulation of interest and ownership of learning by learners are high priorities for the phase which remain elusive.

> General education (traditionally known as 'academic education') is the dominant form of education for 14–19-year-olds. In fact, it is so dominant quantitatively, politically and culturally, it is almost as if it cannot be questioned or discussed. This has certainly been the attitude of the Government since its 2005 14–19 White Paper (DfES: 2005), with its politically inspired defence of GCSEs and A levels, on the grounds that they are well known nationally and internationally. Instead, reform and policy attention has been almost entirely focused on vocational qualifications and, in particular, on the new 14–19 diplomas.
>
> Yet, even the most cursory analysis of the role and nature of general education in the 14–19 phase in England reveals problems. It is selective, particularly post-16, casting a shadow over 'alternative' vocational provision, which is populated with 'refugees' from GCSEs and A levels. The focus on preparation for GCSE and A level examinations encourages mechanical and instrumental learning habits in young people. Its individual subject approach also fails to support a broad and coherent curriculum: which by the A level stage is reduced for most learners to three areas of study. The policy emphasis on examinations, exacerbated by their use in performance tables in England, contributes to learner alienation and drop-out. For those who do not succeed in general education pre-16, there is no real option to continue with it post-16. Moreover learners of all abilities who do remain in this route because of its status and progression opportunities, are often unchallenged and bored. All of this amounts to a systemic 'crisis' of general education.
>
> *(Nuffield 2008: 2)*

A consensus appears to have been reached across all parties and professions from Tomlinson onwards that new more effective relationships must be forged with all learners and especially those who have proved most difficult or impossible to reach in the past. In addition, flexible access to further challenges for high achievers in the current system and to applied learning for individuals which is relevant to their interests and future aspirations is an attractive prospect.

Learners as individuals within society

So the definition, treatment and subsequent experience of the learner as individual will be dictated by underlying positions relating to beliefs, practical and personal factors taken by those funding, designing and delivering the curriculum. Just as we should remain aware of the impact of this wider perspective, we should also take care to avoid minimising the agency of the teacher.

RESEARCH FOCUS

Armitage (2007) provides insight in relation to contested areas of definitions and perceptions of purpose for education with some implications identified. What is interesting for teachers in this context is the relevance of this post-compulsory oriented discussion to current debates about 14–19 learners and their individual learning. Clearly there are fundamental questions to be addressed before progressing to issues of individual differences, support and development. This is not the case with the increasing numbers of PCE teacher educators and trainers influenced by 'critical theory'. Critical theorists and their followers see the challenge of PCE teaching and training as making 'classrooms more open in language practices', which means that, 'Differences of gender, culture and outlook should be celebrated as part of a democratic endeavour' (Harkin et al. 2001: 135).

Martin Bloomer's somewhat artificial notion of 'studenthood' comes out of this school of thought. He notes that 'studenthood' conceptualises the ways in which students can begin to learn independently and recognise 'the problematic nature of knowledge' (Bloomer 1996: 140) through reflection on their own learning experiences. The consequence is that they can begin to 'exert influence over the curriculum' in 'the creation and confirmation of their own personal learning careers' (p. 140). Bloomer's conceptualisation of PCE teaching situations might be an example of what is often called 'praxis' or 'practical wisdom'. The result of these individualistic application of what were originally Marxist ideas is not radical because it leaves students engaging in a critical self-reflection that is a sort of therapy (see Therborn 1978: 125–8). The appeal of this to some PCE teachers and trainers is a false sense of being able to solve social problems through 'the enlightened efforts of critical students and scholars' (Therborn 1978: 139).

This radical view of the potential of teachers, trainers and students has a parallel in a more conservative view of PCE and one that is widespread. Radical teacher trainers may see education as transformative for individuals, but management and government policy makers are more likely to promote the idea that FE, in particular, can regenerate the economy. We can call this the Bilston College Fallacy as that college did much to promote this view in a series of publications (see Reeves 1997 and, for a critical assessment, Bryan 1998). (Ironically Bilston College went into severe financial difficulties shortly after the publication of their well-known book.) Both the radical and conservative views of FE overestimate the role of education in, respectively, politics and the economy.

(2007: 11)

WHAT DO YOU THINK?

Having trained for your professional role through a relatively individualised process of self-reflection and development, do you find yourself influenced in your practice by this particular approach to effective and dynamic learning?

What pitfalls can you identify in relation to a highly personalised approach to pupil/student learning?

As a committed professional, do you find yourself drawn to the notion of solving wider social problems through your work with learners as individuals? Do you agree that such a perception of broader agency is a 'false sense'?

How far and in what ways do you 'see education as transformative for individuals'?

In support of a more balanced approached Huddleston and Unwin (2002) shift the focus to one where individual learning models are not allowed to distort our under-standing of quality learning for individuals.

> We have paid a great deal of attention . . . to the needs of individual students'
> [and to] how different those needs can be. By bringing students together,
> they can begin to learn how their own needs compare and contrast to others
> and develop shared strategies for enhancing their own learning and for
> overcoming problems. Learning in groups can often be much more fun than
> singly and can facilitate the continuation of learning once the formal session
> has ended. Students may continue to discuss ideas outside the classroom or
> workshop and apply themselves creatively to group tasks.

Interestingly the writers shift attention and the weight of argument away from issues of direct teacher pupil/student interaction and towards quality and type of individual learning experience within a context. We should not lose sight of this amid the rhetoric of reform and new qualifications.

> Given the emphasis in FE on individual learning, and the increasing use
> of ICT, there is a danger that learning in colleges may become too
> individualised. Although groups of students may be together in the same
> space, they might all be working completely separately on different tasks or
> units of competence.

(2002: 105–6)

The learner as individual, isolated and not advantaged, may be found in the centre of any group or in mechanistic tutorial ticking boxes. A worthwhile group session may have a huge impact on the learning of all individuals involved due to good planning, high-quality group interaction, stimulus and peer support as well as teacher actions. It may simply be a question of providing quiet space for reflection by learners within an intense activity. Individual learning, by definition, does not have a single instructional model but requires relationship, understanding and foresight.

The value of the group and of social and shared and formal learning as appropriate should not be diminished in favour of over-personalised and near therapeutic models.

Further discussion along these lines can be found in the work of Ecclestone and Hayes (2008).

WHAT DO YOU THINK?

Having read the views of the writers above on how individuals learn through groups and benefit from the social and collective setting and how learners can be, in many senses, learning alone, i.e. to individual plans – within group contexts:

- Create your own list of the needs both core and additional of learners as individuals (as a group or individual activity).
- Consider which of these could be met, or would be better met, in group settings and which require only individual attention?
- In what ways might the 'danger' of learning that is 'too individualised' be manifested? Have you seen any evidence of this?

Most recently, Frank Coffield's (2008) paper in a series for LSN (the Learning and Skills Network) expresses some widely held views when he makes the case for placing teaching and learning at the heart of the educational system. This work will be considered further on in the chapter.

Learners as individuals and applied learning

What is applied learning? It crosses what in simplistic terms can be seen as the traditional divide between vocational and academic education. The Diploma qualification aims to provide an experience for learners which does not narrow down their choice too early by making the learning very specifically work-related. The idea of this qualification and of many teachers using other qualifications is that a young person should be able to change their focus, and their learning should have been flexible enough to ensure that their achievement remains relevant.

The **LSIS** (Learning and Skills Improvement Service) Diploma support material for teacher development, defines applied learning as follows (notice how strong a focus is placed on the individual):

Applied learning:
- is learning that takes place within practical contexts
- connects with learners' interests and aspirations
- is learning that can be applied to life and work outside the classroom
- helps to build knowledge, skills and understanding which are of personal relevance to the learner
- unites theory with practical activities
- involves practice in real contexts that gradually develops understanding of underlying principles.

*www.diploma-support.org/.../Diploma-support-**Applied**-**learning**-teaching-**learning**-strategies.doc*

LSIS suggest the following example of applied learning activities.

Society Health and Development Foundation level		
Principal learning outcome	**Teaching strategy**	**Applied learning activity**
Be able to communicate verbally and non-verbally (including listening skills) in specific situations (Level 1, unit 4 – Edexcel)	Role-play	Learners take on the role of a member of 'the family' speaking to an occupational therapist, or the role of the occupational therapist. Each learner has a card with detailed information about the patient and the role of the professional.
Understand why it is important to use different methods of communication (Level 1, unit 4 – Edexcel)	Case study	Learners are provided with a case study where communication may need to be adapted to ensure it is effective, such as a nursing home care worker and a stroke victim. Having read through the case study, learners list the barriers to effective communication and how they may be overcome.
Understand how the needs of individuals can be assessed (Level 1, unit 7 – Edexcel)	Problem-solving	Learners select a particular service they are familiar with (doctor, dentist, nursing home, etc.). Problem: how might the quality of this service be improved for both service users and carers/employees?

IN PRACTICE

Does your own teaching focus on individuals in this way? Are there activities you could adapt or introduce which would engage individuals more actively?

How important is relevance – to the individual learner's life, needs and aspirations – in your choice of teaching and learning strategies?

In the latest TDA (Training and Development Agency for Schools) and LLUK (Lifelong Learning UK) Guide to Support the Professional Development of Diploma Teachers (2008) which replaces the previous Training and Development Guidance, the emphasis on **personalised** learning and learners as individuals is clear. It is a primary aim for teachers working in the phase and is further reinforced through the DCSF

(Department for Children, Schools and Families) (2009) professional development support for Diploma consortia. The QCA (Qualifications and Curriculum Authority) website provides learning exemplars across the elements and including those to support learners learning, with illustration on how to incorporate Diploma personal learning and thinking skills (PLTS).

The task for teachers of addressing such a demanding range of learner needs has placed teacher development in the forefront, and specialised support is emerging which is of value for Diploma delivery but has relevance beyond this.

The guide is organised into seven sections to cover the key elements:

- Applied learning
- Assessment for and of learning
- Collaborative working
- Developing reflective practice
- Generic learning skills
- Information, advice and guidance
- Personalised learning.

As the elements clearly demonstrate, the learner as an individual is a starting point rather than a single component. The teacher is focused on modelling and addressing learners in this more individualised way through his/her own process of continuing professional development.

The links are clearly made throughout. For example in the section on Developing Reflective Practice, teachers are directed to 'update and maintain knowledge and understanding of personalised learning and assessment for learning' and to 'continually update subject/applied area knowledge and maintain occupational currency'. In addition, there is an emphasis on ensuring that experienced referral networks are maintained and used to support individual learner needs.

There is an expectation that teachers will supply a combination of externally scaffolded support; access to collaborating institutions and associated professionals, specialists and work-based partners, and that they will nurture the internal development of each learner's independence and capacity for future learning. According to this guide, 'Personalised learning is based on a curriculum of choice and flexibility where individual learning plans and pastoral support and learning guidance are used to help learners navigate their own progress.'

Under Assessment for and of Learning the approach required is expressed in this way: 'Involve all learners in reflecting on their own learning, self assessment and assessing their peers.'

WHAT DO YOU THINK?

Is the description of 'personalised learning' above one which you find sufficient in terms of your own aspirations for your learners?

Or would you go beyond the notion of learner planning and progress navigation, and if so how would you characterise your view?

The guide is aimed at managers responsible for professional development but also for individual teachers in this area. They should ensure that professional development opportunities are available to help teachers to:

1. Be aware of and value the principles and benefits of personalised learning

   - *Promote opportunities for all learners to share responsibility for their own learning through discussion and the use of individual learning plans*

   - Develop learners' understanding of how they learn

   - Identify and support individual learner needs and ensure an inclusive provision to meet the needs of all learners, including those with special educational needs and disabilities, those from minority ethnic backgrounds and those who are looked after or in care

2. Use strategies to personalise learning

   - *Develop their ability to set tasks in real contexts of use that engage all learners in collaborative working with others*

   - Use, and appreciate the benefits of using, initial assessment with all learners

   - Develop a range of active learning techniques to motivate and engage all learners in applied learning

   - Involve learners in planning learning, including generic learning integrated across the curriculum and the Diploma project

   - Provide opportunities for all learners to use individual learning plans that help them reflect on their learning progress

   - Identify and agree targets with all learners that are realistic and achievable

3. Provide pastoral support and learning guidance to help all learners progress and overcome barriers to learning

   - *Identify the forms of pastoral support and learning guidance available in a partnership*

   - Develop their own role and ability to provide pastoral support and learning guidance to all learners

   - Identify and implement strategies for effective mentoring of all learners

   - Identify when and where to refer learners to specialist guidance and support available in the partnership

(TDA/LLUK 2009)

IN PRACTICE

Select one of the bullet points from each of the three categories above and describe a specific action you could take or request from management to develop and improve your approach to personalised learning.

The debate surrounding the differences between learners who are children and learners as adults is longstanding and it reaches a heated level in the 14–19 arena when education claims a powerful influence on the nature and pace of this transition.

Should individuals be directed and trained or allowed to retain what many would regard as an unrealistic sense of infinite choice? This latter position emphasised in many late-twentieth century consumer-led economies has been blamed for a vast range of social ills and can be characterised as counter-productive. Some popular media voices cite the growth in cultures of binge drinking, increased suicide rates, violence, mental-health problems and other serious symptoms of social dysfunction to highlight perceived faults in the parenting, education and social care of the present generation. In order to address the social issues underlying these problems, government and its agencies have generated a vast proliferation of initiatives and long-term policy reform designed to increase personal and social responsibility.

Whatever view we may take ourselves, it is clear that for the practical foreseeable future, education policy and practice will be dominated by the overarching agendas of re-engineering for economic and social change.

In terms of qualifications reform, Diplomas are promoted as spearheading the case for the learner as individual. The recent QCA publication (2008) makes a clear statement in the summary:

> The purpose of this paper is to advise practitioners of the research that has informed the development of the Diploma. It is intended to contribute to the understanding of all those involved in Diploma planning and delivery by providing a brief summary of key research. The paper draws on some key theories of learning that suggest that learners benefit from a range of different, but connected, contexts that involve interactions with a variety of others. Motivation and achievement are increased when tasks have purposes that are relevant to the individual and 'real-world' contexts, including the workplace, and when learners are actively involved, and supported, in shaping their learning experience. Selective references are given for those wishing to explore further the different theories, as well as more practical resources that support teaching and learning in ways that can help learners make the most of the rich and varied experiences offered by the Diploma.

For a very useful set of links to relevant Diploma sites including the range of learning lines and sector skills bodies see Appendix 5.1. There is also reference in this for the individual learner.

The learner's individual voice

If we wish to engage more effectively with individuals as learners, then the teacher must make time and opportunities for learners to feedback so that their point of view and active engagement can be elicited and employed. Depending on the teacher's approach through theory to practice, this may take the form of structured channels for communication, or it may be a central tenet of practice and operate as a key factor in design and planning of teaching and learning.

While there are always elements of dialogue and shared agency both formal and informal, the dominance of reflective practice approaches would suggest that a greater degree of student autonomy and input to sessions should be more widespread in both school and college contexts. More developed humanistic models have produced a range of ways to describe and improve professional practice aimed specifically at the learner as an individual.

Brookfield (1986) uses the metaphor of the 'critical lens' to express the critical points of view relevant to a learning professional, and the learner voice/point of view is one of these alongside and equal to the teacher, the colleague and theory/literature perspectives. This takes the notion of learner as individual into the reflective space where a stepping away from self into a more empathic relationship with the individual learner moves the professional away from models of control and delivery where learners as groups or individuals are simply recipients rather than participants.

Writing on reflective practice professional development, Malthouse and Roffey-Baretson (2009) provide some telling examples of teachers attempting to access the views and responses of their learners as individuals.

IN PRACTICE

Involving the individual learner's critical voice

Example 2:
I teach National Diploma/Certificate courses in art and design. As part of the Historical and Contextual Studies Unit, I felt it was important to develop resources on pictorial representations of gender, (dis)ability and ethnicity, as I found that some of my students' experiences are very limited. Latest government legislation and emphasis on diversity requires a closer look at how these categories are represented in art.

This starting point prompted the teacher featured in Malthouse and Roffey-Baretson's work on reflection to engage in action research, involving close contact with the experiences of learners as individuals resulting in a more participative and democratic way forward. Following pilot sessions with unfamiliar and quite challenging resources the following responses were elicited:

In the closing stages of the class, learners were asked the questions 'Why is it important to study the ways in which disabled people are represented?' Their replies showed that they were aware by the end of the class that images of disability play a significant part in shaping attitudes to the disabled.

When they were asked to speculate about the reasons why some of the artists decided to challenge negative images of disability, most responses were framed in terms of social justice but one or two student in both groups asked whether those artists were themselves disabled. One suggested that the disabled have to be able to speak for themselves. This remark echoed ▶

IN PRACTICE *CONTINUED*

David Hevey's contribution to a discussion of Witkins's work on the BBC2 programme, Late Review. *He insisted that images such as 'Il Santo Oscuro' would eventually become unacceptable but only when disabled people themselves have a voice in the discourse (BBC2, 1996).*

In both sessions learners were able to compare the images related to disability with those studied in previous classes on equality issues: one student, for example, made the point that a white photographer could no longer degrade a black person in the way that the able-bodied Witkin had treated his disabled models. From next year the topic and material will become incorporated into the historical/contextual curriculum. I also propose to enlist the students' help in developing the slide resources at our disposal by asking them to collect pictures from art, advertising or the media that they feel might be relevant to the subject.

WHAT DO YOU THINK?

- Have your own active engagements with individual learners extended to gaining their critical feedback on their own experience of your teaching?
- How are strategies appropriate when undertaking such an exercise?
- If you have used such a direct approach, what value did it have?
- How would you or did you feel about this?

CASE STUDY

Queen Elizabeth's School in Louth has engaged in a student observers' scheme with very positive results.

A group of students were selected to act as observers of staff and teacher trainees. The project involved training sessions for the students and a confidential ungraded 'constructive feedback' approach was used to establish dialogues around teaching, learning and critical perspectives. The students can speak on the topic in a very mature way and the experience has been very positive in terms of developing new respect and responsibility in teaching and learning relationships. Many other schools are interested in such initiatives.

Such innovative work really draws the learner as an individual into the centre of discussion about serious issues of great import in their life. The message sent to these individuals reinforces their sense of worth to the wider institution.

Source: Pearson Education Ltd. MindStudio

Photo 5.2
Ideally the student will 'learn how to learn' as an individual

Teaching learners as individuals

(Chapter 8 covers the key area of learner development and difference in relation to teaching – andragogy and pedagogy.)

For teachers and their learners, the theory and research are of most value where they really inform the practice and have a positive effect in the work, lives and relationships of the professional environments for learning. It is true that educational researchers, establishments, authorities, awarding bodies and even parents, employers, governments and their agencies may share, promote and profit or lose as a result of the work done in schools, colleges and beyond. It is also true that theory, research and related policy creation, testing and debate concerns us all and particularly those engaged directly with learners. But many professionals feel increasingly and unwillingly detached from their core relationship with individuals in their learning environments because of the pressure to fulfil so many other functions in ever more prescriptive systems and role definitions.

There is a clear case to be made for the reclamation of teacher individuality as a prerequisite or at least a means towards achieving real engagement with the learner as individual. Like health, social work and other public service professionals, there is a strong sense that new 'professionalisation' covers an over-specified and controlling culture of compliance in which consultants and quangoes have too much influence and where commercial-vested interest acts freely to the detriment of real progress. It is no coincidence that low recruitment, retention and morale in these professions mirror to some extent key areas of concern relating to learner achievement.

Most teachers would take issue with anyone who said that they treated learners in any other way, but would acknowledge that the individualisation of learning has come to mean a range of approaches and entitlements which support learner choice and increase the relevance of learning for each pupil/student. However convinced and committed teachers might be to acting on the principles of learners as individuals, there are often institutional, contextual and personal barriers which stand in the way. In such circumstances the rhetoric of reforms and new qualifications is not translated into practice, and the effects of lip service to transformative practice without results can be detrimental to all concerned.

On the other hand, there is evidence of very innovative practice emerging which takes the usual individual engagement through tutorial, class activity and assessment for learning to another level. The research is also less established, but there is great enthusiasm for the quality of teacher and learner experience for those who have initiated such work. It is of course enthusiastically undertaken by those with enthusiastic and often passionate commitment to what can be very intensive and demanding programmes. However, for this kind of teacher /institution the feeling is often expressed that a costly, in terms of time and dedicated effort, initial investment stage is more than repaid in terms of ultimate impact on the experience for learners as individuals and groups.

One interesting feature of innovation affecting individual learners is the use of cross subject and external project integration generated by students. This can be effectively instigated through both group and individual activity. One school built on their experience of supporting and reintegrating a learner who had long-term health issues.

The short table below provides some general ideas gathered from a range of schools, colleges and vocational centres working with 14–19 learners.

Approaches	Note
Auto/biographical work	Care, training and preparation required
Holistic group approaches to curriculum	Planning and design can generate creative responses from learners and support personal involvement beyond the formal setting
Frequent personalised life guidance	Conventional or even extended IAG
Reduction in boundaries between education and social life	Advance on the reduction in boundaries between work experience and education
Learner autonomy strategies	Flexible systems to allow scope and pace adjustment
Critical learner feedback on teaching	Learners need to be given security and structure to express this and teachers need support

Approaches	Note
Use of learner beliefs, fears and issues in learning contexts	Potential in many schools to build on existing initiatives (e.g. anti-bullying)
Peer related programmes of activity	Peer mentoring and observation
Focus work on the individual within groups	As above – building on schemes in place e.g. buddies cross-phase
Social networking sites to seek involvement from individuals	Enabling individuals to shift their learning approaches and identities among peers – needs training and support
Relaxation of restrictions around settings for student learning – increased choice	Developing outwards beyond formal school councils, etc.
14–19 learner reflective writing	Risk assessments are key to this and resources can be costly initially
Peer teaching – to increase emphasis on the learner as an individual agent	Examples of learners running sessions on how others can enter volunteering

DISCUSSION POINT

Using the table above as a starting point and adding examples or potential strategies from your own background and practice, add your own suggestions or approaches.

Be aware of the need to think laterally and to ensure that diversity and equality matters are given due consideration. As an earlier example demonstrates, this can provide a fruitful starting point rather than an afterthought in terms of learners as unique individuals.

RESEARCH FOCUS

Coffield (2008: 7) provides a very personal and informed perspective on this area with several points of focus for consideration in practice.

From all the many theories, models and metaphors of learning in existence, I have chosen to focus in this short pamphlet on the two approaches that dominate current practice and research: the metaphors of acquisition and participation.

RESEARCH FOCUS: *CONTINUED*

The Acquisition Metaphor

The acquisition metaphor is familiar to anyone who has studied or taught in the formal education system, where learning is seen as gaining possession of knowledge, skills and qualifications, just as people acquire cars, watches and houses. It is also the unacknowledged metaphor behind government policies in education and the basis on which schools and colleges are judged by Ofsted. Some of the key words in this approach are: delivery, transmission, internalisation, achievement, accumulation and transfer. The acquisition metaphor also tends to assume that learning is individual; that it is the direct result of teaching which is seen as a simple, technical process; and that 'good practice is infinitely transferable' (James and Biesta 2007: 104).

The Participation Metaphor

In contrast, the participation metaphor locates learning not in the heads of individuals, but in the simultaneous social processes of: learning to belong to different 'communities of practice' (a term which I will explain in a moment); learning to recognise changes in our identity because learning changes who we are; learning to create meaning out of our experiences; and learning what it means to know in practice. This fresh look at learning shifts the focus from the individual to learning as participation in 'communities of practice', which are 'groups of people informally bound together by shared expertise and passion for a joint enterprise' (Wenger and Snyder 2000: 139).

I am, for example, simultaneously a member of the following 'communities of practice': Newcastle United season ticket holder (for my sins, of which there must be many), the British Educational Research Association, a local health club, a book club, a village community association, the University and College Union, the Parish Council, etc.

The key words in this approach are: community, identity, meaning, practice, dialogue, co-operation and belonging. Learning is viewed as a process of participation in a variety of social worlds, and the learner is seen as someone being: 'transformed into a practitioner, a newcomer becoming an old-timer, whose changing knowledge, skills and discourse are part of a developing identity – in short, a member of a community of practice' (Lave and Wenger 1991: 122).

(Coffield 2009)

Coffield (2009) emphasises the importance of 'maximising the agency of learners' and is critical of what he describes as:

Post-compulsory education is expected to pick up the deep-seated problems created by those schools that have ignored youngsters unlikely to gain five good GCSEs; these are structural problems caused in large part by the target and performance culture imposed by government on schools. And yet the great, unsung achievement of the post-compulsory sector is to re-engage in learning so many of these young people and adults whom no one else is keen to teach. Such teaching is, however, highly intensive and demanding; it also requires high levels of support staff and so needs to be much more favourably resourced than it is at present.

According to Coffield, consultation and dialogic approaches are vital particularly in circumstances where learners are likely to disengage or have already underachieved and become lost to learning. He balances his criticism of schools' record with an acknowledgement of the power and efficacy of the 'pupil voice movement' in schools as:

> *well researched by Ruddock and McIntyre, who claim that 'pupil consultation can have a very powerful beneficial impact on life and learning in classrooms' (2007: 150). The benefits of successful practice in this area are identified as a learning opportunity for post-compulsory education.*

He provides the following summary of benefits, adapted from Ruddock and McIntyre (2007: 152), with a caveat that 'the authors being careful to point out that they do not yet have evidence that they lead to improved attainments'. You can find evidence, however, that 'a focus on learning can enhance performance, whereas a focus on performance can depress performance' (2009: 28).

Learner consultation

tends to

Enhance learner commitment through strengthening self-esteem	Improve tutors' teaching and capacity for learning through tutors' greater awareness of pupils' capacity
+	+
enhancing attitudes to college and learning	gaining new perspectives on their teaching
+	+
developing stronger sense of membership	renewed excitement about teaching
+	+
developing new skills for learning	transformed pedagogic practices

and to

Transform tutor-learner relationships

from passive and oppositional to more active and collaborative

and so is very likely to

IMPROVE LEARNING

(Coffield 2009)

DISCUSSION POINT

- What, if any, is your own experience of learner consultation – extensive and well-established or minimal? Do you agree with Coffield that learner consultation is chiefly located in schools or can you identify strong practice in colleges or other post compulsory settings?
- Can you see positive results or describe issues arising?
- Would the practice you have observed or engaged in transfer to the school or college setting?

SUMMARY

For the learner to gain greater independence and a more integrated sense of what education can mean, the teacher must surely bring this concept to life through their own evident awareness, attitudes and practice. In a system with a greater emphasis on compliance and yet subject to new and shifting structures, this can be a burden for many professionals. While it may be disappointing to see the disillusionment that can result from ambitious visions of individualised learning when they produce little more than a mechanised recording of predetermined responses, there are many success stories, particularly in individual cases. Let us hope that the shared enthusiasm of numerous dedicated professionals and their learners will produce positive change as we approach 2011 with further challenges to face.

Find out more

Specialist Schools Advisory Trust research on: Can **effective individual** learning plans be part of assessment, learning, support and achievement? Very useful and recent material available on this site including a pilot study on the topic by author: Emma McCLelland submitted: 2008/2009 **www.ssatrust.org.uk/ specialism/appliedlearning/Pages/ Effectiveindividuallearningplans.aspx**.

Useful government information providing a simple introduction to the diplomas in an easily accessible format which uses FAQs. Good quick reference and should be updated. **www.direct.gov.uk/en/ EducationAndLearning/QualificationsExplained/ DG_070676**.

The link below provides access to a template Individual Learning Plan for 14–19-year-olds designed for a college context: **www.iagworkforce.co.uk/files/.../5d/ ILP_prompt_Colleges.doc**.

Bibliography

Armitage, A. et al. (2007) *Teaching and Training in Post-Compulsory Education*, 3rd edn, Maidenhead: Open University Press/McGraw-Hill.

Bloomer, M. (1996) Education for studentship, in Avis, J. et al. (eds) *Knowledge and Nationhood: education, politics and work*, pp. 140–67, London: Cassell.

Brookfield, M. (1986) *Understanding and Facilitating Adult Learning*, Milton Keynes: Open University Press.

Coffield, F. (2008) *Just suppose teaching and learning became the first priority*. Learning Skills Network.

Curzon, L. (2003) *Teaching in Further Education: principles and practice*, London: Continuum.

DCSF (2009) *Delivery 2009 and Beyond: professional development support for Diploma Consortia*, available at: **http://www.dcsf.gov.uk/14-19**

Donovan, G. (2005) *Teaching 14–19: everything you need to know about teaching and learning across the phases*, London: David Fulton Publishers.

Eccleston, K. and Hayes, D. (2008) *The Dangerous Rise of Therapeutic Education*, London: Routledge.

Fielding, M. (2008) Personalisation, education and the market, *Soundings*, 38, Spring: 56–69.

Harkin, J. (2007) *Excellence in Supporting Applied Learning*, London: TDA/LLUK.

Harkin, J., Turner, G. and Dawn, T. (2001) *Teaching Young Adults. A Handbook for Teachers in Post Compulsory Education,* London: RoutledgeFalmer.

Hodgson, A. and Spours, K. (2008) Issues Paper 10, General education in the 14–19 phase, Nuffield Review of *14–19 Education and Training*, available at: **www.nuffield14-19review.org.uk**

Huddleston, P. and Unwin, L. (2002) (2nd edn) *Teaching and Learning in Further Education*, London: RoutledgeFalmer.

Lea, J. et al. (2003) *Working in Post-Compulsory Education*, Maidenhead: Open University Press.

Lumby, J. and Foskett, N. (2007) *14–19 Education: policy, leadership & learning*, London: Sage.

Malthouse, R. and Roffey-Barentson, J. (2009) *Reflective Practice in the Lifelong Learning Sector*, Exeter: Learning Matters.

McIntyre, D. and Ruddock, J. (2007) *Improving Learning through Consulting Pupils*, London: Routledge.

Pring, R. et al. (2009) *Education for All: the future of education and training for 14–19-year-olds*, London: Routledge.

QCA (2008) *The Diploma and its Pedagogy*, QCA/08/3908.

TDA & LLUK (2008) *A Guide to Support the Professional Development of Diploma Teachers*, available at: **www.lluk.org.uk**

Therbourn, G. (1978) The Frankfurt School, in New Left Review (ed.) *Western Marxism: A Critical Reader*, pp. 83–189, London: Verso.

Weblinks

DCSF – **www.dcsf.gov.uk/14-19**

QCA – Qualifications and Curriculum Authority: **www.qca.org.uk**

Training and Development Agency for Schools (TDA): **www.tda.gov.uk**

www.diploma-support.com

14–19 Links Document – Diplomas

National websites about Diplomas	Department for Children, Schools and Families – 14–19 website: **www.dcsf.gov.uk/14-19/** QCA: **www.qca.org.uk/qca_5396.aspx** UK Commission for Employment and Skills: **www.ukces.org.uk/default.aspx?page=2860** National Database of Accredited Qualifications (NDAQ): **www.accreditedqualifications.org.uk/**
Phase 1 Diplomas – available from 2008 • Construction and the built environment • Creative and media • Engineering • IT • Society, health and development	**QCA Curriculum guidance:** Construction and the built environment: **www.qca.org.uk/qca_13481.aspx** Creative and media: **www.qca.org.uk/qca_13482.aspx** Engineering: **www.qca.org.uk/qca_13483.aspx** Information technology: **www.qca.org.uk/qca_13484.aspx** Society, health and development: **www.qca.org.uk/qca_13485.aspx** **Qualification specifications:** On the Edexcel website, all five Diplomas offered by that board are at: **developments.edexcel.org.uk/diplomas/draft-specifications/** For AQA the link is: **www.diplomainfo.org.uk/** – then each subject that AQA is offering is at a separate tab For OCR the link is: **www.ocr.org.uk/qualifications/1419changes/diplomas/** – links to all on this page (note: the individual documents are labelled as draft because they have not been finally checked for spelling errors etc., but they are actually **final** in terms of content)

Diploma Development Partnerships:
Construction and the built environment:
www.cbediploma.co.uk/
Creative and media:
www.skillset.org/qualifications/diploma/
Engineering:
www.engineeringdiploma.com/
Information technology:
www.e-skills.com/diploma
Society, health and development:
www.skillsforhealth.org.uk/diploma/

Phase 2 Diplomas – available from 2009
- Business, administration and finance
- Environmental and land-based studies
- Hair and beauty studies
- Hospitality
- Manufacturing and product design

QCA Curriculum guidance:
Business, administration and finance:
www.qca.org.uk/qca_16902.aspx
Environmental and land-based studies:
www.qca.org.uk/qca_16900.aspx
Hair and beauty studies:
www.qca.org.uk/qca_15768.aspx
Hospitality:
www.qca.org.uk/qca_16901.aspx
Manufacturing and product design:
www.qca.org.uk/qca_16903.aspx

Qualification criteria:
www.qca.org.uk/qca_13956.aspx

Diploma Development Partnerships:
Business, administration and finance:
www.baf-diploma.org.uk/
Environmental and land-based studies:
www.diplomaelbs.co.uk/
Hair and beauty studies:
www.habia.org/
Hospitality:
www.people1st.co.uk/14-19-diplomas
Manufacturing and product design:
www.manufacturingdiploma.co.uk/

| **Phase 3 Diplomas – available in 2010**
• Public services
• Retail
• Sport and leisure
• Travel and tourism | Draft final Line of Learning statements for these have now been endorsed for publication. These set the parameters for Principal Learning content and are available to download from the Diploma Development Partnership websites

 Diploma Development Partnerships:
Public services:
www.government-skills.gov.uk/index.asp
Retail:
www.skillsmartretail.com/ categories.php?pages_id=30
Sport and leisure:
www.skillsactive.com/training/qualifications/ 14to19/sport-and-leisure-diploma
Travel and tourism:
www.goskills.org/client/standards_ goskills.aspx?id=29 |
| **Information for learners** | Diploma information website for learners and their parents/carers:
www.direct.gov.uk/diplomas
National list of local 14–19 online learning prospectuses (enable users to view local learning provision, including Diplomas):
www.dcsf.gov.uk/14-19/index.cfm?sid=41
Connexions Direct (information, advice and guidance for 13–19-year-olds):
www.connexions-direct.com/ |

Pearson Education Ltd./Sophie Bluy

PART 2 Teaching for Learning

This part considers the knowledge and understanding required of teachers of the 14–19 age group and the ways in which they need to apply this to a range of aspects of learning.

- Chapter 6 considers the nature of subject knowledge in the sector, the particular characteristics of specialisms, evaluates models of professional development and considers the professionalisation of the sector and the role of professional standards.

- Chapter 7 examines the diversity of learning environments and associated technologies, a diversity, it is argued, which is both enriching and challenging depending on the outlook, expertise, resources and commitment of those involved. There is far wider recognition today, it is claimed, than in previous years, of the need to make learning relevant and to acknowledge that it can and does take place across a wider range of formal and informal environments.

- Chapter 8 offers a critical analysis of key learning style models, the major features of andragogy and pedagogy, the notions of deep and surface learning and the place of applied learning in the vocational diplomas.

- Chapter 9 examines behaviour management, in particular the identification of difficult or unwanted behaviour, teachers' own responses to behaviours, and explores practical strategies for promoting positive behaviours.

- Chapter 10 considers the importance of assessment *for* learning as opposed to *of* learning; the impact of assessment on learning, motivation and achievement; the importance of effective feedback on learning, the principles, methods and types of assessment and the impact of curriculum change on assessment.

Teachers' Knowledge and Development

In this chapter you will:

- Consider the nature of subject knowledge in the sector
- Reflect on the particular characteristics of your specialism
- Examine the requirements of the minimum core and relate them to your subject specialism
- Evaluate models of professional development
- Consider the professionalisation of the sector and the role of professional standards
- Examine the impact of the teacher training reforms on initial training and continuing professional development
- Explore the role and purpose of mentoring as a development process

Pearson Education Ltd./Sophie Bluy

Introduction

When trainee teachers are asked to reflect on the qualities of good teachers they themselves have had experience of, their responses tend to identify qualities in three categories. Firstly, good teachers were those with sound, extensive subject knowledge and high levels of expertise. Secondly, qualities relating to personal attributes, emotions and dispositions are mentioned: teachers were enthusiastic, had good senses of humour, were caring, good listeners, were fair. Thirdly, there are qualities connected with the skills and abilities needed for the teaching task: firm classroom management, good organisational skills, clear explanations. The training and education of teachers has, at different times, put a premium on developing qualities in each of these categories. The development of teaching (in the primary and secondary phases) as a graduate profession is a recognition of the high level of subject knowledge required of teachers. The establishment of employment-based routes into the profession in the 1990s was partly a reaction to the dominance of teacher training by higher education institutions which were seen by some to have over-theoretical and insufficiently practical programmes of training. As we shall see in Chapters 19 and 20, many consider it is the softer people skills associated with high emotional intelligence which the current and future teachers of 14–19-year-olds will need to develop. All trainees agreed, however, that the good teacher has qualities in all three categories.

Teachers' subject knowledge

The extent to which teachers in the lifelong learning sector require subject knowledge is complicated by the diversity and complexity of the curriculum in the sector. The authors of a Joint Institute for Learning and Universities and Colleges Union survey identify in Engineering, for example, 'a multiplicity of subject disciplines from motor vehicle, through electronic engineering to shipbuilding; the diversity is as immeasurable as the industry itself.' The Survey found 787 different qualifications among the 1006 respondents! Although there are now requirements for those in the sector to possess a teaching qualification, there is not the same requirement regarding subject qualifications and the Survey found the following levels of qualifications among its respondents: NQF Level 2 (GCSE) 13%, Level 3 (A level) 25%, Level 4 23%, Level 5 16%, Level 6 (degree level) 10%, Level 7 (master's) 7%, Level 8 4%. So 21% have degree-level qualifications or higher, while the 2003 Ofsted Survey Inspection (2003) found 45% of those on in-service teaching qualifications were qualified to degree level or above.

The types of subject or specialist knowledge a teacher in the lifelong learning sector might require could include:

- factual, empirical information;
- an understanding of key principles;
- personal beliefs or a stance on what the subject comprises, how it should be taught or learned;

- an awareness of current practices in the specialism;
- the ways in which a specialism relates to wider social, economic and environmental concerns;
- knowledge of key current developments in the specialism;
- knowledge of the literacy, numeracy and ICT requirements of the specialism;
- an awareness of new and emerging technologies;
- an understanding of key transferable skills;
- knowledge of where available resources may be obtained.

WHAT DO YOU THINK?

Consider the types of knowledge above. Rate the importance of each for teachers of your own specialism.

Jocelyn Robson (2000) has observed that, for further education teachers in particular, their allegiance to their specialism may be stronger than any other professional allegiance.

> In moving from one occupational area (in industry or commerce) to another (education and training) most further education teachers retain strong allegiances to their first occupational identity – this identity is what gives them credibility (as well as knowledge and skill) and it is understandable that much value attaches to it. They have experienced initial occupational or professional socialisation in one context, and are in the college precisely because this process has been successful and in order to socialise others (the students or trainees) to the same norms and practices.
>
> *(Robson 2000: 14)*

WHAT DO YOU THINK?

What are your own allegiances to your specialism? Do you network with other specialists locally, regionally or nationally via, say, a subject society or Subject Coaches Network? Do you see yourself as a practitioner within your specialism more than as a teacher of it, or does this dichotomy not exist for you?

Traditional academic subjects are occupying a decreasing part of the lifelong learning sector curriculum, particularly in FE. Much of the curriculum comprises areas in which there is a range of patterns of the integration of subject disciplines, often mirroring the structure of occupational sectors. The structure of the diplomas represents the ways

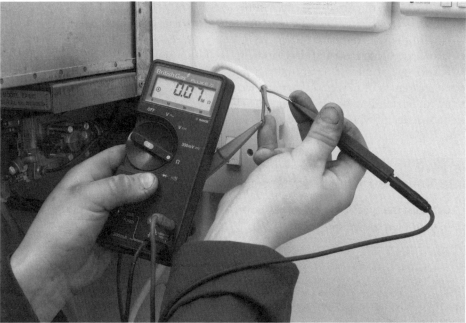

Source: Pearson Education Ltd. Gareth Boden

Photo 6.1
Many FE teachers will have practised a trade before becoming teachers

in which some of those patterns of integration are delivered in practice. Principal learning focuses on the vocational or academic subject area of the diploma line, and, although at least 50% of learning must be applied through practical tasks, principal learning has throughout a broad, sector wide focus. **Generic learning** comprises the functional skills of English, Maths and ICT, as well as personal learning and thinking skills. There is also a project which, requiring students to undertake an individualised research task, represents a further pattern of subject integration. Work experience will represent yet another way in which a student will undertake learning in an integrated way. Additional and specialist learning will consist of optional free-standing courses such as those of BTEC, GCSEs or A levels.

IN PRACTICE

Select one of the programmes you teach on. Consider whether the programme demonstrates a particular type of integration of subjects/knowledge or interdisciplinary approach and the different kinds of knowledge you need to deliver it. An Accounts programme will clearly need mathematical knowledge, while understanding the application and effects of hair dye in Hair and Beauty will require a knowledge of chemistry and biology.

The minimum core

The Ofsted Survey Inspection (2003) found that 58% of in-service Certificate in Education/PGCE students had a GCSE Grade C or equivalent in English, while the figure was 50% for Mathematics. The implementation of the minimum core of language, literacy and numeracy into teacher education programmes for the sector was achieved in 2004. This minimum core was revised and extended as part of the reform of teacher education programmes in 2007 and ICT has now been included. It is intended that the minimum core should be covered through the three units of assessment of the initial teacher education programmes, the Certificate/Diploma in the Lifelong Learning Sector: Planning and Enabling Learning, Enabling Learning and Assessment, Theories and Principles for Planning and Enabling Learning. With regard to the assessment of the minimum core, it was intended that knowledge and understanding relating to literacy, language, numeracy and ICT should be assessed internally by providers while personal skills in English and Mathematics would be assessed by external tests. At the time of writing, it appears that these tests will not be implemented but that those seeking Qualified Teacher Learning and Skills status (QTLS) and Associate Teacher Learning and Skills status (ATLS) would need to hold 'approved level 2 qualifications in literacy/English and numeracy/Mathematics [which] will count as proxy for the personal skills in literacy and numeracy as described in the minimum core' (DIUS/IfL/SVUK/LLUK 2008: 2).

There are two distinct but related issues regarding the minimum core of teachers' knowledge, understanding and personal skills. The first concerns what minimum personal skills *all* need to function effectively as teachers in the sector. All teachers must be effective listeners, for example, express themselves clearly and convey information accurately.

IN PRACTICE

Consider the Personal English Language, Numeracy and ICT Skills as described in *Addressing Literacy, Language, Numeracy and ICT Needs In Education and Training: defining the minimum core of teachers' knowledge, understanding and personal skills*, accessible at:

www.lluk.org/documents/minimum_core_may_2007_3rd.pdf.

For which activities involved in their teaching role would these skills be necessary for all teachers in the sector?

The second issue regarding the minimum core is a pedagogical one: the extent to which teachers of particular subjects will need to teach literacy, numeracy and ICT in or through their subjects. The extract below is from research carried out by the National Research and Development Centre for adult literacy and numeracy on embedding language, literacy and numeracy (LLN) in post-16 programmes and considers the features of teaching where this happens.

RESEARCH FOCUS: FEATURES OF TEACHING AND LEARNING

This broad grouping combines the following features:

- LLN teaching is linked to practical, vocational content and activities.
- LLN materials are contextualised to the vocational area.
- Initial/diagnostic assessment contributes to the integration of LLN into vocational teaching.
- There is differentiation according to LLN needs in the way in which the vocational subject is taught.
- LLN are seen as essential in the development of learners' professional identity and for success in their vocational area.
- LLN development is treated in practice as relevant to all learners, not only necessary for those who are identified with LLN needs.

What these mean in practice varies enormously from one curriculum area to another. For example, on a Level 2 Health and Social Care course, the vocational teacher uses her own experience as a nurse and quotes real life situations to demonstrate the importance of literacy and numeracy for such vocational tasks as measuring drugs and report-writing. On an Entry/Level 1 Motor Vehicle course, the LLN teaching, evidencing and assessment are carried out in practical sessions in an automotive engineering workshop, and differentiated to three levels. On this course, literacy and numeracy are taught by a multi-skilled vocational teacher, who has fully integrated these subjects into his vocational teaching. In a Health and Social Care department, which integrates literacy and numeracy with vocational teaching throughout its courses, LLN is taught not by an individual but by a course team. Here, literacy, numeracy and Health and Social Care are taught in different sessions. One teacher states:

> 'When I look for passages [for reading] they are all health-related. I try to find magazines and newspapers that relate to the course content being covered. So this is literacy with health and care in the literacy session, and then I put it back into a health and care vocational assignment as well.'

This type of provision is driven by experience, commitment, language awareness and recognition of the holistic needs of learners. On a Level 1 Hairdressing course, successful participation in activities that require LLN is treated as part of the vocational training, and as essential to successful achievement of the qualification, to progression into employment, and to future career development in the vocational area. A mature learner on this course said:

> 'At our age if you could read and write it was a bonus but now to get any kind of employment you've got to be computer literate and you've got to be able to do CVs . . . there is a lot of support from the teachers, the salon teacher and [the key skills teacher].'

In fully embedded provision the differing LLN needs and trajectories of all individual learners on the vocational course are taken fully into account. For example, some learners who were aiming for a GNVQ Level 2 in Construction were entered for a full Level 2 key skills accreditation, while another learner on the same course was entered for an Entry 3 Skills for Life qualification in Literacy, and a Level 1 key skills qualification in Application of Number.

'You wouldn't expect a maths teacher to teach plastering . . . ', *Embedding literacy, language and numeracy in post-16 vocational programmes – the impact on learning and achievement*, pp. 30–32 (Casey, H., Cara, O., Eldred, J., Grief, S., Hodge, R., Ivanic, R. 2006), London: National Research and Development Centre for Adult Literacy and Numeracy. Crown Copyright material is reproduced under the terms of the Click-Use Licence.

IN PRACTICE

The extract above describes the complex ways in which literacy, language and numeracy skills can be embedded in vocational programmes. How are LLN skills taught in your institution? Are they taught discretely or are they embedded? Does this vary from one section/department to another, or is there a whole institution policy/strategy? Could this delivery be improved? How do you regard your responsibility for developing your students' LLN skills in the programmes you teach on?

Models of professional development

The most effective model(s) for the development of teachers will be related to notions of what counts as effective teaching and the practical contexts teachers work in. However, the wide range of teaching roles in the lifelong learning sector (LLUK has recognised the distinction between the associate and full roles), as well as the variety of teaching contexts, complicates questions about the training and development required for teachers in the sector.

John Elliott (1993: 16) famously described three perspectives or models of teacher education. The first he conceives of as the traditional Platonic or **rationalist view of teacher education** which

> emphasises the image of a teacher as a *rational-autonomous* professional. Underpinning the image is the basic principle of rationalism; namely that good practice transcends the biased and prejudiced practical cultures of everyday living when it is derived from a theoretical understanding of educational values and principles.

The implication of this view is that priority is given to the development of theoretical understanding at the initial stage, with opportunities to apply this to practice. Once the rationally autonomous individual has been developed, any further in-service development or training would be the responsibility of the teacher. Secondly, Elliott describes the **'social market' view of teacher education** as a production/consumption system. According to this view, 'which applies the production–consumption systems which prevail in the economic sphere of Western democracies to the cultural/social sphere of the public services, including education', the outcomes of teacher training are construed as quantifiable products which can be clearly expressed in objectives prior to training. Elliott is here describing a model of training based on competencies and which has widespread currency in work-based training leading to NVQs. Here, as Elliott points out, theoretical knowledge underpins the demonstration of competence and is evidenced through competencies themselves. Thirdly, Elliott describes a **hermeneutic view of teacher education as a practical science**. This 'highlights the role of "teachers as researchers" in effecting improvements in practical situations construed as complex, ambiguous and unpredictable.' Central to this view then is the role of action research as well as reflective practice. As Elliott shows, this view does not derive practice from theory as in the rationalist view, nor does it reduce theory to practice in the form of competencies, but it is based on what he calls 'situational understanding'.

> [T]he relationship between understanding and action is an interactive one. One does not first understand and then act. Understanding is developed through actions in the situation, and those actions are themselves improved as understanding develops. Hence, from the hermeneutic perspective [Elliott has] outlined, the activity of teaching constitutes a kind of 'practical science'.
>
> *(1993: 18)*

There is a real tension in our sector between training which adheres to the second and third views described by Elliott, between outcome-based competency programmes and those which take a more holistic view of what teacher development is. Historically, this tension has existed between provision made by national awarding bodies and higher education institutions but that would be to oversimplify the current picture: some HEIs are moving to more practical, skill-based programmes while all NAB programmes, as well as HEI programmes, need to be endorsed by Standards Verification UK.

IN PRACTICE

Consider some staff development you have recently been involved in. It may be a longer programme such as Preparing to Teach/Diploma in Teaching in the Lifelong Learning Sector or a relatively short piece of training with section or department colleagues. Can you describe what you believe to be the model of learning/development which underpinned the training you undertook?

Below is a pen portrait of a student who has completed a pre-service PGCE 14–19. What were the key elements of his training and what can you tell about the training model the PGCE was based on?

Background information

The student came to us with a 2.2 degree in Psychology from Goldsmiths College, University of London. He previously worked as a manager of a bar and restaurant.

Early assessment of needs and potential (at interview, via audit)

The student was interviewed in March 2009 for Society, Health and Development and had initially applied for Psychology as a first choice but the course had closed. He was impressive at interview and demonstrated an immediate rapport with the audience. He was also very good at supporting other presenters. His reasons for teaching were sound and his subject knowledge audit highlighted a broad range of strengths and areas for development. The student had researched the Diploma in Society, Health and Development but did not have any occupational experience in any of the four sectors. His diagnostic numeracy test contained few incorrect answers.

Support and interventions provided

There has been an open-door tutorial policy, where the student could access advice and guidance whenever needed, including fast responses to email queries. The curriculum studies sessions are set up in a manner that encourages group discussion of needs and ideas, giving each of the student teachers the opportunity to share professional practice methods and work as colleagues in a support network.

Progress made to date (including IRB and PP1 grades, PI1 grade)

The student has progressed well, developing a creative and fluent style of both writing and teaching. His confidence has increased to the point where he is able to communicate effectively with students and colleagues, building a productive working relationship. His reports from the professional and subject mentors reflect this progress, both mentors at both placements awarding him a 'Good' grade. He listens to advice from tutors at university and school, and integrates these improvements into his practice. This was a new FE placement for this subject and his mentor is keen to take more students in the future. During Curriculum Studies sessions the student has worked innovatively and produced outstanding presentations. He was a key participant and subsequent driver in the development of a 'wiki' as a method of assessing the use of new and emerging technologies. The PI1 investigation was an interesting study of Assessment for Learning in practice and Inclusion, and showed a good understanding of its methods in the classroom, as well as a rigorous investigatory technique, written in an engaging style. The work was awarded 71% at M grade giving a Distinction. After internal moderation, this work was sent to the External Examiner. ▶

IN PRACTICE *CONTINUED*

Summary of overall achievement

The student has made excellent progress across the year, developing an innovative and creative style of teaching. He is an enthusiastic contributor to discussions in classes at university, and the experimental and outspoken ideas can be tested in this environment before being applied in his practice. He has gained a great deal of in-depth knowledge in his curriculum field, having begun the course from a very different background. He has engaged with the subject, both through course materials and those that can be found in the media, making sure that the topics discussed are right up to date and relevant to this rapidly changing field. The relationships he has developed with his students have been the cornerstone of his teaching, and he has focused on the learners and their needs, discovering where they want to go, what they have difficulty with, and working out individual plans for their future progress. In addition to the freedom of expression encouraged in the university classes, the two mentors at the two placements have allowed the student freedom to develop, and his style has progressed from competent content-based lessons early on, through to increased use of ICT techniques, role-plays, use of media, debates, work-related learning and tutorials, resulting in a holistic and varied approach that puts the learner at its focus. His work with students who have special educational needs or difficult backgrounds, as well as those who are high achievers, has shown the effectiveness of the working relationship. The course has given the student the desire to work in FE, a field he wasn't previously considering, but the experiences gained on his placement, as well as the discussions and projects based on the philosophy and theory of FE have given him great enthusiasm for this sector, as evidenced by his offer and acceptance of a lecturer post in an FE college where he will be able to gain both QTS and QTLS in this setting as an NQT. He reported that the innovations offered by this course helped in the interview process, that the knowledge of both school and FE standards were advantageous especially for students making that transition, and that some of the methods used in the course, such as the compilation of a Wiki for a project on ICT were received well.

Professionalisation, professionalism and standards

The publication of *Equipping our Teachers for the Future* (DfES 2004) heralded an unprecedented period of what has been claimed to have been the professionalisation of teachers in the sector. All new teachers and trainers who successfully complete an initial qualification, revised and underpinned by new overarching standards, from 2007, can register with the Institute for Learning and gain a licence to practise as Qualified Teachers Learning and Skills (QTLS) or Associate Teachers Learning and Skills (ATLS). In order to maintain this licence, teachers must complete 30 hours of continuing professional development per year.

Some would maintain that, in spite of efforts to professionalise teaching in the sector, teachers are not and will not perceive themselves, nor will they be perceived of, as professionals. One reason is the audit culture which, some argue, has pervaded the sector. Teachers have become increasingly publicly accountable, via league tables and external inspection, as well as being subjected to increased scrutiny by employers regarding the quality of their work. The notion of the self-assessing, self-evaluating professional is not one that many would recognise in practice. Linked to this audit culture is the tension between the professional and managerialist paradigms (Randle and Brady 2000) Most colleges, it is argued, are dominated by a market ethos: managers through regular surveillance monitor whether performance indicators are being met, and quality is assessed on the basis of inputs and outcomes. Such an ethos lends itself to a process of frequent or continual organisational restructuring, and many FE staff find themselves working in volatile, uncertain institutional contexts. Finally, a range of teaching roles and conditions of service are now widespread in colleges: there are those on temporary or rolling contracts, fractional appointments, sessional staff, agency staff, characteristic of the casualisation rather than professionalisation of the workforce. At the time of writing, many FE staff envy the salary and conditions of their colleagues in schools.

Some of the key features of a profession are described below:

- knowledge and expertise developed during a lengthy training period;
- clear gate-keeping via barriers consisting of qualifications and experience;
- membership of a professional organisation which may have regulatory powers;
- a large degree of operational autonomy;
- subscription to a professional code of practice;
- a commitment to regular or continuous professional updating;
- subscription to a professional code of values and ethics;
- comparatively favourable salary reward.

DISCUSSION POINT

It could be argued that some of the key aspects of a profession above have been met by recent reforms: we now have a professional organisation in the IfL which awards a licence to practise and monitors professional development and updating. We have an initial teaching qualification which is underpinned nationally by the same units of assessment and overarching standards of professional values, knowledge and understanding and professional practice. How far do you believe you operate as a professional in you current role?

In 2007, a new set of occupational standards replaced the FENTO (Further Education National Training Organisation) standards, published in 1999 and providing the basis for initial teaching qualifications which were, from 2001, compulsory for all FE teachers. These new overarching standards, according to Lifelong Learning UK (which succeeded FENTO in 2005),

> supply the basis for the development of contextualised role specifications and units of assessment, which provide benchmarks for performances in practice of the variety of roles performed by teachers, trainers, tutors and lecturers within the lifelong learning sector.
>
> *(LLUK 2007: Introduction II)*

DISCUSSION POINT

You may be familiar with the overarching standards but, if not, you can find them at: **www.standardsverificationuk.org/documents/professional_standards_ for_itts_020107.pdf**.

Do you think the six domains comprehensively cover the range of teaching taking place in the sector? Are there certain domains which you regard as more relevant than others to your professional role and professional context?

The new standards have undoubtedly provided a broader focus for teachers across the sector rather than the narrower FE focus of the FENTO standards. Professional values, knowledge and understanding, and practice have also been integrated into six domains which have explicitly included Professional Values and Practice, Specialist Learning and Teaching (marking the increasing emphasis on subject **pedagogy**) and Access and Progression. However, questions remain about these, as about the FENTO standards, relating to

> how the 1999 [FENTO] standards emerged and have been translated (or not) into the pedagogy of FE teacher education and – what implications this might have for the present attempt to base qualifications and training programmes on a new set of standards.
>
> *(Nasta 2007: 2)*

The first question concerns whether it is possible to set out explicitly the range of knowledge, understanding and abilities expected of a teacher. 'Many authorities', comments Nasta,

> have argued that many aspects of a teacher's practice are based upon tacit (Polyani 1983; Eraut 1994) rather than explicit knowledge and that it is only in the application of knowledge in action that teachers and other professionals shape their craft. In other words teachers 'know' and 'do' much more than they can say or can be written in sets of standards. Their knowledge and performance is in many respects unique and dependent upon the contexts in which they work.
>
> *(Nasta 2007: 4)*

The second question relates to what significance and currency the standards have for trainees: a question as relevant to the new standards as the FENTO standards. To gain FENTO endorsement, awarding bodies needed to show how the *content* of their programmes could be cross-referenced to the standards which did not then need to play a further active part in the trainees' programme. The authors taught several generations of trainees who struggled to make sense of the FENTO standards and relate them to their own practice. As for the overarching standards, there is a danger that they could be the victims of what Nasta calls a 'policy model for reform' which is

> a linear notion that standards must be specified first, then regulations and qualifications must be developed that incorporate the standards and only at the final stage are a curriculum and assessment model to be developed that will form the basis of what trainees experience.
>
> *(Nasta 2007: 8)*

The modules/units of current qualifications must be based on centrally designed units of assessment. Trainees who take these modules will therefore be engaging with the learning outcomes of such units of assessment. But, because the relationship between the units of assessment and the standards is not a transparent one, trainees are unlikely to engage with them and they may turn out to be no more significant to a trainee's professional development than were the FENTO standards.

IN PRACTICE

If you are currently undertaking an initial teacher training qualification, look through your programme documentation. Are there references to the LLUK standards? If so, how do they relate to your programme of study? Ask your tutors what significance the standards had for them in the design of your programme of study.

Initial teacher education

Of the 40,000 or so teachers each year in the sector who are undertaking a programme of initial teacher education, only a small proportion are pre-service students. The majority are undergoing training while employed or volunteering as teachers and are therefore technically in-service students. This leads to a very wide diversity of trainees undertaking programmes, from new tutors with small sessional teaching loads to full-time staff with many years of experience. This is arguably the major challenge to teacher trainers in the sector.

The intention of the reforms of initial teacher education in the sector, implemented from September 2007, can be summarised in Ofsted's conclusions to their 2003 survey inspection report as well as the then DfES publication *Equipping Our teachers for the Future* (DfES 2004). According to Ofsted, ITE should do the following:

- Give substantially more attention to developing trainees' expertise in teaching their subject.
- Ensure that the trainees' practical teaching is made more central to their training and assessment.
- Integrate ITT with their overall management of human resources, including the professional development of staff.
- Ensure the provision of workplace mentoring to support trainees in developing the necessary skills to teach their specialist subjects.
- Work with SVUK to identify those of the current standards which are most appropriate to the initial training of teachers across the lifelong learning sector.

Key DfES recommendations were the following:

- All ITT candidates will require an appropriate subject mentor.
- Students who complete may be registered with the Institute for Learning who will award the status ATLS or QTLS and monitor ongoing CPD (30 hours of CPD will be compulsory to maintain QTLS).
- Assessment of Need and Individual Learning Plans will be negotiated in conjunction with the employer – for in-service students and a personal tutor.
- Overarching professional standards to be produced by LLUK, and cross-referenced with TDA standards.
- Eight teaching observations will be required for the Diploma qualification – to be conducted by a range of appropriate people.
- CPD options will be made available through Initial Teacher Training programmes.

RESEARCH FOCUS

The remarks below are drawn from research conducted involving trainees in Adult and Community Education who were undertaking the first year of a teacher training programme incorporating the reforms described above and teacher trainers who were delivering it.

In a general sense I have no difficulties with the overall standards and the general philosophy of the teacher training programme as regards general theory and practice. However, I am aware of the fact that, particularly in the area of assessment, the description of objectives and the planning of teaching, that much of the content is more dictated by the political objectives of the current government than an actual concern to meet the needs of learners and an understanding of what it is to teach adult learners. The concern expressed by the current government to raise standards is more a concern to educate a potential workforce through adult education on the cheap rather than properly to allocate resources to meet social needs . . . I hasten to add that my comments do not spring from any party political standpoint.

Student

I agree with the drive to improved standards in teaching and therefore learning. Many tutors, who may have considerable specialist skills, may not necessarily have good teaching skills. If we are to offer value for money professionally delivered courses then the standards and the training programme is key to the overall aims. However, it should be added that the course offering should be matched to the market need and not the current political focus.

Student

I believe that there should be more relevance to 'softer learning outcomes' and less emphasis on targets. Education should be offered for its own sake more than for strictly measurable targets.

Student

Although I am reluctant to subscribe to the NVQ style of assessment which seems prevalent across the PCET sector, I can see value in having parity of standards across the ITT programmes . . . However, I would like to see more scope for creativity being valued in teaching – i.e. that which cannot be measured, necessarily in terms of product outcomes but which we know changes lives.

Teacher trainer

I am afraid that the tone and tenor of the new Teaching Awards have become too instrumentalised . . .

Teacher trainer

IN PRACTICE

You may recently have undertaken or be currently enrolled on an ITE programme, or you may know colleagues who are. How far has your or their experience reflected the intention of reforms as identified by Ofsted and DfES above?

Continuing professional development

The importance given in the teaching reforms to professional formation and development is an important element in the professionalisation of teachers in the sector the reforms have sought to bring about. All teachers are now required to complete 30 hours of CPD per year (or a proportion according to their teaching commitment). This will hopefully lead to a wider range of opportunities, activities and strategies than the frequently minimal staff development activities on offer to FE college staff which will often relate to teachers' statutory or quality management responsibilities.

IN PRACTICE

Below are a range of staff development activities. Consider:

a) which would be of relevance to you in your professional role;
b) which might be available to you within or beyond your institution.

Staff development activities

- Subject network group/network meetings
- First degree opportunities
- Master's degree opportunities
- Training in emerging technologies
- Professional/occupational updating
- Action learning sets (a group of work-based colleagues who meet regularly – at each, one presents a work-related problem and the others, guided by a facilitator, discuss and analyse this problem)
- Appraisal
- Peer review
- Attendance at conferences
- Self assessment/evaluation
- Short courses
- Consultancy
- Training by externals
- Consortium training activities
- Action planning
- Recording experiences, meetings, professional activities, thoughts/ideas
- Sharing with peers and others: experiences, meetings, professional activities, thoughts/ideas
- Learning visit to industry/commercial organisation, public services
- Secondment
- Project
- Shadowing/observation
- Mentoring

An important additional national resource has been the establishment of Centres for Excellence in Teacher Training (CETTs). These are networks or partnerships of training organisations varying in size from a CETT with 17 partners to one with over 50 with the majority with membership in the twenties. Currently the total number of partners is 288.

Source: Pearson Education Ltd. Naki Kouyioumtzis

Photo 6.2
Peer learning is just one of a range of development activities staff can engage in

CETTs operate in different areas in England. Most of the CETTs are led by universities; two are led by colleges and two by other organisations in the learning and skills sector. According to the Quality Improvement Agency:

> The main activities of the CETTs focus on the development, support for and provision of ITT and CPD. The activities are understandably diverse and, to some extent overlap, but there are different emphases within each CETT.
>
> All CETTs are involved in mentoring, but some with different aspects such as research, training or support.
>
> Other activities include action research, communities of practice – whether face to face or virtual, ILP development, networks – new, existing or specialised, task groups, VLEs/websites, working with employers and work placement.
>
> The target groups also overlap and include AVC/community groups, ACL, ESOL, Offender Learning, students with learning difficulties or disability, vocational and work-based learning staff.
>
> The communication tools vary and include conferences, academic journals – paper and electronic, newsletters, seminars, workshops, teacher education forums, summer schools, and graduation events.
>
> *QIA – Centres for Excellence in Teacher Training*

There is some concern that CETT activities and resources are regional rather than national in nature and that they are unevenly distributed geographically: there are three in the North East and two in the South West, with the North West and South East relatively poorly served. This raises the issue of access for those outside CETTs and in specific areas of England. Nevertheless, they represent a considerable national investment in training in the sector and the range of their activities after the first year of their operation was impressive (see **http://excellence.qia.org.uk/page.aspx?o=cettsnews**).

The recording of CPD has benefited from the Institute for Learning's innovative 'Reflect', an online record of professional development. This enables teachers to record action plans; activities such as workshops, conferences, training courses attended; significant professional meetings such as appraisals and meetings with managers and colleagues; thoughts recorded as journal entries, notes, ideas, a blog; an ability – the gaining of skills or expertise; an achievement such as an award and important professional experiences. All can be managed within a CPD record, with entries tagged as relating to institutional context, learning and teaching or subject specialism. There are facilities for the sharing of 'assets' with others and for them to comment, review or collaborate.

As mentioned above, it is hoped that the teacher training reforms will bring about a considerable enhancement of the CPD available to staff in the sector. However, some are calling for an entitlement to:

- Support, in the form of finance and time, from employers to undertake focused and relevant continuing professional development.
- Have CPD activities accorded the space and status needed in order to be viewed as integral and central to professional practice.
- Information on the full range of professional development opportunities available to them, including that about the quality, transferability and relevance of each.
- Ongoing opportunities, within work time, for reflection, networking and private study.
- The support needed to be able to provide their own rationale, and measures of effectiveness and impact, for planned CPD activities.
- Encouragement, in the context of the Children's Plan announcement in relation to school teachers, to undertake relevant study leading to relevant Master's level qualifications.
- Institutional support to access the means needed to update any knowledge and skills outlined in a CPD plan.
- The opportunity to avail themselves, over a number of years, to a full range of CPD activities.

(Hafez et al. 2008: 8)

The Universities' Council for the Education of Teachers Occasional Paper goes on to make a series of recommendations relating to CPD in post compulsory education:

- Department of Innovation Universities and Skills follows the lead set by Department of Children Schools and Families and facilitates opportunities for teachers in the post-compulsory sector to secure relevant Master's level qualifications.
- Opportunities to achieve graduate status should be made available to those teachers without degree-level qualifications.
- The Association of Colleges and LSC encourage employers to provide sufficient support to allow their staff to undertake professionally relevant, and focused, continuing professional development.

- IfL, LLUK, DIUS and others encourage a diversity of development opportunities and share information (covering availability, quality, relevance and transferability) about each (while refraining from endorsing, by deed or implication, any particular form of provision).

- IfL monitor the effectiveness of different forms of professional development and adjust its requirements accordingly.

- DCSF, DIUS, LLUK and TDA take action to improve synergy between the initial training and professional development of teachers in the schools and post-compulsory sectors.

- Universities and FE colleges consider the relationship between each sector in regards the provision of HE-level teacher education programmes.

- Teacher education institutions, with the support of CETTs, review their professional development programmes to ensure their continued relevance and synergy with initial training provision.

- DIUS to ensure that resources provided by CETTs are available on a national rather than a regional basis.

- Centre for Excellence in Leadership (or any successor body) should align its programmes to ensure synergy and read-across to those offered by the HE sector and other providers.

- Support, consistent with the values and ethos of higher education, be provided (in a non prescriptive way) for teacher educators and opportunities for teacher educators to secure Master's level qualifications.

(Hafez et al. 2008: 9)

WHAT DO YOU THINK?

How far do you support UCET's recommendations as outlined above?

Mentoring

Both the Ofsted Survey Inspection Report (2003) and *Equipping Our Teachers for the Future* (DfES 2004) emphasised the importance of mentoring and, in particular, mentoring in a teacher's subject discipline as a key dimension of the professional development of teachers in the sector. The effectiveness or otherwise of mentoring in initial teacher training is a headline issue in the reports of the inspection cycle of post compulsory ITE providers undertaken by Ofsted from 2004 to 2008. The lifelong learning sector, unlike the secondary and primary phases, has not had a history or culture of mentoring, but this is changing. Major initiatives such as the CETTs and the Subject Learning Coaches programme are now impacting on ITE and CPD in the sector. SLCs are trained regionally and the expectation is that they will return to their institutions and operate using a cascade model with their colleagues. Examples of best practice indicate that colleges which have been successful in the use of their trained SLCs have been able to integrate coaching or mentoring into their staff development programmes and ensure that these complement their quality assurance procedures.

ACTIVITY

Below are listed a series of roles that teachers thought mentors might have.

a) In small groups, select six of these and place them in a priority triangle with what you regard as the most important role at the top, followed by the next two below and the next three below them.

b) When you have completed this exercise, compare and contrast triangles: do any roles occur in all? How prominent were they?

c) Look at the adaptation of Klasen and Clutterbuck's diagram (Figure 6.1). There are three axes: directive – non-directive, active – passive, stretching – nurturing. Now take your six roles and plot them on the diagram. This will indicate broadly the overall role you believe a mentor should have.

ASSESSOR, APPRAISER, TEACHER, LEADER, EXPERT, COACH, INSTRUCTOR, DISCIPLINER, DEVELOPER OF TALENT, SPONSOR, TRUSTED GUIDE, PROTECTOR, GUARDIAN, ROLE MODEL, MOTIVATOR, HELPER, OPENER OF DOORS, FACILITATOR CONSULTANT, COLLEAGUE, FRIEND, COUNSELLOR, ADVOCATE, DIAGNOSER

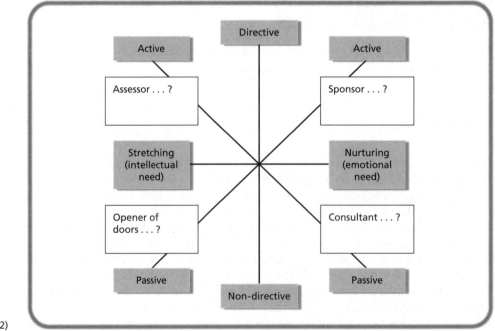

Figure 6.1

(Adapted from Klasen and Clutterbuck 2002)

There are two areas of concern regarding the implementation of mentoring. The first relates to the emphasis on subject pedagogy. As we saw above, the sector curriculum is a diverse and complex patchwork of very many subject disciplines which will often be delivered in an integrated or interdisciplinary way. It may therefore be very difficult to find an exact mentor/mentee match and this raises the question about whether the wood trades lecturer can effectively mentor the plumbing tutor, even though both work in the curriculum area of Construction. Furthermore, it is by no means clear whether individual subjects, or indeed larger curriculum areas, have a distinctive pedagogy. A video of best occupational practice, an interactive DVD about work roles, a matching exercise or a Health and Safety at work test, might all have content which varies from one curriculum area to another, but the teaching strategies and learning processes involved are likely to be identical. The second area of concern relates to clarity about the role and purpose of mentoring. Where the key purpose is for the mentee's professional development, the process is likely to be non-directive and non-judgmental on the mentor's part and the relationship will thrive on trust and professional candour. However, many colleges use mentoring as part of their quality assurance processes. And staff whose performance is judged as unsatisfactory following observation may be allocated a mentor under what is clearly a deficit model, with mentoring as a means of addressing poor performance. The consequence of this could mean that the mentoring relationship is formed on a directive and judgmental basis.

SUMMARY

The lifelong learning sector has a diverse and complex curriculum which comprises areas in which there is a range of patterns of the integration of subject disciplines, often mirroring the structure of occupational sectors. The Ofsted Survey Inspection (2003) found that 58% of in-service Certificate in Education/PGCE students had a GCSE Grade C or equivalent in English, while the figure was 50% for Mathematics and a minimum core of language, literacy, numeracy and ICT has been incorporated into teacher education programmes. There is a real tension in our sector between outcome-based competency programmes and those which take a more holistic view of what teacher development is. There is a very wide diversity of trainees undertaking initial training programmes, from new tutors with small sessional teaching loads to full-time staff with many years of experience, which is arguably the major challenge to teacher trainers in the sector. The importance given in the teaching reforms to professional formation and development is an important element in the professionalisation of teachers in the sector the reforms have sought to bring about, with all teachers now required to complete 30 hours of CPD per year (or a proportion according to their teaching commitment). Unlike schools, lifelong learning institutions have not had a culture of mentoring as part of initial and continuing professional development but major national initiatives like the initial training reforms in 2007, the CETTs and the Subject Learning Coaches programme are changing this.

Find out more

Dreyfus, H. L. and Dreyfus, S. E. (1986) *Mind over Machine.*
Dreyfus and Dreyfus conceived of a five-stage model for the development of expertise, from novice to advanced beginner to competent, proficient and expert. Consider whether you think teaching expertise develops in this staged fashion or whether a teacher's development might have a more spiky and uneven profile.

Nasta, T. A. et al. (2009) *The knowledge that you do every day – easing the transition for those who enter teaching from vocational backgrounds.*

Nasta et al. identify three categories of capability which apprentice vocational teachers develop on their journey to being expert teachers: specialist teaching, general teaching and organisational aspects. These overlapping categories were integrated in a project using a resource for teachers and their mentors and through a development process resembling the spiral curriculum. The implication is that such development does not necessarily happen in a linear manner as Dreyfus and Dreyfus might suggest. Available at: **www.loncett.org.uk**

Bibliography

Casey, H., Cara, O., Eldred, J., Grief, S., Hodge, R., Ivanic, R., Jupp, T., Lopez, D. and McNeil, B. (2006) *You Wouldn't Expect a Maths Teacher to Teach Plastering . . . Embedding literacy, language and numeracy in post-16 vocational programmes – the impact on learning and achievement*, London: National Research and Development Centre for Adult Literacy and Numeracy.

Cunningham, B. (2005) *Mentoring Teachers in Post-Compulsory Education*, London: David Fulton Publishers.

DfES (2004) *Equipping Our Teachers for the Future.*

DIUS/IfL/SVUK/LLUK (2008) *Evidencing the Personal Skills Requirements for teachers, tutors and trainers in the lifelong learning sector*, London: LLUK.

Dreyfus, H. L. and Dreyfus, S. E. (1986) *Mind over Machine*, Oxford: Basil Blackwell.

Elliott, J. (ed.) (1993) *Reconstructing Teacher Education*, London: Falmer Press.

Eraut, M. (1994) *Developing Professional Knowledge and Competence*, London: Falmer Press.

Hafez, R. et al. (2008) *CPD for Teachers in Post-Compulsory Education* Occasional Paper No. 18, London: Universities' Council for The Education of Teachers.

LLUK (2007) *New Overarching Professional Standards for teachers, tutors and trainers in the lifelong learning sector*, London: LLUK. Available at:

www.standardsverificationuk.org/documents/professional_standards_for_itts_020107.pdf

Nasta, A. (2007) Translating national standards into practice for the initial training of further education (FE) teachers in England, *Research in Post-Compulsory Education*, 12(1) March 2007: 1–17.

Nasta, T. A. et al. (2009) *The Knowledge that You do Every Day – easing the transition for those who enter teaching from vocational backgrounds*, London: London Centre for Excellence in Teacher Training, University of London Institute of Education. Available at: **www.loncett.org.uk**

Ofsted (2003) *The Initial Training of Further Education Teachers: a survey*, HMI 1782, London: Ofsted.

Polanyi, M. (1983) *The Tacit Dimension*, Gloucester: Peter Smith.

QIA – Centres for Excellence in Teacher Training. Available at: **http://excellence.qia.org.uk/page.aspx?o=cett**

Randle, K. and Brady, N. (2000) Managerialism and professionalism in the 'Cinderella service', in Hall, L. and Marsh, K. (eds) *Professionalism, Policies and Values*, London: Greenwich University Press.

Robson, J. (2000) A profession in crisis: status, culture and identity in the further education college, in Hall, L. and Marsh, K. (eds) *Professionalism, Policies and Values*, London: Greenwich University Press.

CHAPTER 7

Environments for Learning

In this chapter you will:

- Consider what is meant by the phrase 'environments for learning'
- Examine some approaches to where we teach and how this affects learning, i.e. the creation and use of environments for learning
- Reflect on the characteristics of the settings in which we teach
- Examine issues relating to the use of e-learning technology and its impact, i.e. virtual learning environments extending the space for learning
- Explore the implications of these in relation to your own practice
- Examine recent developments to extend and adapt existing concepts of where learning can occur
- Consider the implications of increased partnership work on the learning space

Pearson Education Ltd./Sophie Bluy

Introduction

This chapter looks closely at the very important area of the places physical and virtual in which learning takes place. It is of course at once a straightforward definition and at the same time full of potential and some challenges. To give a simple teaching example, it would not have been possible a few years ago to teach Information Communication Technology without very expensive equipment in a specialised environment. Now this might occur with students using remote and mobile devices, phones and intenet access with netbooks and so on.

The space in which teaching and learning occurs is less limited than we may think, and the chapter will explore this kind of potential for expanding our ideas about where and how our learners can learn, as well as retaining a realistic sense of the issues arising in terms of what works best.

Finally we should remember that learning of an informal but very valuable kind may be located in an out-of-hours volunteering session, a part-time job or a performance put on for pleasure. All of these need to be seen as a relevant part of the environments in which we learn.

The chapter builds on the examination of contexts to be found in Chapter 1, Contexts for Learning, and introduces discussion and activity relating to the wider territory explored in Chapter 13, Collaborating to Promote Learning, Chapter 16, Learning Technologies, and Chapter 17, Extending Partnerships.

Developing the concept of environments for learning

The phrase 'environments for learning' can refer to so many locations, activities, groupings and situations that its value can be lost in generalities. Previous generations of teachers and learners were accustomed to quite clearly delineated definitions of appropriate learning environments based on functionality. Academic teaching took place in a classroom with books, writing materials and minimal display facilities. Practical activities involving crafts or skills from art to engineering and from sport to hairdressing could be located in a workshop, studio or outside facility. Even in the relatively narrow range of the 14–19 phase, this term may now refer to anything from a virtual learning environment to a learner-generated social business enterprise.

This diversity is both enriching and challenging depending on the outlook, expertise, resources and commitment of those involved. There is far wider recognition today than in previous years of the need to make learning relevant and to acknowledge that it can and does take place across a wider range of formal and informal environments. The creative and media learner who sets up a space in a social network site and uses feedback to evaluate photograpy and artwork they have produced and then exhibits in a virtual gallery is operating in an enriched environment with stimulating contacts and a very real engagement with potentially commercial activity.

The emphasis on applied learning so central to Tomlinson (DfES Report 2004), whose report was concerned primarily with ensuring that 'all young people are equipped with the skills and knowledge they need to succeed and progress in education, employment and adult life' is now embedded into the Diplomas. This demonstrates a clear attempt to move from a polarised academic and vocational divide. The idea in the UK that certain subjects requiring mainly intellectual activity (mathematics, history, languages, etc.) have a higher value that those involving practical hands-on and perhaps workshop-based subjects like sports, craft skills or construction and/or perhaps home economics or catering, is wrong-headed but quite prevalent. Where there is to be any measure of success in achieving changes in opportunity and attitudes, the environments for learning can be pivotal.

By placing learners, especially those who are young and capable of being excited or even re-engaged by fresh experience, within a stimulating and well-selected environment with all the appropriate support and planning, we can effect startlingly rapid and yet deep and enduring learning. However, there are potential dangers. Certain changes have been driven solely by the need to economise on resources: e.g. questionable assumptions that online learning saves teacher time and money. This can result in learners being disappointed and poorly served.

For trainees and professionals developing work in the 14–19 phase, it may appear hard to find the environment specifically discussed even in some popular standard texts. Geoff Petty (2009) whose *Teaching Today* is a best-seller provides only one very short section which uses this explicit heading and yet the topic is implicit throughout. The learning environment is more than setting out a classroom and ensuring good ventilation, important though these features are. It should in our planning cover a whole range of elements from access and flexibility to proximity to other facilities, and from the ownership and control of the space by learners (can they adjust things, introduce changes?) to learning which takes place in other people's spaces (workplaces, partner schools, FE Centre of Vocational Excellence in construction). This would take us beyond the useful but limited advice in Petty (2009: 32):

> Is the teaching situation distracting or noisy? Is it the last lesson on Friday afternoon? You may need to consider such factors in your preparation and lesson planning. Students who are tired, hungry or thirsty will find learning difficult.

The positioning of learning in appropriate environments in order to enable learning through experience, application and real situations receives greater attention in relation to planning for the 14–19 phase. However, if this interest in making learning more relevant to the wider world is taken seriously, the quality of learning must be well considered.

All students should benefit from more imaginative places and approaches to learning, not just those participating in new qualifications. If we are not careful, then fresh approaches to learning environments, like team-building adventure events, could remain one-off fixes to re-engage learners defined as the NEETs (those not in education, employment or training). In fact the challenges, risks and potentially valuable outcomes of reform cry out for more thoughtful consideration of environments for learning and for collaboration with partners who could help to provide them.

A study of current trends in the promotion and selection of environments for learning can provide one of the most obvious indicators of political, social and economic agendas. Both the drive for global competitiveness and expansion and now its successor, the fight for economic survival, have resulted in similar governmental preoccupations. Huge emphasis is placed upon learning for employment and this underpins the development and introduction of industry-oriented environments for learning right across the 14–19 phase (from sports centre management to firefighting, fashion design to finance). This means that we as teachers need to learn how to manage learning in more varied settings. Our learners may also be coming together in these environments from several different schools and colleges, and we need to design sessions for the environment and the learners.

Creating appropriate environments for learning

According to the DCSF, environments for learning fall into a number of categories. *Positive Behaviour and the Learning Environment* (at: **www.standards.dcsf.gov.uk**) considers how educators can develop the learning environment, which is understood as comprising four factors:

- physical
- relationships
- structures and expectations, and
- language and communication.

The definition of the environment is ultimately wide enough to include community and social aspects as well as the more usual physical features.

Every Child Matters ECM (2003), which applies to teaching and learning in the 14–19 phase, should have an impact on environments for learning.

ECM is an approach to the well-being of children and young people from birth to age 19.

The government's aim is for every child, whatever their background or their circumstances, to have the support they need to:

- be healthy
- stay safe
- enjoy and achieve
- make a positive contribution
- achieve economic well-being.

This means that the organisations involved with providing services to children – from hospitals and schools, to police and voluntary groups – will be teaming up in new ways, sharing information and working together, to protect children and young people from harm and help them achieve what they want in life. Children and young people will have far more say about issues that affect them as individuals and collectively.

'An appropriate environment is key both to safety and to effective learning and development' (DfES 2006).

The Learning Environment involves both the people and the space in which children develop and learn. An appropriate physical environment is one where children feel safe, cared for and relaxed because they are in the continuous care of one, or a small number of, adults who are responsible for them (this includes a childminder's home). An appropriate physical environment offers access to an outdoor as well as an indoor space and should provide a place where children have opportunities to explore, learn and develop with the support of sensitive, knowledgeable adults. Knowledgeable adults who children trust and who observe and respond to their needs are an essential part of the Learning Environment.

(DCSF 2007)

What is clear in this reporting is the concern with the needs of each child and, increasingly, each young learner in a more holistic sense. *Every Child Matters* (2003) set out the direction for policy makers and encapsulated the drive to promote a wider and deeper approach to childrens' services by connecting agencies from education to health and social care. This extended and enriched approach has certainly gained ground and now informs practice and training.

CASE STUDY

The case study below is an example of how the whole feel of an environment and its links with the community and setting have been designed to ensure that the public uses the site and the students are not isolated within it. Ideally environments for learning will be designed to reduce not increase barriers.

Everest Community College's landscape scheme was created to encourage the integration of the school campus with the public realm, minimising any perceived barriers to encourage wider community use.

This design project was supported by CABE, the government's adviser on architecture, urban design and public space.

The college, located on a previously rural site in Basingstoke, Hampshire, is an 11–16 mixed comprehensive school for 750 students which opened in September 2007.

Hampshire County Council has a long history of innovative school grounds design, with the county's landscape architects actively involved in the design of Everest from an early stage to ensure the grounds were developed as a learning, as well as social, resource.

IN PRACTICE

How does the school or college environment in which you work or are placed for training make you and your learners feel? Perhaps you could survey this?

Have you considered what changes in the environment might improve the learning experience? For some learners gardens or open space are vital, while for others changing art work and music may support learning indirectly.

Is there easy access to your site and do the public feel welcome to become involved in the life of the school or college?

Sharing environments

In the more usual sense we would ask if an environment is fit for purpose and what this is. For example, many have often been designed to fulfil a single purpose and rather specific requirements: from swimming pools to catering kitchens, running tracks to music rooms. While this is necessary, it can be exclusive, expensive and logistically difficult to manage. More partnership schools and colleges share this kind of facility these days, not only with each other but also with the wider community, and this provides scope for creative approaches to learning: e.g. learners volunteering in a shared library or museum space or experiencing work in a nursery.

Older-style language laboratories with their fixed furniture and dated equipment went out of favour as too fixed and limiting, being replaced with online programmes and more flexible communicative approaches.

Others, intended to serve two or more purposes, fail to achieve either or any to a high standard. General halls pressed into second-rate service for sport and theatre work, or the characterless multi-purpose school or FE college classroom, with its multitude of transient occupants through the day, can provide sad examples of shortfalls in environments. A carefully zoned learning resources centre, however, can become a favourite area for young people to socialise and work together as well as alone in comfortable and welcoming surroundings.

IN PRACTICE

How often have you directed and facilitated your learners to work elsewhere?

If you frequently use a range of settings to allow for group and individual working, then you might extend this by considering contact with the community. If your idea of the learning environment has been very limited, discuss the practicalities of expanding your learners' experiences with colleagues or tutors and plan some alternative settings.

If we are indeed aiming to prepare young people to apply higher-level skills and to develop their talent as an investment for work and society, then there are far more major infrastructure issues as yet unexplored. The imposition of requirements to work in partnership is fairly recent and goes against many decades of support for a system based on high levels of competition among stakeholders both for learners and for resources. Diplomas, for example, currently require schools and colleges to be partners. If a key purpose of the learning environment is to enable collaborative activity (see Chapter 13) working in teams and problem-solving, then real accessibility and a sense of joint ownership of facilities and spaces is vital.

These are difficult enough to achieve within one institution and even more so when usage extends to diverse learners coming together across institutions on a relatively limited basis, as is envisaged in the strategies for the 14–19 phase. In many Diploma partnership situations a scarce or very important resource, like an engineering workshop or a well-equipped sports centre or theatre space, may be shared, and transport

Source: Pearson Education Ltd. Ian Wedgewood

Photo 7.1
All aspects
of learning
environments
require ongoing
consultation

for learners from other partners, timetabling of staff and students can present logistical challenges to be overcome. Best use of environments requires commitment and management support.

In recent decades institutions have been much more concerned to showcase superior facilities than to plan for joint ownership through shared vision. This tends to lead towards a reduction in attention on real learner needs in outward-facing environments. One young learner in an innovative engineering project when asked for a comment about his experience said, 'I really enjoy it when I'm not being asked what I think about it all the time.'

WHAT DO YOU THINK?

Who comes first – learners or facilities? How do we balance the needs of children and young people 14–19 with institutional pressures in work or work-related environments? For example, the need to provide additional time to stretch learners with exciting activities or fit flexible links with workplaces or other schools and colleges and still meet the demands of whole-school timetabling.

Making environments work for learning 14–19

What are we trying to provide in an effective environment for learning? Responses are often expressed in terms of specific experiences, resources and opportunities and can build into checklists similar to the one below:

- Work-related experience and skills
- Learning to learn
- Opportunities for individualised achievement
- Team learning
- Life skills development
- Problem-solving in applied settings
- Contact with local working environments and community
- Stimulation and engagement for all
- Re-engagement for the disaffected.

In serving the 14–19 phase, teachers and learners are currently working in a huge range of environments many of them far from ideal in either design or practice. Some initial examples are set out below.

Environment for learning	Examples
Informal social settings/home	Parenting, earning and learning, music, communication and e-skills through social networking
Classrooms in the traditional sense	Academic subjects
Field trips and residential settings	Languages, travel and tourism, history, science
Work-based learning	Construction, social care settings, in actual work environments
Work-related learning	Catering, sport in dedicated facilities, i.e. college kitchen area, school enterprise
External formal environments	Extra-curricular programmes: HE, Duke of Edinburgh, cadet forces, coaching qualifications
Tutorial/support settings	One-to-one, peer support
Individual learning	Separate workspaces, storage and study areas, mobile/flexible ICT access instruction one2one
Practical class/workrooms	ICT, Geography, Food technology
Workshops	Construction, motor vehicle workshops
Studios	Art, Drama – adaptable spaces
Simulated learning environments	Travel agency, salons . . . in a college
External project working	Voluntary service, young enterprise
Visitors	Theatre groups, peer groups, community agencies, business
Virtual learning environments	Distance learning as additionality, enhancement for stretch, learner autonomy through VLEs
Extended projects	Links with local charity, media, arts projects, learner-generated citizenship initiatives
Apprenticeship settings	Fully established or providing taster experience, e.g. engineering or construction firm

The descriptions above provide brief reference to the often rather compartmentalised perspective prevalent in much of our 14–19 provision. Clearly, the range of subject disciplines and vocationally related courses have generated a tremendous variety in terms of settings, locations and resources deemed suitable for learning in the 14–19 phase. The fact that policy is dictating greater choice for all learners poses logistical problems not only for local government and education providers but also for professionals whose practice must adapt to their own changing environment for teaching. On the positive side, there is rich potential for exciting and rewarding experience and learning to take place in different environments.

Sadly, there is far less attention paid in mainstream discussion and planning to the provision of appropriate environments for meeting the widest range of need for all learners. This means optimising access in a physical sense and creating a welcoming environment from a wide range of backgrounds with support and learning shaped to their needs. Advice points with information and staff time made available to listen to problems and direct learners to support are all part of the environment.

Post-compulsory teaching and training serves so many diverse groups of adults and young people working and learning, that it has long acknowledged and attempted to meet serious challenges in very difficult environments. Lea et al. (2003: 24) provide some useful background on disability and disabling environments where perhaps access or attitudes may reduce a learner's motivation and success.

ACTIVITY

You will certainly have some, even if not very extensive, experience of the environments for learning set out in the table above.

Consider the environments you experience as a teacher – are they similar or can you add other examples to the table?

Then provide a short case describing your experience of a well or poorly planned environment for learning. What key characteristics of an effective learning environment emerge? Did the environment suit the teaching aims and objectives?

Learning with e-learning

Information and learning technologies (ILT) can be creative and liberating or constraining and irrelevant. Issues relating to the development or selection of environments can prove costly but may be resolved in very simple ways. One example of this was a school and college collaboration with an HEI over creative and media environments which resulted in mutual benefit and reduced costs for all. Students used facilities and worked alongside HE students, supporting and acting as extras in film projects. This was very inspiring for the younger learners, many of whom chose to consider this as a future career.

Not least among the advantages for learners in this kind of situation is increased exposure to a range of learning environments and positive messages around collaboration. Environments are powerful vehicles for certain kinds of change.

Source: Pearson Education Ltd. Studio 8

Photo 7.2
Learning
in virtual
environments is
increasingly
important

Virtual learning environments are part of ILT (information learning technology); more commonly used now in schools and colleges, they provide another example of rapid change. Their use and misuse has contributed significantly to innovation and debate in this area. Their impact on the theory and language of learning environments has been extensive, and as technological change continues apace their impact cannot be underestimated. Blended learning (that is, a learning solution created through a mixture of face-to-face and online learning delivered through a mix of media) depends on the existence of technology-related approaches and solutions to learning and teaching and brings to the debate a host of imaginative routes to integration and coherence.

CASE STUDY

Bexley College – improving learning through VLE use

Summary

'Sparks', Bexley College's Moodle-based virtual learning environment (VLE), was not a popular platform by September 2008 and was underused by both lecturers and learners. John Jackson, e-Learning and VLE Professional Tutor, and Dave Byrne, ILT Training and Development Co-ordinator, set out to discover what could be done to turn this situation around and start to embed e-learning across the College. Over 60 staff and 1,750 learners, representing a wide range of programmes from basic education, access to higher education, Business, ICT, Beauty,

ESOL (English for Speakers of other Languages), Art and Design and Construction, were involved in the drive to extend and enliven e-learning at Bexley College.

The challenge

Recognising it had **an underused and unloved virtual learning environment**, Bexley College agreed a four-point action plan to turn the situation around. They set out to:

- discover why the VLE was currently unpopular and underused;
- address any immediate concerns around usability, which could improve take-up of the VLE;
- provide proactive and ongoing advice, support and training to lecturers to enable them to make best use of the VLE; and
- continue to improve and develop the VLE and e-learning in the College, ensuring its relevance and effectiveness in teaching and learning.

Methods used:

- awareness-raising in team meetings;
- Sparks training provided at all cross-college and departmental training days;
- drop-in advice and training sessions, including one-to-one sessions to address individual needs. These sessions have also provided inspiration for staff seminars;
- development of a 'Smarter Teaching' area on Sparks to provide online support to lecturers; and
- distribution of useful eTools (USB sticks and CD-ROMS) to those attending seminar and advice sessions. These included a variety of 'portable apps' such as Audacity (audio recording), Lightscreen (screen grabber) and Gimp (image editing).

The outcomes

- **Greatly increased use of Sparks** measured by both the number of 'hits' and numbers of unique users
- **Greatly increased number of courses on Sparks** – and more sophisticated tools and techniques (e.g. using streaming audio and video, interactive quizzes, discussion forums, chatrooms, assignment setting and marking, including anti-plagiarism tools, and effective group and one-to-one communications)
- **Use of video proving popular** with learners, lecturers and external and internal verifiers. Around 160 instances of video now embedded in the VLE
- **Very positive feedback from training sessions** and one-to-one advice and support sessions
- **Very positive feedback from current users of Sparks** – both lecturers and learners.

The impact

Bexley College now has a VLE that is proving popular with learners and lecturers:

- there is an increasing tendency for lecturers to put Sparks at the centre of their teaching and to use it imaginatively to the benefit of their learners;
- increased use of streaming video is also proving very popular, particularly for student presentations, debates and for practical subjects such as Beauty and Construction; and
- Bexley College has now reached the stage where previously reluctant users are embracing the VLE and where e-learning is supported and encouraged by their peers.

(www.excellencegateway.org.uk/page.aspx?o= 292398&c=casestudies)

There can be very few occasions on which the teacher is able to exercise much control over the physical environment in which he or she works. The shape of the classroom, its situation in relation to other rooms, its general facilities, cannot often be altered. But the important details which have a direct effect on the process of instruction – the layout of the room, the relative positions of the teacher and students, seating arrangements, position of teaching aids, temperature, illumination, ventilation – that is, the accommodation arrangements, require organisation.

Curzon (2003: 186)

What do you think? How far do you agree with this? There are those who address the actual location of teaching and learning through very innovative means, including moving the learner from a traditional to a more relevant environment. Workplaces, social situations, the learner's home and a virtual environment, are just a few of the possible and sometimes very successful alternatives.

Curzon (2003: 186) goes on to take the position, obvious to those trained in recent decades and especially those who have worked in post-compulsory, practical and vocational settings, that the physical relation of learners and teacher should be dictated by the requirements of the learning activity and not by some traditional arrangement 'hallowed by time'; 'the best position from which to speak, from which to control the class, has to be discovered by individual experiment.' Even within such a statement there are assumptions we may question relating to the desirability of notions of control within an environment rather than individual autonomy and of hierarchies of speech and communication. There is a case to be made for allowing environmentally driven learning methods to take precedence over conventionally directed instruction. In other words, take account of and prioritise where the learners are in the widest sense rather than how you prefer to teach.

Curzon is exploring the impact of environment on students as individuals and in groups. How have your own classroom arrangements affected student learning? Do you believe that the environmental issues – including space, proximity to the teacher, layout and even colour and mood – influence the quality of learning significantly?

Conventional studies of learning environments in both school and college settings for post-14 learners have been chiefly classroom-focused. The following provides a summary of Curzon (2003) on broad findings:

1. There seems to be a direct increase in student participation in the teaching-learning process, with a decrease in distance between teacher and student.

2. Where there is a traditional classroom arrangement – teacher: front/centre standing – a 'triangle of maximum interaction' may be discerned (see Figure 7.1 below). Davies suggests that, where the teacher is able to make such arrangements, the 'more introverted', reticent students should sit within and the more 'extrovert' without this area. The area may shift if the teacher moves for a relatively lengthy period.

3. U-shaped class arrangements with teacher centred in the gap encourage high participation.

4. College students tend to dislike standard seating arrangements and prefer less rigid arrangements

5. Students can be 'territorial' about places when they have become established in a space.

WHAT DO YOU THINK?

Thinking about your own experiences, either as a teacher or a student, how accurate do you think Curzon's findings are? Would you disagree with any of these conclusions? Why/why not?

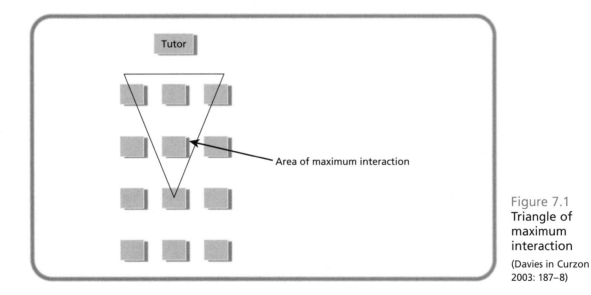

Figure 7.1
Triangle of maximum interaction
(Davies in Curzon 2003: 187–8)

Learning environments for work

Not all students can have extended experience of actual work, but through placements, facilities which replicate realistic work conditions and settings (like college restaurants, salons and shops) and through schemes and links with employers which provide experiences to do real work, they can experience work-based learning.

Work-based learning refers to any form of learning in the workplace; often for employees who are learning, placements are temporary and could be in a block of time or slot in over a longer period with, for example, a day each week.

Work-related learning aims to:

- enable young people to develop an understanding of the knowledge and skills which relate to a particular industry sector;
- provide learning with direct relevance to the world of work;
- give students opportunities to be involved with real projects directly related to real businesses;
- provide a wide range of progression opportunities into further learning.

In each case the raising of young people's skills and preparation for work is a key objective, but the extent to which they are engaged with the environment will differ. This could be because for some learners it is not practical to set up full working experience, for others they are not ready and would not cope. The choice of environment should of course be driven by the learning and learner needs.

It is worth remembering that there is often scope for compromise. With younger learners, there may be benefit in getting access to an FE college simulated environment: for example, use of software that replicates a travel agency booking set-up which can be used in conjunction with role-play. This kind of environment is far more interesting than textbook and hand-out work.

A recent Ofsted report (2009) on the identification of good practice for leisure, travel and tourism in colleges makes six recommendations. Three of these relate to the importance of environments for learning:

- develop further the opportunities for learners to access realistic learning environments, to enhance their understanding of industry requirements while working under supervision with as wide a range of participants as possible
- review the role that real work environments play in travel and tourism courses, in particular the opportunities available for learners to experience working in the industry
- develop further the use of virtual learning environments and other technologies to support learners in these areas.

A fourth recommendation concerns the significance of ensuring that teachers keep up to date with industry practices and this emphasis overlaps with the agenda informing the points above.

Environments in which work-based learning is located are now subject to increased scrutiny and may be accessed by younger learners. Such change may be exciting and positive but it presents new challenges for the management of a learning environment that is also an adult working environment. The very features which provide interest and stimulation and bring learners in touch with the public and with fellow workers are usually those which pose threats to the health, safety and the well-being of learners.

At the far end of the spectrum, this practice includes the traditional and more modern apprenticeship models through the use of work placements and can include all kinds of structured and unstructured environments with very different supervision and management processes in place. For example the apprentice will be working with experienced adults and the public and benefiting from exposure to the commercial world. This interaction with customers and work with a superior in semi-employment cannot be replicated in a college workshop. The risks accompanying external learning of this kind are usually outweighed by the tremendous benefits of such activity. The ultimate reward for an apprentice is the achievement of full working status.

Suggestions as to precisely what the teacher might do to address threats or barriers inherent in the environment, like the interpersonal conflict that might arise for a work placement learner with a manager, are far less frequent than general advice exhorting teachers to take such things into account. The real thorny questions – such as, where does responsibility lie and how far does a teacher's professional role extend where environmental concerns arise? – are commonly sidestepped. In fact the teacher's role, even when student supervision is shared, is all about taking responsibility for the learning, being aware of all the factors and participants and ensuring that they come together. The teacher should have time to enter the environment of the learner and understand it in detail. For example, one very unhappy student was helped by a teacher who negotiated a safe place for him to leave his bike each day after it had been damaged. This was done in the garage with his motor vehicle supervisor and the setting helped to reinforce wider learning about communicating in the workplace, not just the classroom.

Improving quality in environments for learning

Factors for consideration in relation to improving quality within environments for learning include:

- The quality and commitment of teachers in terms of their experience in multi-environment management
- Specialised CPD (continuing professional development) and training for teachers and support workers to work in teams across learning environments
- Cross-institutional integration of mixed-learner cohorts where learners move from one site to another – college to school and off-site together
- Shared protocols for teachers and learners working cross-institution
- Sharing of specialised facilities and the expertise that goes with it – e.g. Media centre, hairdressing salon, catering kitchen, company contact and business link placements
- Learner integration with working adults, mentors and sponsors in their own location

- Safety and security – safeguarding children and learners in real and e-environments with appropriate policies, monitoring and training
- Access to individualised tracking and monitoring information within diverse environments
- Equality and accessibility issues addressed appropriately
- Time and resources to ensure coherence.

After considering the factors above, there could seem to be a great deal too much to take into account in relation to establishing the best environment for particular activities or longer-term teaching and learning. In fact each situation will present different opportunities and challenges and it is usually best and often a requirement to discuss these with colleagues or a mentor to test out your ideas and take on any constructive criticism.

IN PRACTICE

Consider introducing new or evolved environments for learning: for example, one student group from an art and design class worked with construction and drama students on a joint project to transform a drama studio. This changed the space to provide a flexible set and moveable staging and new scenery materials with multiple uses. The teamwork and creativity was inspirational and the outcomes long-lasting and extending far beyond a conventional change in physical environment could have done.

What potential benefits, risks or cost could be incurred? How responsible are you for implementing more radical change of this kind? What role might you play in actively lobbying for changes like increased collaboration?

Learning environments have been extensively researched from certain angles and largely neglected from other perspectives (see the example above relating to student rather than teacher/external environment creation). The new focus on more collaborative, real-world and active learning environments are generating new awareness and interest in the notion of environments for learning. As will be seen throughout the chapter, professionals are now far more concerned with synthesising a whole-person approach to this work which focuses on learner development rather than control and management. However, in the past interest has centred on specific issues like classroom behaviour, results and concentration.

The principal research both from the UK and beyond relates to fairly predictable physical environment factors such as building design, noise, light and organisational processes, but surely environments for learning are more than just places. They need to reflect and define purpose and mood, to welcome, stimulate and inspire, as well as to incorporate a sustainable blend of trained and committed staff in accommodation which meets and adjusts to need, and a thoughtful approach to wider design principles which supports real learning communities.

Source: Pearson Education Ltd. Mind Studio

Photo 7.3
Learner views must be included in the design of environments

RESEARCH FOCUS: THE IMPACT OF SCHOOL ENVIRONMENTS: A LITERATURE REVIEW

The Design Council commissioned a literature review of school building programmes in the UK carried out by a team of researchers at the University of Newcastle upon Tyne. This identified a variety of lessons to be learned from previous phases of school building if the government's £2 billion flagship Building Schools for the Future (BSF) programme is to succeed. The team, from the Centre for Learning and Teaching at Newcastle University, conducted two in-depth studies to assess the impact of school environments on learning, and its implications for the BSF programme.

Physical elements in the school environment can be shown to have discernible effects on teachers and learners. In particular, inadequate temperature control, lighting, air quality and acoustics have detrimental effects on concentration, food, well-being, attendance and, ultimately, attainment.

The research team found that sub-standard environments had a detrimental impact on learning, but that once adequate standards were reached the complexity of environmental interaction comes into play.

An attempt at improving acoustics in a classroom, for example, by deadening echo noise through the use of hangings, may actually decrease the air quality, through increased dust particles.

RESEARCH FOCUS: *CONTINUED*

They concluded that, in many cases, small and relatively low-cost alterations to the learning environment, such as changing the colour of classroom walls, could make a significant difference to the classroom experience.

Above all, evidence showed that learner involvement was a key element in defining and solving design problems in schools, with solutions that are individualised, organic and local.

The most successful approaches to learning environment design are likely to be those which are seen as interim solutions and which have within them elements of flexibility and adaptability for new cohorts of learners and teachers, new curriculum demands and new challenges.

ACTIVITY

The review above uses the five categories below to provide a series of summaries indicating the evidence of effect of environment:

1. Attainment: improvements in curriculum attainment measured by standardised tests or exams as monitored by teacher observation
2. Engagement: improvements in levels of attention, more on-task behaviours observed, decrease in distracted or disruptive behaviour
3. Affect: improvements in self-esteem for teachers and learners, increased academic self-concept, improvements in mood and motivation
4. Attendance: fewer instances of lateness or absenteeism
5. Well-being: impacts on the physical self, relating to discomfort as well as minor and major ailments.

What, if anything, would you adjust or add to these indicators?
How applicable might they be within your own environments for learning?

 ## CASE STUDY

The shared, specialised environment for learning

This example illustrates a more joined-up approach to providing work-related experience, employability and many other valuable social life and indeed academic skills. Its success

relies on the participation of local schools' employers.

Sunderland Futures Centres
Harraton and Pallion Centres have been designed and developed to offer students in Sunderland broader learning

opportunities within their home school option choices. Courses within these Centres of Excellence are based around areas of study that provide a direct and relevant link to business, industry and the world of work. The courses are delivered through a variety of exciting and stimulating programmes, leading to valuable qualifications in today's competitive world.

Students studying at the Centres will find that the environment has been designed to encourage students' independence, personal responsibility and maturity in preparation for their progression to future studies and chosen career path.

When students apply for their chosen course, they are interviewed by Centre staff and Business Ambassadors to ensure that the course selected is appropriate for the individual student's needs. This process reflects working practices within business and industry and forms an essential element of work related learning.

WHAT DO YOU THINK?

How important is realistic interview as an introduction to the environment for learning? Why do think this may/may not encourage students to commit to the learning experience?

Sunderland Futures is committed to the provision of a high level of teaching and learning, offering outstanding facilities and resources.

The Centres have an ethos of success and the expectations of students attending the Centres are high. Students are required to show outstanding commitment to work, respect for staff and fellow students, and maturity in their approach to work.

Every student is asked to read, accept and sign a contract which clearly outlines the expectations and the quality of teaching and provision they can expect from the staff of Sunderland Futures Centres. Parents and carers of students are asked to fully support and encourage their child and are asked to sign the Parent Contract in supporting the Sunderland Futures Centre staff in working in partnership with the student.

Integrated within Sunderland Futures Centres is the aim to develop real working environments in which students will develop their skills and experience within a business and enterprise culture. The Centres work in partnership with business and commerce to provide work-related learning experiences, and students are supported by Business Ambassadors to update them on latest developments within their area of study.

(http:sun1419.net)

WHAT DO YOU THINK?

How willing would you be to work as a partner teacher in this kind of environment? What questions might you ask? Perhaps you could consider researching opportunities to access more work-related environments in your own area.

The unique partnership has enabled collaborative timetabling across schools but the demands of the courses may require students to work within a different time frame during sessions at the Centres. Students may start or finish later than usual and may have a reduced lunch time. As part of their commitment to the course, and their own success, students need to demonstrate excellent punctuality and attendance. Students may have to take responsibility for their own transportation to the Centre that they attend, which again, is part of the development of maturity and responsibility.

IN PRACTICE

What elements of the case study above have you experienced in your own professional practice? Is the environment a vital factor in such provision or not?

Select an existing (or outline a plan to establish) learning environment in collaboration with a partner provider, i.e. a school or college in the same consortium. This could well be a Diploma-focused environment/combination of related environments as above or one with another purpose. Explore the specific advantages and difficulties anticipated or encountered for learning in such a situation.

SUMMARY

Environments for learning are both complex and highly influential. The widest possible definitions encompass teacher and learner attitudes, social and economic contexts as well as physical factors. Given the intense focus in some political and economic quarters on environment as powerful in its own right, it is as well to consider the implications of such opinions for teaching. If exposure and practice through placement, instruction and associated support is sufficient for the purposes of certain stakeholders, is the work environment seen as a substitute in part or perhaps even in full for many post-14 learners? The latest legislation on the leaving age raises as many familiar and historical questions relating to environments for learning as it answers. Will young people really be supported in a range of environments to continue learning? What role will we have as teachers in maintaining continuity within the new arrangements.

Find out more

Armstrong, P. and Hughes, M. (2000) *Developing Skills: realistic work environments in further education,* **at: https://crm.lsnlearning.org.uk/user/ order.aspx?code=002128.**
Further education has a long tradition of providing realistic work environments (RWEs) that offer opportunities for training and assessment. But what is their contribution to skills development? This report presents the results of a survey of all FE sector colleges to establish the prevalence and perceived value of RWEs. It provides clear evidence of the potential of RWEs to develop skills for the competitiveness agenda.

McCrone, T., Wade, P. and Golden, S. (2007), *The Impact of 14–16 year olds on Further Education Colleges,* **Slough: National Foundation for Educational Research.**
This provides a helpful look at some of the implications and impact for young learners within these particular environments for learning. It can also support further study on the context for collaborative working as this

highlights the development and effects of younger learners working in further education colleges.

Eraut, M. (2007) *Learning in the Workplace – research summary for House of Commons Committee,* **available at: www.niace.org.uk/lifelonglearninginquiry/docs.**
Professor Michael Eraut provides a very interesting perspective on this important aspect:

All learners from 14 onwards should be learning in a variety of contexts as essential preparation for lifelong learning, since learning in the workplace is very different in kind from learning in school or college learning in one context will not easily transfer to the other, nor will knowledge and skill transfer without being resituated in the new context. A significant amount of preparation for work will have to be undertaken in employment in the absence of greater variety of learning contexts. To pretend otherwise would be to deceive the public and limit the quality of the outcomes of general and vocational education.

Bibliography

Curzon, L. (2003) *Teaching in Further Education: principles and practice,* London: Continuum.

DCSF (2007) *The Early Years Foundation Stage – Effective Practice: the learning environment,* London: DCSF.

DfES (2004) *14–19 Curriculum and Qualifications Reform.* Final Report of the Working Group on 14–19 Ryorm (**www.dcsf.gov.uk**).

DfES (2006) *Early Years Foundation Stage Consultation Document,* Nottingham: DfES (ref.SESCO6_18).

DCSF (2008) Children and Young Peoples' Workforce Development consultation, available at: **www.everychildmatters.gov.uk/deliveringservices/ childrenandyoungpeoplesworkforce/**

Donovan, G. (2005) *Teaching 14–19: everything you need to know about teaching and learning across the phases,* London: David Fulton Publishers.

Hillier, Y. (2005) *Reflective Teaching in Further and Adult Education,* London: Continuum.

Lea, J. et al. (2003) *Working in Post-Compulsory Education,* Maidenhead: Open University Press.

Lumby, J. and Foskett, N. (2007) *14–19 Education: Policy, Leadership & Learning,* London: Sage.

Ofsted (2009a) *Identifying Good Practice: a survey of college provision in leisure, travel and tourism,* London: Ofsted.

Petty, G. (2009) *Teaching Today: a practical guide,* 4th edn, London: Nelson Thornes. Available at: **www.ofsted.gov.uk/Ofsted-home/ Publications-and-research/Browse-all-by/ Documents-by-type/Thematic-reports/**

Ofsted (2009b) *Virtual Learning Environments: an evaluation of their development in a sample of educational settings,* London: Ofsted. Available at: **www.ofsted.gov.uk/Ofsted-home/ Publications-and-research/Browse-all-by/ Documents-by-type/Thematic-reports/**

Race, P. (2001) *The Lecturer's Toolkit: a resource for developing learning, teaching and assessment,* London: Kogan Page.

Rogers, A. (1996) *Teaching Adults,* Buckingham: Open University Press.

In this chapter you will:

- Acknowledge the ambiguity of 'learning styles'
- Attempt to devise a learning style profile for yourself and your students
- Become familiar with key learning style models
- Consider the key features of andragogy and pedagogy
- Understand the distinction between deep learning and surface learning
- Appreciate the place of applied learning in the vocational diplomas

Pearson Education Ltd./Sophie Bluy

Introduction

One of the difficulties in considering learning styles is the range of cognate terms used in discussions of them. Coffield et al. (2004b: 3) note some of them:

'learning strategies' and 'approaches to learning' (as well as) 'models', 'instruments' and 'inventories' . . . other terms in constant use (include): '*cognitive* styles', '*conative* styles', and 'cognitive structures', 'thinking styles', 'teaching styles', 'motivational styles', 'learning orientations' and 'learning conditions'.

Furthermore, 'learning styles' can have a number of distinct meanings, as Pritchard (2005: 53) points out:

a particular way in which an individual learns; a mode of learning – an individual's preferred or best manner(s) in which to think, process information and demonstrate learning; an individual's preferred means of acquiring knowledge and skills; habits, strategies, or regular mental behaviours concerning learning, particularly deliberate educational learning, that an individual displays.

You need only Google 'learning styles' to discover what Coffield and colleagues (2004b: 2) describe as:

a large commercial industry promoting particular inventories and instruments. Certain models have become extremely influential and popular: in the US, for example, the Dunn, Dunn and Price Learning Styles Inventory (LSI) is used in a large number of elementary schools, while in the UK, both Kolb's Learning Style Inventory (LSI) and Honey and Mumford's Learning Styles Questionnaire (LSQ) are widely known and used.

It is easy to understand the attraction of the notion of individual learning styles to teachers, trainers and institutions faced with the challenge of meeting the learning needs of a range of individual learners. This is particularly so in the lifelong learning sector with its increasingly diverse range of learners situated in so many differing learning contexts. It is very tempting to believe that the administration of a particular learning style inventory to students will produce clear individual profiles which can then be used to determine teaching strategies to be used with them. However, some studies have called into question the value of such measures. Coffield and colleagues (2004b), for example, selected 13 key models from 71 identified in the literature. Of these, only three met their criteria for consistency, reliability and validity, with some of the best-known and most-used models failing to meet these criteria.

Learning style profiles

Eric Jensen (1996) suggests that aspects of learning styles are influential at different stages of the learning process. The first aspect will be related to the context for learning, the second to the type of input preferred, the third to the processing of information and the final aspect to the way in which the learner responds to what has been learned. Jensen's aspects are summarised in the table below:

Contextual factors

- Field dependent v. Field independent

Field dependency maximises the importance of the context in which learning takes place: students learn best in real-life contexts such as field trips and practical experiments. NVQs and other work-based learning programmes are reliant on a high level of field dependent learning. For field independence, the context for learning is unimportant and could be a PC station, library or classroom.

- Flexible environment v. Structured environment

Some students learn effectively in a variety of different environments in which variable such as lighting, temperature or noise levels make no difference. Others prefer a well-ordered, controlled environment with a minimum of variation.

- Independent v. Dependent v. Interdependent

Some students prefer to work alone while others thrive on interacting with others. Interdependency is the capacity to work both alone and with others.

- Relationship-driven v. Content-driven

Students can be relationship-driven in that they prefer to like the presenter of the information, while others find the content more important than the source of the information.

Input preferences

- Visual external v. internal

Visual learners respond well to pictorial explanation, overhead transparencies, PowerPoint presentations and handouts, whereas others prefer to create internal pictures, to visualise situations, events and ideas.

- Auditory external v. internal

Prefers external auditory input, needs to be told, informed, able to listen, absorb, is sensitive to aspects of speech such as tone, pitch, emphasis. Or can/need to hold conversations with themselves, engaging in self-talk.

- Kinaesthetic tactile v. internal

These are practical, hands-on, have-a-go, committed to activity, learn through doing. Kinaesthetic internal learners rely on intuition, inference, on what is not said, are sensitive to body language, more physically than verbally expressive.

Processing format

- Contextual global v. Sequential detailed/linear

Contextual global learners need the bigger picture, need all the details together in a holistic gestalt fashion. More likely to be able to multi-task. Are inferential and intuitive in processing information. Often referred to as 'right-brain' learner with preference for processing in pictures, symbols, icons and themes. The sequential detailed linear learner prefers to work in sequence of steps, also wants an agenda, a timetable of what's coming up. Is analytical and word-based, often known as a 'left brain' learner.

• Conceptual – abstract v. Concrete – objects and feelings

The abstract learner is intellectual, academic, theoretical, whereas the concrete learner wants to touch and manipulate things. Needs specific examples and hand-on experience.

Response filters

• Externally referenced v. Internally referenced

The externally referenced response is one which is concerned with what others think, what their expectations are, whereas internal referencing is based on the learner's own views and values.

• Matcher v. Mismatcher

The matcher notes similarities, agrees more easily, likes consistencies. The learner will approve of something tried and tested, whereas the mismatcher notices differences, what's missing. They look for inconsistencies, for flaws in arguments.

• Impulsive experimental v. Analytical reflective

The impulsive experimenter acts immediately on thoughts, employs trial and error, focuses on the present. The analytical reflector responds internally, absorbs information, processes it reflectively, is pragmatic, stands back.

(Adapted from Jensen 1996)

IN PRACTICE

Look through the aspects affecting learning in each category above and see if you can select from each category those which you might expect to find in a learner of a particular type and which might be grouped together to make up a learning style. For example, you might think that someone who learns best in a structured environmental context is independent and content-driven, is also likely to be auditory external driven, a sequential detailed/linear left-brained learner who is a mismatcher and analytical reflective.

Now, taking the aspects in each of Jensen's categories, profile yourself as a learner. In doing so, try to make a judgement about whether this profile has always been fixed or changes over time or in different contexts.

Photo 8.1 Some students may prefer to learn kinaesthetically, with more than one sense being engaged simultaneously

Source: Pearson Education Ltd. Jules Selmes

IN PRACTICE

Good practice in FE and schools will often be represented in a group or class profile, which will pick out the general features of the group and add any specific learning needs individuals may have. They will rarely extend to individual learner profiles. Select one student from a group you are currently teaching or have recently taught and attempt to profile him or her as you did yourself above.

The reflection and application exercises above will have introduced you to some of the key questions about learning styles which it is hoped we can address in this chapter. Firstly, is it possible to group together a consistent series of features of an individual's learning such that we can call it a 'style'? Secondly, are the instruments which claim to measure learning style able to do so, and do so consistently? Finally, what are the implications for the teacher of an understanding of their students' learning styles?

Learning style models

Coffield et al. (2004a) identify five families of learning styles. The first three assume that such preferences are fixed and stable. These may be 'constitutionally based' such as that of Dunn and Dunn (1992) and Gregorc (1982), 'reflect deep-seated features of the cognitive structure' as in Riding's (1991), or be related to personality types as in the Myers-Briggs (1998) model. The remaining two families allow for more flexibility in as far as they allow for change over time or between contexts. These will include those which conceive of learning styles as 'flexibly stable learning preferences' such as those of Kolb (1984) and Honey and Mumford (1992), and a wide-ranging family of 'learning approaches, strategies, orientations and conceptions of learning' (Coffield et al. 2004b). This family will include the models of Entwhistle (1988) and Marton and Säljö (1976) (whose work we shall return to below when we discuss deep and surface learning).

The learning style measured by the Myers-Briggs Type Indicator (MBTI) is based on an assessment leading to an ascription of personality type underpinned by Jung's theory of personality types (Jung 1971). Subjects respond to a series of questions which place them on four bipolar or dichotomous scales relating to their favourite world, or their attitudes, their acquisition and processing of information, their pattern of decision-making and their lifestyle:

Extraversion E --Introversion I
Sensing S --Intuition N
Thinking T --Feeling F
Judging J --Perceiving P

Subjects' overall responses ascribe them to one of 16 personality types:

ISTJ	ISFJ	ISTP	INTP
INTJ	INFJ	ISFP	INFP
ESTJ	ESFJ	ESTP	ENTP
ENTJ	ENFJ	ESFP	ENFP

A series of descriptors is related to each type. ISTJ, for example, might be described as someone who is serious and quiet, but nevertheless practical and matter-of-fact, highly responsible and someone who is a logical organised thinker, is loyal and traditional. Some have regarded the generation of 16 personality types as a positive aspect of the MBTI, reflecting the relative complexity and range of individual differences and offering more comprehensive accounts of learning styles than the more restrictive range of other models. Further, MBTI recognises that learning is not simply a cognitive matter but requires the complex interplay of the cognitive with the emotional, attitudinal and other aspects of personality.

There are, however, reservations. MBTI as a personality inventory is not about learning at all. Any account of how an individual might learn based on personality descriptors requires a further judgment about how they might impact on individual learners in practice. There are concerns (reported by Coffield et al.) that the bipolarity of each scale has not been established, or that each end of the scale does not represent a true opposite and that it would be possible therefore for subjects to score highly at each end. Finally, the appropriateness of the forced questions has been called into questions, with critics arguing that true bipolarity would emerge even if questions were not either/or.

Kolb's learning style model (1984) follows from his conception of the process of experiential learning which is a four-stage model involving four learning modes: *concrete experience, reflective observation, abstract conceptualisation* and *active experimentation*.

Firstly, concrete experience (CE)/abstract conceptualisation (AC) and secondly, active experimentation (AE)/reflective observation (RO) comprise what Kolb calls 'two distinct dimensions, each representing two dialectically opposed adaptive orientations' (Kolb 1984: 41). The first dimension, CE-AC, represents what Kolb sees as *prehension*, or two different ways of grasping experience in the world, either through conceptual interpretation (or *comprehension*) or through tangible immediate experience (or *apprehension*), while the second dimension, AE-RO (or *transformation*) represents two ways of transforming that grasp, either through internal reflection (or *intention*) or active manipulation of the external world (or *extension*).

Kolb's *Learning Style Inventory* (LSI) asks the respondent to rank four statements in a way that best describes his or her learning style. One word in each statement corresponds to one of the four learning modes: CE (e.g. feeling), RO (e.g. observing), AC (e.g. thinking), AE (e.g. doing). The LSI 'measures a person's relative emphasis on each of the four modes of the learning process – plus two combination scores which indicate the extent to which the subject emphasises abstractness over concreteness and action over reflection' (1984: 68). This emphasis leads to a learning style profile which very specifically describes the individual in relation to the learning modes and ascribes to them a particular composite of four basic learning styles.

The **Convergers** (**AC-AE**) emphasise problem-solving, decision-making and the practical application of ideas. The converger performs best in conventional learning situations such as intelligence tests where there is one closed answer. S/he uses hypothetical-deductive reasoning and prefers dealing with technical tasks and problems rather than interpersonal issues.

The **Divergers'** (**CE-RO**) learning strengths are opposite to the convergers'. Divergers rely on imaginative ability and awareness of meaning and values. Concrete situations are seen from many angles, and meaningful wholes, or gestalts, are synthesised from parts. Divergers flourish in situations where alternative ideas are sought or brainstorming is used. They are people, feeling and imagination oriented.

The **Assimilators** (**AC-RO**) reason inductively, create theoretical models and assimilate diverse ideas into an integrated explanation. This orientation, as in convergence, is less focused on people and more concerned with ideas and abstract concepts. Ideas are, however, judged less on their practical value and more for their logical soundness.

The **Accommodators'** (**CE-AE**) learning style stands in opposition to Assimilation in so far as it prizes doing things, carrying out plans and tasks and getting involved in new experiences. The accommodator likes risk-taking and adapting to rapidly changing circumstances. Where theory or plans do not fit the facts, the accommodator will discard the plans while the assimilator will disregard or re-examine the facts. Accommodators are intuitive rather than analysts.

While Kolb's learning style model, like the Myers-Briggs, is heavily influenced by Jung's theory of psychological types, Kolb (1984: 63) allows for the possibility of change over time but particularly in changing circumstances:

> The implication of the contextualist world view for the study of human
> individuality is that psychological types or styles are not fixed *traits* but stable

states. The stability and endurance of these states in individuals comes not solely from fixed genetic qualities or characteristics of human beings; nor, for that matter, does it come solely from the stable, fixed demands of environmental circumstances. Rather, stable and enduring patterns of human individuality arise from consistent patterns of transaction between the individual and his or her environment.

WHAT DO YOU THINK?

Teachers are veteran learners. Following the self profile you completed above, consider the extent to which your learning style represents a 'stable state' as described above, or whether this has varied over the years or from one learning situation to the other.

Andragogy and pedagogy

The notion that adults and children learn in different ways is of crucial importance to teachers of 14–19-year-olds because the age phase arguably marks the transition from childhood to adulthood. Malcolm Knowles (2005) developed the theory of andragogy 'the art and science of helping adults learn' as opposed to pedagogy 'the art and science of teaching children' (2005: 61). According to Knowles, there are six key ways in which pedagogy and andragogy differ. The first relates to the need to know. According to pedagogy, learners are pragmatic in that they need to learn what the teacher requires them to learn to be successful, whereas adults need to know why it is necessary for them to engage in learning. The second assumption of andragogy is related to the learner's self-concept. The adult has a deep-seated need to be self-directed, to be responsible for and in control of their own learning. This self-concept develops as learners mature and the child is therefore typically non-self directed and dependent. Thirdly, pedagogy would regard the experience of the learner as of little value to their learning, whereas adults bring to learning both a breadth and depth of experience and it is this which for Knowles leads to the emphasis in adult learning on experiential techniques – techniques that tap into the experience of learners, such as group discussion, simulation exercises, problem-solving activities, case methods, and laboratory methods instead of transmittal techniques (2005: 66). Fourthly, learning readiness is an important aspect of adult learning. Adults will have passed through all the developmental stages of their lives which makes them open to many areas of learning, whereas children's learning readiness will be restricted by age, developmental stage and curriculum level. Fifthly, Knowles argues that whereas children are subject-centred in their orientation to learning, which they see as the acquisition of subject content, adults are life-oriented: 'they learn new knowledge, understanding, skills, values, and attitudes most effectively when they are presented in the context of application to real-life situations' (2005: 67). Finally, although adults are responsive to some external motivators – promotion, qualifications, for example – the strongest motivators are internal ones such as self-esteem, achievement, satisfaction, stimulation. Children's motivation, on the other hand, is largely external.

RESEARCH FOCUS

Two of Knowles's assumptions about andragogy are questioned below.

2. Experience: *As a person matures he accumulates a growing reservoir of experience that becomes an increasing resource for learning.* The next step is the belief that adults learn more effectively through experiential techniques of education such as discussion or problem-solving (Knowles 2005: 43). The immediate problem we have is the unqualified way in which the statement is made. There may be times when experiential learning is not appropriate – such as when substantial amounts of new information are required. We have to ask the question, what is being learnt, before we can make judgements.

A second aspect here is whether children's and young people's experiences are any less real or less rich than those of adults. They may not have the accumulation of so many years, but the experiences they have are no less consuming, and still have to be returned to, entertained, and made sense of. Does the fact that they have 'less' supposed experience make any significant difference to the process? A reading of Dewey (1933) and the literature on reflection (e.g. Boud et al. 1985) would support the argument that age and amount of experience makes no educational difference. If this is correct, then the case for the distinctiveness of adult learning is seriously damaged. This is of fundamental significance if, as Brookfield (1986: 98) suggests, this second assumption of andragogy 'can arguably lay claim to be viewed as a "given" in the literature of adult learning'.

3. Readiness to learn. *As a person matures his readiness to learn becomes oriented increasingly to the developmental tasks of his social roles*. As Tennant (1996: 21–22) puts it, 'it is difficult to see how this assumption has any implication at all for the process of learning, let alone how this process should be differentially applied to adults and children'. Children also have to perform social roles.

Knowles does, however, make some important points at this point about 'teachable' moments. The relevance of study or education becomes clear as it is needed to carry out a particular task. At this point more ground can be made as the subject seems relevant.

However, there are other problems. These appear when he goes on to discuss the implications of the assumption. 'Adult education programs, therefore, should be organised around "life application" categories and sequenced according to learners' readiness to learn' (1980: 44).

First, as Brookfield comments, these two assumptions can easily lead to a technological interpretation of learning that is highly reductionist. By this he means that things can become rather instrumental and move in the direction of competencies. Language like 'life application' categories reeks of skill-based models – where learning is reduced to a series of objectives and steps (a product orientation). We learn things that are useful rather than interesting or intriguing or because something fills us with awe. It also thoroughly underestimates just how much we learn for the pleasure it brings (see below).

Second, as Humphries (1988) has suggested, the way he treats social roles – as worker, as mother, as friend, and so on, takes as given the legitimacy of existing social relationships. In other words, there is a deep danger of reproducing oppressive forms.

Source: Smith, M. K. (1996, 1999) *'Andragogy': the encyclopedia of informal learning*

WHAT DO YOU THINK?

Considering the above as well as your views on Knowles's other assumptions relating to the need to know, the learner's self-directness, real-life learning and motivation, do you believe, on the basis of your own experience and your knowledge of your students, that the distinction between pedagogy and andragogy is a sound and useful one?

Deep and surface learning

Marton and Säljö (1976) found that Swedish university students given an academic prose text to read approached the text in one of two ways. The first group had tried to memorise key facts in the text, while the second group took a more holistic approach, attempting to grasp the big picture and understand the writer's overall argument. The learning of the first group was designated 'surface learning' while the second group had engaged in 'deep learning'. Surface learning accorded with the first three conceptions of learning Marton and Säljö later identified: increasing knowledge, memorising or storing information and acquiring facts. Deep learning exemplified the further three conceptions: making sense of or abstracting meaning, interpreting to understand reality and changing as a person.

Entwhistle (1987) later refined and extended the features of deep and surface learning.

DEEP LEARNING	SURFACE LEARNING
Intention to understand	Intention to complete task requirements
Vigorous interaction with content	Memorises information needed for assessments
Relates new ideas to previous knowledge	Failure to distinguish principles from examples
Relates concepts to everyday experiences	Treats task as an external imposition
Relates evidence to conclusions	Focuses on discrete elements without interpretation
Examines the logic of the argument	Non-reflectiveness about purpose or strategies

IN PRACTICE

Consider the following points in relation to your own learning and that of your students:

Does the deep and surface learning dichotomy characterise the learning of any of your own students?

Do the curriculum models of the programmes you teach on invite a deep or surface approach?

Do the deep and surface approaches depend less on the individual student's learning preference and more on the strategies used by the teacher? Is it possible, for example, to teach for deep learning and, if so, what kinds of teaching strategies would encourage this?

Applied learning and the diplomas

A key feature of the 14–19 diplomas, implemented from September 2008, is the central importance of **applied learning**. For the Qualifications and Curriculum Authority, applied learning

> is essential to the vision for the Diploma. At least 50% of principal learning has to be applied. This means that learning cannot take place in the classroom but must be in a work-related environment, whether real or simulated. Applied learning is the practical application of theory that allows

learners the opportunity to actively engage with the curriculum they are studying. It is relevant and meaningful to learners as it allows for learning within different contexts and environments. Applied learning allows the learner to interact with teachers, other learners and individuals from outside the classroom.

Applied learning encourages:

Linking understanding and learning activities to job roles
Interaction with professionals
Real life investigations and active enquiry
Learning through doing
Interaction with other learners through group work
Learning in different environments.

QCA Applied Learning

The most important aspect of applied learning as described above is the necessity that it takes place in a vocational rather than in a classroom context. Harkin (2007: 35) conceives of applied learning in a rather broader way:

Applied learning is about active engagement with subjects, teachers, other learners and the world beyond. It is about doing, being an agent of change, influencing one's own life and the world, being a citizen, as well as potentially an employee. It is about excitement in following one's interests and therefore about some power to make informed choices.

And Pring (2008: 2), in a discussion of Applied Science, points out that ' "Applied" means something different from "vocational", "practical" or "relevant" although there may well be much in common between these.'

Source: Education photos

Photo 8.2
Work-based contexts offer many opportunities for applied learning to take place

The emphasis on applied learning in the diplomas raises two important issues in relation to student learning styles. Firstly, many of the aspects of the broader notion of applied learning as described above by Harkin would be best suited to an andragogical approach to learning in its emphasis on self-directedness, experience as a prime focus for learning and real-life situations as desirable learning contexts. Secondly, will the emphasis on the active, experiential dimension of applied learning lead to those with certain learning profiles, Kolb's divergers and accommodators, finding this approach to learning more preferable and disenfranchise the convergers and assimilators who would be less suited to it?

SUMMARY

It is easy to understand the attraction of the notion of individual learning styles to teachers, trainers and institutions faced with the challenge of meeting the learning needs of a range of individual learners. It is very tempting to believe that the administration of a particular learning style inventory to students will produce clear individual profiles which can then be used to determine teaching strategies to be used with them. However, some studies have called into question the value of such measures. By considering a range of learning style models, the question has been posed as to whether it is possible to group together a consistent series of features of an individual's learning such that we can call it a 'style'. The instruments which claim to measure learning style have been examined and their claim to be able to do so, and do so consistently, scrutinised. Finally, the implications of andragogy, pedagogy, deep and surface learning and applied learning for teachers of 14–19-year-olds have been considered.

Find out more

Two reports for the Learning and Skills Research Centre by Frank Coffield and colleagues have been influential in shaping the views of practitioners about the value of the use of learning styles, learning models, inventories and questionnaires with students:

Coffield, F., Moseley, D., Hall, E. and Ecclestone, K. (2004) *Should We be Using Learning Styles: what research has to say to practice* and *Learning Styles and Pedagogy in Post 16 Learning: a systematic and critical review*. London: Learning and Skills Research Centre. Available at: **www.lsrc.ac.uk/**.

In spite of a highly critical analysis of 13 key learning style models in the second report, the authors come

to some very positive recommendations about the potential of using investigating learning styles:

A reliable and valid instrument which measures learning styles and approaches could be used as a tool to encourage self-development, not only by diagnosing how people learn, but by showing them how to enhance their learning.

We wish to recommend that consideration be given to developing for schools, colleges, universities and firms new programmes of study focused on human learning and how it can be fostered.

The tutors/trainers who involve their students/ staff in dialogue need to be knowledgeable about the strengths and limitations of the model they are using; to be aware of the dangers of labelling and discrimination; and to be prepared to respect the views of students who may well resist any attempts to change their preferred learning style.

(pp. 132–3)

There are many learning styles questionnaires available online, many of which are free. The Honey and Mumford questionnaire can be accessed at: **www.peterhoney.com/**

Bibliography

Boud, D. et al. (1985) *Reflection – Turning Experience into Learning*, Milton Keynes: Open University Press.

Brookfield, M. (1986) *Understanding and Facilitating Adult Learning*, Milton Keynes: Open University Press

Coffield, F., Moseley, D., Hall, E. and Ecclestone, K. (2004a) *Should We be Using Learning Styles: what research has to say to practice*, London: Learning and Skills.

Coffield, F., Moseley, D., Hall, E. and Ecclestone, K. (2004b) *Learning Styles and Pedagogy in Post 16 Learning: a systematic and critical review*, London: Learning and Skills Research Centre.

Dewey, J. (1933) *How We Think*, New York: D.C. Heath.

Dunn, R. and Dunn, K. (1992) *Teaching Secondary Students Through Their Individual Learning Styles*, Needham Heights, MA: Allyn and Bacon.

Entwhistle, N. (1987) *Styles of Learning and Teaching*, London: David Fulton Publishers.

Gregorc, A. F. (1982) *Gregorc Style Delineator: development, technical and administration manual*, Columbia, CT: Gregorc Associates Inc.

Harkin, J. (2007) *Excellence in Supporting Applied Learning*, London: TDA/LLUK.

Honey, P. and Mumford, A. (1992) *The Manual of Learning Styles*, Maidenhead: Peter Honey Publications.

Humphries, B. (1988) Adult Learning in social work education, towards liberation or domestication, *Critical Social Policy* No. 23: 4–21.

Jensen, E. (1996) *Brain-based Learning*, Del Mar, CA: Turner Point Publishing.

Jung, C. G. [1971] *Personality Types, Collected Works of C.G. Jung*, edited by Read, H., Fordham, M. and Adler, G., London: Routledge and Kegan Paul.

Knowles, M. (2005) *The Adult Learner* (6th edn), Burlington, MA: Elsevier.

Kolb, D. A. (1984) *Experiential Learning*, Englewood Cliffs, NJ: Prentice Hall Inc.

Marton, F. and Säljö, R. (1976) On qualitative differences in learning: 1 – outcome and process. *British Journal of Educational Psychology*, 46: 4–11.

Myers, I. B. and McCaully M. H. (1998) *Manual: a guide to the development and use of the Myers-Briggs Type Indicator*, Palo Alto, CA: Consulting Psychologists Press.

Pring, R. (2008) *Applied Learning: the case of applied science*, Oxford: Nuffield Review of 14–19 Education and Training.

Pritchard, A. (2005) *Ways of Learning*, Abingdon: David Fulton Publishers.

QCA *Applied Learning*, at: **www.qca.org.uk/ qca_13477.aspx** [accessed 18.07.08].

Riding, R. (1991) *Cognitive Styles Analysis User's Manual*, Birmingham: Learning and Training technology.

Smith, M. K. (1996, 1999) *'Andragogy' – the encyclopedia of informal learning*, at: **www.infed.org/ lifelonglearning/b-andra.htm** [accessed 17.07.08].

Tennant, M. (1996) *Psychology and Adult Learning*, London: Routledge.

In this chapter you will:

- Consider what we mean by the term 'behaviour'
- Explore feelings of self-efficacy when dealing with unwanted behaviours
- Consider the influence of social policies and attitudes on the education agenda and the effects on young people
- Identify difficult or unwanted behaviour
- Identify and analyse your own responses to behaviours, in particular that of diffusion and escalation
- Explore practical strategies for promoting positive behaviours

Pearson Education Ltd./Sophie Bluy

Introduction

Behaviour management is a key topic for debate within both secondary and further education. It is also one of the most requested areas for continued professional development (CPD) and training. It is clearly an area for concern for both experienced and newly qualified teachers, as well as those teachers who are in training, despite the plethora of information, guidance and general literature available. This may be because it has such an impact on the way in which we, as individuals, feel about ourselves and of course about our effectiveness as a teacher.

Behaviour is necessarily complex and the structure of this chapter reflects its multifarious and intricate nature. Thus, the chapter starts with an overview of common support systems and structures found within further education and secondary schools. It then explores the emotional impact of challenging behaviour in terms of teacher self-efficacy – that is, a person's belief in themselves to effect change. This is followed by a brief consideration of external influences such as political drivers and exploration of the somewhat conflicting ideologies and beliefs concerning the purpose and practice of education. The chapter is designed in such a way as to allow the reader to explore a variety of theoretical aspects as well as more practical activities to improve their own skills in dealing with difficult behaviour. The final section of the chapter is more practical in nature and aims to discuss strategies for preventing or reducing unwanted behaviour and fostering a climate that is conducive to the learning of all learners.

Source: Cartoonstock

Whilst the turbulence of the teenage years can be challenging, it is important to remember this is a temporary phase

Overview

Behaviours are often described and discussed within and outside of the work setting but rarely, do we as teachers, *analyse* behaviours in such a way that we can interrogate either our own role in the behaviours, or the roles of others. We rarely stop to consider the reasons behind the behaviour, the events that lead up to the behaviour, the development or '**ontogeny**' of the behaviour, or, perhaps crucially, the function of the behaviour – that is, 'what does the individual get out of it' (Timbergen 1963 in Martin and Bateson 2007). By analysing and evaluating classroom incidences, teachers can develop their own understanding of how and why the behaviour may have occurred, and so identify and implement strategies which may reduce the unwanted behaviours. It is equally important to evaluate when teaching goes well – if you can identify why a particular activity, or approach, has worked it is likely that you can optimise your chances of reproducing positive learning and teaching experiences.

One of the difficulties of managing behaviours is that every situation is unique. There are no fixed answers. This requires flexibility from the teacher in terms of their response to different situations and differing 'players' (students/pupils).

It is also important to recognise when an individual requires specialist help. As a teacher, you are responsible for creating and maintaining positive environments that are conducive to learning – you are not a counsellor, psychologist or psychiatrist. An essential skill of teaching is to be aware of your own limitations and to know when to refer students to specialist services, wider professional support or other agencies. This is particularly important in relation to counselling, which requires specialist input from trained and experienced experts.

WHAT DO YOU THINK?

- What is the difference between '**advice**' and '**counselling**'?

Ensure you have a clear definition of these and know when to refer students to specialist support services

Support systems

Secondary schools generally have comprehensive access to a variety of specialist services including the school nurse, sexual health nurses, educational psychologists and specialist literacy teachers, for example.

The **SENCo** (Special Educational Needs Coordinator) takes responsibility for the onward referral of pupils to the appropriate support such as an educational psychologist. 'Special educational need' is a legal term to ensure those pupils who 'have a significantly greater difficulty in learning than the majority of children the same age, or have a disability which prevents or hinders them making use of educational facilities of a kind generally provided to children of the same age in schools which fall within the area of a local authority' (SEN code of practice: p. 6 section 1.3) are supported and enabled to learn and make progress. Under the law, *every* pupil's education is *equally* important. 'Pupils with SEN may need extra help because of a range of needs, such as in thinking and understanding, physical or sensory difficulties, emotional and behavioural difficulties, or difficulties with speech and language or how they relate to and behave with other people' (DCSF 2009b). The key principle when assessing pupils is to decide whether they require additional support to meet their needs, beyond the normal differentiation strategies a teacher might use to meet the needs of all learners. The identification of special educational needs does not automatically mean a pupil will be statemented. A **statement** is a formal document outlining the pupil's needs and how this *legal entitlement* will be met. These are needs that the school is unable to meet on its own. It can be a lengthy process and involves information from a variety of sources including the school, parent, carers, educational psychologist, a doctor or social services. Around 2.7 per cent of pupils are formally statemented and in secondary schools SEN rose from 17.4 per cent in 2008, to 19 per cent in 2009. More boys than girls have SEN, the rates for black and white pupils remain the same (20 in every 1,000 pupils), and pupils from poorer background continue to be overrepresented at 25 per cent. The benchmark for this is a pupil's eligibility for free school meals (FSM). 'Around 40 per cent of pupils eligible for FSM at KS4 are identified as having SEN – double the rate of their non-FSM peers' (DCSF 2010: 11). SEN is graduated according to level of need and triggered by a pupil being unable to make adequate or sufficient progress. **School Action** identifies a pupil who requires further, additional or different support to that provided as part of the school's normal differentiated curriculum offer. All pupils with SEN require individual educational plans (IEPs), which should identify personalised targets, the teaching strategies to be used, the nature of the provision, review dates and success criteria/outcomes. **School Action Plus** normally signifies the need for help from external specialists.

> The triggers for School Action Plus could be that, despite receiving an IEP and additional support, a pupil
>
> * Continues to make no or little progress in specific areas over a long period
> * Continues working at national curriculum levels substantially below that of pupils of a similar age
> * Continues to have difficulty in literacy or numeracy skills
> * Has emotional or behavioural difficulties which substantially and regularly interfere with their own learning or that of the class group, despite having an individualised behaviour management programme . . .
>
> *(SEN code of practice: p. 71 section 6. 64).*

Worryingly, despite these measures and support systems in place within secondary settings, many pupils are arriving at colleges of further education with undiagnosed learning needs and difficulties. The recognition of a more coherent phase of 14–19 education must include the further development of clearly articulated transition planning and systems for the continued identification and support of pupils and young adults who require additional learning support.

Wider support networks within further education organisations can be more difficult to navigate, particularly for new members of staff, as different colleges will have
approaches and systems unique to their own organisations. Further education colleges
do provide access to specialist and additional learning support for students with
disabilities: for example, physical difficulties, visual or hearing impairments, or more
general difficulties such as mental health problems or dyslexia. Many also offer comprehensive referral systems to resources such as counsellors who are available in the
community rather than on-site. A range of support systems is important to ensure that
all needs are met and so do not act as barriers to learning.

IN PRACTICE

- Identify the key support personnel and departments in your own organisation,
  or an organisation you have experience of.

- Design an activity for students to complete which promotes their awareness
  and understanding of the support and guidance they can access. This should
  include finance, future choices, physical and emotional health, sex and
  relationship education and specialist screening services.

Additional learning support within both schools and FE often involves **learning support
assistants**. These are specially trained members of staff whose primary objective is to
support the student and teacher within the classroom. LSAs or classroom assistants are
a valuable resource and should be utilised effectively to promote teaching and learning.
This requires clear lines of communication between the teacher, the LSA and the
student about expectations, needs and the way in which support will be provided.
Clarity about the difference in roles between the LSA and the teacher are important.
A key feature of the relationship between the LSA and the pupil is one of trust. It is
important to remember your role as a teacher includes that of being a leader. Expecting
the LSA to be overly authoritarian, for example, can reduce the trust between LSA
and pupil and reduce your *authority as the teacher* in the eyes of the pupil. In practice,
ensure you avoid delegating the responsibility for pupil learning to the LSA. Planning
collaboratively can ensure you are both clear over your:

- roles
- tasks
- strategies and
- how you will implement these to promote learning, progress and best outcomes
  for the pupil.

IN PRACTICE

Either:

Set aside 15 minutes after the end of five sessions in which you are allocated a learning support assistant. It is important to be rigorous about the amount of time spent as this will help you both retain your focus and clarity of outcomes or solutions.

- Spend five minutes reviewing the session – make this targeted and specific. Identify three ways in which things went well and three ways in which they did not go well.
- Spend five minutes discussing ideas for changes and alternative strategies.
- Spend five minutes agreeing on three changes and strategies to implement in your own practice to ensure you are both clear about your role and task.

Or:

observe an experienced teacher and identify:

- Three differences between the role of the teacher and the role of the LSA – who takes responsibility for what?

And

- One effective strategy you can learn from this experience to implement into your own practice. You will need to justify this – why will your use it? How will it support learning and teaching?

Defining behaviour

'Behaviour' refers in the psychological sense to the way in which an individual reacts to external or internal stimuli or conditions.

When dealing with students, the definition above can be helpful in reminding ourselves that a student is *reacting* to a situation, the student is not 'doing something' to 'you', 'the teacher', on a personal level. This point is important because of the emotional impact negative behaviours can have on the teacher.

As teachers, it is therefore important to focus on the positive behaviours of a group or individual as, all too often, our judgments can be impaired through negativity. This negativity can in fact prolong and even promote unwanted behaviours. Petty (2007) refers to this negative trend as the 'vicious spiral':

1. You dislike the behaviours of the student
2. You become less likely to have a positive attitude towards the student and may become increasingly unfair towards the student

3. The student in turn increasingly dislikes you and your classes
4. The student misbehaves more and so the cycle resumes and continues . . .

The way you feel and demonstrate your feelings will and does have an effect on the 'feel' of groups, and on group and individual behaviour. One of the problems with unwanted behaviour is that it feels personal. In addition, many unwanted behaviours are often spontaneous, leading to reactive, rather than planned responses, from both the student and the tutor. Planning can of course have a considerable impact on one's self-belief in managing that behaviour or similar behaviours. A planned response can help us to keep calm, objective and to ensure we are following all guidelines and procedures with confidence. Reactive responses can of course *become* planned if they have been successful, and form part of your own behaviour toolkit. This mostly occurs when dealing with common and repetitive sources of unwanted behaviour. This is one of the reasons why more experienced staff often seem more confident and, indeed, capable of managing a variety of behaviours. Effective skills are increased, developed and improved over time and experience. Unfortunately, for the practitioner and our students many of these skills are developed or learned as a result of our mistakes.

Self-efficacy

Notions of **self-efficacy** – a belief in your own ability to effect change – are particularly important when considering behaviours. For teachers, a lack of self-efficacy can often be the cause of not only anxiety but also, increasingly, a negative downward spiral of despair, hopelessness and helplessness. You begin to believe that *nothing* you do can or will make any difference, so why even try. Thus, 'people's beliefs about their abilities have a profound effect on those abilities. Ability is not a fixed property; there is huge variability in how you perform. People who have a sense of self efficacy bounce back from failures; they approach things in terms of how to handle them, rather than worrying about what can go wrong' (Bandura 1996).

The above may paint a bleak picture of both teaching and indeed students, but it is important to recognise the emotional impact of teaching and learning and that *perceptions* of unwanted behaviour may not always reflect the *actual* incidences of unwanted behaviour. 'Violence in schools is popularly depicted as an escalating problem of global proportions . . . Increasing numbers of teachers and head teachers report encountering both low level disruption and violent behaviours among pupils and towards themselves. *However* (author's emphasis) they [also] consistently report that it is a *small minority* of pupils who behave in this way' (Munn et al. 2007: 52).

It is important to remember that incidents of actual violence and extreme violence are rare. The most common problem that teachers express concerns over is that of low-level disruptive behaviours. The key issue with this type of behaviour is that it is extremely annoying and tends to 'gnaw' away at your patience. It is important to recognise your own reactions to these types of behaviours as well as recognising what they are. Common low-level disruptive behaviours include:

- Talking – particularly within friendship groups
- Using mobile phones

- Students trying to access inappropriate websites or social networking sites
- Off-task behaviour
- Refusing to work or needing to be 'nagged'
- Low-level defiance or questioning of teachers' instructions
- The 'constant questioner' – usually a means of task avoidance
- Listening to music – with or without headphones.

IN PRACTICE

List three of the low-level disruptive behaviours you have to manage on a daily basis.

- Identify how you manage these.
- Discuss these types of behaviours with at least three different colleagues and exchange ideas.

Identify how and when you will implement one of these ideas into your own practice and why.

Discussing behaviours with colleagues is important in several ways:

1. It helps you feel less isolated.
2. It can be cathartic.
3. You can develop your range of 'responses'.
4. You can be a source of help and advice to your colleagues.

The impact of continuous change, such as the relentless raft of reforms, guidance, pilots, policies, legislation and statutory requirements can also have a detrimental effect on teachers in terms of self-efficacy, as they can be overwhelmed by the sheer magnitude of all of these additional requirements. Feelings of impotence can have a marked impact on the tutor's motivation to even try and address behaviours, as they may feel that nothing they do makes any difference or that they have tried everything. Change has an impact on all those who experience it. For some of us this can lead to excitement and increased motivation, for others it can create high levels of anxiety. This can be because of a perceived or real increase in teaching workloads, or simply confusion over what is required, what is good practice, or even what is allowed.

Attitudes to challenging behaviour: social and political influences

Conflicting approaches towards managing or dealing with challenging behaviour within educational settings and at a political level are also perplexing. Much confusion exists with regards how we, as teachers, should respond to unwanted or challenging behaviour. Should we take an authoritarian/discipline based approach or more **humanistic** approaches rooted in self-development and encouragement when responding to and dealing with difficult behaviour, for example?

Simplified, authoritarian approaches rely on an assumption of the teacher as a superior, to whom pupils should defer. It is directive and requires obedience and is often associated with traditional teaching methods. Humanistic approaches to education can be described as 'student-centred', building on the work of influential American psychologists Carl Rogers and Abraham Maslow. They are rooted in more holistic ideals of pupil self-development, awareness that recognise the importance of emotions and feelings as well as academic knowledge.

Approaches as to how to deal with and respond to difficult behaviours are made even more complex by differing social attitudes towards problematic behaviour and the people who have to deal with it. This is similar to the rift found with the penal system and whether its purpose is to punish or rehabilitate.

Your own values as regards the purpose of education can therefore be of considerable influence in terms of your approaches to behaviour(s). This conflict over the purpose of education has been noted elsewhere – Bernstein in his seminal article 'Education cannot compensate for society' (1970) and Frank Furedi's article in the *Telegraph* (2003) 'Teachers are not social workers', for example. Thus, the socialising aspect of education is hard to separate from its academic purpose. Many have argued that education is simply an instrument used for reproducing inequalities in society (Willis 1977, Illich 1972), for producing docile workers or as a means of 'dumbing down' and 'breaking the spirit' (Holt 1964, Gatto 2002). An instrumentalist approach, that is task-orientated and often linked to extrinsic motivation, does of course fit in with the skills and training agenda, which was a clear priority for the Labour government from 1997. This agenda is reflected in the following government strategies and White Papers such as *21st Century Skills: realising our potential, individuals, employers, nations* (DfES 2003c) and more recently *Investing in Potential, Backing Young Britain* (DCSF 2009a). An interesting aspect of these documents is the curious mix of a skills or training agenda combined with the need to address wider aspects of education, such as the whole-child approach of realising potential and the recognition of the importance of the emotional aspects of learning. This latter approach complements a number of polices including the *Every Child Matters* agenda (DfES 2003b) and Secondary SEAL: Social and Emotional Aspects of Learning (DfES 2007).

WHAT DO YOU THINK?

Consider the following extracts from newspaper articles and ask yourself questions that follow.

1. There are two fundamentally different views of education. On the one hand, there is the emphasis on the child. The insistence that everything must be relevant to the child's experience and to the perceived needs of society. The argument that the teacher should be a mentor or a coach who facilitates the growth of the child's understanding. The current obsession with personalisation. On the other, there is the belief that the school is an institution in which

children are initiated by teachers, who are authorities in their subjects, into a body of knowledge which has no immediate connection to their lives or necessary relevance to the problems of society. I believe in the latter.

(Curtis, P. *The Guardian* 12 May 2009: 'Don't say I was wrong'. Interviewing Chris Woodhead)

2. The current fashion for 'child-led' and 'personalised' learning is part of a misguided philosophy that is corroding intergenerational relations. Children are taught to mistrust teachers; teachers are taught to mistrust themselves. No one has confidence to extol or exert the simple authority of adulthood and scholastic knowledge. Discipline breaks down, leading to moral panic and even greater pressure on schools to fix the 'broken society'.

(Behr, R. *The Observer* 2009, quoting Furedi 2009)

a) Should education be holistic and meet the wider needs of the child?
b) Should teachers personalise the learning for every pupil?
c) Do you feel that teachers lack authority and/or respect – what could be done differently?
d) Should the focus of education be on
  • imparting knowledge; or
  • developing socially responsible and socially adept members of society?

'Education is big because it is seen as an engine for economic growth, a sure fire route to future prosperity and victory in a global competition. The belief for education runs deep and wide beyond our political classes, replacing socialism as the great secular faith of our age' (Wolf 2002). The purpose of education is thus perceived as a tool to boost a nation's economy (DfES 2003c), rather than a means of personal enrichment or growth.

Consideration of the 'purpose' and 'how' of education may seem odd within a chapter on behaviour. However, in terms of child well-being, the UK ranked 24th out of 29 European countries, based on data from 2006 (Bradshaw and Richardson 2009) and in addition 'the mental health of teenagers has sharply declined over the last 25 years' (Collishaw et al. 2004). Policy, cultural and societal expectations and norms can and do have an impact on the children and young people within that society.

WHAT DO YOU THINK?

Consider the following statement. Does this fit with an authoritarian or humanist approach to managing behaviours?

We adults destroy most of the intellectual and creative capacity of children by the things we do to them or make them do. We destroy this capacity above all by making them afraid

(Holt 1964)

Defining 'unwanted behaviour'

As with other terms that are in general use, we rarely consider what these mean in a wider sense and to ourselves. In general terms, behaviour can be defined as what an individual (or group) does, or the way in which an individual (or group) responds to a situation or the environment. It can be conscious or unconscious, planned or reactive.

The regulation of human behaviour, that is, behaviour that is deemed 'normal' or acceptable, is through the historical development of social **mores** or norms and established systems of social control through the law, for example.

This latter notion is important as it suggest that attitudes towards behaviours are socially constructed: thus behaviour only becomes unwanted when it is interpreted as unwanted. Interpretation necessarily involves the use of emotion – usually to make a judgement.

When we refer to behaviour within educational settings, this normally refers to negative or challenging behaviour that is out of our normal range of experiences or expectations. In this way, negative behaviour can be self or socially constructed. This has importance when considering personal reactions to behaviours and whole school or organisational approaches to behaviour in terms of consistency. For example, some teachers may not mind or even notice language which could be considered offensive by colleagues and therefore not address the use of unwanted language by pupils. This can lead to feelings of injustice by pupils when being disciplined by other teachers for language that is considered acceptable in some teachers' classrooms. This can escalate what might otherwise be minor problems or concerns.

Teacher's expectations of behaviour can sometimes be idealistic. This can be particularly true within FE where many trainee teachers have unrealistic expectations of student behaviours and their motivation for being in college. Many prospective trainee FE tutors when asked why they wish to teach in FE as opposed to the secondary sector commonly respond that they believe the students choose to be there and are interested in the subject. Faced with these expectations, the reality of teaching 14–16-year-olds on link programmes, 16–17-year-olds on resits, or key or functional skills to apprentices, can be daunting and somewhat bewildering. While many students appear to have choice, in reality this is not always the case. Faced with minimal employment opportunities, lack of income and societal pressure to achieve 'skills', many 16-year-olds attend college simply because they lack viable alternatives.

All 14–16-year-olds are legally required to attend 25 hours education per week, although at Key Stage 4 there is some flexibility in the type of provision: for example, this can be a combination of work and school-based learning, which can include attendance on vocational programmes at a college of further education.

The impact of disengagement of behaviour

The Education and Skills Act 2008 raised the participation age: education will be compulsory for 17-year-olds from 2013 and for 18-year-olds from 2015. These and other changes within the 14–19 curriculum offer have in part been driven by the recognition of disaffection among Key Stage 4 students. A key focus of the new diplomas has been work-related or work-based learning that is deemed *relevant*.

Disaffection and disengagement are often associated with unwanted behaviours and lack of achievement. It is estimated that around 12 per cent of Year 9s are disengaged, rising to 19 per cent of Year 10s and 20 per cent of Year 11s. The likelihood of young people engaging in other risky behaviours such as truancy, drinking and smoking increase with disengagement. They are also more likely to get involved in fights or public disturbances (DCSF RR 178, 2009). Poor behaviour can have long-term social impacts on the individual, particularly that of reduced life chances, and on society. Research conducted on behalf of the DCSF (2009) identified that the 'characteristics most associated with underachievement were being male, White British, being entitled to free school meals and having Special Educational Needs – particularly **School Action Plus** and living in a deprived area' (DCSF RR 086, 2009: 1).

The impact of relationships and behaviour

One of the key protective factors in reducing both underachievement and disengagement is the quality of relationships within school settings. This can include the relationship between peers, between peers and teachers, between parents and teachers, and parents and schools.

Educational establishments are necessarily complex particularly with regard to the relationships played out within them. Considering the interplay between teachers and teachers, students and students and of course teachers and students, added to the confined nature of the teaching rooms, large numbers of diverse personalities, and then mixed with a little adolescent turbulence, it is little wonder that tensions and conflicts can sometimes ensue. Bill Rogers, an expert in behaviour management, observes that 'in any school the same students may behave differently in different settings, with different teachers. The teachers' behaviour and the students' behaviour have a reciprocal effect on each other and the ever present "audience" of peers' (Rogers 2006: 7).

> **Schools need 'back to basics' approach to discipline**
>
> **'Chav' culture blamed for teacher burnout**
>
> **Poor teaching responsible for pupils' bad behaviour**
>
> **Problem pupils' parents to be taken to court**
>
> **A quarter of teachers report experiencing violence from pupils**
>
> **Pupils run amok**

Figure 9.1 Media portrayal of teens and adolescents often focuses on the negative behaviours displayed by a small minority

The impact of a positive teacher–student relationship is therefore crucial – many students who are disengaged from education perceive their teachers to be too controlling or domineering and many 'feel unfairly treated and blamed for any trouble in class' (DCSF RR 178, 2009: 6).

Most practitioners react to 'explosions'. These situations are charged with emotions from both the practitioner and the student(s) involved. Experienced practitioners can often 'feel' the tension levels increasing and recognise changes in behaviour, and are mostly able to diffuse situations before the explosive stage. Once a situation has started to escalate, it becomes increasingly difficult to diffuse. However, 'explosions' rarely come from nowhere and if you can identify these at the early stages, you can help to avoid them.

IN PRACTICE

Read the following and with a colleague 'finish' the scenario. You can do this through the production of a written script or enactment through role-play.
Context: Year 11, Maths class

> A student is staring out of the window, looking decidedly bored and fed up. The teacher walks over to him and asks him 'why he hasn't started his work'. The student replies 'cos I aint got a pen'.

> (Adapted from Rogers 2006)

Identify how you as a teacher could diffuse this situation and then, perhaps drawing on your own experiences of other teachers, identify how a teacher's responses could escalate this situation.

Practical strategies for promoting positive behaviours

Whole school or organisational approaches when dealing with behaviour are important. These should be transparent, fair and applied consistently. Learners need to feel secure in their learning environments in order to allow learning to take place. An interesting study in Dewsbury College asked students and teachers to produce a list of the qualities of the 'ideal teacher'.

Positive teacher qualities identified by teachers	Positive teacher qualities identified by students
• explains points clearly and at the appropriate level • conveys enthusiasm and interest for the subject • pays attention to revision and exam techniques • makes lessons interesting • has high expectations for students' work • teaches for understanding rather than rote learning • is confident • is constructive and helpful	• keeps order by being firm but not intimidating • explains things clearly • treats all students fairly and equally • is friendly and humorous • gets to know learners' names/treats them as humans • tries adventurous strategies/variety of techniques

(LSDA 2007: 9–10)

The similarity in terms of desirable qualities between the two groups is striking. Equally interesting is that teachers did not identify disciplinary approaches in their qualities, but the students did. Disciplinary approaches are important for establishing expected norms and behaviours. These should be mutually agreed between learners and teachers. The way or manner in which these rules are imposed should also be considered. An overly authoritarian approach from the teacher can lead to rebellious behaviour. Conversely, an overly cooperative or even submissive approach from the teacher can be perceived as a weakness by the students. The problem with this approach is that the teacher ends up taking the lead from students, rather than the other way round. The development of leadership qualities that are fair and democratic as opposed to authoritarian is important. Leadership is strongly linked with pupils' or students' recognition of a teacher's authority.

'Authority' and leadership traits do not have to be imposed. They can be 'voiced' in both verbal and non-verbal communication and practice. For example, clear explanations about the purpose of a session, and your expectations of student outcomes within that session, can support learning in terms of memory and the filing and retrieval of information. However, at a non-verbal level, they also convey your 'authority' as the professional responsible for student learning and your leadership qualities in terms of directing student learning. This can also increase students' confidence and trust in you as a 'professional'. A student or pupil's acceptance of the legitimacy of a teacher's authority optimises cooperative behaviour.

Self-confidence or the appearance of self-confidence is crucial when teaching students. If you do not appear confident in yourself, than how can you expect your students to have confidence in you? If necessary, practise acting with confidence by holding eye contact or changing the tone of your voice. Try to avoid nervous habits. Another useful strategy for developing assertiveness is deciding the outcome and asking for this in a calm and measured way, and expecting compliance. Deliver the instruction and turn your attention to another student, or the next part of the lesson. Moving on in sessions in this way can help to reduce 'argumentative' behaviours (both yours and your students'!). The way in which you challenge poor or unwanted behaviour is as important as the challenge itself. Be clear about the outcome you wish to achieve. If the student consistently refuses to comply, consider whether you need to take the conflict 'off stage', that is outside of the classroom. This can often reduce the audience and thus the student's 'fuel' in terms of 'showmanship' or 'clowning'. It also allows a means by which the students can back down without losing face in front of their peers.

Your awareness of what is happening within the classroom is important in terms of nipping behaviours in the bud. It is important to deal with challenging behaviours quickly, otherwise this can send a message to students that says 's/he got way with it, why shouldn't I?' The greater your awareness of a class, the more likely it is that you will be able to intervene early to both reduce unwanted behaviours and promote wanted behaviour. Notice desirable behaviour and reward with praise.

Many teachers get 'locked' into a negative spiral and only notice the negative aspects of a group or individuals. This is damaging for all.

IN PRACTICE

Make a note of the times you make a negative comment and the times you make a positive comment in one of your sessions. This is often more difficult than it sounds as these negative responses may be so habituated they have become an unconscious part of your dialogue and relationship with students. If possible ask a trusted colleague to do this – this often gives a more accurate picture. Teachers who complete this exercise are often shocked by the amount of negativity they express in a session.

This exercise can be particularly useful in motivating teachers to make more use of positive comments and praise. While praise is important in motivating students to achieve, it is important to ensure this is meaningful. If you are overly nice all the time, the student will not connect appropriate behaviours or attitudes at a personal level or attribute this to their own efforts or abilities: they may think 'you say that to everyone'. A student's self-belief in the regulation of his or her own behaviours and ability to achieve is paramount in terms of serving as an incentive. Thus, a student's belief in their own self-efficacy and ability to change or attain is as important a factor in the promotion of positive behaviours as your belief in yourself as an effective teacher.

Careful planning of your lessons is crucial. This includes the timing, sequencing and pace of activities as well as the activities themselves. Setting the scene at the start of the session conveys your authority and your leadership skills in terms of telling the students what is going to happen. It also allows the students to start processing and thinking about this information. Friendship groups can be particularly problematic to address, as the members will frequently join forces in terms of the behaviour – task avoidance, for example. Male friendship groups can often appear to be far more intimidating than they actually are. You can control some of these groupings by planning a range of activities – individual, paired and group work, in which you decide beforehand on the groups or pairs.

SUMMARY

Dealing with unwanted behaviour is as complex as the individuals and groups who exhibit these behaviours. Defining unwanted behaviour is difficult and can change according to the individuals concerned and the emotional states of the individuals concerned. Every situation is unique and thus demands a unique response. The way you feel about yourself and your students, and the way you respond to these behaviours, really does make a difference. Some of our most difficult days as teachers are the results of challenging behaviour, but this is part of the challenge of what it means *to be* a teacher. Many of our most vulnerable young people display behaviour that is unwanted: much of this is an expression of unhappiness or underlying anger; it is rarely personal. Government policies and social attitudes towards education influence the curriculum, teaching approaches and our understanding and willingness *or otherwise* to make a real difference to the lives of our students. This is of particular importance during the current economic climate, where attainment is considered to be of more importance than any other indicator of progression, and where cuts inevitably have the most impact on those who are the most vulnerable. Pupils with SEN such as those who fall within the continuum of autistic spectrum disorders (ASD), or school phobics and others with multiple difficulties are likely to be the most disadvantaged.

Value your students enough to unravel the reasons for unwanted behaviour and promote positive behaviour for learning. Trust your skills and commitment to promote the learning and progression of all pupils in their academic, social, moral and behavioural outcomes.

Find out more

For information relating to the Every Child Matters (ECM) agenda the following website is useful: **www.dcsf.gov.uk/everychildmatters**.

Key policy drivers to promote pupil engagement and attainment have included:

- 14–19: Extending opportunities, raising standards
- Increased Flexibility Programme – developed to enhance the vocational offer available to KS 4 pupils with access to college programmes on a part-time basis
- 14–19 Education and Skills White Paper
- The Children's Act 2004
- Education and Skills Act (2008)
- the raising of the school participation age (RPA).

The SEN code of practice can be downloaded from: **www.teachernet.gov.uk/docbank/index.cfm?id=3724**.

Secondary Seal guidance booklet can be found at: **nationalstrategies.standards.dcsf.gov.uk/node/ 157981?uc=force_uj**.

The behaviour4learning website (**www.behaviour4learning.ac.uk/**) is full of useful information – in particular, a video that shows how a teacher can escalate a situation instead of diffusing it. This is even more interesting given the time the video was made in 1947 – how little things really change! **www.behaviour4learning.ac.uk/ viewarticle2.aspx?contentId=13454**.

Dave Vizard's book on how to manage behaviour in further education is a particularly good resource which is full of practical strategies that we have used and found to be of benefit – Vizard, D. (2007) *How to Manage Behaviour in Further Education*, London: Paul Chapman Publishing.

The Steer Report available at: **www.teachernet.gov.uk/_doc/13514/8208-DCSF-Learning%20Behaviour.pdf** provides a useful review of behaviour issues within secondary settings.

The LSDA Report *What's your problem: working with learners with challenging behaviour* can be downloaded from: **https://crm.lsnlearning.org.uk/user/order.aspx?code=062543**. This was a follow-up report from one issued in 1998 *'Ain't Misbehaving'* – advocating the need for whole organisational approaches and consistency to deal with disruptive behaviour in FE.

Bibliography

Bandura, A. (1996). *Self-efficacy: the exercise of control*, New York: Freeman.

Behr, R. (2009) Wasted: why education isn't educating (Furedi, F.) *The Observer*, Sunday 15 November 2009. Available at: **www.guardian.co.uk/books/2009/nov/15/wasted-education-isnt-educating-furedi** [accessed 29.01.10].

Bernstein, B. (1970) Education cannot compensate for society, *New Society*, 26 February 344–7.

Bradshaw, J. and Richardson, D. (2009) An index of child well-being in Europe, *Child Indicators Research*, 2(3): 319–51. Available at: **http://php.york.ac.uk/inst/spru/pubs/social.php** [accessed 29.01.10].

Collishaw, S., Maughan, B., Goodman, R. and Pickles, A. (2004) Time trends in adolescent mental health, *Journal of Child Psychology and Psychiatry* 45(8): 1350–62 quoted in Roberts, Y. (2009) *GRIT: the seeds of success and how they are grown*. The Young Foundation available at: **www.youngfoundation.org/files/images/publications/GRIT.pdf** [accessed 29.01.10].

Curtis, P. (2009) Interview with Chris Woodhead 'Don't say I was wrong'. *The Guardian*, 12 May 2009 available at: **www.guardian.co.uk/education/2009/may/12/chris-woodhead-teaching** [accessed 29.01.10].

Dawson, M. and Sheppard, J. (1998) 'Psychology in the schools of the United Kingdom and the United States: an introduction', *Educational and Child Psychology*, 15(1): 6–14. Available at: **www.bps.org.uk/downloadfile.cfm?file_uuid=3B16EAF7-1143-DFD0-7EAC-A390FB3731E2&ext=pdf** [accessed 16.10.09].

DCSF RR 086 (2009) *Pupils with Declining Attainment at Key Stages 3 and 4.* Callanan, M., Kinsella, R., Graham, J.,

Turczuc, O. and Finch, S. National Centre for Social Research, available at: **http://publications.dcsf.gov.uk/default.aspx?PageFunction=productdetails&PageMode=publications&ProductId=DCSF-RR086&** [accessed 28.01.10].

DCSF RR 178 (2009) *Disengagement from Education among 14–16 year olds.* Ross, A. National Centre for Social Research, available at: **http://search.publications.dcsf.gov.uk/kbroker/dcsf/dcsfpubs/search.ladv?sr=0&cs=UTF-8&sc=dcsfpubs&nh=10&sb=0&ha=144&hs=0&fl1=publicationshop%3A&op1=1&ty1=0&tx1=2986&fl0=&op0=1&ty0=0&ucSearchControl%3ASimpleSearchButton=Search&fl8=contributor%3A&op8=1&ty8=0&tx0=RR178&tx8** [accessed 28.01.10].

DCSF (2009a) *Investing in Potential, Backing Young Britain*, HMSO.

DCSF (2009b) *Special Educational Needs* (SEN): *a guide for parents and carers*, revised 2009. Crown Copyright. Available to download at: **http://www.teachernet.gov.uk/_doc/3755/4163_A5_SEN_GUIDE_WEB[4].pdf** [accessed 03.07.10].

DCSF (2010) *Breaking the Links between Special Educational Needs and Low Attainment: everyone's business*, Crown Copyright. Available to download at **http://publications.dcsf.gov.uk/eOrderingDownload/00213-2010DOM-EN.pdf** [accessed 03.07.10].

DfES (2002) *14–19: Extending Opportunities, Raising Standards'*, London: HMSO.

DfES (2003a) Working Group on 14–19 Reform. *Principles for Reform of 14–19 Learning Programmes and Qualifications*, London: HMSO.

DfES (2003b) *Green Paper: Every Child Matters*, London: HMSO, available at: **www.dcsf.gov.uk/ everychildmatters/about/background/background/** [accessed 30.01.2010].

DfES (2003c) *21st Century Skills: realising our potential, individuals, employers, nations*, HMSO.

DfES (2004) *Every Child Matters: change for children*, London: HMSO, available at: **www.dcsf.gov.uk/ everychildmatters/about/background/background/** [accessed 30.01.10].

DfES (2007) *Secondary SEAL: social and emotional aspects of learning*, National Strategy for School Improvement, Guidance Booklet. Available at: **http://nationalstrategies.standards.dcsf.gov.uk/node/ 157981?uc=force_uj** [accessed 30.01.10].

Furedi, F. (2003) Teachers are not social workers, *Telegraph*, 8 November, available at: **www.telegraph.co.uk/education/educationnews/ 3320912/Teachers-are-not-social-workers.html** [accessed 29.01.10].

Gatto, J. T., Moore, T. and Albert, D. (2002) *Dumbing us Down: the hidden curriculum of compulsory schooling*, New York: New Society Press.

Holt, J. (1964) *How Children Fail*, New York: Pitman Publishing.

Illich, I. (1972) *De-schooling Society,* Harmondsworth: Penguin.

Learning and Skills Development Agency (2007) *'What's Your Problem? Working with learners with challenging behaviour'*. Impress Gillingham available at: **https://crm.lsnlearning.org.uk/user/ order.aspx?code=062543** [accessed 29.01.10].

Martin, P. and Bateson, P. (2007) *Measuring Behaviour: an introductory guide*, Cambridge: Cambridge University Press.

Munn, P., Johnstone, M., Sharp, S. and Brown, J. (2007) Violence in schools: perceptions of secondary teachers and headteachers over time, *International Journal on Violence and Schools*. No. 3 available at: **www.ijvs.org/files/Revue-03/52-80--Munn---IJVS-n3.pdf** [accessed 26.08.09].

Petty, G. (2006) *Evidence Based Teaching – a practical approach*, Nelson Thornes (**www.geoffpetty.com**), available at: **http://www.geoffpetty.com/downloads/ WORD/ClassroomManagement.doc**

Rogers, B. (2006) *Classroom Behaviour: a practical guide to effective teaching, behaviour management and colleague support*, London: Paul Chapman Publishing.

Willis, P. (1977) *Learning to Labour: how working class kids get working class jobs,* Farnborough: Saxon House.

Wolf, A. (2002) *Does Education Matter? Myths about education and economic growth*, London: Penguin Books.

10 Assessment for Learning

Schools today are not a humanizing or an educational force as much as a credentialing agency, sorting people out who do not fit into the regular channels of educational development. Schools function to certify that someone is not harmful rather than to develop the potential of all.

(Miller 1968)

In this chapter you will:

- Examine the purpose of assessment and explore why we assess
- Consider what is meant by assessment *for* learning as opposed to *of* learning
- Reflect on the impact of assessment on learning, motivation and achievement
- Consider the impact of feedback (formative assessment) on learning
- Explore the principles and integrity of assessment
- Consider methods and types of assessment
- Reflect the tensions and impact of curriculum change on assessment

Pearson Education Ltd./Sophie Bluy

Introduction

Assessment is a measure of the knowledge or competence an individual has gained during a period of instruction. It can be formal, for example, an end-of-year exam, or informal, through use of teacher questioning or observation during a lesson. Most learning happens informally and is not formally tested – for example, social **mores**, learning 'on the job', by doing (experience), or the vast amount of knowledge we 'pick up' along the way from the mass media. Part of what it is 'to be human' is our ability to make judgements about ourselves, our performance, and others and their performance. These acts of assessment are so inherent to our nature, they become 'invisible', that is, not consciously planned, considered or evaluated.

For many of us, as individuals, assessment can prompt feelings of negativity and in particular anxiety. Assessment can often be *felt* to be a measure of what we 'cannot do' and 'do not know', as opposed to what we 'can do' and 'do know'.

When we consider and recognise the integral role of assessment to the teaching and learning process, the notion of assessment as a negative and demotivating process is completely at odds with the positive role assessment *can* play in the development of both teaching and learning.

Gregory Kimble (1961), an American psychologist, defined learning as 'an experience which produces a relatively permanent change in behaviour, or potential behaviour, therefore excluding changes that take place due to biological factors such as maturation, and teaching as the "delivery of planned activities to promote learning" ' (Long 2000: 10). For both the teacher and the student the vital question of what and how much has been learned/taught follows. Assessment is therefore integral to the teaching and learning process.

Source: Pearson Education Ltd. Mind Studio

Photo 10.1
Exams can cause high levels of anxiety for pupils

IN PRACTICE

As a teacher, I am always surprised at the range of interpretations 25 different pupils can bring to one essay title. This can lead to feelings of frustration as, despite my best efforts, some of the students do not appear to have understood the importance, or even grasped key concepts, principles or terminology. In terms of evaluating my own teaching, *this is the most objective, useful and direct feedback I ever receive from my pupils.* It allows me to evaluate and assess what I have taught effectively and, crucially, the areas that I have not. This, more than any other type of information or feedback, informs the changes I need to make to my delivery, subject material, or how I assess pupil learning and progress.

- Consider the first time that you marked pupils' work to assess their learning and understanding at the end of a topic you have taught.
- How many pupils 'answered' the question according to your expectations?
- How many interpreted the questions in a different way to that which you had *intended*?
- How many 'omitted' key terms?
- How many have misunderstood key terms or concepts?
- What, why, how and when will you change your
  - delivery methods
  - explanations and tasks/activities
  - resources and
  - assessment
  the next time you teach this topic?

While distinct in their own right, teaching and learning are not one-way processes and should not be viewed in isolation. Assessment needs to be conducted in order to determine how effective the learning *and* teaching has been. This allows the tutor to utilise assessment as a means of facilitating learning: that is, the information they gain allows them to identify what individuals have learned and what they still need to learn to achieve the outcomes, rather than simply a measure of what has been learned.

Assessment is vital to your learners as a means of checking their progress and understanding, and to you as a teacher in informing you about their levels of understanding. This allows you to evaluate your sessions and to adapt them according to group and individual need.

So why do we assess?

Assessment is used for a variety of differing purposes: at a base level it could be argued that we assess 'because we are required to' (Scales 2008: 175). It can also be used as a means of gathering information about how much a student (or students) has learned, or even to identify if any learning has taken place. It is used to recognise formal achievement in terms of accredited outcomes and certification. It can be used to provide initial or baseline data and to diagnose – for example, specific areas of weakness or strength. Within school settings **streaming** or banding has traditionally been used to identify differing levels of ability. Armitage and Renwick (2008: 5) note the increased role of assessment 'in the selection and admission of FE students' based on the research of Martinez and Munday (1998). While accurate initial and diagnostic testing is important to match students to the right course for their ability, and thus promote retention, it is also important to be aware of the dangers of **labelling**, its links to **self-fulfilling prophecies**, also known in educational terms as the **Pygmalion effect**, and underachievement – in particular for gender, race and class (Keddie 1973, Ball 1981, Gillborn and Mirza 2000).

RESEARCH FOCUS

In 1968 Robert Rosenthal and Leonora Jacobson published *Pygmalion in the Classroom: teacher expectation and pupils' intellectual development.* This was based on research in a school, Oak School, that supported their hypothesis of the link between teacher expectations of pupils' outcomes, ability and attitudes and their actual outcomes. In short, when a teacher expects pupils to do well, pupils do well; when they do not expect pupils to do well, pupils do not.

- Find a summary of this research and identify one *change* to your own practice, as a result of your reading, that you can implement immediately.

In an increasingly controlled environment, perhaps rather dishearteningly, assessment can, and often is, used to regulate and make judgements on the teacher, the student and the organisation. Notions of autonomy within education are being progressively eradicated as professionals are constantly being forced to evidence what they are doing, instead of concentrating on what, after all, they have been *trained* to do. The first decade of the 1800s saw the introduction of the monitorial system as advocated by the British educators Andrew Bell and Joseph Lancaster. The Bryce Report of 1895 recommended a single register for all teachers based on academic and professional qualifications. The McNair Report of 1944, *The Supply, Recruitment and Training of Teachers and Youth Leaders*, recommended the rationalisation of teacher-training provision. In post-war Britain, teacher shortages were acute, the situation worsening with the raising of the school-leaving age from 14 to 15 (in 1947). In response to this shortage, training programmes were introduced in 1945. A total of 76 new training colleges were opened by the early 1950s. Within the FE sector, although many vocational and academic staff were trained, the *requirement* to be trained to teach in the FE sector was not formally implemented until 2001, using Further Education National Training Organisation (FENTO) standards. From 2007, in an attempt to promote parity with

QTS teachers (Qualified Teacher Status), teacher training within the lifelong learning sector, including FE, and the status Qualified Tutor Learning and Skills (QTLS) was introduced. The idea that teachers should be trained and regulated is not therefore new, although the length and content of teacher-training programmes, and how they should be regulated, is a subject of ongoing debate and change.

As teachers, it is important to 'remember that the primary objective is about learning and that this, after all, is what all the teaching is for . . . the careful planning, implementation and recording of assessment are central to what the lesson is about. It's not just about teaching; it's about learning. The teaching is only a means to an end' (Wallace 2007: 168). Tummons (2007: 5) too argues there are six reasons to assess:

- to find out if learning has taken place
- to diagnose students' needs
- to provide public acknowledgement or certification of learning
- to allow processes of selection to be carried out
- to provide a way of evaluating programmes and
- to motivate and encourage learning.

Assessment for learning (AfL)

Assessment for learning supports the learning and *continued* learning and progress of pupils by providing constructive feedback. This allows the pupil to understand what it is they are doing well (affirmative), what they need to do (informative), in order to achieve a higher grade (for example, the difference between a GCSE grade D or C, or the difference between a merit and distinction), and how to do it (constructive). **Summative** assessment merely comments on how well a pupil has achieved, or not.

IN PRACTICE

Think about the way in which you mark pupils' work. Do you indicate 'good' points with a tick, and 'bad' points with a cross?

While this may tell a student what s/he has got 'right' or 'wrong', it does not tell them why, or what to do about it.

A simple strategy to improve your pupils' knowledge and understanding of a topic, which in turn will lead to improved results, is to replace 'ticks, crosses or grades' with comments.

These do not need to be long, complicated or over-detailed.

This notion of using assessment to motivate and encourage further learning may seem at odds with your own experiences of learning and assessment, especially if you have had negative experiences, or if you view assessment as simply a means to 'getting a qualification'. Assessment for learning, and its use of **formative assessment** to improve attainment, was clearly articulated in the work of Paul Black and Dylan Wiliam in 1998. This research was undertaken after the research of Derek Rowntree (1987) who formalised the distinction between formative and summative assessment, and of Ruth Butler (1988) who demonstrated the effectiveness of comments only feedback as opposed to grades. Guidance and toolkits for whole school approaches on the implementation of AfL have been sited within the national strategies website and available since 2004.

Assessment for learning places the students' development at the heart of teaching and learning. It is 'the process of seeking and interpreting evidence for use by learners and their teachers to decide where the learners are in their learning, where they need to go and how best to get there' (Assessment Reform Group 2002). Assessment for learning is much more than simply informing a student how well, or not, they have completed a task. The key characteristics of assessment for learning should be used *within* and *throughout* every teaching and learning session. Assessment for learning is **formative** (it informs the teacher and learner); it encourages and builds on students' existing knowledge through constructive (useful) *and developmental* **feedback** (the pupil is able to progress).

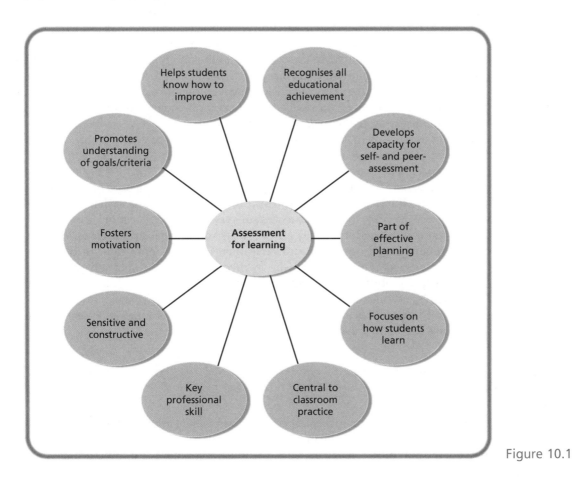

Figure 10.1

The research carried out by Black and Wiliam (1998) suggests improvements to student learning and attainment can be made through the following simple measures:

- The provision of effective feedback
- Active involvement of students in their learning and assessment
- The utilisation of information from assessment to adapt/change planning to improve student learning
- An awareness of the negative impact assessment can have, particularly on self-esteem, confidence and motivation
- Clear communication systems between teacher and learner, so the learner knows what is required and how to achieve this.

Deep and surface learning

The core ethos of assessment for learning is to encourage greater learning and understanding. Within classroom settings, teachers are continually making judgements about the differing levels of student learning, from little or no knowledge to comprehensive understanding. This latter notion relates to deep as opposed to surface learning and is an important consideration when selecting appropriate methods of assessment.

Expressed simplistically, deep learning is associated with a greater understanding of concepts – the ability to analyse for example and the ability to link and connect this knowledge with existing knowledge and apply it to unknown situations to problem-solve.

Surface learning is often associated with rote learning or recall. Perhaps the easiest way to define the difference is the student's ability to apply and use theory (deep learning) rather than merely recite theory (surface learning).

In terms of assessment, an AfL approach tends to encourage deep learning, whereas assessment of learning generally fosters a surface approach to learning. Surface and deep approaches to learning are also linked to motivation. **Intrinsically** motivated students, students who value their learning as a good in its own right, generally assume a deep approach to learning while **extrinsically** motivated learners, that is, students who are motivated by the consequences, in this case a qualification, can adopt a surface approach. Atherton (2009) also explores the strategic approach to learning, or the extremely 'well organised' surface learner. Here the motivation is to achieve high marks or grades. It is a learner who in effect has 'learned to play the game'. This is of particular importance when you consider the purpose of assessment in terms of formal accredited outcomes – it is clear, with the focus on high-stakes testing in the secondary, FE and HE sectors, that a strategic approach to learning rather than a deep approach is becoming inherently embedded.

Motivation and feedback

As a teacher it is important to remember that all assessment activities have an emotional impact on learners. This can be motivating or demotivating. The emotional aspects of assessment should be considered when planning assessment and in particular when providing feedback. 'Motivation refers to the psychological processes that lead us to do certain things' (Long 2000: 104). Thus, motivation turns intentions into actions. The way in which you deliver your feedback could therefore be a deciding factor on whether students act on your feedback or disregard it. It could also have an impact on how students tackle future tasks. Students with a fear of failure, for example, may tackle easy tasks which they know they can achieve. They may also tackle extremely difficult tasks because they can point to the level of difficulty if they fail. In both these situations, nothing new is learned. They will not tackle moderately difficult tasks as this may 'expose' them. Assessment tasks need to be sufficiently challenging and achievable for new learning to take place (Csikszentmihalyi 1990).

In order to encourage students to tackle new tasks, it is important to build the confidence and self-esteem of students, particularly when providing feedback. Psychologists such as Albert Bandura (1977) have also noted the need for 'explicit, proximal and affirmative' feedback, that is, clear, immediate, relevant and delivered in a manner that promotes self-esteem.

By providing constructive and developmental feedback, you can help motivate your students.

Feedback to learners should:

- Form the basis of ongoing discussions and dialogue with all learners
- Be timely – immediate feedback when possible
- Be explicit – remember it is just as important to explain how and why a piece of work is good, as it is to correct errors
- Be ongoing throughout the learning programme and each session
- Be honest – ensure this is tactful
- Be constructive and developmental – offer strategies and advice on *how* to improve, not simply 'what' needs improving
- Be motivating.

Goals and deadlines can often help a student achieve long-term goals, especially when these are broken down into manageable steps. Remember that feedback need not simply describe and advise – e.g. 'you have done this . . . you need to . . '. It can also challenge – 'why do you think that is the case; what is your evidence?' Challenging questions are especially important for extending knowledge and understanding. You can also use feedback to encourage learner self-evaluation – for example, what did you enjoy; why, or what would you do differently in the future? Questions play an integral role in assessment for learning.

IN PRACTICE

1. Consider a time when you have received positive feedback – identify how and why this helped to motivate you, or helped you to achieve your goals.
2. Now consider a time when feedback has had a negative impact on you. Identify what this was and then consider what you would have done differently were you that teacher.
3. Identify one change in your own practice as a result of this reflection.

Principles of assessment

We have considered the importance of assessment for learning, and the 'what', 'when' and 'how' of assessment are equally important. As teachers delivering programmes, we are not at liberty to change formal assessment requirements and are constrained by the demands and dictates of the examining/awarding body. This can of course lead to conflict between students and tutors, as tutors impose a means of assessment that is seen as invalid or, increasingly in a profession where *evidence* has become the primary driver, over-burdensome. This can cause anger in the student and in many cases create classroom relationships that are damaging, as the student 'blames' the tutor for what may perhaps be perceived as unnecessary or unwarranted assessment.

Questioning of assessment can relate to the perceived validity or purpose of the assessment task – for example, is it a fair assessment, or why are you assessing in this way at this time? What's the point of this assessment? Does it contribute to my final grade?

Questioning from students can also be an indicator of underlying anxiety about the assessment or, perhaps more specifically, fears about failing. Before you act in a defensive manner to such questions, or make judgements about your students' behaviours, it is therefore important to ask yourself the questions below and to have a clear idea about the purpose and relevance of the assessment task you are setting.

IN PRACTICE

Consider a time when a student has questioned either your assessment of a piece of work, or why they are being assessed in a particular way.

Answer the following questions:

- Why was the student asking these questions?
- Did this have an impact on the student as an individual, a small group or the whole group?
- If yes, in what way?
- Did this have an impact on you – if yes, in what way?
- What would you do differently the next time: for example, had you been clear about the purpose of assessment and/or made the assessment process transparent?

If students are questioning the purpose of assessment, it is likely that they do not see the relevance or the *validity* of the assessment. **Validity** is one of several principles of assessment. When designing assessment these principles should be taken into account (see the table below by Race 1995b). The validity of an assessment relates to whether it is 'fit for purpose' and measures what it intends to measure. These should relate to the learning outcomes. Remember that in addition to skills and knowledge you can also assess behaviour.

In order for a test to be valid, it is important that you have a clear idea of what is to be measured. Principles of assessment are also considered by Ofsted when inspecting – 'a basic principle of gathering first-hand evidence is "fitness for purpose". Inspectors should ask: what is needed to investigate particular issues or assertions made by the school? The inspections are intended to be tightly focused and efficient but they must also ensure that the judgements are valid and securely based upon sufficient evidence' (AAIA 2007: 2).

The following table from Phil Race's *Making Learning Happen*, (1995b) highlights some of the key principles of assessment.

Validity	Ensure that what is being assessed is actually being measured
Reliability	Ensure it is consistent and produces similar results with similar students on re-test Ensure that all staff will be marking to the same criteria and standard
Transparency	Don't surprise your students! Ensure that the links between learning outcomes and assessment criteria are obvious to the students
Fairness	Ensure that students have equal opportunity to succeed and that these are seen to be fair (e.g. anonymity)
Equity	No discrimination between students should occur and no individual should be disadvantaged
Incrementally	Progressive assessment – feedback to students should be continuous to facilitate students' learning
Redeemable	There should be opportunities for redemption from failure if things go wrong
Demanding	Assessment systems should stretch students to ensure quality

In addition, and particularly when producing portfolios, you should consider sufficiency – this considers how much 'evidence' is required, or how many times a learner should demonstrate their knowledge before they are officially, or formally, deemed 'proficient'.

The utility or practicality of assessment is also important. This includes the costs and ease of application of assessment, as well as the most efficient use of staff and resources. The authenticity of assessment refers to the appropriateness of assessment and how accurately the tasks reflect those which would actually be experienced in the workplace. Authenticity of student work relates to whether the work is the original work of the student.

Differentiation of assessment

It is important that you ensure differentiation within assessment. This relates to equity of assessment and is an important principle of assessment. This means that, as tutors, we need to use a range of assessment types and methods to accommodate differing student need, and to ensure students are able to demonstrate achievement in a variety of ways. If we want to test a skill, we need to ask students to demonstrate this. If we want to assess knowledge, then we can ask them to explain in an essay, for example. Assessment tasks should be designed to allow students to demonstrate their skill or understanding of a topic, not as an assessment of their skill in completing a particular method of assessment such as written exams.

It is important to remember that we are not talking about lowering standards to compensate but are allowing them the opportunity to demonstrate their skills and understanding in a variety of ways. Assessment should therefore be carefully thought out – students should be provided the questions in their first language, for example, or care should be taken to ensure that the material/content is not overtly eurocentric; make assessment questions clear – de-jargonising is not lowering standards.

Schemes of assessment

A scheme of assessment is a planned summary or overview of all the assessment activities, informal and formal, that you will implement as part of a topic or unit. This is normally found with your scheme of work, which helps support short, medium and long term planning and sequencing of lesson content.

When designing schemes of assessment, it is important to take the principles of assessment into account to ensure the assessment process is fair, aids development and progression and is meaningful and relevant. Teachers will need to use their professional experience to make decisions about what is to be assessed and how. This may include reducing the authenticity of assessment in order to make it practicable. For example, if a learner was enrolled on an equine-care programme it would be highly authentic for a real horse to be used when practising a standard health check. However, it may not be practical to do this in a classroom!

Assessment schemes are important to ensure logical sequencing of assessment, appropriate selection of methods, and adherence to formal assessment processes. They should allow for flexibility and the opportunity to revisit topics.

An assessment scheme should ideally be embedded into your scheme of work. A scheme of work is a skeletal plan which sequentially outlines the teaching of a particular topic, including:

- what you are going to cover and how (teacher/student activities)
- the syllabus or programme learning outcomes and requirements
- any resources you may need (this is of particular importance when you need to book an item of specialist equipment in advance, or will require permission slips and medical information for younger learners), and
- assessment – this should include formal and informal assessment activities.

The relationship between the learning outcomes or requirements of the programme and teaching and learning is of importance when planning your scheme of work. The learning outcomes describe what must be learned; you then devise and plan activities that will teach the students the 'what' of what is to be learned. The information gathered through formal and informal assessment activities can be used in order to make judgements about how much the students have learned. This data and information can then be used to shape and formulate how you will teach the topic next time, or identify the changes you need to make to the next lesson in order to ensure student understanding and progression. Changes can be made to short and longer time planning, including revisions to your scheme of work. It is important to remember that like all planned activities the scheme of work is a 'live' document. Thus, the learning outcomes are your starting point when planning, followed by your learning and assessment activities.

Types of assessment

There are many types of assessment. It is important that you select the most appropriate type of assessment in order to meet your requirements or purpose.

- Initial – the range of information and data you have about a student before you meet them. Initial assessment information is of particular importance during transition stages such as that from school to college. It may include results of past assessment such as SAT scores or GCSE results. It can also include more general information about attitudes, behaviours and aspirations and individual needs.

- Diagnostic – used to identify weakness and strengths, usually in the key skills and functional skill areas of literacy, numeracy or ICT. Diagnostic assessments are also used quite extensively to diagnose specific learning difficulties and to identify support needs.

- Formative – assessment designed and implemented to inform teaching and learning during a course or programme of study. It is most often informal. It is used to identify what has been learned and what needs to be learned. Formative assessment is planned and designed by the teacher, and so the information from assessment can be used to identify *how* learning can be improved: for example, by the introduction of smaller, bite-sized pieces of knowledge. This type of assessment lies at the heart of assessment for learning. It should be ongoing and used to improve teaching and learning.

- Summative – generally associated with assessment *of* learning, this assessment takes place at the end of a programme, unit or module. It assesses or tests what has been learned (or not).

- Formal – assessments used to record the final outcome of a period of study: those which lead to the public recognition and accreditation of achievement from the awarding body. These are assessments which directly lead to the qualification.

- Informal – assessment tasks designed by the teacher to develop learner knowledge, skill or understanding. These provide autonomy for the teacher in terms of the 'what', 'how' and 'when' of assessment. These are often spontaneous and do not provide accredited outcomes.
- Ongoing – all of the *informal* assessment activities that are set and undertaken occur during a programme of study.
- Continuous – all of the *formal* assessment activities taking place throughout a period of study which contribute to the final outcome or qualification.

Formal or summative assessments tend to make comparisons of a pupil's performance against national averages, for example, or against set criteria. This is known as referencing. Referencing is important if we wish to make a relative judgement about a student's attainment. These can be idiographic, that is, relating to an individual's uniqueness as opposed to a comparison to other defined criteria. Ipsative (from the Latin *ipse*: the self) assessment allows a judgement to be made about an individual's current performance based on their previous performance or achievements. It is most commonly used for self-improvement – such as exceeding personal bests. It is often more appropriate to utilise ipsative assessment when working with pupils and students with SEN (special educational needs) or AEN (additional educational needs), as these can be more relevant and purposeful than comparison of national averages, for example. Nomethic assessment makes general comparisons to other defined benchmarks: in criterion referencing, for example. Norm referencing compares an individual's performance to that of their peers – this may be within the group, year or national cohort. This is most commonly used in public examinations such as GCSEs and A and AS levels.

Methods of assessment

A method of assessment is the activity by which you assess a pupil's learning. Thus, the *type* may be formative, but the method you choose is that which is the most appropriate to measure the progress and learning of a pupil in a defined area. It may be more appropriate to ask a student to *demonstrate* (a method of assessment) a skill, for example; but to test their theoretical knowledge, a written explanation or *essay* may be more appropriate. A range of assessment methods is therefore crucial to ensure you can test a variety of skills, knowledge and understanding in the most appropriate way. In order to do this, you need to be clear about the aims and objectives of the programme so you can select the most appropriate assessment method to identify whether (or not) these have been met.

Role-plays can be an effective way of measuring performance, but many teachers are reluctant to use these as many pupils can feel anxious, exposed and thus vulnerable. Many teachers tend to use the assessment methods they have experienced or that they are most comfortable with. There is a danger here of selecting assessment methods through habit rather than appropriateness. Research (Ecclestone and Pryor 2003, Torrance et al. 2004) suggests that some students will select a programme of study according to its assessment methods – particularly in the avoidance of summative exam-based programmes. Methods include essays, exam, question and answer, portfolios and presentations.

ACTIVITY

Look at the following table adapted from Armitage et al. (2007). Identify the most effective method to meet the learning aims and objectives. Number 1 has been done for you.

Table 10.1

Aims	Objectives	Method
A To exercise overall command of emergency services throughout a major incident	Can maintain clear and accurate communications through changing circumstances	1 Interview
B To reflect on clinical practice	Can evaluate positive and negative aspects of interactions with patients	2 Audio/video taping
C To handle TV interviews effectively	Demonstrate an ability to use appropriate body language on camera	3 Objective/ multiple test
D To develop and retain knowledge of costs of building materials	Know the costs of a variety of types of bricks	4 Log/diary
E To bring about an awareness of health and safety issues	Can indicate where fire exits are	5 Display
F To converse fluently in Spanish	Can conduct a one:one conversation about everyday topics	6 Exam consisting of long essays
G To identify major literary themes	Can trace and describe ideas of kingship in Shakespeare's history plays	7 Demonstration of skills/routine (e.g. resuscitation)
H To be able to support clients in expressing their emotions	Can draw out client's feelings about a traumatic incident	8 Seminar presentation
I To develop an argument and defend own views	Can present an analysis of the cause of inflation and respond to questions from colleagues	9 Role-play
J To develop a sense of design	Is able to use colour, shape and image to present a concept visually	10 Simulation exercise

Briefing: assessment and curriculum change

The range and extent of assessment activity is extensive and complex. This necessarily reflects the complex nature of learning. Assessment has undergone a marked shift in focus over the past three decades, and it is useful to have an understanding of these changes particularly that from summative to formative based practice.

Curriculum change can have a key impact on the way in which students are assessed and therefore the assessment activities and regimes of the tutors. The Nuffield Review (2006) 'Policies for 14–19 education 1976 to the present day' provides an extremely useful and in-depth overview of the key polices and their impact on education. A key driver in these changes was the recognition that traditional summative exams were not appropriate for the testing of skills associated with a mixed academic and vocational curriculum. The nature of what is taught within schools and colleges is firmly entrenched in the political landscape. Labour prime minister James Callahan's speech at Ruskin College, Oxford in 1976, for example, sparked off what became known as the 'great debate'. This was in response to perceived 'falling standards' and the lack of 'relevance' of the curriculum to prepare young people for the 'world of work'. The DES (Department for Education and Science) Green Paper (1977) *Education in Schools: a Consultative Document*, argued for a more vigorous use of assessment – particularly that of initial and diagnostic assessment, but the idea of national testing was rejected at that time. The national curriculum with the emphasis on core or common standards was finally introduced in schools in 1988 following the Education Act of that year. This also saw the introduction of a national system of assessment at ages 7, 11 and 14 (Standardised Attainments Tests: SATs) and inspection. This was a significant move away from the liberal ideals of education of the late 1960s and early 1970s, which saw education as a means of optimising social justice and opportunity (Newsom 1963, Plowden Report 1967), to a far more prescriptive regime.

Vocational 'usefulness' became, and indeed remains, a key focus for debate with regard to the curriculum and, of course, young peoples' 'readiness' for the world of work. In 1978 the Youth Opportunities Programme was introduced which targeted youth unemployment and provided work experience and training. This was highly criticised and was widely believed to be an attempt to mask the increasing numbers of the unemployed. The year 1983 saw the introduction of vocational qualifications – TVEI (Technical and Vocational Education Initiative) and the CPVE (Certificate of Pre-Vocational Education). These changes in the nature of the curriculum led to changes in the way learners on these programmes were assessed. Validity and authenticity played a key role in these changes. It was no longer appropriate to test vocational knowledge or skills via the use of summative traditional exams.

The idea of 'competence' was introduced following the establishment of the NCVQ (National Council for Vocational Qualifications) as a result of the De Ville Report (MSC/DES1986). This led to the development of a new system of National Vocational Qualifications (NVQs). Critics of this approach argue that the nature of competence-based learning ignores the 'subjectivity of people and dynamics' (Stitt 1998: 9); we are simply reduced to 'can' or 'cannot do', 'competent' or 'not yet competent'. In other words, it focuses on the end outcomes or product, as opposed to the journey and process of learning for the person.

WHAT DO YOU THINK?

Go back to the quotation at the start of this chapter – do you agree with Miller?

From 1999, draft regulations were introduced which allowed for the part-time attendance in FE or within the work base for Key Stage 4 students, particularly those who were displaying signs of disaffection. This reflected the need for the curriculum to engage students and reiterated the need for skills and employment relevance. In 2002 the Green Paper (DfES) *14–19 extending opportunities, raising standards* introduced the idea of an overarching matriculation diploma. The emphasis was on flexibility and the option to mix and match a greater range of subjects, including work-based learning. The first of the specialised diplomas were introduced in 2008. By 2013, 14 different specialised learning lines will be available. There will be three levels – Foundation (equivalent to 5 GCSEs grades D–G), Higher (equivalent to 7 GCSEs grades A*–C) and Advanced (equivalent to 3.5 A levels). The diploma covers principal learning related to the specialist subject, generic learning – including functional skills and those that promote PLTS (personal, learning and thinking skills) – as well as additional and specialist learning.

One of the fundamental principles of the new diploma is the development of an offer that is able to be personalised, is flexible, relevant and engaging, and which includes work-related opportunities. In addition, it makes clear the importance of 'assessment for learning and development of meta-cognitive capabilities, such as reflection, that promotes deeper learning and the making of connections between contexts and subjects' (QCA 2008). It is difficult to imagine how this will be assessed in a manner that is consistent and reliable, given the amount of variables for each student. However, there is a clear emphasis on assessment for learning and the use of constructive feedback to promote deep learning.

Tensions in assessment

It can be easy to become cynical and demoralised as a tutor by the ever-prescriptive demands of the role and the ever-increasing monitoring of the profession. While notions of professional responsibility and accountability should be fully endorsed, this should not be at the expense of professional autonomy. 'Quality is a feature of professional practice that is nurtured by freedom and discretion but compromised by restraint and standardisation' (Kushner in Elliot 1993: viii). Kushner's is a useful account of how quality in the sense of outputs only serves to enforce accountability of the individual to the system, rather than the system's accountability to the individual.

In schools in particular the issue of high stakes testing has become a key area for debate. 'High stakes testing' relates to a test that has important consequences for the person being tested on a personal level, such as progression or entry to employment routes such as a professional qualification; or for a group or organisation, such as the consequences of a school being named and shamed for having lower than average SAT results. Opposition to SATS led to calls for teacher boycotts and SATS for 14-year-olds were scrapped in the autumn of 2008 following a 'fiasco' over the marking and reporting of results.

The problem here is that, viewed in isolation, summative results do not portray the whole picture of the student's journey or achievement. The assessment reform group argue that 'to avoid the negative consequences of using high stakes summative assessment to evaluate teachers and schools, systems of school accountability should not rely solely on the data derived from summative assessment of pupils and that the monitoring of standards of pupils' achievement should be derived from a wider base of evidence than test results from individual pupils' (ARG 2006: 1).

'If tests are confined to what is measurable, what is not measurable tends to be neglected . . . the tangible results are not the only ones that matter; what is important in such work is the quality of the experience that lies behind it and this can hardly be summed up in quantitative terms' (Handbook of Suggestions for Teachers (1944: 154)).

The research by Black et al. (1998, 2002) strongly argued that continued testing does not equate to, or promote, greater attainment. For a significant number of pupils, attainment potential can be undermined by low expectations and negative attitudes to education. Many students are strongly influenced by peer values and fear ridicule within their subgroups. Paul Willis in *Learning to Labour* (1977) explored why 'working class kids got working class jobs' and found evidence that home and cultural values influenced academic attainment, and that there is a stronger correlation between attainment and cultural influences than hereditary or biological assumptions espoused by eugenicist theorists such as Francis Galton (1822–1911) in his book *Hereditary Genius* published in 1869.

SUMMARY

Within this chapter you will have explored the purpose of assessment – why we assess and how we assess. You will also have considered a range of different types and methods of assessment. No one assessment method or type is sufficient: therefore a selection and range of assessment activities should be planned to promote learning, motivation and achievement, which are fit for their intended purpose.

It is important to remember that, although teachers may not have control over the *formal* assessment of learners, we are, and through the isolated nature of the work, will necessarily continue to be, autonomous within the classroom and are able to determine *how* a topic can be delivered. This is crucial to the teacher and their ability to plan according to individual and group need, *as well as* meeting the dictates of the awarding body. This also allows the tutor an element of choice – we may be constrained by what is to be taught, but we are not constrained or limited by this, or how we teach. Tutors can therefore move away from assessment as a means of mere accountability, or evaluation, to assessment for purer 'educational ends' (Kelly 2009: 147). These 'educational ends' can be selected by the tutor, informed by their own values or past industry experience and the interests of the students.

Find out more

The Assessment Reform Group (ARG), which originated in 1989 as the policy task group on assessment, has a useful site which also includes helpful and practical downloads for teachers: **www.assessment-reform-group.org/**. A link to the Nuffield research is also available from this site Assessment Systems for the Future: the place of assessment by teachers (ASF).

A useful site with a range of strategies is the National Strategies website. You will find a range of useful materials and resources, including targeted secondary material for assessment. It can be found at **http:// nationalstrategies.standards.dcsf.gov.uk/secondary**.

The widely influential work of Paul Black and Dylan Wiliam *Inside the Black Box: raising standards through classroom assessment*, London: nferNelson is a must for developing teachers' insight and understanding of assessment for learning.

Self-fulfilling prophecy – initially based on a sociological theory by Robert Merton in 1948, where Merton describes a self-fulfilling prophecy as having three stages – the initial suggestion or prophecy is presented and believed even though this is false; this leads to the second stage where new or changed behaviour occurs in accordance with that prophecy; which leads to the final stage where the expected event actually occurs and the prophecy is 'fulfilled'.

Derek Gillard has an interesting and informative website 'A brief history of the education of England'. This site contains many useful links to original documents and government reports and can be found at: **www.educationengland.org.uk/index.html**.

Useful websites

Association for Achievement and Improvement through Assessment (**AAIA**): **www.aaia.org.uk**.

Office for Standards in Education, Children's Services and Skills (**OfSTED**): **www.ofsted.gov.uk/**.

Qualifications and Curriculum Development Agency (**QCDA**, previously Qualification Curriculum Authority **QCA**): **www.qcda.gov.uk/**.

Office of the Qualifications Examinations Regulator (**Ofqual**): **www.ofqual.gov.uk/**.

Bibliography

Armitage, A. and Renwick, M. (2008) *Assessment in FE*, Continuum International Publishing Group.

Armitage, A. et al. (2007) *Teaching and Training in Post-Compulsory Education*, McGraw Hill. Open University Press.

AAIA (2007) *Recording and Tracking Pupils' Attainment and Progress – the use of assessment evidence at the time of inspections*: **www.aaia.org.uk/**

Assessment Reform Group (2006) *The Role of Teachers in the Assessment of Learning*, available online at: **www.assessment-reform-group.org/ ASF%20booklet%20English.pdf** [accessed 02.08.09].

Assessment Reform Group (2002) *Assessment for Learning: 10 principles*, available at: **www.assessment-reform-group.org/CIE3.PDF** [accessed 10.10.08].

Atherton, J. S. (2009) *Learning and Teaching: deep and surface learning* UK, available at: **www.learningandteaching.info/learning/deepsurf.htm** [accessed 17.07.09].

Ball, S. J. (1981) *Beachside Comprehensive: a case study of secondary schooling*, Cambridge: Cambridge University Press.

Bandura, A. (1977) Self-efficacy: toward a unifying theory of behaviour change, *Psychological Review*, 84: 191–215.

Bidner, C. (2008) A spillover based theory of credentialism, University of Columbia, UNSW Australian School of Business Research Paper No. 2010 ECON10.

Black, P. and Wiliam, D. (1998) *Inside the Black Box*, London: nferNelson.

Black, P., Harrison, C., Lee, C., Marshall, B. and Wiliam, D. (2002) *Working Inside the Black Box*, London: nferNelson.

Butler, R. (1988) Enhancing and undermining intrinsic motivation: the effects of task-involving and ego-involving evaluation on interest and performance, *British Journal of Educational Psychology*, 58: 1–14.

Central Advisory Council for Education (England) The Newsome Report (1963) *Half our Future*, London: HMSO, available at: **www.educationengland.org.uk**

Central Advisory Council for Education (England) The Plowden Report (1967) *Children and their Primary Schools*, London: HMSO, available at: **www.educationengland.org.uk**

Coultas, J. and Torrance, H. (2004) LSRC Research Report: Do Summative assessment and testing have positive on negative effect on post 16 learners motivation for learning in the learning and skills sector? **www.sussex.ac.uk**

Csikszentmihalyi, M. (1990) *Flow: The Psychology of Optimal Experience*. New York: Harper and Row.

DfES (2002) *14–19: Extending Opportunities, Raising Standards'*, London: HMSO.

Ecclestone, K. and Pryor, J. (2003) 'Learning careers' or 'assessment careers'? The impact of assessment systems on learning, *British Educational Research Journal*, 29(4): 471–88 **http://dx.doi.org/10.1080/01411920301849** [accessed 30.10.08].

Elliott, J. (1993) *Reconstructing Teacher Education*, The Falmer Press.

Galton, F. (1869) *Hereditary Genius: an inquiry into its laws and consequences*, London: Macmillan.

Gillborn, D. and Mirza, H. (2000) *Educational Inequality: mapping race, class and gender – a synthesis of research evidence*. London: Ofsted (**www.ofsted.gov.uk**).

Hayward, G., Hodgson, A., Johnson, J., Oancea, A., Pring, R., Spours, K., Wilde, S. and Wright, S. (2006) *Nuffield Review Annual Report 2005–06*, Department of Educational Studies. University (pdf) Full Report and available at **www.nuffield14-19review.org.uk/cgi/documents/documents.cgi?t=template.htm&a=129**

Keddie, N. (1973) *Tinker, Tailor . . . The Myth of Cultural Deprivation*, Harmondsworth: Penguin.

Kelly, A. V. (2009) *The Curriculum: Theory and Practice* (6th edn), London: Sage.

Long, M. (2000) *The Psychology of Education*, London: RoutledgeFalmer.

Martinez, P. and Munday, F. (1998) *Voices: student persistence and drop out in further education*, Further Education Development Agency Study. **www.guidance-research.org**

Miller, S. (1968) Breaking the credentials barrier *NASSP Bulletin*, 52(329): 38–46.

Mirza, H. S. (1998) Race, gender and IQ: the social consequence of pseudo-scientific discourse, in *Race, Ethnicity and Education*, 1(1): 109–26.

MSC/DES (1986) *Review of Vocational Qualifications in England and Wales*, London: HMSO.

Newsome Report (1963) *Half our Future: a report of the Central Advisory Council (England)*, London: HMSO.

QCA (2008) *The Diploma and its Pedagogy*, available at: **www.qcda.gov.uk/libraryAssets/media/The_Diploma_and_its_pedagogy.pdf** [accessed 27.07.09].

Race, P. (1995a) The art of assessing, *New Academic*, Autumn 3–5 and Spring 1996 3–6.

Race, P. (1995b) *Making Learning Happen*, London: Sage.

Reece, I. and Walker, S. (1997) *Teaching, Training and Learning: a practical guide* (3rd edn), Sunderland: Business Education Publishers Limited.

Rosenthal, R. and Jacobson, L. (1968) *Pygmalion in the Classroom: teacher expectation and pupils' intellectual development*, New York: Rinehart and Winston.

Rowntree, R. (1987) *Assessing Students: how shall we know them?*, London: Kogan Page.

Scales, P. (2008) *Teaching in the Lifelong Learning Sector*, McGraw Hill/Open University Press.

Stitt, Dr. S. (1998) Mediocrity finds safety in standardisation. Paper presented at the British Educational Research Association Annual Conference.

The English Education Act of 1918, the 'Fisher Bill': Background and Forecast of the Bill.

Torrance, H. and Coultas, J. (2004) *Do Summative Assessment and Testing have a Positive or Negative Effect on Post-16 Learners' Motivation for Learning in the Learning and Skills Sector?*, Shaftesbury: Learning and Skills Research Centre.

Tummons, J. (2007) *Assessing Learning in the Lifelong Learning Sector* (2nd edn), Exeter: Learning Matters Ltd.

Wallace, S. (2007) *Teaching, Tutoring and training in the Lifelong Learning Sector*, Exeter: Learning Matters.

Willis, P. (1977) *Learning to Labour: how working class kids get working class jobs*, London: Saxon House.

Wolf, A. (2002) *Does Education Matter? Myths about education and economic growth*, London: Penguin Books.

Wright, S. and Oancea, A. (2006) *Policies for Education and Training in England 1976 to the present day: a chronology*. Nuffield Review of 14–19 education and Training available at: **www.nuffield14-19review.org.uk/cgi/documents/documents.cgi?a=21&t=template.htm** [accessed 26.07.09].

Appendix 10.1

> ## Suggested answers for matching of assessment methods to learning aims and objectives activity in Table 10.1

A – 10	F – 1
B – 4	G – 6
C – 2	H – 9
D – 3	I – 8
E – 7	J – 5

> ## Dates of the changes of name for the Department of Education

DES – Department of Education and Science (1964–July 1992)

DfE – Department for Education (July 1992–July 1995)

DfEE – Department for Education and Employment (July 1995–June 2001)

DfES – Department for Education and Skills (June 2001–June 2007) split into two departments the DIUS (Department for Business, Innovation, Universities and Skills, targeted adult education) and the DCSF

DCSF – Department for School, Children and Families (June 2007–May 2010)

DfE – Department for Education May (2010–)

3 Enhancing Teaching for Learning

This part builds on the previous section by examining five aspects of professional practice seen as key for those working in the sector.

- Chapter 11 focuses on the importance of reflecting on learning as an activity in the development both of the student and of the practitioner.
- Chapter 12 looks at the role of research in professional contexts and the links with practice, arguing that research and enquiry are key tools of professional development.
- Chapter 13 considers the different levels of collaboration individuals and organisations are increasingly engaged in across and beyond their institutions.
- Chapter 14 examines inclusion and its importance in the 14–19 transformation agenda.
- Chapter 15 looks at the teacher's repertoire, particularly the teaching methods, teaching styles and range of key teaching roles which that repertoire is composed of.

Pearson Education Ltd./Ian Wedgewood

In this chapter, you will:

- Understand the debate about the effectiveness of reflective practice as a tool for teacher development
- Become familiar with the key principles of learning from experience
- Be acquainted with the views of two key theorists, Schön and Brookfield
- Examine the qualities of effective reflective practice
- Consider the process of recording reflection

Pearson Education Ltd./Ian Wedgewood

Introduction

We saw in Chapter 5 that Elliott (1993) distinguished between three models of teacher education. The first of these was a rationalist view which saw teachers grasping the theory and principles of education and applying them in practice. The second model Elliott describes is the 'social market' view of teacher education as a production/consumption system. According to this view, 'which applies the production–consumption systems which prevail in the economic sphere of Western democracies to the cultural/social sphere of the public services, including education', the outcomes of teacher training are construed as quantifiable products which can be clearly expressed in objectives prior to training. The third model Elliott calls a hermeneutic view of teacher education as a practical science. This 'highlights the role of "teachers as researchers" in effecting improvements in practical situations construed as complex, ambiguous and unpredictable' (Elliott 1993: 18). Central to this model is the notion of the reflective practitioner. Over the past 20 years, the merit of each model has been central to the debate over what makes a good teacher and what composes effective teaching. The conflict can be seen dramatically in Chris Woodhead's 1999 Ofsted Lecture, when he was HM Chief Inspector of Schools, entitled *The Rise and Fall of the Reflective Practitioner* in which he excoriates against this model which he holds responsible for falling standards, recommending instead a model underpinning government attempts to raise standards of teaching, attempts which he claims are 'pragmatic, unsentimental, hard nosed'.

> It is a vision of teaching as a vitally important, and, to do well, immensely difficult craft. A craft that depends upon an understanding of the knowledge and skills which must be taught, of the structure which must be followed if progress is to be made, of the classroom competencies which enable teachers to relate positively to each and every one of their children. A craft which has to be learnt.
>
> *(Woodhead 1999)*

WHAT DO YOU THINK?

Do you agree with Woodhead that teaching is a craft which has to be learnt or is professional development as a teacher more complicated, involving research and reflection on the part of practitioners?

Learning from experience

Kolb (1984) developed a four stage cycle of learning modes as indicated below and Gibbs (1988) gives the following examples of how the cycle might characterise experiential learning. Firstly,

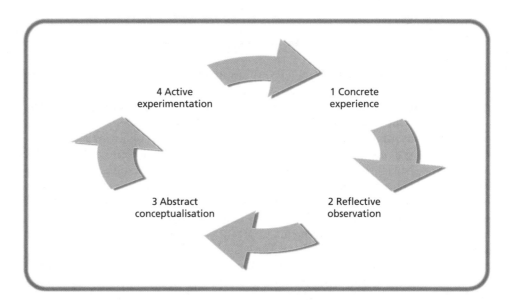

Figure 11.1

A trainee nurse might start learning how to lift a patient by taking part in supervised practice with a dummy, which would give experience of (a simulation of) what it is like (stage 1 in the diagram).

The charge nurse might then ask: 'How did that feel? What might you have done differently?' to encourage the nurse to be reflective about the experience (stage 2).

That night the nurse could look up, in a textbook, how to lift patients and read about the reasons for doing it in particular ways (stage 3).

Next day, confronted with a real patient to lift, the nurse would think: 'As a result of what happened yesterday, and because of what I read last night I ought to do it like this' (stage 4). This would provide a new experience and start the nurse on the next learning cycle.

Secondly, the sequence of learning of a chemistry course might be as follows, with 1–4 and 5–8 each representing one revolution of the cycle:

1. Taking notes in a lecture about a type of chemical reaction
2. Designing and running an experiment to test whether this type of reaction occurs with a particular group of elements
3. Gaining the experience of seeing what happens in the experiment
4. Looking at the results and comparing these with others' results
5. Discussing possible explanations of these results
6. Designing and running an experiment to test these alternative explanations
7. Gaining the experience of seeing what happens in this experiment
8. Looking at the results and comparing them with previous results

and so on, round and round the cycle, until an adequate understanding of the nature of the chemical reaction has been arrived at.

(Gibbs 1988)

Source: Pearson Education Ltd. Trevor Clifford

Photo 11.1
The sequence of learning of a chemistry course might be an illustration of learning from experience

IN PRACTICE

Take a sequence of learning activities either your students or you as a learner have undertaken. This might be activities from a session you have taught or from staff training or development activities you have taken part in. How far did they reflect the experiential learning cycle above?

Reflective practice

Schön (1983) describes his model of professional knowledge as supplanting and contrasting with Elliott's first model mentioned above, a technical–rationalist one which involved professionals applying theory in a systematic scientific fashion to practice. Schön identifies what he calls 'knowing-in action'. This know-how can be conceived of as being *in* the action concerned or demonstrated by it:

> [A] tight-rope walker's know-how, for example, lies in, and is revealed by, the way he takes his trip across the wire, or . . . a big league pitcher's know-how is in his way of pitching to a batter's weakness, changing his pace, or distributing his energies over the course of a game. There is nothing in common sense to make us say know-how consists in rules or plans which we entertain in the mind prior to action. Although we sometimes think before acting, it is also

true that in much of the spontaneous behaviour of skilful practice we reveal a kind of knowing which does not stem from a prior intellectual operation.

(Schön 1991: 50)

This knowing-in-action shares features with what Polanyi (1967) called 'tacit knowing', the kind of knowing for which we cannot adduce principles or evidence for what we know. Polanyi uses examples from the recognition of faces: if we know a person's face, we can pick it out in a crowd or we can recognise different moods in it. In neither case would we be able to identify explicitly how or why the recognition takes place.

However, as well as knowing-in-action, we may also have the ability to adjust, change our action or performance on the spot as we go along, responding to feedback. This, Schön (1991: 55) calls '**reflecting-in-action**' –

If common sense recognizes knowing-in-action, it also recognizes that we sometimes think about what we are doing. Phrases like 'thinking on your feet', 'keeping your wits about you' and 'learning by doing' suggest not only that we can think about doing but we can think about doing something while doing it. Some of the most interesting examples of this process occur in the midst of a performance.

Schön contrasts reflection-in-action with **reflection-on-action**, the conscious reviewing of experience, action or performance which may follow our demonstration of practice.

IN PRACTICE

Can you think of a professional activity you have recently been involved in, lesson planning, explaining, group management, management of an individual student, for example, when you might describe yourself as reflecting in action – when you confronted a new situation, a problem, feedback which required you to change, adjust, reframe what you were doing? Try to describe the different stages of that process.

For Brookfield (1995), the process of critical reflection on teaching takes place through four 'lenses': our autobiographies as learners and teachers; our students' eyes; our colleagues' experiences and theoretical literature. Consulting our biographies as learners puts us in the role of the 'other', according to Brookfield, and has important implications for how we teach. Our approaches to teaching may have been developed, consciously or unconsciously, from our experiences as learners. We may attempt to replicate our positive experiences for our learners and avoid those experiences which were negative. The authors have met many teachers in the sector whose teaching vocation has emerged from early negative experiences, followed later in life by very positive experiences which have given them the spur to enter the sector to replicate those positive experiences for other students.

Seeing ourselves through our students' eyes

is one of the most consistently surprising elements in any teacher's career. Each time we do this, we learn something. Sometimes what we find out is reassuring – but often, we are profoundly surprised by the diversity of meanings students read into our words and actions.

(1995: 34)

Seeing our practice through students' eyes does, Brookfield argues, help us to teach more responsively. It gives us direct access to their understanding and experiences, offering a yardstick for measuring the effectiveness of specific teaching methods.

'Talking to colleagues about what we do unravels the shroud of silence in which our practice is wrapped,' Brookfield claims of this third lens, 'our colleagues [serving] as critical mirrors reflecting back to us our images of our actions that often take us by surprise.' There is value in sharing and comparing experiences which helps us to reconsider, reframe and adjust our own theories of practice. There is also an important dimension of emotional sustenance in this process of sharing experience and knowing that we are not alone in our struggles.

Finally, 'theory can help us – to [illuminate] the general elements of what we may think are idiosyncratic experiences [and can] help us realize that what we thought were signs of our personal failings as teachers can actually be interpreted as the inevitable consequences of certain economic, social and political processes [which] stops us falling victim to the belief that we are responsible for everything that happens in our classrooms' (1995: 36). Theory can illuminate aspects of our practice. Brookfield gives an example of student hostility which might be interpreted as a response to an individual teacher but which theories of cognitive and moral development might suggest resistance on the part of students to change aspects of themselves which they would rather not happen. Brookfield recognises that educational theory can be inaccessible for practising teachers who might also find it hard to apply it directly to their practice.

WHAT DO YOU THINK?

Consider the following points relating to Brookfield's lenses:

1. Are there critical incidents or specific experiences either as a learner or teacher which have impacted on your own practice as a teacher?
2. In which ways do you share experiences with colleagues? Is this largely done formally or informally? What kind of communication with colleagues is of most value?
3. In which ways do you take student feedback into consideration when evaluating your practice?
4. Do you consider educational literature of any value to you in your work? If so, what kind – the official literature of legislation and policy, subject specialist literature such as specialist journals, literature produced by your institution, works of general educational theory, practical handbooks?

Reflective activities

The nature of reflective activities will depend upon their role and purpose in professional development. They might be required as part of a structured initial teacher training or CPD programme, as evidence of professional formation for the Institute for Learning, or as routine evaluation of practice, for example. The structure and content of the reflection will be determined by the focus chosen, the stance taken by the reflector towards the object of reflection, the conclusions reached through reflection and any future intended consequences.

Focus

The focus of reflection could be on a particular context of practice: a lesson, a conversation with colleagues or assessment of student work. The focus might be on a critical or, what has been called, 'significant' incident, an incident which itself exemplifies an issue to be investigated, such as an individual's unwanted behaviour, a group response to a learning activity or a barrier to learning common to a class. Reflection might focus on the teacher's interpersonal or intra-personal skills, their emotional response to student behaviour. It may seek to uncover a teacher's hidden and overt assumptions. The object of reflection could be on the deployment of a resource or the management of the learning environment. Hillier (2005) distinguishes between contextual, dispositional and experiential reflection. In contextual reflection, 'an episode of experience is reviewed in terms of contextual forces, e.g. time, place, race, class, policies, which have influenced and shaped it.' For dispositional reflection, 'it is a person's orientation which influences the action, e.g. preferences, aspirations, feelings and personal reactions to purposeful activity.' And in experiential reflection, 'the person reflecting on the purposive activity tries to think back to what the event was like as an experience. It focuses on the 'whatness' of the experience' (2005: 9).

Stance

The stance of the reflector will be expressed in the way they interpret, conceptualise or give meaning to their experience. It will be determined by the relationship they have with the object of reflection and what they do in and through their reflection. Their approach may be comparative: what did I do differently this time to get that result? They may be exploratory, examining aspects of their practice they have not considered before. They may question their own decisions or actions, be confrontational with themselves. They might use theory in an attempt to understand events. Their stance might be highly analytical. It could offer hypotheses about events or behaviour.

Conclusions

The conclusions of reflection concern what has been learned through it, what the key insights or understandings of the activity have been. This awareness will often be arrived at through a process of judgements and evaluations. I realise that my students' motivation is directly affected by the sequence of learning activities I am asking them to participate in, or it appears that the animation of my PowerPoint slides is distracting rather than illuminating or illustrating their content.

Consequences

The consequences of reflection are concerned with what will now happen or not happen as a result of conclusions reached, judgements made. What will I do differently? What new strategies shall I try? What transformation do I expect of my practice? Have I developed new perspectives both on the object of reflection and on related issues?

Effective reflection will therefore have a number of features. The focus of reflection should be appropriate for the issues explored. I would want to monitor student learning throughout a taught module if I am interested in my delivery of the module topics in a new sequence, or the critical incident of a student storming out of the room would provide an appropriate focus were that event typical of the student's behaviour. The stance of the reflector should be that most likely to lead to conclusions regarding the issues being examined or the problem to be solved. I am not able to explain myself why some of my interactions with students turn out as they do: perhaps applying theory drawn from transactional analysis or neuro-linguistic programming might help me here. The conclusions or judgements I come to need to follow from what I have experienced and lead logically to any consequences: I have now understood my difficult interactions with students as the result of crossed transactions and I am going to try to initiate interactions with my students in different ways.

CASE STUDIES

Below are three extracts from reflective journals. In each case, comment on their effectiveness as reflections, bearing in mind the focus selected, the stance taken, the conclusions reached and the consequences following. You might want to consider what advice you would give to each teacher.

1. Leanne

Leanne is an English graduate on a pre-service PGCE programme on teaching practice in an FE college.

I have had real lateness problems with the AS class I teach first thing Tuesday and Thursday mornings. Early in my practice I tried being firm with latecomers – I would tell them they were late and demand a reason why they were: this often led to a long silence when there was no particular reason why they were late, or me backing down when they produced a good reason for being late, like public transport problems which the rest of the students backed them up on. I also applied official college policy of not admitting any students after 15 minutes of the session but that seemed like a terrible waste. I did have a hunch that the students were less bothered about being late for my lessons because I was a student teacher and not to be taken as seriously as employed members of staff. But Moira, who is their regular teacher, says their lateness with me is no worse than their lateness with her. So – I am going to try keeping late students back at the end of the session. It's not an ideal solution – some of them are on quite tight ▶

 **CASE STUDY** *CONTINUED*

timetables with only 45 minutes for lunch – but at least it takes back some of their free time, which might act as a deterrent.

2. Deborah

Deborah is a full-time Hair and Beauty tutor in an FE college, having run her own hairdressing business for 10 years. She is in her 2nd year of teaching and has just begun a Diploma in Teaching in the Lifelong Learning Sector programme.

For my Professional Values and Practice assignment, I am required to consider an issue relating to professional values in my own subject area. A thing which struck me from day one of my teaching was how varied the students are in their professional attitudes: some very laid back and casual with customers, others more formal, some being far more prescriptive when offering advice to customers, others carrying out exactly what the customer asks for. I could only think that the reason for these differences lay in the different salons students went to for their work experience. So, I decided on my work experience visits to interview work experience supervisors about the professional attitudes they expected of trainees. Some were very clear about company rules on professional behaviour, others unable to articulate these and expecting trainees to pick up the atmosphere and house style of a salon themselves. The conclusion I came to was that good stylists are not always the best work-based learning supervisors. But I also wondered whether my concern about common workplace practices arose from my own work experience which, although extensive, is limited to one place of work and did I therefore have a hang-up about such variation? As a consequence of my findings, we are going to spend more time

in college sessions using the varied experience of students comparatively when considering professional issues.

3. Tim

Tim teaches Art & Design at several adult and community learning centres. Although he enjoys the teaching, his major interest is his own work as a painter. His reflection follows an observation and feedback from his line manager.

I had a sense this observation was not going to go very well. I was criticised for having a vague lesson plan but I argued that the nature of the subject means that each student is continuing with their work and that having an overall plan for the group was difficult. I didn't have my aims and objectives for the session on the board – well, frankly, I think that sort of stuff is just going through the motions in case we have an inspection. As is the idea that the art room was not a very stimulating environment: we have people's work up there – I can't see what could be more stimulating than that. Again – I didn't use a variety of teaching and learning strategies: well, that just wouldn't be appropriate – people want one-to-one commentary on their work – I give them what they come for. And, as for them not learning anything during the session – well, how does he know? I know how their work does or doesn't develop through one course or from one course to the next. And anyway, students come for reasons other than just learning: they come because they enjoy themselves or to socialise with the group. My classes are always full because they get what they want from them and they come back again and again. It's all about bums on seats, he's always saying. Well – that's what I deliver.

Recording reflection: a reflective journal

A useful way of framing reflective writing is to respond to a series of prompt questions relating to the area of professional practice which is the focus of reflection. The questions below were set for the following areas of reflection on a pre-service PGCE (post-compulsory) programme.

Theory and practice

- What theory/theories seem(s) to be most valuable at this stage in terms of preparation for teaching?
- How do you feel your own attitude to being assessed, to communication, and to managing the learning of others has altered in the light of recent university sessions, reading and discussions?

Professional role and values

- What core values do you hope to take into placement and why?
- What has pleased or inspired you about your experience to date?
- Can you describe your 'teacher identity' or is it still evolving?
- What type of teacher do you hope to become – why? What does it mean to be a professional?
- Identify your own personal code of professional practice and justify your choices.
- Consider your role within the lifelong learning sector – what are your boundaries?
- Have you experienced any professional conflict with regard to your own values and that of the curriculum requirements?
- What is an inclusive environment?
- List three strategies that you use to promote equality.
- How do you manage the work/life balance?
- Select a newspaper article relating to education from this week's news. Summarise the article and produce a critical response, identifying any implications for the teaching profession or your own subject specialist area.

Peer collaboration

- Have you shared your experience with your peers (e.g. through the VLE)?
- Reflection does not have to be a solitary activity! Comment on the ways in which shared discussion and evaluation could help to improve your own development, colleagues' development or the development of your learners. Provide examples to illustrate. What are the advantages and/or disadvantages of collaborative planning, delivery and evaluation? Provide some examples from own practice.
- Which teachers do you admire in your placement or from your own learning experiences – why and how have they influenced you?

Photo 11.2 Peer collaboration can be a useful way of reflecting on practice

Source: Pearson Education Ltd. Ian Wedgewood

Subject specialism

- Recommend a website for your own subject specialism; place this on the VLE with a short justification.
- List the different programmes you have taught on throughout the PGCE programme. What have you enjoyed – why? How has your own specialist knowledge developed over the course of the programme – have you engaged in any subject specific development – e.g. feedback from exam boards?

Own learning and development

- Complete a SWOT analysis. What strengths and weaknesses do you have at this stage of the programme and what opportunities and threats do you foresee?
- Reflection – why bother? What are the advantages of reflection – should these be formal or informal, systematic or on an ad hoc basis? What system of reflection works for you and why?
- Identify your own CPD needs and opportunities for development.
- Teaching is a very demanding profession – how have your expectations differed from the experience?
- What has been the most useful piece of advice you have been given? How will you employ this in your own development?
- What has concerned or disappointed you about your experience to date? How are you going to address this?
- Describe one issue you feel uncomfortable about – what is it? Why is this an issue? How can you overcome this?

- Reflect on your own learning in the light of what you are observing and experiencing concerning the learning of others

Programme and lesson planning

- What is the difference between aims and objectives?
- List three reasons why sequencing is so important.

Own career

- Have you surveyed the employment market, found out about agency working, discussed opportunities with staff in placement?
- What tips or advice could you offer to new entrants to the profession?

Own organisation

- What has your widening view of the organisation as a whole contributed to your learning?
- Consider your placement organisation and the range of services it offers – how are students referred to the wider support networks? Are these sufficient? How are students referred to outside organisations, e.g. Youth Offending Teams, Social Services, Connexions or charitable organisations such as those that help with housing issues?

IN PRACTICE

Considering your teaching over the past two weeks, select a focus for reflection. Develop a series of prompt questions similar to those above and write a 500-word reflection.

Jenny Moon, describing a generic framework for reflective writing, specifies 'four "levels" of depth of reflection'. The fourth level is described as follows:

Description now only serves the process of reflection, covering the issues for reflection and noting their context. There is clear evidence of standing back from an event and there is mulling over and engagement.

The account shows deep reflection and it incorporates a recognition that the frame of reference with which an event is viewed can change. A metacognitive stance is taken (i.e. critical awareness of one's own processes of mental functioning, including reflection).

The account probably recognizes that events exist in a historical or social context that may influence a person's reaction to them. In other words, multiple perspectives are noted.

Self-questioning is evident (an 'internal dialogue' is set up), deliberating between different views of personal behaviour and that of others.

The view and motives of others are taken into account and considered against those of the writer.

There is recognition of the role of emotion in shaping the ideas and recognition of the manner in which different emotional influences can frame the account in different ways.

There is recognition that prior experience and thoughts (own and others') interact with the production of current behaviour.

There is observation that there is learning to be gained from the experience and points for learning are noted.

There is recognition that the personal frame of reference can change according to the emotional state in which it is written, the acquisition of new information, the review of ideas and the effect of time passing.

(Moon 2006: 162)

WHAT DO YOU THINK?

Using Moon's description above, assess the extent to which your peer's 500-word reflection is at the fourth level.

SUMMARY

Kolb (1984) developed a four-stage cycle of learning modes: a learner's concrete experience is reflected on, either through discussion with a peer, tutor, or supervisor, for example. Through further enquiry such as reading, the abstract aspects of the experience are considered, leading to a further active experimentation, which itself becomes a new concrete experience and so begins a further cycle. Schön identifies what he calls 'knowing-in action', conceived of as being *in* the action, concerned or demonstrated by it, which he distinguishes from *reflection-on-action*, the conscious reviewing of experience, action or performance which may follow our demonstration of practice. For Brookfield, the process of critical reflection on teaching takes place through four 'lenses': our autobiographies as learners and teachers; our students' eyes; our colleagues' experiences; and theoretical literature. The nature of reflective activities will depend upon their role and purpose in professional development. And the structure and content of the reflection will be determined by the focus chosen, the stance taken by the reflector towards the object of reflection, the conclusions reached through reflection and any future intended consequences. Jenny Moon contends that reflective writing is carried at a series of levels, at each of which there is greater depth of reflection.

Find out more

Schön, D. A. (1983) *The Reflective Practitioner,* **Aldershot: Arena, Ashgate Books.**
As well establishing some of the key concepts which underpin our understanding of reflective practice such as *reflection-in-action* and *reflection-on-action,* Schön's 1983 work is notable for the way his theorising is related to a whole range of professional contexts, from science-based professions such as medicine through town planning, architecture and engineering rather than simply to educational contexts which a great deal of work on reflective practice focuses on. This is useful for teachers in the sector who may wish to explore how reflective practice might be applied by their own students in different curriculum areas or vocational contexts.

Moon, J. (1996) *Reflection in Learning and Professional Development,* **London: Kogan Page.**
Many trainees and teachers find the recording of their reflection on practice particularly challenging and Part 3 of Jenny Moon's book provides practical advice and support for them to develop their writing. The provision of a framework to enable them to do so at different levels has been found especially helpful by teachers we have worked with.

Brookfield, S. D. (1995) *Becoming a Critically Reflective Teacher,* **San Francisco, CA: Jossey-Bass.**
Stephen Brookfield's work is notable in the literature of reflective practice, which can often be abstract and over-theoretical, for the use of one of his own four lenses, key autobiographical incidents, to present his observations of them in an open, accessible way. Brookfield is a teacher's teacher who speaks directly to their experience.

IfL (www.ifl.ac.uk/)
The Institute for Learning is the professional body for teachers, trainers, tutors and student teachers in the lifelong learning sector. If appointed in the sector after September 2007, you will be required to gain one of the new teaching qualifications, progress to licensed practitioner status and remain in good standing by undertaking and recording 30 hours of CPD. At the centre of this process of professional formation is the notion of reflective practice and the IfL tool used for recording this reflection is Reflect. You can gain an understanding of how this works at **www.ifl.ac.uk/cpd/reflect**, but whatever your professional status as trainee or teacher in the sector, you would be advised to join the IfL and gain full access to the Reflect process.

Bibliography

Bolton, G. (2006) Reflective *Practice: writing and professional development* (2nd edn), London: Sage.

Boud. D., Cohen, R. and Walker, D. (eds) (1993) *Using Experience for Learning,* Buckingham: Open University Press.

Boud, D., Keogh, R. and Walker, D. (1985) *Reflection: turning experience into practice,* London: Kogan Page Ltd.

Brookfield, S. D. (1995) *Becoming a Critically Reflective Teacher,* San Francisco, CA: Jossey-Bass.

Elliott, J. (ed.) (1993) *Reconstructing Teacher Education,* London: The Falmer Press.

Gibbs, G. R. (1988) *Learning by Doing: a guide to teaching and learning methods,* London: Further Education Unit/Oxford: Oxford Polytechnic.

Hillier, Y. (2005) *Reflective Teaching in Further and Adult Education* (2nd edn), London: Continuum.

Kolb, D. A. (1984) *Experiential Learning,* Englewood Cliffs, NJ: Prentice Hall Inc.

Loughran, J. J. (1996) *Developing Reflective Practice,* London: The Falmer Press.

Moon, J. (1996) *Reflection in Learning and Professional Development,* London: Kogan Page.

Moon, J. (2006) *Learning Journals: a handbook for reflective practice and professional development,* London: Routledge.

Pollard, A. (2005) *Reflective Teaching* (2nd edn), London: Continuum.

Polyani, M. (1967) *The Tacit Dimension,* New York: Doubleday and Co.

Schön, D. A. (1983) *The Reflective Practitioner*, Aldershot: Arena, Ashgate Books.

Schön, D. A. (1991) *The Reflective Turn: case studies in and on educational practice*, New York: Teachers Press, Columbia University.

Tummons, J. (2007) *Becoming a Professional Tutor in the Lifelong Learning Sector*, Exeter: Learning Matters.

Woodhead, C. (1999) *The Rise and Fall of the Reflective Practitioner*, London: Ofsted.

Investigating Learning

In this chapter you will:

- Reflect upon the need for investigating learning in the 14–19 education phase
- Examine the role of the teacher-researcher
- Consider potential research themes in relation to your professional practice
- Consider factors impacting on your project

Pearson Education Ltd./Ian Wedgewood

Introduction

In this chapter we will be considering the importance of investigating learning for professional development. We will explore the role of the teacher as a researcher and examine some of the factors that may influence this type of investigation.

This section is not meant to discuss educational research in terms of methodology or research methods: this can be done by consulting the wide variety of publications available on this topic. This chapter is to introduce the concept of research offering practical advice and examples for the 'regular' teacher-researcher practising in the 14–19 context.

Why investigate learning?

Investigating learning is considered an integral part of a practitioner's professional practice, whether teacher or lecturer or in any other capacity that involves teaching and learning. The link between research and learning is obvious in the sense that there can be no learning without an initial query or a need or desire to know the 'what' or 'how and why' of a subject matter or learning process. To a certain extent, teachers investigate learning every time they plan a session, devise an activity, step into a classroom, assess learners, or discuss issues of students' progression with their colleagues. This means that investigating learning can happen in our day-to-day teaching but also in a more formal manner.

Investigating learning encourages the teacher to consider, question or deepen teaching and learning as part of his/her professional development. Still, professional development is somewhat limited to continuous professional development (CPD) of subject specialism which often takes the shape of courses, exam board's activities or training days initiated by the school or college we work in. Conversely research is often seen as an additional venture that requires extra time, resources and efforts beyond a practitioner's capacities. It is safe to say that few practitioners have the opportunity to undertake investigations about their students' learning, and most educational research seems 'reserved' to universities' educationalists and other research-based institutions. In fairness, using research papers can help us inform, compare, confirm or question our practice. Yet, there has been growing encouragement of a more practice-based research, enabling teachers to investigate issues applicable to their own practice and in their own professional context.

There is great need to involve 'front line' practitioners to contribute to the investigation of issues and the building of knowledge for the development of the 14–19 teaching phase. The development of teaching and learning should not be exclusive to professional researchers who, despite their ability to examine an issue from a different perspective, may lack the expertise that teacher-researchers have in their day-to-day practice. It is crucial to 'hear' from practitioners about their 14–19 teaching and learning experiences in order to build a better picture of the development of 14–19 education.

WHAT DO YOU THINK?

- Have you ever considered researching issues influencing your professional practice? Which issues have you identified?
- Why are they worth investigating?

Which type of investigation?

Investigating learning in professional educational settings can take several forms: from personal reflection to formal enquiries, such as thinking over a lesson which did not work, as well as finding out why your students' punctuality is erratic. To some extent we could consider reflective practice as a means of investigation. It allows practitioners to identify an issue and use own experience and knowledge to establish cause and effect and find an appropriate solution. The practitioner's reflection is not an 'official' type of research as it is unlikely to be formally recorded. It is aimed at helping us to think about our practice, and relies on what we experience in the classroom. It is by no means less valuable than 'proper' research and it could be seen as one of the stages of a more formal investigation.

We could say that using a simple cycle of reflection invites the practitioner to investigate further and in a more formal manner. For instance, the reflection you have undertaken after an unsuccessful teaching session could lead to a more formal investigation of pedagogical approaches. You may wish to refer to Chapter 11 for further reading on reflective practice.

ACTIVITY

From the list of issues you have identified in the 'what do you think' feature, choose one issue and answer the following questions:

- What do I want to find out and for what purpose?
- Who will benefit from this investigation?'

It is likely that what you want to investigate is quite complex. Very few issues have a simple answer and your interest in the matter may require time and resources to be investigated. You may be offered solutions by colleagues or by your institution to develop or improve the 'issue'. However, you should not be discouraged to examine the issue from another perspective. Being involved with research enables you to develop as a critical practitioner.

Photo 12.1 We are constantly involved in informal research – think about what investigations you might be involved in during a typical day's teaching, like planning a lesson or reviewing a student's work

Source: Pearson Education Ltd. Mind Studio

The teacher-researcher

The notion of the **teacher-researcher** has grown in recent years mainly within an action-research format. **Action research** is a form of enquiry enabling the teacher to become a researcher in order to investigate an issue and learn directly from his/her own practice. The researcher and author Jean McNiff identifies action research as:

> [A]n enquiry by the self into the self, undertaken in company with others acting as research participants and critical learning partners. Action Research involves learning in and through action and reflection.
>
> *(McNiff and Whitehead, 2002: 15)*

Action research is about: involvement, understanding and improvement of practice (Robson 2002: 215). John Elliott defines its aim as 'to improve practice rather than to produce knowledge' (Elliott 1991: 49). Within action research the teacher is seen as a 'teacher-researcher' and is encouraged to formulate his/her own theory or theories about the learning issue and the overall research experience. In the past few years action research has become more prominent in classroom research due to its practical aim to improve own teaching and learning context but also to empower the practitioner as a 'constructor of own theory'.

For example, let us go back to the issue of 'students' erratic punctuality' mentioned earlier. The example is not anecdotal: issues of punctuality have a significant impact on learning and deserve further thought. As a practitioner you may wish to discuss the problem with colleagues or consult various classroom management textbooks offering tips on how to control or prevent the situation.

However, this issue originates from your students and is happening in your classroom. Who might be the best person to investigate the issue other than you? We are not suggesting here that you are the cause of such an issue but there is a strong case for you being at the centre of the investigation as you are the one who is experiencing the issue. As a result of an action research, you may be able not only to generate a 'theory' explaining why your students tend to be late but also to plan and test some solutions to the problem.

As such, action research 'informs professional judgement and thereby develops practical wisdom, i.e. the capacity to discern the right course of action when confronted with particular, complex and problematic states of affairs' (Elliot 1991: 52), and as a result reinstates the practitioner as an expert within his/her own profession. Action research puts the practitioner researcher at the heart of the research. Whitehead suggests that the 'I' *'should be placed at the centre of educational enquiries, not as an abstract personal pronoun but as real-life human being'* (McNiff and Whitehead 2002: 72).

Factors to consider throughout your action-research project

Identifying the 'issue' from your practice

You have previously selected a range of issues which had an impact or which influences your professional practice. The issues may not be necessarily negative and it is more than likely that you will come into action research from an 'improvement of practice' angle.

ACTIVITY

The following 'I' questions have all been used for action-research projects:

- How do I use ICT to enhance my History lessons?
- How do I integrate study skills within the Engineering curriculum?
- How do I use more target language in my GCSE Spanish sessions?
- How do I apply differentiation with large groups of students?
- How do I make Health and Social Care lessons more relevant to students' life?
- How do I make more use of the learning assistant's skills during group work?
  Now, formulate your own question using the 'How do I' format:
- How do I ....?

Planning and process

You have now identified the issue to be researched and formulated your research question. Now you can start thinking of how this will be done. The process evolves around the reflection-action-evaluation cycle (see Figure 12.1) but some models may include more precise steps such as:

- I experience a concern
- I reflect upon the reason for this concern
- I imagine a solution to that concern
- I take action
- I gather evidence to see if my action influences the situation
- I evaluate the outcome of the solution
- I modify my practice in the light of the evaluation
- I evaluate the outcome of the modification, and so on.

(adapted from McNiff and Whitehead 2002)

It may also be useful to add: 'I research and read any paper or book with regard to this "concern" or "issue" in order to gain a better contextual knowledge of the situation'. Textbooks offer a more in-depth theoretical approach whereas journals may give a better picture of actual practice.

IN PRACTICE

Using literature to inform the 'issue'

- How can I use more target language in my GCSE Spanish sessions?

You can start the research by identifying which organisation/institution may hold publications on the matter. For example the CILT, the National Centre for Languages, have a wide selection of research papers, statistics and surveys on language learning (**http://www.cilt.org.uk/home/research_and_statistics.aspx**).

Consulting language journals is useful to gain access to research from practitioners and researchers. For example articles on 'Value added Modern Languages in the classroom: an investigation into how teachers' use of classroom target language can aid pupils' by Crichton, 2009, or 'The use of target language at GCSE' by Buckby, 1999, both in *Language Learning Journal* can be informative for the topic of 'target language'. They may not specifically focus on the language you teach but they will give you insights of other practices. The 2002 textbook *A Course in Language Teaching: Practice and Theory*, by Penny Ur, can support both theoritical and practical aspects of modern foreign language teaching and acquisition of language. You can use the findings to reflect upon the issue you are researching at the initial stage of the planning and/or for the writing of your paper, if you intend to use the results of your research for publication or essay purposes.

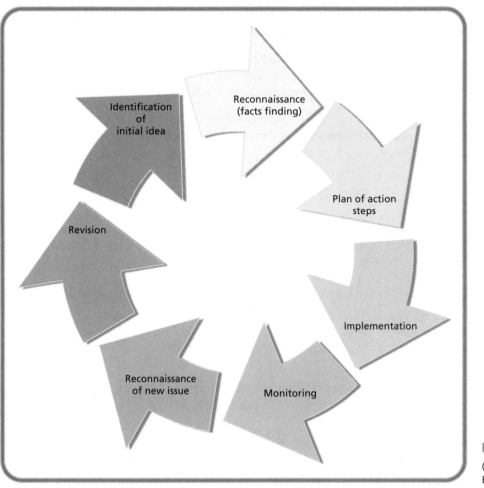

Figure 12.1

(Adapted from Elliot 1991: 71)

Action research should not follow a rigid process. It is meant to be flexible and organic and adapt to the pace of your investigation. However Figure 12.1 can give you some idea of how you could proceed.

There is ample literature which has been written about the collection and evaluation of information and data for your action research. In 'Find out more', we suggest a range of manuals providing an extended theoretical and practical research basis for research. However, in action research there are a few basic things to consider:

- This type of research implies you are putting yourself and your learners at the heart of the research.
- You are undertaking this type of research in order to develop your practice and therefore improve the learning.
- As a teacher-researcher you will be an 'insider' researcher, as you will be fully involved as researcher but also as an 'actor' of your own investigation.

WHAT DO YOU THINK?

An insider researcher is someone who is undertaking research within her/his own institution. As a teacher-researcher you will not only carry out research in your place of work but you are also likely to be involved with your own students within your own practice.

• Can you think of the advantages and disadvantages in being an insider researcher?

Ethical behaviour

The advantages of being an 'insider' researcher are numerous: you will have an in-depth understanding of your work context; trust will be established; and you will have easy access to students, staff and information needed for your research.

On the other hand, this 'proximity' may hinder the research in the following ways:

• Relationships with colleagues may be uncomfortable or affected
• There may be issues of confidentiality difficult to manage
• Objectivity may be difficult to maintain.

(Robson 2002)

The task of any researcher is to ensure that the research abides with ethical guidelines throughout. You should therefore consider some the following ethical issues while undertaking any type of research:

• informed consent – ensuring the participants understand the research and their role within the research
• the right to withdraw – participants must be given a choice to withdraw their contribution at any stage of the research: for example, this could mean you would not be able to use someone's interview as evidence for your project
• issues of confidentiality and privacy – if you write a report, participants should not be directly named or be easily identified: the use of a pseudonym is standard practice
• respect for participants – participants are entitled to their opinion regardless of possible conflict with yours
• sensitivity to power relations and professionalism – as teacher-researchers, you need to acknowledge the impact you may have on your students and whether this can affect your project.

(Hillier and Jameson 2003).

You would also need to follow guidelines and protocols set up by your institution.

IN PRACTICE

You will need to ask the project's participants to fill in the form to confirm they agree to take part in your project. The following letter could act as an 'informed consent' form.

Dear . . .

I am currently involved in a project focusing on the use of ICT in the teaching of A-level History. The research will help me devise appropriate activities for the teaching of the programme. Your participation is appreciated and the information given will be used within the frame of the research, respecting your anonymity. All data will be kept confidential and no name will be identified

Please sign this form and return it to me or in my pigeon-hole room in room C234

I have been informed about the aim of this research and understand that the information will be used for educational purposes. I understand I may not wish to participate in all the project's activities and may withdraw my participation at any stage. I understand my name will not be used in the final report.

I would like/would not like to take part in further research on this topic (delete as appropriate) (if yes, please enter an email and/or phone number you can be contacted on)

Email: _____

Mobile number_____

Name _____

Signature   Date

You may also wish to talk directly to your students, underlining that the project is not just about the activities, it is about evaluating their usefulness for your teaching and their learning.

Gathering information

Because learning is central to this type of research and researching learning is not a straightforward task, collecting information for your project will involve gathering a variety of information. There are pros and cons for every method. There is an ongoing debate around the use of **quantitative** and **qualitative** approach of gathering data. The teacher-researcher tends to adopt a pragmatic view to data/information collection and will consider using what is available and what suits the particular focus of the project. This approach may not satisfy all researchers who may feel more comfortable with a structured approach, but it will enable you to gather various types of evidence that can support your overall project.

The clue is to link the method to what you are trying to find or try out. For example, if you are trying to make more use of the learning assistant scheme for group work (Activity 2), you may have introduced weekly meetings with the learning assistant which enable you to identify precise roles and tasks. Gathering information to see if this has worked may take several forms. For instance, you may wish to talk about the impact of the planning process with the learning assistant. You may also wish to have a look at the outcomes of the group tasks, comparing these with your own.

The table below provides an indication of how you could gather specific pieces of information.

Information needed	Ways of recording data
Students' behaviour/attitude	Observation
Students' opinion	**Questionnaire**, interview, **focus group** conversation, end-of-course evaluation
Teacher-researcher's experience	Diary, evaluation of lesson plan
Learning taking place	Students' work, exam results, **progression data**

Photo 12.2
What useful information could you collect using face-to-face interviews with your students?

Source: Pearson Education Ltd. Studio 8

Selecting tools to gather data is not an easy task. You will probably need to test them and talk about it with a critical friend. For example, for a questionnaire, we suggest you first use a small group of participants. You could evaluate the effectiveness of the questionnaire by asking them to fill it in. Their responses may give you some indication of how well they understand the questions. You may also decide to discuss it with them after completion to get an overall evaluation. An effective questionnaire needs to be easy to understand, clear and relevant. Poor questionnaire design can lead to misunderstandings that risk distorting the results of the research.

ACTIVITY

Focus of action research: How do I integrate study skills within the Engineering curriculum?

Abdul teaches Engineering at level 3 in an FE college in Shropshire. He has been working on a project focusing on a better integration of study skills within his curriculum. Before devising a 'solution', he has designed a questionnaire for colleagues to gauge their opinion on the matter.

- Consider the following questionnaire. How could this questionnaire be improved?

1. How important do you think the following statements are for your level-3 students while they study on their course? (on a scale of 0–5) (0 irrelevant to 5 essential)

Some understanding of subject	☐	Planning skills	☐
Being able to structure an essay	☐	Good communication with fellow students	☐
Communication with staff	☐	Independent skills	☐
Research skills	☐	Reflection and evaluation of own performance	☐

You may have underlined some of the following points:

- The 'How important' question is not very clear. It needs to be simplified – e.g., How important are the following for your students' studies?
- There is not enough choice of statements. Teachers answering this questionnaire are likely to say they are all important for studying at level 3.
- Lack of cohesion between statements, e.g. 'Communication with staff' and 'Some understanding of the subject' do not relate directly to the issue of study skills.

An additional question could be added to ensure an opinion is recorded, e.g.:

11. Is there anything else that you would like to include in the above list which you feel is important for successful Engineering studies at level 3 (e.g. exam practice)?

Choosing a critical friend

The concept of a critical friend to support your project is widely recommended for action-research projects. Critical friends do exactly what they 'say'! They provide a 'critique' (and not criticism . . .) and enable you to gain another perspective on your project. At first hand, choosing a critical friend may seem simple. However, you need to consider the following:

- You must trust the critical friend's judgement. This does not mean that you cannot disagree with them, only that you accept what they have to say about your project.

- Some critical friends may be too 'close to home'. You may be working in the same department or on the same course or there may be a hierarchal issue. You will need to discuss conflict of interest with your critical friends to avoid problems during your project. Your critical friend does not have to be from the same institution or even a teacher but it sometimes help to have someone who understands the context of your project.

What do I do with my findings?

In teacher action research, the findings may help you tackle the initial issue but they are also likely to initiate others. Action research is an ongoing cycle: it does not really end as it is part of your professional practice. Whether you decide to continue to explore these issues on a formal basis is something for you to consider. However, the dissemination of your findings will be relevant within your institution and may be of interest to the wider education community. You could discuss the outcomes at staff meeting or organise a more formal session for colleagues to attend. You may also wish to contact local education authorities or local universities to see if they have a 'platform' for you to feed back your project.

 **CASE STUDY**

Mel is a lecturer in literacy entry 1 to level-2 students in a large FE college, in Kent. She has completed an action-research paper aiming at improving the use of a spelling, punctuation and grammar scheme by students. The project, 'Exploration of professional practice through action research in context of college marking scheme', was undertaken over a year while Mel was teaching at the college. Mel's 'issue' was the lack of use of a student handbook on spelling, punctuation and grammar. She had realised that the handbook was seldom used by students to review their own work. From her initial dialogue with students, she found out that the handbook was too complex but she also realised that students did not grasp the concept of ownership of their own writing: they too often relied on the teacher to correct their work without having to use the handbook. Mel's action was to revise a new handbook to ensure it became more 'democratic' and accessible to students. Throughout her action research she consulted with students and her 'critical friends' as well as colleagues on various drafts of a new version for the marking scheme. Mel felt her greatest achievement was to have raised awareness regarding the need for students' involvement in their own literacy. The project also underlined the importance of clarity and the consideration of 'audience' in devising such a handbook. In this case study we can see that Mel was partly confronted not only by the practical modification of the handbook but also by the need to change attitudes towards the use of the handbook. Mel realised that the real aim was to engage students with their literacy progress. As a reflective practitioner, Mel demonstrated her commitment to develop her practice. As a teacher researcher, she proved her project could have an impact on learning. Mel disseminated her findings and recommendations at a local university conference, which gave her the opportunity to present her project to her peers.

Exploring issues beyond the classroom settings

So far we have examined the role of the teacher-researcher. You may also wish to focus on areas beyond the boundaries of your classroom and explore what is happening in the 14–19 educational and institutional contexts (school, college or academy). For example:

- From school to academy, the case study of changes in learning practice
- The challenges of implementing widening participation in my school
- How can my sixth-form college improve students' AS results?
- Examining the impact of education maintenance allowance (EMA) in year 11.

Or explore the development within the 14–19 education sector:

- Exploring partnership within the X region
- Implementing the 14–19 Diploma in X partnership: opportunities and issues
- Should FE colleges focus on vocational education?

Or examine some pedagogical issues within your subject specialism:

- Improving the teaching and learning transition between AS and A2 Sociology
- Exploring the role of problem-solving activities in the development of critical thinking on BTEC in Business and ICT courses.

Or perhaps other issues that are more generic:

- Using Drama to manage students' behaviour
- Do school trips improve learning?
- Gender issues and teaching 'role models' at KS4.

Becoming involved in research

Except for teacher action research, which can be organised within you own institution, you may already have identified some potential barriers to undertaking research alongside your role as tutor/teacher – a lack of time is one, but problems can also be experienced concerning gaining consent, finding willing participants and managing to secure all the necessary resources. The value of research as part of your ongoing professional development should not be underestimated, but unfortunately many schools and colleges are underequipped to deal with such projects or deployment of staff.

The following bodies and institutions may enable the researcher to formulate, support and fund a potential piece of research:

- The Research Inform Teaching project is aimed at linking research to teaching more closely in higher education. The Higher Education Funding Council (HEFCE) also funds research projects in further education institutions offering higher education courses. For further information visit the HFCE website: **www.hefce.ac.uk**.

- The National Teacher Research Panel offers research participation in current research in 14–19 education context, but could also sponsor a research paper. For more information contact NTRP at: **www.standards.dfes.gov.uk/ntrp**.

- The General Teaching Council's research of the month **http://www.gtce.org.uk/teachers/rft/** provides a concrete example of the type of research a practitioner-researcher can undertake.

- The Institute for Learning, the professional body for teachers and trainers in further education (FE) and skills, welcomes post compulsory education practitioners' involvement with research and will 'support practitioners to develop their own research skills and conduct action research' (IFL's 5-year strategy) **www.ifl.ac.uk**.

- It might also be worth checking with local universities to see if they have any conferences you could disseminate your research to. Most Higher Education Teacher Training or Education Studies departments have an interest in teacher research.

SUMMARY

In this chapter we have been exploring the role of the teacher-researcher. We have provided an overview of issues to consider while undertaking a research project. Undeniably, investigating a particular issue within teaching and learning brings a range of benefits to the researcher and its immediate educational context. Research projects are also beneficial to your own professional development. They not only encourage you to be more critical about your practice, they also highlight some of the issues arising in educational settings. Teacher-research projects may also generate a 14–19 education research culture needed to contribute both to the overall development of professional teachers and to education as a whole.

Find out more

Colin Robson (2002) *Real World Research*: a comprehensive and accessible research companion from theory to practice, from planning to the research writing. The book also offers exemplars which can be adapted to own research. An essential book to cover all types of research.

Jean McNiff, Pamela Lomax and Jack Whitehead (1996) *You and Your Action Research Project*: a very practical book guiding you through every step of the action research process.

John Elliott (1991) *Action Research for Educational Change*: the book critically discusses the nature of action research and its role for change within the educational context. It also contains informing case studies of specific action research projects.

Bibliography

Bell, J. (2005) *Doing Your Research Project* (4th edn), Milton Keynes: Open University Press.

Cohen, L., Manion, L. and Morrison, K. (2000) *Research Methods in Education* (5th edn), London: Routledge Falmer.

Elliot, J. (1991) *Action Research for Educational Change*, Buckingham: Open University Press.

Hillier, Y. and Jameson, J. (2003) *Empowering Researchers in Further Education*, Stoke on Trent: Trentham Books.

McNiff, J. and Whitehead, J. (2002) *Action Research: principles and practice* (2nd edn), London: Routledge.

McNiff, J., Lomax, P. and Whitehead, J. (1996) *You and Your Action Research Project*, London: RoutledgeFalmer.

Open University (2001) *Research Methods in Education*, Milton Keynes: Open University Press.

Robson, C. (2002) *Real World Research* (2nd edn), Oxford, Blackwell Publishing.

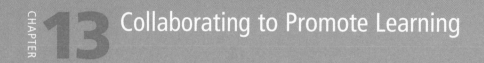

CHAPTER 13 Collaborating to Promote Learning

In this chapter you will:

- Consider what is meant by collaboration to promote learning
- Explore some of the factors that produce effective collaborations and those which may have a negative influence
- Examine specific examples of different forms of collaboration, e.g. schools with colleges, workplace, HE, home or community settings
- Consider how the impact of collaboration might be measured and how you might inform your own decisions for collaborative teaching and learning
- Critically examine ideas of collaboration in relation to your own practice

Pearson Education Ltd./Ian Wedgewood

Introduction

What is collaboration and why has it become so significant for teachers? Put simply, it is individuals working together to achieve a common purpose. Teachers have always done this to some extent within schools and colleges, but the increasing importance of learner choice and self direction, the challenge of wider partnerships and new structures makes this area far more exciting and demanding than before.

Qualification reform has placed the work of teachers, learners and organisations working together at the heart of 14–19 developments. Great value has been attributed to good communication, joint efforts and coherent approaches among all those involved in teaching, supporting, advising and potentially employing young people.

This policy approach seems to define ideal collaboration as planned and coherent localised endeavours directed towards raising the achievements of pupils and students wherever they are based. In Chapter 17, the structures and operation of more formal partnership management is explained and discussed. In this chapter we will be looking at the situation for teachers and learners who have to work together for success. In the 14–19 context, reforms promise more control over choices and outcomes and this is intended to result in greater cooperation among those providing qualifications so that, for example, expertise in a skills area or subject is shared, not limited to learners in one specialised school or college setting.

While there are always many different ways in which similar outcomes might be achieved and disagreement between political parties and among teachers about what works and why, most would agree that educators, parent and employers should provide good role models of collaborating where this serves the best interests of learners. By the end of this chapter you should feel better equipped to shape your own views on what continues to be a complex and important area for your practice.

Background

Diploma qualification developments have raised the profile of collaboration. The Diploma requires teachers to work together across groups of institutions and to draw in employers, communities and learners. The qualifications also expect learners to collaborate with others, and so teachers and all those involved should really be modelling constructive collaboration in order to support pupils and students as they move into adult work and life.

The sense of mutual working beyond traditional boundaries is captured in some of the material used to promote and explain these qualifications. The emphasis is frequently on joint working, with collaborative approaches given prominence in relation to both development and delivery of learning. Teaching approaches for this phase are best matched to promote learning through both content and modes of delivery which model collaborative practice. As the principles suggest, Diplomas involve:

- Education (*not* training)
- Composite Qualifications

- Lines of Learning (*not* subjects)
- Curriculum based
- Collaboration and partnership to develop
- Collaboration and partnership to deliver
- A new approach to learning
- Mixing applied and general learning
- Emphasising skills as well as knowledge.

QCA (Qualifications and Curriculum Authority) Presentation 2008

'Collaboration is not a new idea and we want to build on existing good practice, such as that developed in the 14–19 Pathfinders and the Increased Flexibility Programme. However, collaboration would need to happen more systematically if all learners are to have access to a range of options, delivered in institutions with appropriate facilities and expertise.' The Tomlinson Report (DfES 2004) gained widespread support when it expressed in clear terms issues and proposals obvious to many professionals. Schools and colleges had been driven over many years to compete rather than to cooperate with one another, and cultures of competition may be seen as influencing parents who change post codes to gain access to certain schools and in some of the well-publicised cases relating to selection. The report, published on 18 October 2004, sought to ensure that 'all young people are equipped with the skills and knowledge they need to succeed and progress in education, employment and adult life' (Press release 18.10. 2004). It proposed a range of reforms, including a new Diploma framework and many elements which would require far higher levels of collaboration than had previously been found.

For example, some of the Tomlinson Report (DfES, 2004) proposals below could be considered in terms of their implications for teachers and students working together across institutions or more collaboratively within one school or college:

- Vocational courses and pathways would become part of the single diploma framework. This would allow students to move between courses while accumulating transferable credits and could support progress to higher education courses.

- Improved differentiation for advanced level students as more difficult options will be added to examinations to add 'stretch'. These would be introduced firstly to the existing system as A-plus and A-double plus grades before the diploma was introduced.

- On 'graduating' students would receive a transcript of all their achievements, including a breakdown of individual module marks. These would be available to universities via an online system.

- The curriculum should develop personal skills including problem solving, teamwork and study skills. Also students would be encouraged to use their skills and knowledge creatively and to think for themselves.

- The extended project would allow the development of investigation, planning, research, analysis and presentation skills.

So what is meant by collaborating to promote learning? In the most straightforward sense this type of collaboration should mean thoughtful, well-planned and flexible systems to increase opportunities for learners, to share resources including teachers and facilities and to enable professionals and learners themselves to work together rather than in competition. As can be seen from the example above, effective collaboration aims to stretch and challenge learners by extending the scope and context of their experiences and by putting them in new situations made available through collaboration.

The proliferation of policy, theory and practice literature racing to capture and label all aspects of this rather arbitrarily defined phase has resulted in a confused and ill-defined currency of terms. The language used in some education-related contexts can cloud rather than clarify our views of the various aspects of this relatively new territory. In this chapter the focus will be on the actual conditions and relationships which constitute and affect teaching and learning in order that readers can form their own opinions and explore some of the concepts in practice.

Partnerships of different kinds both formal, as for example a school which is a member of a Diploma consortium, and informal, where for example cooperation occurs without contracts or financial transactions, are necessary to establish and maintain collaborative activity, and ideally they should not act as barriers to the real business of learning. Collaboration can occur outside longer-term partnerships so the two terms are not just interchangeable. It is important to take a broad and open view of the term in order to encourage initiative and experiment at all levels of collaboration rather than to wait for local authorities, head teachers or government to set up large-scale and permanent systems. Collaboration encompasses all types of joint working towards shared goals, including ongoing teaching and learning activities, their evaluation and resulting relationships. The choices which determine how and with whom we work should be informed by both near and far perspectives if we wish to do our best for all learners in these challenging times.

In one area this may be as simple as a shared trip for pupils studying drama to a local theatre for a performance followed by a workshop at which they get to hear a wider range of views than usual and to enjoy learning with a different group of peers. Two teachers can save on costs and gain in learning terms on many levels just by trying something different. This is a real and far from uncommon example; another involves the occasional shared use of photography equipment and a specialised teacher to enrich art and design sessions. In neither case was there a formal school partnership, though such small beginnings can flourish and produce mature and very productive partnerships over the long term.

Making collaboration work

Recent education reforms have been rapid and frequent, and teachers can find that the parameters for planning, delivery and evaluation of teaching, learning and assessment change year on year in both major and minor respects. Funding matters have a significant impact on what can be accomplished and who should be involved, and the agencies and government departments concerned are themselves being dissolved and reformed at a time when consistent frameworks and shared agendas should be of paramount importance. The formal partnerships for training teachers, supporting learners and delivering new and revised qualifications have themselves been strained by economic factors and future uncertainties relating to education policy.

For example, 14–19-year-olds may be taught by both qualified and unqualified teachers who may work together in one school but whose training, qualifications and continuing professional development will differ significantly. Collaborative-working relationships for both newly qualified and very experienced staff can become strained under circumstances where pay, conditions and training arrangements are very different. Graduates new to teaching do not always value the extensive and often equivalent experience and qualification of colleagues from the learning and skills sector with vocational and occupational backgrounds, and this can be a barrier to good working relationships and exciting projects for learners.

Parents, learners, local government and education professionals can all be affected by the shifts, developments and confusion that policy and initiative overloads can create. It is beyond the scope of the writing here to address such overarching issues but we must acknowledge the impact and irony stemming from failures of collaboration at the highest levels over recent times. Good teachers will naturally collaborate where they perceive potential benefits for their learners.

Collaboration is vital to the success of recent reforms in the 14–19 phase which aim to establish maximum choice and sound foundations for work and life within key group of young people. The benefits for the economy and wider society as well as for individuals have been widely promoted but the implementation of reform has been fraught with difficulties and, in some vital areas, by a dearth of joined-up strategy. Given the high ideals and the commendable achievements and progress made in some areas, the stakes are very high as each piece of legislation is signed off and each funding round passes. Significant investment in all forms, political and professional reputations and, most importantly, the futures of young learners are all in the balance.

The Pathfinder Programmes were an important trial of wider collaborative working and produced some durable partnerships and positive outcomes still influencing current developments. The 14–19 pathfinders were first proposed in the Government's Green Paper *14–19: Extending Opportunities, Raising Standards*.

Their objective was to test the local delivery of 14–19 education in a range of settings, and to identify and spread good practice. There were 39 pathfinders who took part in the programme, which ran from January 2003 until August 2005 (**www.dfes.gov.uk/ 14-/dsp_pathfinders**). Their importance was the way in which they highlighted the significance of extended collaboration for achievements in this area.

In their evaluation of the second year of the 14–19 Pathfinder programmes, Higham and Yeomans (2005) examine the progress achieved across the pathfinders and raise key issues from the evaluation for practitioners and policy makers. In summary, one of the key findings was 'the positive impact of the continued development of extensive collaborative arrangements which provide a strong basis for further development' (p. 3).

CASE STUDY

Collaborative approaches to 14–19 provision: an evaluation of the second year of the 14–19 Pathfinder Initiative

The importance of institutional collaboration in developing a flexible, coherent 14–19 phase has been a central feature of the reform agenda. Therefore pathfinders are required to work closely with a wide range of local partners including Local Learning and Skills Councils* (*The Learning and Skills Council has managed Further Education in England 2001 until March 2010 when it was replaced by the Young Peoples Learning Agency and the Skills Funding Agency under the DCSF and DBIS. With a budget of around £13 billion, it was the largest agency funding education – and was structured around 47 local councils across the regions*), local education authorities, employers, colleges, schools, training providers, higher education institutions and the Connexions service. Pathfinders are also expected to show how they propose to take account of the views of young people in developing and implementing their plans.

Key points

- Collaboration remains at the heart of the 14–19 Pathfinder initiative
- The vast majority of pathfinders continue to report good progress in collaborative working
- The forms which collaboration takes in individual pathfinders is brought about by interaction between national, local and institutional policies and local contextual factors* (*such as employment opportunities, types of schools and specific issues in, for example, regeneration areas or Education Action Zones*)
- Collaboration in an individual pathfinder varies in institutional inclusivity* (*whether institutions will allow very full or only partial access to others and/or allow its learners/staff scope to work outside*), the levels at which it operates, its substantive focus and its geographical scope
- It is still too early to assess the impact of collaboration on student participation, retention, achievement and progression but it has brought a significant broadening of curriculum provision and has enhanced student information, support and guidance processes

(Higham 2005)

*added notes

DISCUSSION POINT

How far do you agree with the identification of collaboration as a central success factor in 14–19 reform? Does your own experience lead you to believe that small-scale collaboration between teachers or across schools is having/can have a significant impact on learning? What factors from the chapter so far suggest threats or opportunities for collaboration?

What seems to have emerged from the complex and extended processes of policy research, consultation, debate, introduction, qualifications development, marketing and revisions within sectors is an approach which combines new freedoms with the previously familiar tight specifications. Although schools and colleges are still constrained by the need to compete for learners, to achieve to quotas and targets and be business-focused, there seems to be a more pragmatic acceptance emerging that for real collaborations to work across such complex and different contexts, support and encouragement must be given to all kinds of inter-professional and cross-institution relationships and to the establishment of more sustainable working approaches in those communities and agencies involved in young learners' lives. Perhaps each school and college does not have to stand alone in business terms and we may see far more supportive joint working and real collaboration for the benefit of learners and ultimately society.

As Hodgson, Spours and Wright (2005) clearly pointed out when arguing for strong collaboration, it must be 'focused on the needs of a local learning area rather than simply on the individual needs of any one of the partners.'

Two specific examples of such collaborations for the promotion of learning are included here; from careers guidance to a school initiative to support learners collaborating with their peers, both provide some illustration of the variety and scope of this kind of work.

CASE STUDIES

Collaboration to meet local need

In two schools set in a rural location without good transport links, collaboration has been used to bring pupils together out of school by involving them in community-work-based projects over a wide area. Clearing and cleaning of a nature reserve and some restoration in a club room enabled staff and students to get to know one another through the projects and to set up curriculum-related initiatives. IT equipment was installed in the new facility and shared and peer support activities were undertaken through a buddy scheme which helped link up local young people who had been more isolated.

The improvement in relations between the pupils and the schools is still producing many benefits and seems to have improved attendance for some learners. Enthusiasm and time on the part of the teachers who initiated the work was required since the pupils involved volunteered but this in itself was a positive as it promoted independence and provided some good role models for others.

In another school there had been a number of problems around good careers advice and guidance for some of the more specialised vocational routes and it was felt by staff and some parents that the learners were not being best served. A collaboration was developed with a local college which allowed access not only to improved advice but also to taster sessions and some placements in established employer links. This resulted in progression routes being opened up with high-quality information and better liaison to ensure that places were appropriate for the students.

College learners also benefited and there are plans to extend the placement and taster initiatives.

The examples above may serve to illustrate that collaboration can be simple, relatively quick to set up and yet very effective. They may help you to identify similar opportunities in future.

Evaluating collaboration to promote learning

It seems clear from teachers engaged in working with others, and from those in positions of authority attempting to make such work easier and more widespread, that there are many opportunities and challenges. In order to review what kinds of activities might be found and what issues can arise when these are put into practice, the table below may be helpful. See overleaf for an in-practice application.

Some features of collaborative approaches for promoting learning	Barriers and additional issues relevant to collaborating for learning
<ul><li>Learning environments open to outsiders</li><li>Learners move into external learning environments – work-based and field contexts, other schools, colleges and community settings</li><li>Teachers enable learners to work independently with a range of people</li><li>Mixed school, college and work-based cohorts</li><li>Mixed age and qualification aim groups</li><li>Active involvement with progression partners – employers, universities, colleges</li><li>Modelling collaboration for young people and developing their peer support for learning</li><li>Regular group engagement with families, not just individual parents/carers</li><li>Frequent opportunities for trips and shared informal, social activities</li><li>Use of technologies for joint working</li></ul>	<ul><li>Resource implications – increased administration</li><li>Perceived and real bureaucratic barriers (e.g. ensuring learner safety but overcoming/finding solutions to outdated regulations if they are no longer appropriate)</li><li>Training and development costs</li><li>Location and distance</li><li>Risk assessments, communication across appropriate professionals and with homes/individual learners</li><li>Vetting and supervising, duty of care to ensure the safety of learners in external settings</li><li>Coherence and consistency re equality and diversity requirements</li><li>Monitoring and tracking issues</li><li>Issues arising from joint work on flexible design and planning of approaches (see Chapter 14 on individual learning)</li><li>Safeguarding issues must be carefully addressed, and compatibility can be an issue</li></ul>

WHAT DO YOU THINK?

Which of these are most likely to have an impact in your own context? Would you be put off by the barriers and issues; consider what strategies you might employ to overcome them?

What other features or issues can you add?

IN PRACTICE

You could use this to do an informal survey of what kinds of practice you can identify in your own placement/area or wider region. Compare notes with others for collaborative learning. If you are training, it may form the basis for a useful investigative project

The advantages and disadvantages of collaboration are often more complicated to assess than they appear to be. For example, you will often hear about the time and expense involved in organising and implementing what are seen to be more innovative approaches to learning. However, where there are long-standing partnerships and well-tried networks and relationships – in relatively small communities or in centres where circumstances have driven cooperation forward as a necessity – then the very factors which initially seem to mitigate against joined-up working may lay the foundations for sustainability.

Cornwall College (which will also provide a more detailed case later in the chapter), the largest provider of FE in the UK, has, for example, grown its provision for learners of all ages by working in a highly collaborative way across multiple sites; it provides learning for this phase alongside schools and progression to HE in order to serve a widely distributed population in a region where the geography has an impact on the access to learning of many students.

 CASE STUDY

Cornwall College has made extensive use of collaboration in a positive way to provide 14–19 and especially 14–16 opportunities. On its website, collaboration is highlighted from the point of view of promoting learning:

As the 14–19 agenda gathers pace it is important for Cornwall College to provide opportunities to learners and schools in order to make learning more flexible at Key Stage 4, as well as provide flexibility post 16.

> As a result of our commitment to this, we operate two Increased Flexibility Programmes (IFP) – one in East Cornwall, the other in the St Austell area. We are partners in the other two Cornish IFPs, one led by Truro College the other by Penwith.
>
> This collaboration means that each of our seven campuses are involved in providing the broadest possible curriculum to 14–16 year olds within the County. In addition we offer individual schools the opportunity to develop other partnerships with us and provide a range of options outside the Increased Flexibility Programme [see Appendix 13.3 for detail of IFP].
>
> **(www.cornwall.ac.uk/)**

The wider reputation of an effective network spreads over time. Volunteers may become involved in projects which settle into community life and time can be given freely. Processes for Criminal Records Bureau (CRB) and other checks are set up and become more accepted and understood. Where support and information are clear, then issues that might have become barriers tend to disappear. The advantages in terms of relationship-building and opportunities for modelling collaborative working within a community can be invaluable in terms of setting a positive and constructive example for children and young people.

> We know that different learning environments and institutional structures have a significant effect on learners themselves. But there are many discontinuities between school, further education, higher education and the workplace. Perhaps more effective learning contexts and linkages could be created. Such developments would emphasise the need for critically reflexive teachers, tutors and other staff who can support learners' adaptation to new environments and respond to a diverse range of students.
>
> *(Hodkinson and Colley 2006)*

Learning environments that support **deep learning** processes are likely to require extensive collaboration between different types of providers, whether schools, colleges or workplaces. Whether collaboration is facilitated or constrained is itself a system-wide issue. To meet the varying needs of pupils and to open a wider range of vocational options to more people, some proposals for reform presuppose a much greater degree of collaboration between schools, colleges and workplaces than we see today. Policy levers, funding and support all need to be in alignment if this ambition is to be achieved. Collaboration is expensive, while other policies, and factors such as the existence of performance tables, may act as a spur to competition between schools and colleges.

Collaborative home and school/college working becomes truly participatory when parents and carers are drawn in to contribute together with staff rather than simply being informed or consulted through fixed channels. In such situations talents are shared and weaker areas addressed, and the kinds of tensions which might undermine learner progress are more easily overcome. Parents and carers who have a voice learn to make more effort and remain involved. The contacts gained through personal links can result in access to work experience, employment opportunities and expertise for projects as well as promoting the learning of individual pupils and students.

Source: Pearson Education Ltd. Lord and Leverett

Photo 13.1
Working in real
employment
settings

Creativity – approaches to collaboration

IN PRACTICE

Creative responses to support collaboration – based on successful examples:

- Changing attitudes to encourage and celebrate shared projects and long-term partnerships – enhancing of extended school work, learner enterprises, use of new technologies, international links/exchanges

- Maintaining links to learning in both social and formal strands of learner experience – through teacher/pupil teams and school councils, college representation

- Developing forms of peer education to suit particular school/college/external contexts

- Developing from existing strengths – institutional and individual existing collaborations and cross-curricular work; or sport, arts, leisure and voluntary work activities which may provide opportunities to support more formal learning – e.g. student journalism

- Enabling young learners to take the initiative and develop their own ideas in collaboration with their contemporaries – charity and volunteering work, events organisation, school policies and council work, participation in national forum work, problem-solving activities
- Establishing wider cross-institution and workplace relationships for effective collaboration (see Chapter 17, Extending Partnerships)
- Building expectations among all parties involved – promoting parental, community and employer initiatives, e.g. small business and charity schemes and sponsorship
- Ensuring that the outcomes from the learning are shared and celebrated.

How far has your own school/college (placement) travelled in terms of collaborative practice beyond the institution?

What further innovation would be possible and potentially beneficial for your learners? Could any of the ideas above apply, and if the case does reflect practice that you have experienced what benefits can you identify or what issues have you encountered?

By working towards fully or partially shared goals and enjoying support through interaction and effort invested in the pursuit of common interests, teachers and learners gain more than just a fixed set of outcomes from a completed project. Most of us are aware of the value inherent in the participation itself. Tensions develop and dissolve, barriers are perceived and overcome, and participants commit and move on. The learning process experienced by those involved is often quoted as being the most powerful aspect of this kind of relationship.

As developing teachers, we are clearly well aware that the values represented in collaboration to promote learning are deeply embedded in the standards for teachers in both sectors. Hodgson and Spours (2005) asserted that Tomlinson's more unified and fully collaborative system was of greater value in the minds of the majority of practitioners than the partial approach finally adopted in the 14–19 reforms. This approach meant that only some institutions and some staff, chiefly those involved in vocational education, were fully involved. Full collaboration in the original sense would have included the full range of vocational, academic and applied learning with teachers, employers and wider community participation.

In later work a more detailed examination of 14–19 learning systems is undertaken and produces a Nuffield Review of 14–19 Education and Training (for further details on the Nuffield Review, see Appendix 13.2) seminar paper on 14–19 Collaborative learning systems (2005a) in which Hodgson, Spours and Wright claim to

> make an initial attempt to develop a concept of '14–19 collaborative learning system' as a way of focusing on learning and learner needs; the relationships between providers in a local area and the respective roles of local and national policy in 14–19 education and training.

> [I]n the paper we identify six key dimensions of 14–19 collaborative learning systems through which we compare the Government's 14–19 White Paper 'partial routeway' approach and the Tomlinson Final Report 'unified system' approach. We argue that an effective and inclusive 14–19 collaborative learning system is closer to the second than the first but that there are overlaps between the two and potential for movement from the first to the second. We conclude the paper by arguing for strong collaboration focused on the needs of a local learning area rather than simply on the individual needs of any one of the partners.

The Nuffield Foundation funded a six-year independent review of 14–19 education and training from October 2003 to September 2009. The team brought to the Review extensive networks of research and development – the many schools and local education authorities associated with the Institute's London Region Post-14 Network, the ESRC Research Centre on Skills, Knowledge and Organisational Performance (SKOPE), directed jointly by Oxford and Cardiff, the incomparable links between UCAS and schools and higher education institutions.

This learning system model was produced from a focus on collaborative learning. The table below lays out the two versions (weak and strong) of the learning system, clearly illustrating full and partial collaboration to show the differences.

Dimensions of the learning system	Partial route-based/weakly collaborative approach	Unified system/strongly collaborative approach
Vision, purposes and underpinning principles	Academic and a new strong vocational route. Main purpose: participation up to 19 and employability. Principle: choice of route way and entitlement to the 'basics'.	Vision: comprehensive system with transformation of secondary and upper secondary education and training as a whole. Main purpose: preparation for adult life and lifelong learning. Principle: entitlement to common 'formation' and choice within this.
Curriculum, qualifications and assessment	Divided curriculum and qualifications arrangements with separate but clearer progression routes based on individual free-standing qualifications. Credit-based Framework for Achievement does not apply to general/academic qualifications.	Unified credit-based diploma system for all 14–19 learners based on holistic learner programmes, with clear ladder of progression and high degrees of local innovation and discretion.
Planning and organisation in a 'local area'	Specialisation, competition and collaboration with the possibility of clear distinctions between institutional types (e.g. grammar schools and FE colleges); area planning primarily focused on the vocational route.	Focus on planning comprehensive provision across a local area and the possibility of rationalisation and specialisation within the unified framework. Clearer limits to institutional autonomy and possible changes to governance arrangements.

Dimensions of the learning system	Partial route-based/weakly collaborative approach	Unified system/strongly collaborative approach
Professionalism, pedagogy and leadership	Capacity building primarily for vocational learning. Tolerance of different conditions of service and professional development for those working in FE, schools and work-based training. Main focus on delivery and recognition of a vocational route with the aspiration to involve employers more fully.	Capacity building for innovative general and vocational learning and assessment to support the new unified system and the transformation vision. No distinction between conditions of service and professional development for those working in FE, schools and work-based training. Focus on delivery and recognition of all types of learning, including wider activities and learning in the community.
Physical learning environments and communications systems	Main focus on new vocational learning environments and communications systems aimed mainly at tracking achievement and supporting choices across a divided system.	Focus on learning environments for both general and vocational learning and communications systems aimed to create new relationships between learning, assessment and personal progress.
A progressive accountability framework	Top-down levers (e.g. performance tables, targets, inspection, funding) to drive institutional behaviour; mainly based on individual institutional performance but including 'progression targets'. No local quality assurance development – standards assured through national external exams.	Emphasis on bottom-up 'aspirational' targets; main focus on monitoring performance across an area at 19 based on collaborative targets for participation, achievement and progression; creation of local, transparent quality assurance systems alongside national awarding and validating systems.

(Hodgson and Spours 2005)

RESEARCH FOCUS

Using the table above which provides a summary and framework for analysis relating to structures and strategies supporting 14–19 provision, consider the following questions:

What aspects of the Hodgson and Spours Dimensions of Learning System (illustrated above) are most evident within the 14–19 provision as it stands today?

Can it be characterised as weakly or strongly collaborative in each of the six possible dimensions of the system set out? (2005: 9)

Finally, how far, if at all, does the following judgement still apply? The work from the Nuffield Review used above and below provides one strong view of what is wrong and what should be done. Do you agree with the authors?   ◗

RESEARCH FOCUS: *CONTINUED*

Currently, the Government approach lacks consistency – it wants to micro-manage institutional behaviour while supporting institutional autonomy within a rhetoric of collaboration. This approach we have termed 'weakly collaborative'.

The logic of 14–19 collaborative learning systems requires three inter-related national policy shifts – a more unified curriculum and qualifications approach; a supportive accountability framework for strong collaboration focused on the needs of a learning area rather than on the individual needs of any one of the partners; and reciprocity of local and national policies which provides genuine space for local determination.

(Hodgson, Spours and Wright 2005)

Promoting learner collaboration

Modelling high-level collaboration can be achieved as described through the establishment of quality partnerships, but the real work of collaborating to promote learning takes place over time through positive and constructive relationships. In order to benefit learners, we should ask them to do as we do rather than just placing them in difficult and poorly managed practical situations, and then expecting them to collaborate with one another, work in teams and develop PLTS. We may be team teaching and drawing in student mentors who can be tremendously valuable in generating and sustaining motivation and providing knowledge and guidance. Paired and team teaching acts as a powerful model of how students and pupils should work together for common goals, and is all the more significant when it is cross-institutional.

> The way we work with our learners is of paramount importance . . . But we also need to think about the ways in which we work with other members of staff at colleges, training centres or adult education institutions.

(Tummons 2007)

Peer collaboration can open doors to learning for all kinds of students. Young disaffected learners can be re-engaged and others can provide mutual support, inspiration and networks. The sense of well-being experienced by successful peer mentors and mentees is very empowering and affects young learners not directly involved in such projects. The ripple effect of delegating responsibility and trusting children and young people should never be underestimated. There are many highly effective professionals who will testify to the fact that the more you expect from learners and believe they can achieve, the more they will produce. Such achievement where real and independent learning has been generated is of greater long-term value to the individual in their life and work than any quick-fix strategy or incentive, however attractive.

CASE STUDY

European project with a focus on collaboration to promote learning

Five European partners (including universities and professional learning providers) from Denmark, UK, Romania, Italy and Poland are participating in a European project involving young learners in schools. The PRESTO (peer related education supporting tools) Project focuses on two key areas: 'Learning to learn' and peer education in various forms and in different national settings/learning environments.

It aims to:

- Promote the learning to learn competence among European students aged 14+ using peer education
- Contribute to reducing early school leaving and insufficient school completion in EU schools.

Peer education, familiar in UK practice, refers to a variety of different activities that you are likely to have already had experience of implementing and managing in your school, such as peer mentoring, peer teaching, peer learning, peer assessment, student voice facilitation and support from external agencies.

The connection between the two focus areas of such a project is clearly very important, because learning especially in the 14–19 phase should involve increasing learner autonomy as each young person develops and prepares to move into adult life and work. This means that they can manage their own learning as they develop their skills and knowledge.

Far from being mutually exclusive, collaborative work and independent working are interrelated and mutually supportive facets of the learning journey. Young learners value the society and support of peers, and individual engagement and communication rests on the wider relationship with the whole of a learner's sphere. This is acknowledged to be their home, health, interests, background and beliefs, but it is just as important to include their friends and classmates.

The project is highly collaborative in principle and in practice. In this case collaboration works on several levels. There is the obvious high-level cross national and institutional structure which will ensure the maximum dissemination and professional benefit from project outcomes and learning. In turn each country is employing collaborative approaches using existing schools, colleges or other learning providers in order to reach appropriate teachers and learners.

Shared guides and activities are produced and evaluated and a website has been set up through project participants from each country. For example, video work from students can be shared along with blogs and reflections relating to peer learning.

In particular the core aims relate to the development of peer education as it promotes learning, and this growing field has generated many very positive examples of learner autonomy and effective practice relating to inclusion, behaviours for learning and raised achievement.

Participating schools may concentrate on developing a particular area of peer education involving selected learners and colleagues during the project period. As the work progresses they join with other education professionals to exchange experience and expertise across Europe. Sharing practice and the transfer of experience across contexts and systems can then develop into further collaboration to benefit greater numbers of learners. The project involves school-based activities and sharing of resources in various forms that will be displayed on the project website. The website has areas for students and staff, and resources range from videos to student journals. The UK partner is Canterbury Christ Church University.

Source: Pearson Education Ltd. Rob Judges

Photo 13.2
Learning
new skills for
employment

Increasing numbers of school students are studying in FE and work settings. Their experience can be highly successful and very rewarding but there are also many narratives of failure, difficulty and poorly managed risk. As a low status, low resource option this kind of provision so central to the collaborative spirit and planning of decades of 14–19 reform work will never succeed. The organisation, commitment, staffing and infrastructures must be of high quality. Where this is the case, learners do progress and the collaboration of professionals results in learners collaborating to learn.

CASE STUDY

Cornwall College – school students in FE 14–16

This case study illustrates how the collaboration modelled by professionals and institutions concerned to promote best practice can result in real learning improvements.
(from *Teaching 14–19-year-olds in college in Cornwall College* **'teach'** *resource – a*

collaborative production from the Advisory Teacher Team at this large multi-site college. David Degenhardt shares his success teaching 14–16 learners in a construction department:

In the Construction Department at Cornwall College St. Austell we have about 160 students aged 14–16 coming to us from schools and studying on the Future

Pathways programme. I have been responsible for organising this programme for the last four years so I have had the opportunity to consider the differences, for the teacher, between these 14–16 groups and over-16 learners. I believe there are definite differences in the learners' attitude to their course, and following on from this, there are also differences in the ways in which we need to approach teaching them.

. . . One characteristic of these learners . . . is that the 14–16 year olds typically come to us from school with a real fear of theory lessons. We have attempted to alleviate this anxiety by ensuring that there is a ratio of 70% to 80% practical learning against 20–30% theory. The learners never spend more than 25 minutes in the classroom,

however they must understand that this is necessary to ensure their understanding of practical work and the assessment. All theory discussed in the classroom is always reinforced through the practical session which follows.

Many of our students have real difficulties with writing, and one way in which we attempt to overcome this is getting them to work in small groups, where they can support one another. This also has the advantages that they learn to take turns and that they all have the opportunity to develop leadership skills.

The small groups are carefully chosen by the teacher in the first instance to avoid potentially troubled partnerships. This secures good working relationships in these groups right from the very beginning.

Professional collaboration for teacher development

Teachers who collaborate for their own professional learning are better able to promote learning in their pupils and students. They reflect on practice and make valuable contacts to support their work. There is a huge variety of valuable networks and associations providing frameworks and support for collaborating professionals. These range from established national and local subject specialism groups, through the activities for development and shared delivery within consortia, federations, etc. to broader networks for representation and bodies supporting and sometimes funding a wide range of research in teaching. Of vital importance is the promotion of professional collaborations for learning at all levels and for a range of purposes. Membership of appropriate networks and organisations support practice through shared research, events, shared member contributions, project participation and collaborative working initiatives. Continued professional development can be both formal and informal, run through school, college or university providers and be accredited in some cases, or far more personalised to the individual's professional context. Whatever the case, there is fertile ground across the sectors to participate in action research or to engage with others in activities related to collaborating to promote learning. (See Appendix 13.1 for contacts and details.)

It is important to consider what kind of role professional collaboration can play in the long-term promotion of learning. As can be seen from the short sample list above, networks and organisations can gather professionals together at all kinds of levels, nationally and internationally in order to stimulate and support ideas exchange, research and relationship-building within disciplines and phases or cross-cutting boundaries. The purposes of subsequent collaborations and participations are as diverse but very often fruitful, and at their best such interaction and engagement is reported as having a high impact on teaching and learning. World-class education should be research-informed and keen to open itself to critical collaboration, debate and change. The best teachers are motivated to be better and tend to seek out inspiration, advice, best practice and challenging colleagues.

The example below outlines the aims and approaches of one professional network. This is an interesting example of a more extended approach to collaboration, with action research at its heart and a very broad inclusive view of potential contributing professional collaborators. (For a collaborative professional case study, see Appendix 13.4.)

CASE STUDY

Economic and Social Research Council Teaching and Learning Research Programme transforming learning cultures in further education: TLC

This project was established to understand and transform learning cultures in further education through four partnerships between FE colleges and universities. The TLC project was funded by ESRC and part of the Teaching and Learning Research Programme. It identified collaborative relationships with employment as one of the key issues with implications for policy making in 14–19 vocational education and training.

Vocational education and training (VET) programmes require relationships with their relevant employment sectors. There should be a close relationship between the knowledge, skills and understanding needed in the sector and the curriculum of a VET course. VET courses provide either progression from the course into related employment, or relevant off-the-job

education for trainees already working in a firm. These two purposes are linked, but making them work is fraught with difficulty. For example, many students' original job-related expectations were not realised in four of the VET programmes studied in the TLC project. In another programme, students claimed that their job prospects had improved but not because of increased understanding of the workplace.

Each situation brings different strengths and weaknesses. The most effective VET provision is likely to be found when college and employer links are close and synergistic. Fuller and Unwin (2003) showed how such close links can work well in a modern apprenticeship scheme in the steel industry. Our research showed equally effective provision for nursery nurses that was college-led. In both cases, on-the-job training experiences and college-based off-the-job VET were mutually supportive. Both were valued by all concerned – employers, tutors and students. In the case of nursery nursing, the two-year period on the course helped the majority of students who completed to progress easily into employment.

This very success revealed associated problems. Existing values and practices in the sector were difficult to challenge. There were occasional tensions, as when the college tutors helped students to understand and adopt principles of equality of opportunity, while some students routinely encountered racist attitudes in their work placements. Other issues could not be raised, because close links with the workplace rendered them invisible. Key among these was female gender stereotyping, associated with low status and low pay. A linked issue was emotional labour. By this we mean that nursery nurses must bottle up and constrain their feelings, regardless of their own emotional well-being, yet acknowledge and deal supportively with intense emotional pressures and demands from the children (Colley 2006).

Where links between college and employers are less close, there can be different problems. On a male-dominated engineering day-release course, many students struggled to see the value and relevance of what was taught in the college. Their identity was formed at work, and they did not regard themselves as students. This situation may allow college tutors to introduce theory and methods not found at work, and thus challenge aspects of existing working practices. However, the risk is that the more they do this, the less notice some students will take. Here too, emotions played a role in inclusion and exclusion, as students completed or dropped out according to their ability to cope with the demands of college work in addition to full-time employment and family responsibilities (Colley et al. 2003).

An increasing number of VET courses have no substantial employer links or even work experience. This was the case on a GNVQ business education course and is likely to be the case in many successors to GNVQ programmes including vocational GCSEs. Students enrolled on the full-time course intending to learn skills to get them good jobs in business. Business-related knowledge, skills and understanding were taught successfully and tutors were unconstrained by employment practices. However, it proved difficult to inculcate ways of working appropriate for employment into the students. Many had no practical experience of the business sector with which to relate what they were taught. The successful ones learned how to be good students of business studies, not how to be business employees. The lack of local employer links made progression into related employment difficult (Walhberg and Gleeson 2003).

Sometimes the college just provides NVQ assessment or verification. What is learned depends almost entirely on the employers, and there can be problems because working practices are too narrow to allow the full range of NVQ competence to be developed. One college tutor took it upon herself to work with the trainees and their employers to fill as many of these gaps as possible. The result was relatively high pass rates. These were achieved by adding college teaching in the workplaces. This was not officially part of her job, and the college was not funded to provide it, but it was an essential ingredient in the success of the programme. College decisions to move to online assessment (reflecting a broad national trend) closed down the space for such 'underground' tutor–student contact and the learning opportunities it could generate (Colley et al. 2003).

WHAT DO YOU THINK?

The cases described above demonstrate the importance of real collaboration and the communication required. If there are strengths in one area, there may well be weaknesses elsewhere as in the final example, but with timely and effective collaborative work by the teacher (as in the last example) the learners were well served. What stands out here is the lack of financial support and recognition for the work and achievement.

The case studies show between them how important it is to get the balance right. Here, this lies between education and work, the learner needs and those of the employer. It is for teachers to make the judgements, develop the collaborative relationships and promote learning.

Have the case examples made you think differently about practical aspects of collaboration? For example, the time and effort required? Perhaps you might consider how a team of staff could address this, and what might be developed over time even with limited resources?

Collaborations enable professionals and their learners to make changes; to take owner-ship of their own situations; to be heard and to promote the kind of learning that is most valued and most effective. How such judgements are informed and allow the professional education sector practitioners to benefit learners and one another is an equally important aspect of collaboration. Research undertaken with others and funded at appropriate levels is a vital element in the promotion of ideas, approaches and attitude changes in that, done well, it supplies the foundation for real dialogue and case-making among those most closely involved and the key decision makers for an area.

SUMMARY

If the future as described by the government's Childrens' Plan in *Raising Expectations: supporting all young people to participate until 18* (2006) is to become reality, then real collaboration at all levels must be supported.

The prospectus, containing an integrated Common Application Process (CAP) and Individual Learning Plan (ILP), will enable learners to select learning courses and programmes and to submit applications. Informed by accurate and timely management information, local areas will better align learning provision with demand . . . For young people this will mean clear information about what's on offer, and a choice of courses which are accessible and flexible enough to meet their demands.

(DCSF 2006)

Find out more

Information on developing a vocational curriculum with another school, college or training provider on:

- The benefits of collaboration
- Who you could collaborate with
- Managing collaboration and partnership
- How to fund and cost a collaborative activity
- The different roles partners can play
- Examples of projects which involve collaboration.

Available at: **www.excellencegateway.org.uk/ page.aspx?o=131137**.

OFSTED (2007) *The contribution made by centres of vocational excellence to the development of vocational work in schools.*
This is an Ofsted report of a small-scale survey to find out how centres of vocational excellence (CoVEs) in further education colleges were supporting vocational work in schools, particularly as it related to the development of the 14–19 Diplomas and to identify barriers to developing this support.

Hardman, J. (2006) *Collaborating for Success: collaborative arrangements for 14–19 provision in the West Midland: summary and analysis of research findings from six case studies*, available at: **lsn.org.uk.**
These findings from six case study areas in the West Midlands examine: how 14–19 collaborative arrangements have developed and changed in response to local circumstances; the impact of the developments and changes on the curriculum offer, learner choice and participation; and the factors that make 14–19 collaborations effective.

Featherstone, G. (2010) The new Diploma: learners and teachers give their view, *Impact* 3.
Articles in this journal from NfER are based on independent, reliable research, and in this case we are given the voice of the learners and teachers themselves as the author looks at the feedback from the ground on diploma delivery as it is experienced by those directly involved.

Bibliography

Brown, A. and Pollard, A. (2006) *14–19 Education and Training: a commentary by the Teaching and Learning Research Programme*.

Colley, H. (2006) 'Learning to labour with feeling: class, gender and emotion in childcare education and training' in *Contemporary Issues in Early Childhood* 7(1): 15–29.

Colley, H., James, D., Tedder, M. and Diment, K. (2003) 'Learning as becoming in vocational education and training: clase, gender and the role of habitus' in *Vocational Education and Training* 55(4): 471–98.

DCSF (2006) The Children's Plan *Raising Expectations: supporting all young people to participate until 18*, London: DCSF.

DfES (2002) *14–19: extending opportunities, raising standards*, London: DfES.

DfES (2003) *14–19: opportunity and excellence*, London: DfES.

DfES (2004) *14–19 Curriculum and Qualifications Reform: final report of the Working Group on 14–19 Reform*, London: DfES.

DfES (2005) *14–19 Education and Skills*, London: DfES.

Fuller, A. and Unwin, L. (2003) 'Fostering workplace learning: looking through the lens of apprenticeship', *European Education Research Journal* 2(1): 41–5.

Higham, J. and Yeomans, D. (2005) *Collaborative Approaches to 14–19 Provision: an evaluation of the second year of the 14–19 Pathfinder Initiative*, London: DfES.

Hodgson, A. and Spours, K. (2004) *14–19 Education and Training: politics, policy and the role of research*, Nuffield Review Working Paper 18 [online]. At: **www.nuffield14-19review.org.uk/documents**

Hodgson, A. and Spours, K. (2005) *Building a strong 14–19 phase in England? The Government White Paper in its wider system context*, Nuffield 14–19 Review. Seminar Paper presented at the Nuffield Foundation on 20 April 2005.

Hodgson, A., Spours, K. and Wright, S. (2005a) *From collaborative initiatives to a coherent 14–19 phase?*

Paper presented at the Nuffield Review of 14–19 Education and Training.

Hodgson, A., Spours, K. and Wright, S. (2005b) *The Institutional Dimension of 14–19 Reform in England: 14–19 collaborative learning systems*, Nuffield Review of 14–19 Education and Training Discussion Paper 10.

Hodkinson, P. and Colley, H. (2006) *Transforming learning cultures in further education* TLRP. Available at: **www.tlrp.org/pub/documents/14-19**

Pring, R. (1993) A philosophical perspective on 14–19 curriculum change, in Tomlinson, H. (ed.), *Education and Training 14–19: continuity and diversity in the curriculum*, Harlow: Longman.

Tummons, J. (2007) *Becoming a Professional Tutor*, Exeter: Learning Matters. At: **http://education.exeter.ac.uk/tlc/** website for the Transforming Learning Cultures in FE project.

Wahlberg, M. and Gleeson, D. (2003) 'Doing the business: paradox and irony in vocational education – GNVQ business studies as a case in point', *Journal of Vocational Education and Training* 55(4): 423–4.

Appendix 13.1

Organisation/Resource	Contact
UCET: The Universities Council for the Education of Teachers	**www.ucet**
Subject Learning Coach website is a portal for managers, teachers and trainers throughout the learning and skills sector to access Teaching and Learning Programme information.	**subjectlearningcoach.net**
CARN: Collaborative Action Research Network	**www.did.stu.mmu.ac.uk/carnnew**
APTE: Association for Partnership in Teacher Education	**www.apte.org.uk**
TLRP: The Teaching and Learning Research Programme	**www.tlrp.org**
Teachernet	**www.teachernet.gov.uk**
Excellence Gateway	**www.excellencegateway.org**
TTRB: The Teacher Training Resource Bank new improved website and search facilities	**www.ttrb.ac.uk**
CETTs: Centres for Excellence in Teacher Training	**http://excellence.qia.org/**
IfL: Institute for Learning	**www.ifl.org.uk**
Becta: Government agency promoting the use of ICT; news, projects and resources on lifelong and special education	**www.becta.org.uk**
Becta: Schools Advice and projects on ICT in schools	**schools.becta.org.uk**
BERA: The British Educational Research Association is a high-profile national network	**www.bera.ac.uk**
SCETT: Standing Committee for the Education and Training of Teachers	**scett.org.uk**

Appendix 13.2

The Nuffield Foundation funded a six-year independent review of 14–19 education and training from October 2003 to September 2009. The Nuffield Review was carried out by a Directorate of Richard Pring and Geoff Hayward from the University of Oxford Department of Education, Ann Hodgson and Ken Spours from the Institute of Education, University of London, Jill Johnson from UCAS, Ewart Keep from SKOPE, based at Cardiff University and Gareth Rees from Cardiff University.

The team brought to the Review extensive networks of research and development – the many schools and local education authorities associated with the Institute's London Region Post-14 Network, the ESRC Research Centre on Skills, Knowledge and Organisational Performance (SKOPE), directed jointly by Oxford and Cardiff, the incomparable links between UCAS and schools and higher education institutions. In addition, the Review established close links with the extensive research and development of the Learning and Skills Network (LSN) and of the National Foundation for Educational Research (NFER).

The Review has produced a number of publications, including a series of Issues Papers, focusing on various topics within 14–19 education, and earlier Annual Reports. These publications, and papers commissioned by the Review, are available on this website under 'documents'.

The final report of the Review was published by Routledge in June 2009.

Source: **http://www.nuffield14-19review.org.uk/**

Appendix 13.3

What is IFP?

The Increased Flexibility Programme (IFP) for 14–16-year-olds is a programme that aims to increase vocational opportunities in schools by allowing pupils to take a range of GCSEs in vocational subjects and other related qualifications. The programme is currently in place in 60 per cent of maintained secondary schools. IFP is used by more than 280 LSC-established partnerships in England. These partnerships consist of colleges, schools and other education-related organisations.

What does it mean for me and my school?

It means that over 100,000 Year 10 and Year 11 pupils nationally are now undertaking vocational learning, spending one day a week in a college, with a training provider or with an employer. Early figures suggest that the IFP is reaping benefits in a range of ways, including improved attendance and behaviour.

Most recently, research by the National Foundation for Educational Research revealed that the Increased Flexibility programme has exceeded its targets for encouraging 14–16 students to continue into further education. A total of 90 per cent of students embarking on new vocational GCSEs in subjects such as healthcare and IT skills have continued their education post-16.

CASE STUDY

Collaboration in research: a network example

CARN: Collaborative Action Research Network

The quality of our work in the professions depends upon our willingness to ask questions of ourselves and others, and to explore challenging ideas and practices, including the values that underpin them.

*The **Collaborative Action Research Network** (CARN) is committed to supporting and improving the quality of professional practice, through systematic, critical, creative inquiry into the goals, processes and contexts of professional work.*

CARN was founded in 1976 in order to continue the development work of the Ford Teaching Project in UK primary and

CASE STUDY *CONTINUED*

secondary schools. Since that time it has grown to become an international network, drawing its members from educational, health, social care, commercial, and public services settings.

CARN aims to encourage and support action research projects (personal, local, national and international), accessible accounts of action research projects, and contributions to the theory and methodology of action research.

CARN sets out to promote:

Recognition

- that professional development requires critical inquiry into past, current and future practice;
- that practitioners themselves should be actively and creatively involved in defining and developing professional practice;
- that practitioners themselves should contribute to the growth of valid professional knowledge and theory;
- that all relevant communities (including service-users, students, clients, etc.) need to be involved in developing the provision of services;
- that action research provides a powerful means of developing worthwhile professional and institutional practice.

Support

- for professional staff carrying out action research, individually and in collaboration with others, in their place of work;

- for professional development through action research as a lifelong focus throughout all phases of professional careers;
- for collaboration and dialogue between those concerned, to develop research-based professional practice, and practice-based research.

Networking

- through sharing accounts of action research, in the bulletins, on the CARN website, in the Educational Action Research Journal, and through other CARN publications;
- through attentive personal encouragement and critical feedback;
- through engaging with CARN colleagues at steering group meetings, regional events and at the CARN annual conference.

Discussion

The inter-professional (e.g. education/health/ social care) connections supported through the Collaborative Action Research Network are very much in tune with current thinking for promoting learning in children and young people. To what extent do you think such a network and action research approach might be of value in your own context?

What kind of research-based collaboration would inform/improve your own teaching/ promoting learning either now or in the future? Would you involve other new colleagues or approach more senior staff? Perhaps you could contact your university or professional organisation?

Source: http://governors.lsc.gov.uk/Programme+areas/Increased+Flexibility+Programme.htm

14 Including All Learners for Independent Learning

In this chapter you will:

- Reflect on some definitions of inclusion and independent learning
- Consider the policy background to current developments in inclusion
- Review some key approaches informing practice through strategies to support learning to learn approaches and be introduced to some theory for teachers
- Examine some actual examples of good and poor practice in relation to learning
- Consider key strategies for inclusion in learning to learn, and reflect on those which you adopt in your own practice
- Consider how research and theory might impact on your own teaching and learners

Pearson Education Ltd./Ian Wedgewood

Introduction

This chapter introduces two vital aspects of teaching and learning in parallel precisely because they are inextricably entwined. In order to move learners towards a mature and more autonomous approach to learning for their lifetime, it is essential to ensure that the different profiles, needs and aspirations of all individuals are recognised and included in the learning. An independent learner will be able to make choices, seek appropriate advice from relevant sources and learn from both success and failure. They will be able to move forward and remain open to development and continuous learning with pleasure rather than trepidation.

In this chapter we will explore the challenging area of addressing the many differentiated levels and requirements of the 14–19 phase and using the opportunities for this kind of growth to **independent learning** for young people. In order to enable individuals to learn how to learn they must be fully included and their unique talents and needs acknowledged and supported as contributing to the best learning environments.

The law in this country does not allow discrimination by any state or private provider of education in relation to sex, sexual orientation, disability or race. This applies to employing staff, admissions, exclusion and access to service. In some circumstances relating to faith, age and specific disabilities there are exceptions. In the case of state schools and colleges there are even more detailed requirements or duties set out as additional legal responsibilities.

A useful guide, *Legislation on Equality and Diversity: a guide for the action that maintained schools need to take to comply with equality and diversity legislation* is currently available.

This can be accessed at: www.teachernet.gov.uk/_doc/11059/Equality_legislation_guide_for_schools_V2 2 1.pdf.

Definitions and discussion of inclusion and independent learning

Inclusion can mean different things to different groups, professionals and policy makers but there is much common ground. The TDA (Training and Development Agency for Schools) summarise the position with three principles which can be translated into practice:

1. Setting suitable learning challenges
2. Responding to pupils' diverse learning needs
3. Overcoming potential barriers to learning and assessment for individuals and groups of pupils.

www.tda.gov.uk/upload/resources

As teachers, our practice should be positively anti-discriminatory. The TDA provides the following simple set of headings to show what such practice will contain:

- Diversity and the valuing of difference
- Self-esteem and positive identity

- Fulfilment of individual potential
- Full participation of all groups.

The Centre for Studies on Inclusive Education provides a useful and more descriptive overview of what this might look like in your school or college context.

- Valuing all students and staff equally.
- Increasing the participation of students in, and reducing their exclusion from, the cultures, curricula and communities of local schools.
- Restructuring the cultures, policies and practices in schools so that they respond to the diversity of students in the locality.
- Reducing barriers to learning and participation for all students, not only those with impairments or those who are categorised as 'having special educational needs'.
- Learning from attempts to overcome barriers to the access and participation of particular student s to make changes for the benefit of students more widely.
- Viewing the difference between students as resources to support learning, rather than as problems to be overcome.
- Acknowledging the right of students to an education in their locality.
- Improving schools for staff as well as for students.
- Emphasising the role of schools in building community and developing values, as well as in increasing achievement.
- Fostering mutually sustaining relationships between schools and communities.
- Recognising that inclusion in education is one aspect of inclusion in society.

IN PRACTICE

How many of the points above can you recognise in the vision and practice of your own school or college? What examples can you give to support your thoughts? Which areas of practice have you seen which might benefit from further consideration in the light of the above? Are there any of these you would remove from the list, or change?

There is a clear link between full participation of all students and pupils and ensuring that individuals can become independent and fulfilled as learners for life. Equally clear is the link between educational and social inclusion assumed in so many aspects of this approach.

Like most areas of this relatively new phase, there is much fluidity and even contradiction evident in the constantly changing language. Inclusion as a term can appear to mean many things but for teachers it reflects our increasingly multi-faith; multi-race; multi-culture; multi-ability experience in learning environments. This does not mean that all schools work with diverse groups, nor that such contexts present the greatest challenges. Inclusion can be more difficult where diversity is less apparent and schools are enriched by their diversity.

In their front-line role, teachers become facilitators of sensitive discussions, promoters of openness and tolerance which remains mindful of the rights of others and instigators of action to ensure the safety and success of pupils and students. For good professionals this relationship-based inclusiveness defines the term most closely. They aim to prepare young learners for the uncertainties and doubts as well as for the known situations, challenges and opportunities.

For many teachers, there is too little time built in to allow for the kind of constructive and more extended interaction with individuals through which effective long-term learning relationships could be developed. In order to achieve increased participation and attainment for all young people and reduce the inequalities which exist between different groups, teachers are working with more individual learning plans, longer-term local projects and wider community links as well as developing their connections with employment, further and higher education.

You can find further relevant discussion of this area in Chapter 5, Learners as Individuals. Topics are further developed and additional important aspects explored in more depth.

Policy background

We live in a society where individuality appears to be highly prized. Rights, freedoms and entitlements are increasingly claimed and enshrined in legislations, codes and policy initiatives, some would say at the expense of responsibilities to others and a sense of wider society. We will learn in training from many texts (Berry 2007) about, for example, our responsibilities as teachers in place of the parent, 'in loco parentis' and other legal matters. Pupils and parents have more rights than ever, and for some the balance has tipped too far in favour of these individuals and away from those of the profession. You can consider some aspects of this area of debate through the activity below.

WHAT DO YOU THINK?

Should pupils have more or less rights as individuals in school and college settings?

Advocates of pupil rights tend to forget that the teacher–pupil relationship is not an exact parallel to the one of producer and consumer in a market. The pupil is given no right as to whether he or she wishes to attend school.

Legal obligations are imposed upon schools to accept pupils to an extent regardless of their behaviour. State schools cannot easily exclude pupils permanently. Although doctors have recently been given the right to refuse to treat violent patients, no such rights exist for teachers, unless they are asserted de facto by unions such as mine. The right to an education is sometimes abused by unreasonable parents, who insist that their offspring attend their first-choice school regardless of behaviour.

Anyone placed in authority can make mistakes. Like referees in a football match, instant decisions have to be made. Enhancing individual rights can easily make life impossible for the teacher. If teachers get it wrong, they must be corrected by management. This is best done on the quiet, and not in front of the children. The general good requires the authority of teachers to be maintained. A teacher consistently getting it seriously wrong deserves dismissal. Giving pupils too many individual rights could erode the sensible use of authority in schools. In practice everyone, including pupils, have rights which must be respected. Some are governed by statute and common law and are fairly obvious. As pupils grow up they are effectively given more rights and treated increasingly as adults. In return they are expected to exercise increased responsibility for themselves.

Practice will vary according to individual circumstances. It would be difficult to legislate for all pupils to have the same rights, no matter the local circumstances. This is an area for sound professional judgment. The last thing teachers need is enhanced rights for pupils laid down either by statute or the (dreaded) Government guidance which often amounts to the same thing.

(De Gruchy, N., *TES* 1999. Nigel de Gruchy is general secretary of the National Association of School-masters Union of Women Teachers.)

Do you believe that young learners need more boundaries in order to learn how to be self-disciplined individual citizens and lifelong learners, or more freedom?

What of the individual learning? Do you engage your pupils or students in learning purely for the advantage or enjoyment they might gain from the process, or in the interests of some common national economic or social good connected with their citizenship of a nation or of a threatened planet? Before you can consider the best approach for your individual learners, you must surely first think about where you stand in relation to the values underlying the current education system. Armitage et al. (2010) lay out a useful introduction to philosophies of education and the role of vocationalism in education.

Whatever our level of experience as teachers, we are contributing to the future and, at least on the face of things, have many new opportunities to make our voice heard through online consultations, social networking and discussion groups. Government and professional associations canvas for public and professional opinion far more than in the past. The same is true for parents and learners who, depending on their age, would once have considered their local or national vote to be their main instrument of expression. Now they can make their voice heard in quite powerful ways through the media with communication channels like Facebook, Twitter and YouTube which ensure that individuals can at least seem to be influential in the decision-making.

Policy makers can seem more concerned to seek public approval by managing media messages and marketing their views than by taking action. For example, 'fear of crime' has been portrayed as being more significant than crime itself at times. The kind of activity this produces shows that the attention of policy makers is not really directed at listening to individuals nor to taking account of public wishes or needs but at polling and marketing; spinning and selling in a kind of democratised consumerism where we can choose how best to position ourselves as producers and products in competitive markets.

In this chapter it is important to understand that inclusion relates to the high profile of the individual's needs and wishes in our society and the widespread notion that we have many rights. Alongside this come responsibilities, and the 14–19 phase teacher supporting learners with decisions about their futures is working in a challenging context. Inclusion is now central to educational principle and practice (The National Curriculum Inclusion Statement, DfEE/QCA 1999) and it is valuable to give critical consideration as to how we view the implications of this in our work as teachers.

DISCUSSION POINT

What can **inclusion** achieve?

Inclusion requires that schools and teachers establish ways of working that actively secure the fullest participation of all learners – both in curricular and social terms. It is incumbent upon institutional and individual attitudes to change, rather than an expectation that a pupil who is at risk of marginalisation because of issues of 'race', religion, gender or sexual orientation will be moulded to 'fit' pre-existing conditions and arrangements within a school.

Commentary

The concept and practice of educational inclusion has become the prevailing initiative in education systems throughout Western Europe. It has been driven by a commitment to the rights of all learners to secure those opportunities to enable them to function as equal participants in twenty-first-century society.

Inclusive practice in education has been influenced by far wider and international notions of human rights. In the past few years increasing importance has been placed on inclusive principles by national and local governments. A significant number of academics, administrators, politicians, parents and practitioners have come to regard the approach as the single most effective means of combating discriminatory attitudes, creating welcoming communities and building an inclusive society (Multiverse 2009).

Do you agree with the final statement? You may wish to research alternative views on effective approaches: for example, the view that questions attempt to include or fit the excluded groups and individuals within the existing structures which originally excluded them. Instead consider the case for changing the society and its structures more radically.

For a range of views, read Edwards and Armstrong (2001), Labonte (2004) and Jupp (1992).

The message about inclusion for an individual can, however, be difficult and contradictory. A young learner with no qualifications, a poor track record of individual achievement as measured through tests and exams, a fractured home life and any associated issues of criminality or health may well feel that with low scores and no certificates they might be considered by some to be at the lowest point in a society where these things count so much, and yet will see high-profile campaigns promoting the message that every child and every learner matters. It is teachers who turn this message into reality through the quality of the relationships formed in learning.

According to current DCSF (Department for Children, Schools and Families) information, the 14–19 Reform agenda will support the development of policies to increase participation and attainment for all young people. At present, data shows significant inequalities in participation and achievement among young people.

> The 2007 Final Report of the Equalities Review [*an independent investigation*
> *of the causes of persistent discrimination and inequality in British society,*
> *commissioned as part of the Government's commitment to creating a society where*
> *everyone can achieve their full potential, free from prejudice and discrimination*]
> confirmed that most people think educational attainment is critical to life
> chances and equality. Therefore, as new 14–19 policies are developed and
> rolled out, looking at the impact of those policies on young people of
> different race, disability and gender is not only a legal requirement but a
> valuable lever for change.
>
> *http://archive.cabinetoffice.gov.uk*

Within classrooms and wider learning environments, the strategies to support inclusion and independent learning for every individual are becoming more centrally directed. Provision for 14–19 is now subject to assessment of its suitability in terms of race, disability and gender impact: in other words, how effective delivery will be in terms of participation and attainment for all.

The Equality Act 2010 is designed to provide a framework in law to protect the rights of individuals and advance equal opportunities for all. It intends to create a fairer and more equal society.

It contains provision to extend the protection for individuals against discrimination and increases the responsibilities on public bodies in many areas including education. It also provides for monitoring and impact assessment to ensure the effectiveness of the new Act. All this is aimed at removing discrimination, and directly addressing issues like those illustrated below.

- Less academically able, but better off children, overtake more able, poorer children at school by the age of six.
- The gap between the employment rate of disabled people and the overall employment rate has decreased from 34.5% to 26.3% since 1998, but disabled people are still more than twice as likely to be out of work than non-disabled people.
- If you are from an ethnic minority, you were 17.9% less likely to find work in 1997 than a white person. The difference is still 13%.
- Six out of 10 lesbian and gay schoolchildren experience homophobic bullying and many contemplate suicide as a result.

WHAT DO YOU THINK?

Have you encountered an issue relating to any of the points above within your own practice?

How might you/did you address this?

There is some important additional protection (Equality Act 2010) for the rights of those with learning disabilities which should be of interest to all education professionals.

The government has placed the five outcomes of the *Every Child Matters* (DFES, 2003), the Green Paper for children's services, which included proposals to provide education, health, and social care around the needs of the child rather than the needs of professionals at the centre of work for the 14–19 phase. Colleges and schools must ensure that they support learners to be healthy, stay safe, enjoy and achieve, make a positive contribution and achieve economic well-being. The responsibility for this set of requirements extends across the whole curriculum and this means getting to know learners as individuals and ensuring that they are fully included.

Our aim as teachers is to participate in and help to develop an education system where all young people have the opportunities to learn in ways that motivate and stretch them: a system where, through their own hard work and that of people who work with them, young people are able to qualify themselves for success in life.

The *14–19 White Paper* (2003) introduced reforms like the Diploma qualification which have been designed to provide all young people with entitlements and opportunities across a wide range of areas, both academic and vocational, and prioritised core skills – English, mathematics and ICT. It also focused on teamwork and other personal skills, to prepare young people for study at a higher level or for employment. In short, they will be given a curriculum which should motivate and engage them as it prepares them for life and work.

The interesting extension to all this lies in the wider agenda and the stated aims which are both economic and social. For reference the government's work across this phase can be found in the *Youth Matters* Green Paper (2005) relating to 13–19-year-olds and the subsequent consultation *Youth Matters: next steps, something to do, somewhere to go, someone to talk to* (2006) which provided a major consultation exercise with more than 19,000 responses from young people and more than 1,000 drawn from organisations, professionals and parents. The title summarises the young people's view of what is wanted, and the promotion of social mobility through improved life chances clearly links this to *Every Child Matters, change for children.*

The Green Paper, *Every Child Matters*, set out the then government's proposals for reforming the delivery of services for children, young people and families. It builds on existing measures to ensure that we protect children at risk of harm and neglect from negative outcomes and support all children to develop their full potential. In each case it is made clear that wider social and economic problems will be addressed through solutions focused on individual children and young people.

The views of the government today continue to reflect earlier policy on children and youth and to influence strategy on inclusion and the closely related approaches to developing independent learning. Social change and addressing the 'big picture' is an approach which seems to be acknowledged as vital in order to make real advances in including all children and young people in a successful future.

> What happens outside of formal education and training is equally important and of concern to us all. We (DCSF Department for Children Schools and Families) want all young people to have happy, enriching, diverse experiences. We will ensure that a wide range of activities are made available for them to develop the personal, social and emotional skills needed to thrive in today's society and economy.
>
> We recognise that some young people face difficulties and hardships in their lives that can limit the opportunities available to them and impact upon their wellbeing and progress. They may also need help to steer clear of risks. The Government has dedicated several programmes of work to help limit the problems associated with substance misuse, offending, teenage pregnancy and homelessness.
>
> The drive is towards supporting the next generation in learning how to learn and to value learning. This has influenced the practice of teachers who spend more time on personalising the learning and getting to know individual learners' needs and profiles.
>
> *Youth Matters: http://www.dcsf.gov.uk/everychildmatters/Youth/youthmatters*

How will we know whether the kind of strategies which have emerged from the Youth Matters and Every Child Matters legislation have been effective? The government will use the following Key PSA (Public Service Agreement) targets to measure success. PSA targets are demonstrable milestones towards any programme or initiative's longer-term aims and objectives:

- reducing teenage conceptions
- reducing substance misuse
- reducing the proportion of young people not in education, employment or training
- increasing the proportion of young people aged 19 achieving level 2 and 3 qualifications.

www.dcsf.gov.uk/everychildmatters/Youth/youthmatters

In practical terms the kinds of initiatives intended to support learners as individuals have had varying levels of success. Among the multitude of research publications on the DCSF (Department for Children Schools and Families) website which relate to the area of individual learning are large numbers on parenting, but the urgency of the focus on immediate and pressing problems so evident today brings education professionals to the fore in addressing contemporary challenges once again.

John Freeman the Director of React, the local authority sector-led support programme for the changes to funding and delivery of education for the 14–19 phase, speaking as part of the LSN Big Debate, a key conference run by the Learning Skills Network on government changes for the 14–19 phase (LSN 2009), recently highlighted the potential benefits for individuals which can only be realised if those charged with managing the provision maintain a strong commitment to every learner.

These, together, if properly implemented, will provide routes for every young person to succeed, so that at age 18 they are able to go into a skilled job or higher education. It's really important to emphasise the inclusive 'every' young person; not all young people will succeed through the academic route, however well taught; we must ensure that every child does achieve all they can through the commissioning of challenging vocational and work-related activities. And while I am on stereotypes, remember that Diplomas and apprenticeships make direct provision for some of our most able young people with progression routes into higher education.

As you can see from Freeman's final comment, he objects to the way in which such qualifications have been branded by some as suitable only for the under-achiever because they are not academic but vocational or applied learning.

WHAT DO YOU THINK?

Do you agree with Freeman? Why do you support the qualification reforms for including all learners? If not, what alternatives do you believe are preferable, and why?

Government strategies to improve inclusion

In this section we're going to look at the impact of government policy in terms of current key areas: reducing the numbers of NEETs (those Not in Education, Employment or Training); providing really effective IAG (information, advice and guidance) for young people preparing for work, further learning and wider life experience; and the use of enhancement schemes in colleges and schools.

Reducing the number of those young people 16–18 not in education, employment or training (NEETs)

As teachers, training and experienced, we may all come across these young people. Whether this encounter occurs directly in classrooms as we teach and support pupils, or indirectly in wider social and professional settings, we will probably have contact of some kind. Young pupils may have family members in this category or be heading that way themselves. The problems are urgent and relevant. This refers to the group of young people not currently included in education, employment or training who are the focus of growing concern in the UK and across Europe. They are excluded from the opportunities enjoyed by their contemporaries and this causes them to lose direction and motivation. It becomes increasingly difficult for such young people to re-engage and learn how to learn independently so their life chances are not undermined. The waste of potential is detrimental for both the individual concerned and the wider society.

Of all European countries we are among those most afraid of our young individuals, who drink more heavily, become pregnant at a younger age and are more likely to perpetrate and become victims of crime. In attempting to break this cycle of negative perception and what many claim to be self-fulfilling prophecies, there have been some powerful and successful initiatives. The use of a negatively expressed label like the ubiquitous term NEETs (those Not in Education, Employment or Training) is at best unhelpful and at worst incredibly damaging. It may be factually accurate but denies the many other activities, hopes and achievements of the person thus described. The first word indicated is 'not' rather than a more neutral or positive term, and to be defined by what you are not rather than what you are is in other contexts seen to be against an inclusive and accepting set of values (see below for the NEET strategy). Later on in this chapter, strategies to address this are looked at in more detail as part of the broader focus on including all rather than just some 14–19 learners.

In November 2007, the DCSF published *The NEET Strategy: reducing the number of young people not in education, employment or training*. This outlined the approach to be taken to tackle the significant issues identified.

> Being out of education, employment or training (NEET) between the ages of 16 and 18 is an enormous waste of young people's potential and their contribution to society. It is also linked to a number of other poor outcomes, including low levels of attainment and teenage conception.
>
> Reducing the proportion of young people NEET is therefore one of the DCSF national priorities – our target is to reduce the proportion of 16–18 year olds who are NEET by 2 percentage points by 2010. Local authorities have the lead responsibility for reducing the proportion of young people NEET in their areas and the DCSF welcome the fact that so many local areas have chosen the NEET Indicator for their Local Area Agreement (LAA) with Government.

The latest figures for the end of 2008 show that the proportion of young people aged 16–18 participating in education or training reached 79.7 per cent, an increase of 1.7 percentage points since 2007 and the highest ever rate.

'The proportion of 16 and 17 year olds NEET has fallen for the third consecutive year. At 5.2 per cent, the proportion of 16 year olds NEET is at its lowest level for more than a decade. The proportion of 18 year olds NEET rose by 2.4 percentage points to 16.6 per cent. This caused the overall proportion of 16–18 year olds NEET to rise by 0.7 percentage points to 10.3 per cent.' *Reducing the number of young people not in education, employment or training (NEET): The Strategy* (2007) is structured around the four key themes that are essential to reducing the proportion of young people who are NEET:

- careful tracking to identify early those young people who are NEET, or who are at risk of becoming NEET;
- personalised guidance and support to enable young people to access suitable provision, and to tackle barriers to learning like family circumstances, language and learning difficulties
- a flexible mix of learning provision with many course options and school, college and work experience choices, both pre- and post-16, designed to meet the needs of every young person in every area; and

- an emphasis on rights and responsibilities so that there are clear incentives on young people to re-engage quickly if they drop out. This includes good individual support and mentors in some cases to assist in the development of learning to learn skills and monitoring to ensure that learners progress.

The Strategy also set out a number of additional measures that the Department is taking to support these four themes. The Entry to Learning pilot programme supports young people who are Not in Education Employment or Training (NEETs) to make the best use of high-quality re-engagement programmes delivered via the third sector. Through a range of experiences provided outside school and college, e.g. young fire-fighter, volunteering, creative nail art, DJ training that are different and appealing, the scheme explores ways of improving young people's progression from this provision to more formal learning to ensure that they are able to advance and gain the skills and qualifications they need to succeed. There are four areas in the first phase of the pilot: Brighton and Hove (with East Sussex), Birmingham, Sandwell and Lancashire. This pilot started in November 2008.

For more information on the Entry to Learning pilot programme, see the Department for Children, Schools and Families website at: **www.dcsf.gov.uk/14-19/index**.

As can be seen in the strategy outlined above, there is a clear steer towards individualised approaches as a means to attend to what is so often presented as a group problem. Quite rightly, the advice and policy guidance has exposed the weakness in notions of collective and quick-fix solutions (like some national project initiatives which are not designed to follow students in the medium to long term) in favour of greater attention to individual issues, local contexts and needs, with a long-term focus on retaining contact with the young person through to employment and beyond, and assuring their access to opportunities on an equal basis.

These principles are sound enough but, in a period of rapid change and severe economic constraints, it is hard for many professionals to be as optimistic as they would wish. This means that joined-up approaches to support the work of teachers and school and college staff are increasingly important.

Information, advice and guidance for individuals

The services directing young peoples' choices, aspirations and experiences of work and learning 14–19 make a significant contribution to any strategy attempting to promote inclusion for attainment.

Our ability to ensure inclusion for all learners and to motivate them to learn more independently as they develop rests to a large degree on the establishment of trust in their relationship with those responsible for their education. Successful young people usually quote in retrospect that key factors in their achievements are the confidence and belief placed in them, the support provided and the individual interest and concern shown for them no matter how they may have presented themselves in good and bad times.

Knowing where an individual learner would like to be in two or five years' time; setting achievable but challenging goals, eliciting fears and hopes and being prepared to allow for and support fresh starts, new directions and emerging identity are features of long-term effective approaches to transforming the future of a young person. If only one professional is making this kind of effort, then the inconsistency can undermine all the benefits; but where good communication exists between careers guidance professionals and teachers, the home, support and those involved in recording and managing learning, the chances of ultimate success are greatly improved.

Information, advice and guidance (IAG) involves providing information about a range of learning and work opportunities; helping individuals to interpret information and choose the next step; and supporting in-depth structured planning and action to access the best route forward for them. This provision should be unbiased and for this reason it has increasingly become the province of trained careers and guidance specialists and is located outside educational institutions; but the pressures of a system where funding follows, individuals (each learner represents income for the school or college) can increase the potential for learners to be recruited into courses that are inappropriate; dropped from a school roll if they are likely to fail or just be encouraged to move on because they do not fit a profile. Clearly there are good service providers supporting study, career and experience choices for pupils, but we may have encountered cases such as those just described; and if we are to improve full inclusion for all individuals this must be a key area.

Good Information Advice and Guidance (IAG) does indeed require specialist input and a well-designed process to ensure that appropriate and responsive planning and support are put in place. In order to ensure that guidance and development for a young person is effective, the process must involve a detailed and long-term engagement with each individual and must begin very early in school life. All too often the motivation, preferences and early talents emerging in the primary phase are lost at transitional points. The guidance must be flexible and encourage change and growth and the implementation and monitoring of linked aspiration and education must involve all those directly engaged in the teaching and learning with the pupil or student concerned.

IAG should not be inserted as a limited and rather tardy addition occurring at the end of an individual's successful or failed journey through school. In some cases this will be unnecessary owing to the automatic advantages still accruing to the privileged young whose parents are well educated, connected and informed. In too many others this will be insufficient and serve only as a remedial patch to keep someone off the streets or acknowledge their need for additional effort in areas which should have been addressed long before. The kind of schemes which sometimes target these groups can be far from ideal and in some cases exacerbate problems owing to the tendency to label rather than enable and stretch individuals.

For example, the fact that a young person has committed a series of car-crime offences does not mean that we can assume, as some do, that they must be interested in cars and can be managed in a scheme to race bangers for a month. Perhaps they were coerced into crimes for other reasons which require more knowledge of the individual's case and needs. And a failure to attend school does not always mean that there was something amiss in the life of the pupil: it can be the school itself that is the problem, as those who have dealt with entrenched bullying will be aware.

CASE STUDY

Enhancement in Blackburn College

Blackburn College's enhancement scheme, established to provided a wider set of options and opportunities, gives students experience of particular careers, developing not only their knowledge of careers but also the skills needed for success in employment or higher education. A recognised and respected part of the curriculum, the scheme has become a major selling point for the college.

There are currently four enhancement areas: pre-teaching, pre-medical, pre-legal and outdoor pursuits. The scheme uses ASDAN and ASET awards which are national awarding bodies for vocational and further education courses at a range of levels.

Around half of the 300 first-year A-level students opt for one of the enhancements. There are two groups for pre-teaching and one group for each of the other areas. The enhancements are allocated up to three and a half hours within the most suitable option block. In general the combinations of subjects taken by students do not restrict which enhancements they can take.

Taking on challenges

For the ASDAN Universities Award, students undertake four challenges:

- work experience based on a career indicated by the title of the course (usually half a day per week for about 20 weeks), for example pre-teaching students will gain work experience at a school and pre-medical students might work at a pharmacy or clinic. The students are responsible for finding themselves the work placement.

- preparing a portfolio and making a presentation based on career-related research and experience. This provides evidence for the communication key skill qualification at level 3 (students can also achieve the three wider key skills)

- two other challenges chosen from any area the student wishes. These may be an activity such as learning a foreign language or volunteering at an after-school support club at Blackburn Rovers Football Club, or may provide the opportunity to gain awards or qualifications, such as coaching awards, a driving licence or a sign-language qualification.

Throughout they compile a portfolio, which they are able to draw on for higher education applications and interviews.

Valuable experience

The scheme has been successful in providing students with the opportunity to find out about the demands of a career and whether they are suited to it. For example, some students, after completing their work placement have decided that teaching is definitely not a career option for them.

The scheme is also instrumental in promoting personal growth as students work as part of a team, take responsibility and work with professionals outside the college environment. As one member of staff commented: 'the experience students gain makes them into rounded individuals. They are able to gain wider key skills and work with others . . . all of which contribute to increased confidence. I have seen students grow from their experiences' (**www.qcda.gov.uk/20899.aspx**).

How teachers can improve their inclusion of all learners and promote independent learning

Diversity demands thoughtful, well-structured individual approaches but these are inevitably restricted by limitations of time, training and support, resources, external factors beyond the professional domain of a teacher and many other constraints. In spite of the difficulties faced by teachers in relation to inclusion whether on a large or small scale, the increased awareness of need and the entitlements now written into legislation have increased the potential for effective action in some respects. Identifying need, aspirations and aims, both actual and potential, is a key factor – personal knowledge of individuals is vital for successful inclusive practice. Consider the following checklist of strategies for successfully including all learners. You will notice that most of these are central to all good professional training and can be found in the practice of experienced and effective teachers across sectors.

- Developing relationships with learners in conjunction with an informed and supportive team
- Seeking advice and guidance from colleagues
- Being prepared to make specialist referrals
- Ensuring that your own understanding of relevant legislation and its practical implications for yourself and your learners is current
- Selecting appropriate learning for individuals in terms of learner aspiration and need, qualification, content, form, delivery, environment and other relevant factors

Source: Pearson Education Ltd. Photodisc

Photo 14.1
Encouraging all learners in experimentation with new challenges

- Monitoring progress and ensuring early intervention where necessary to redirect learner efforts/support
- Provision of ongoing training relating to working with a wide range of individuals
- Listening to all learner voices and communicating well in response.

IN PRACTICE

Having considered the list above, can you identify areas where your own practice is strong and areas where you could develop?

What practical examples of your own successful or problematic experience with attempts at inclusive practice can you share with colleagues?

Examples of successful strategies to include all learners

The cases below provide specific examples of successful practice and experience in particular contexts where individual learning and independent learning has been enhanced or enabled but they have a resonance for a wider audience. Such strategies and approaches have potential for transfer and adaptation to suit other individuals.

CASE STUDY

Oakwood Court College – independent specialist college

Oakwood Court College is a residential specialised independent institution supporting students between 16 and 25 with learning difficulties. The college is located in Dawlish on the Devon coast and it was an award winner in the 2009 Next Generation Learning Awards in the Furthering My Learning category.

A video of this case can be accessed at: **http://feandskills.becta.org.uk/display**

Student/child-centred learning is an often-used term, and Oakwood Court shows what it means in practice. Having discovered that students with autism communicated more easily using a web camera and **Skype**, this is now used every day not just to communicate with other students, but also with family at home.

Oakwood Court provides specialist residential education and work-based learning and care to 35 students with a range of learning difficulties. The last year has seen a major redevelopment of its technology provision to increase the use of e-learning, and the College's person-centred approach has been applied to staff and students alike.

All staff have been encouraged to increase their skills through a designated training programme which includes a weekly workshop that encompasses a range of topics from inclusion to Information Learning Technologies and a daily lunchtime drop-in help desk. The curriculum has been revamped to further enhance inclusion, accessibility and e-safety (security and protection for pupils and students using technologies – see Chapter 16 for further information) and is carefully differentiated for each student. As a result, both students and staff are gaining in confidence, and every student is achieving at least two IT certificates a year on their selected pathway.

Staff involve learners in evaluating new learning technologies and resources, and have a 'can do' approach to problems. As an example, Jemima, an outstanding student who nominated the College for this award, had struggled to enjoy listening to music on computer because of her cochlear implant. What looked like an insoluble problem was in fact solved through adjustments to the assistive technology in the system and Jemima is now able to share this experience with her classmates.

Oakwood Court has moved from a fragmented approach to an organisation-wide technology development plan that is pivotal to each student's progression. It identifies four factors as having enabled success: appointment of a full-time ICT Co-ordinator and a Network Manager to ensure an efficient technical service; an effective data management system; inclusive and e-safe curriculum design for students; and, not least, determination!

(Becta, May 2009)

The case study in Appendix 14.1 provides a teacher's description of the background and experience of a pupil from a family with refugee status. Your inclusion issues may be different but this case study highlights the real importance of supporting the pupil through to independent learning skills and illustrates very well how important this is to raising confidence and improving the potential for achievement.

Research and support for training and practice

Issues relating to the inclusion and support of school and college students of this age as they move towards independent learning can be very challenging. Research findings can help you to inform your practice and networks, and specialist advice sources can provide valuable information for particular issues or individual areas of need. If you are training, it is important to make use of professional studies advice and guidance to ensure that you can access accurate information and help. For example, you may find that you are working with individual children who have specific learning needs or refugee status, as in the case study in Appendix 14.1. Both during and beyond training we benefit from ongoing connection with research and specialised support.

Whether you are training or engaging in CPD (continuing professional development) as you strive to improve your teaching for learners, it is worth exploring the research in areas of particular relevance to your own practice. The Multiverse site (www.multiverse.ac.uk) is very useful for teachers, trainees and associated professionals at all levels. It is funded by the TDA (Training and Development Agency for Schools) and has a strong focus on support and resources for NQTs working with pupils with EAL (English as an additional language) and those from minority ethnic backgrounds. Other areas relating to Travellers and Roma, asylum seekers and refugees and a range including social class and religious diversity matters are also explored, and lesson resources as well as access to expert advice is available.

Including all learners to achieve independent learning

The links between effective full inclusion and fostering independent learning as discussed earlier are very important. Good knowledge and understanding of individuals, their backgrounds and needs are a prerequisite for engaging pupils and students in what is often described as self-regulated learning. Learners can work with teachers, other staff and with their peers but do so in a more responsible, motivated and autonomous manner.

The findings of a recent literature review commissioned from the Learning and Skills Network by the DCSF (Department for Children, Schools and Families) included an identification of the key elements outlined below.

It seems that the combination of providing an inclusive environment in which learning relationships can grow and ensuring that the learners are supported to learn in more independent ways are the key to successful outcomes in this phase.

> The key elements of independent learning may comprise factors internal and external to learners. The external elements are the development of a strong relationship between teachers and pupils, and the establishment of an 'enabling environment'. The internal elements are the skills that individual pupils have to acquire – notably cognitive, metacognitive and affective skills.
>
> Cognitive skills include memory, attention and problem-solving. Pupils need to have reached a certain level in their cognitive development, such as being able to decode basic information before they can embark on independent learning. Teachers are able to promote this cognitive development to encourage independent learning.
>
> Metacognitive skills are skills associated with an understanding of how learning occurs, such as pupils being able to state how they learn and pupils being able to identify other people who help them with their learning. Metacognitive skills are necessary for pupils to self-assess their learning.
>
> Affective skills are skills that are related to feelings and emotions, such as developing a value system, then internalising and acting on these values. Motivation is considered the most important affective skill and is directly associated with increased independent learning and can also be an outcome of independent learning.
>
> The strong relationship between teachers and pupils involves trust and a mutual responsibility for learning, which is based on teachers providing explicit messages about learning (e.g. its value and relevance for their career aspirations); teachers being attentive and responsive to pupils' interests and needs, and schools developing a greater consistency in their approach to learning.
>
> To understand the relationship between teachers and pupils it is important to consider pupils' experiences in their family and local community since this allows pupils to relate learning occurring in school to their everyday lives, thus serving as a powerful motivator for pupils to engage in their own learning.
>
> *(Meyer et al. 2008)*

IN PRACTICE

From your experience in practice, do you agree that the inclusion is linked to the successful development of independent learning? Can you see how the use of progressively acquired **cognitive, metacognitive** and **affective skills** may apply in your teaching? Explain how.

SUMMARY

It is important to balance learners as individuals with their participation and potential to achieve in education and, ultimately, wider society. The 14–19 phase is particularly significant in this endeavour. With so much concern both nationally and internationally for the future economic welfare of states and societies, the fear might be that the weakest or most disadvantaged individuals will continue to suffer most in terms of their life chances and quality of life. Teachers have always played a very significant, even transformational, role in the immediate and long-term debates relating to their learners and to their own professional activity. It is surely more important than ever to engage critically and constructively with these issues for our own practice and our young peoples' future.

Find out more

- **Harkin J. (2005)** *Behaving like Adults: meeting the needs of younger learners in further education*, Ref No: 052299, London: Learning and Skills Network publications.

This publication provides more detail on the needs of learners in the 14–19 phase in further education contexts. The project researched views about the learning of 14–16-year-old students in colleges, from the learners themselves, their lecturers and their teachers. The aims of the research were to gauge the capacity of the teachers and their institutions to meet the needs of younger learners – and as far as the project team can tell, it was at the time the only study to attempt to look in the round at the subject from the perspectives of institutions, teachers and, most importantly, learners themselves.

- **Case study – East Sussex 14–19 Learner Voice Strategy 2008–2010**, available at: **https://czone.eastsussex.gov.uk/supportingchildren/ youth/youthparticipation/pupilandlearnervoice/ 14-19agenda/**.

This strategy details how East Sussex County Council aims to ensure that learners are actively involved in decision-making related to their education, training and associated services. In order to fulfil its commitment to prioritising the needs of all learners, the local authority and its partners must support, listen and take action in response to learner voice.

Bibliography

Armitage, A. et al. (2007) *Teaching and Training in Post-Compulsory Education* (3rd edn), OUP.

Becta (2009) Next Generation Awards – Furthering My Learning case study, (accessed May 2009 **http://feandskills.becta.org.uk**).

Berry, J. (2007) *Teachers' Legal Rights and Responsibilities*, Hertfordshire: UH Press.

Centre for studies on Inclusive Education **http://www.csie.org.uk/**

DfES (2003) Every Child Matters, Norwich: DfES TSO.

DfES (2006) *Youth Matters: next steps* (**www.everychildmatters.gov.uk**).

De Gruchy, N. (1999) *Should pupils have more rights? No, Summer debate* (**www.tes.co.uk/article**).

Edwards, R., Armstrong, P. and Miller, N. (2001) Include me out: critical readings of social exclusion, social inclusion and lifelong learning, *International Journal of Lifelong Education*, 20(5).

Equality Act 2010 (access at: **http://www.opsi.gov.uk/ acts/acts2010/ukpga_20100015_en_1**).

Jupp, K. (1992) *Everyone belongs: mainstream education for children with severe learning difficulties*, London: Souvenir Press.

LSN (2009) *The 14–19 Shake-up: ensuring that everyone can flourish* (access at: **www.lsnlearning.org.uk**).

Labonte, R. (2004) 'Social inclusion/exclusion: dancing the dialectic', *Health Promotion International*, 19(1): 115–21.

Legislation on Equality and Diversity: a guide for the action that maintained schools need to take to comply with equality and diversity legislation (**www.teachernet.gov.uk/_doc/11059/Equality_ legislation guide_for_schools_V2_2_1.pdf**).

Meyer, W., Haywood, N., Sachdev, D. and Faradya, S. (2008) *Independent Learning: literature review* (**http://www.dcsf.gov.uk**).

Multiverse (2009) (**www.multiverse.ac.uk/**).

The Inclusion Development Programme: The TDA works with partners to support the development of the school workforce. The National Strategies has developed training resources that aim to provide basic support to raise awareness, confidence and competence of school and early years staff to help identify and meet children's needs. Resources on speech, language and communication needs and dyslexia are currently available, and resources on autism will follow in 2009. (**www.tda.gov.uk/teachers/sen/core_skills/ inclusion_development_programme.aspx**). (**www.tda.gov.uk/**).

National Association for Language Development in the Curriculum (NALDIC)

Pupil Portrait 5
Ubah
Contributed by Jennifer Cornish and Halima Abdi

Ubah joined this mixed Catholic Comprehensive school in October 2003 and enrolled in year 10. She came to England a few months previously from Somalia with her mother and 11 siblings. Her father has been in England for about a year. The family have refugee status and, after living for some months in a hostel, have now been rehoused in a self-contained house some distance from the school. Ubah has four siblings at secondary school with her, in year 11, 9, 8 and 7. Six younger siblings (including twins) are at a nearby primary school. There is a baby at home.

When Ubah started at UK secondary school, it was her first experience of schooling. On account of the war and upheaval in Somalia, the children were denied the opportunity to attend school regularly. Ubah's older sister and some younger siblings attended Koranic school, where they learnt to recognise Arabic letters and to read some words. For family reasons Ubah did not attend this school. She speaks Somali and can neither read nor write it.

Ubah speaks Somali at home, with friends outside the family and also at school with her siblings. There are few other speakers of Somali among the school's students. At break and lunchtime Ubah spends time with her siblings or in the library. She says she feels like an outsider and wants to be part of the school community.

The school has an EAL department of four teachers (full-time equivalent 3.4). In addition the school has a Somali-speaking bilingual assistant for approximately 20 hours per week. The school has 600 students: 63 per cent of students speak English as an additional language and nearly 20 per cent of students are refugees or asylum seekers.

Ubah has attended the school's induction programme for stage 1 new entrants (four hours per week) in the autumn term. She has six lessons per week of the Extra English option for Key Stage 4 students. She has had in-class support or 1:1 literacy from a bilingual language assistant (BLA) for approximately two hours each week.

In January Ubah and her sister in year 11 started an intensive literacy programme for students New to Schooling (funded by Connexions and organised by the authority's EMA team). This is a pilot project in response to demand across the authority for provision for students who present at secondary phase with no prior, or limited, schooling. Such students are defined as:

- having few or no literacy skills in any language;
- lacking basic curriculum knowledge;

- lacking formal learning skills;
- having difficulties in adjusting to institutional expectations;
- having emotional and behavioural problems resulting from frustration and/or poor self-esteem.

The project involves two hours of intensive teaching, four mornings per week for six weeks. The two students are taught by the Somali BLA, who was trained specifically for this pilot project. The course is structured around a real book with complementary activities to develop literacy in English. Midway through the pilot, Ubah has 100% attendance and is clearly enjoying the lessons. (At a recent meeting with her father, he said he could see that she was making good progress.)

Ubah herself feels that she is making progress with her reading and writing. She can now recognise a number of short, high frequency words and she has gained the confidence to tackle longer words. She can find her way down a page of text and recognise familiar words. Ubah can write short words without copying and can spell single syllable words from memory.

Ubah is starting to speak English a little. In class she will volunteer a short answer and she has made friends in her EAL option group. She particularly enjoyed a recent group visit to the local Islamic Centre and was able to read captions on the photos taken. She likes copying English and her letters are well formed and words clearly demarcated. Ubah likes to borrow books from the school library and wants to make progress with her reading.

At school she particularly enjoys PE, cooking and using the computer. (She says she finds Science very difficult because she does not benefit from in-class support in those lessons.) Ubah will log on at every opportunity and uses the computer after school when she can, as do all her siblings in the school. (They do not have use of a computer at home.) They frequently log on to Somali websites and their progress in English is helping them to read Somali.

Ubah has now become accustomed to the routines of school and is benefiting from opportunities to learn English through practical activities: she engages particularly in Food Technology, using the computer and going on educational visits. In terms of her spoken language, she uses single words or short utterances and now needs to develop question forms. Ubah can read many short common words and the gist of sentences, especially if supported by pictures. She is starting to recognise spelling patterns and reproduce them.

For her year 10 work experience placement, Ubah has expressed a desire to spend two weeks with the police. (The school has a full-time officer on site.)

Ubah is a reserved child. While her sister, just one year older, is chatty and forthcoming about what goes on at home, Ubah is reticent. At home, her father tells us, she helps with cooking while big sister is listening to music! Ubah does most of the shopping for home and uses English a little for that. She is serious about her studies and takes care over her presentation, one of the reasons why she likes to use a computer. She would like to be a doctor or teacher.

At first Ubah was extremely dependent on the BLA and would leave class to look for her. She is now starting to be more independent and goes to lessons promptly. She has a good attendance record and has missed only a few days of school. She has made friends with other students from her Extra English option and is starting to feel more settled now after three months at school.

Ubah and her four siblings travel to school together by bus and some weeks ago they were rehoused, which resulted in a new route to negotiate to and from school. (Mum and dad have to escort the younger brothers and sisters to primary school.) The five children have experienced some difficulty in arriving on time every day.

A recent occurrence illustrates Ubah's resourcefulness and her ability to cope with new situations. One day recently Ubah's school bag was accidentally left on the bus. It contained most of her school books and she was concerned about the loss. However, she showed great presence of mind, returned to the bus stop and spoke to a bus driver on the same route (who happened to speak Somali) in her attempt to recover her property. Although clearly upset, she reacted calmly and without fuss. This incident demonstrates her characteristic determination to overcome obstacles and to succeed.

15 A Teaching Repertoire

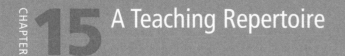

In this chapter you will:

- understand the factors which affect the selection of teaching methods
- review the teaching methods you use
- consider those teaching methods which are likely to bring about the kinds of learning featuring prominently in the 14–19 reforms
- review teacher–student and student–student interaction from the point of view of three prominent communication theories
- consider which factors affect the development of teaching styles
- through completion of a teaching-styles questionnaire, reflect on your own teaching style
- consider key teaching roles and reflect on those which you adopt in your own practice

Pearson Education Ltd./Ian Wedgewood

Introduction

In Chapter 19, there will be a consideration of the overall knowledge, skills and attributes that teachers will probably need in the future if the 14–19 reforms are to be successfully implemented. This chapter will focus on the teacher's repertoire. All teachers will have a range of *methods* they deploy. There will be a number of factors which will influence which of these they use. An important determinant will be the features of the kind of learning they intend to bring about. Another will be the individual *style* or approach which is often expressed in the way in which they engage with their students. The initial training period and early years of their careers will involve teachers developing their professional identities: attempting to become the teachers they perceived themselves to be. Closely related is an individual teacher's interpretation of the various *roles* involved in teaching and, indeed, often an individual's decision that they should play certain roles rather than others. The roles teachers play, the methods they select related to these and the highly individualistic style in which they use these, constitute a teacher's *repertoire*.

Teaching methods

Some of the key factors which affect a teacher's choice of teaching method will include:

- the aims and learning outcomes of the session
- the resources available to them
- the length and depth of their experience and their willingness to take risks
- their knowledge of the group they are teaching and the relationship they have with it
- the nature of the subject/curriculum area.

Rogers (2002) distinguishes between four types of teaching methods:

- **presentation methods**
- **participatory methods**
- **discovery methods**
- **evaluative methods**.

IN PRACTICE

Below are methods that may be used with groups of 14–19-year-olds. Are you able to allocate each to one of Rogers's four types above? Or do you think there are additional categories? Are there any not listed below which you have used? How would you categorise them?

IN PRACTICE *CONTINUED*

Simulation	Game
Lecture	Demonstration
Research project	Educational visit
Workshop	Discussion
Role-play	Seminar
Tutorial	Practical
Residential experience	Design and make exercise
Problem-solving	Presentation
Poster display	Work experience
Experimentation	Observation
Investigation	Estimation exercise
Resource-based learning	Debate
Field trip	Pair work
Video/DVD-based work	

Photo 15.1
Small group work is a method that encourages participation

Source: Pearson Education Ltd. Ian Wedgewood

Key participatory teaching method: role-play

Role-play can be used in a range of learning contexts for a variety of purposes. At its simplest, it puts students in someone else's shoes or gives them a particular point of view ('imagine you are the judge who has to decide the following . . .'). At its most complex, it can form the basis of a highly structured simulation, as in a disaster emergency scenario. But it will always involve students being active by adopting a specific position and interacting with one another. Role theory is central to the social sciences, in so far as they are concerned with an understanding of how individuals act and react to others in particular social contexts. The study in literature and the media of the text will be enhanced by the opportunity for students to gain an active understanding by, for example, playing characters transferred from the text to an alternative or contemporary context. Role-play can simulate the contexts central to learning a modern foreign language. And students taking on the personae of characters at key historical events or engaging in more elaborate living-history projects are likely to gain a much deeper and richer understanding than if they were to be involved in less active forms of learning.

The approach to role-play will depend on the educational purposes for which it is being used. It could be used as the basis for a debrief discussion once students are out of role. A mock interview would give students practice in playing a particular role. Role-play might provide a context in which points of view are adopted and values explored. Theory can be tested, explored, exemplified through role-play in a practical situation. Students can practise decision-making and problem-solving skills in an active context. The following demonstrate a variety of approaches:

- role-play in a fictional setting – local authority officers plan the provision of social amenities in a new town; decisions are taken about resources by shipwreck casualties on a desert island

- students take work-based roles – an editorial team putting together a newspaper or magazine edition; a production team planning a TV/radio programme; a theatre production committee select this season's programme

- individuals take on the roles of interested parties at a meeting to discuss a particular community issue such as crime, transport, redevelopment in the area

- students take the roles of key characters at a historical event – such as the Yalta Conference, the trial of Guy Fawkes, the Diet of Worms

- students are members of one social group – a trade union branch discussing industrial action

- hotseating – one student assumes a role and others in or out of role question him/her

- individuals in role engage a series of encounters with others – characters from a drama meeting 'off stage'; key figures in a social work case.

ACTIVITY

- Take a unit of learning from a programme you are teaching on which you feel may benefit from being the subject of a role-play – this may be a module, a topic or a theme.
- Select a specific group of students.
- Now specify the purpose and the approach of the role-play. You may wish to consider:
  - the setting;
  - the nature of the roles students will play – how will students be briefed on this – role cards, information sheets?
  - how the roles will be allocated – each member of the group a specific role, or the same four or five roles played by students in small groups acting in parallel?
  - the overall structure of the role-play – will it be a single event, such as a meeting, or a meeting in role followed by a discussion in or out of role, a series of encounters between students, a series of events?

Key participatory teaching method: discussion

Group discussions can have a range of purposes. They can be used to:

- explore ideas;
- debate an issue;
- solve a problem, suggest solutions;
- clarify ideas;
- share experiences;
- plan an event or task;
- develop understanding;
- create new ideas.

The key challenge for the leader/manager of a group discussion is to keep the discussion on track while at the same time allowing participants the freedom to express themselves. A good leader/manager:

- has prepared for the discussion via research or information gathering;
- has an agenda or proposed structure for the discussion;
- allows variation in structure according to student interest;
- creates a safe atmosphere in which students feel confident in contributing;
- asks open questions as opposed to closed questions with one acceptable answer only;
- asks prompt questions which are stimulating;
- is able to make any disagreements between students positive and developmental of the discussion;

- is able to control dominant speakers and encourage reluctant ones;
- is an active listener: for example, requests clarification if a student's contribution needs it;
- encourages all students to participate;
- does not dominate the discussion with his/her own views;
- values all contributions and demonstrates this;
- summarises clearly.

A good participant:

- sees a discussion as a shared experience, not a soap box for individual opinions;
- listens to others and ensures they understand what they mean;
- tries not to dominate the discussion;
- contributes relevant points and does not divert or hijack the discussion;
- is brief and clear;
- does not allow the personalisation of interactions with others;
- does not shout others down;
- does not mock or ridicule others' contributions;
- is prepared to state and defend own opinions.

ACTIVITY

- Select a topic, module or theme from a scheme of work you are currently using and which you feel might be useful to base a discussion on.
- Specify what the purpose(s) of the discussion would be.
- Plan the discussion, noting key points or stages and the connection between them.
- Describe what resources you might need for the discussion, such as handouts or whiteboard for key point note-taking.
- Conduct the discussion and then evaluate it using the following key questions:
  - Was the discussion fluent? If it faltered, how did you ensure it progressed once more?
  - Was your preparation thorough enough?
  - Did all group members participate?
  - Did the discussion go to plan?
  - Which aspect of the discussion could have been better handled?

Communication/interaction

Communications theory concerns itself with how messages are communicated between two entities, including how messages are sent and received, and factors that can influence or affect changes in the meaning of the message throughout the process. There is a range of theories and models which may illuminate student–student and student–teacher interaction.

Shannon and Weaver Model

This is a linear view of communication: messages are encoded by a source and sent through a channel. Messages are then decoded by a receiver, who then sends the source feedback. Messages may be disrupted by noise. Schramm (1954) adds the factor of fields of experience of the sender and receiver, life experiences which can enhance communication when they overlap. Shannon and Weaver (1948) were concerned to improve radar and radio transmission. They made the distinction between 'information' and 'information channels', i.e. what the information is about and how it is transmitted.

Key notions were 'noise' and 'redundancy': noise in radio is the jumble of background sound that may prevent us hearing what we are trying to listen to, whereas redundancy refers to an excess deliberately put into the signal to ensure the message gets through. In a teaching context, noise can range from the tone of the teacher's voice to the DVD being played in the next room, the building work outside, or the teacher's distracting clothes. All have the potential to distract from the message. Redundancy implies that a message is so strong it overcomes any noise, so absorbing that everything going on is ignored. In terms of teaching, redundancy can apply to any of numerous teaching and learning strategies used by the teacher.

Transactional analysis

Transactional analysis was first popularised by Eric Berne in the 1960s (Berne 1961 and 1964). It is 'a tool that . . . can be used as a teaching or learning device for understanding behaviour in human interaction' (Quinn: 2000). Berne describes transactional analysis as a system of feelings accompanied by a relative set of behaviour patterns. These are what Berne calls three 'ego states': 'Parent' which is based on transactions which took place in the formative years – the internalised parental 'dos' and 'dont's'; 'Child' based on internal events, positive and negative feelings and responses from the first five years; and 'Adult' exerting control over the world, examining both the parent

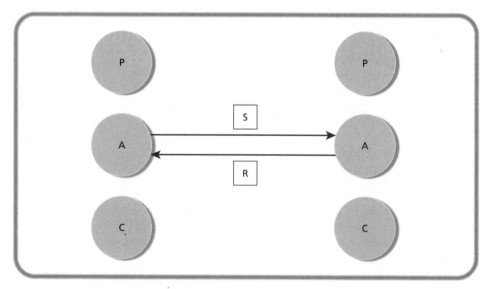

Figure 15.1
An adult-adult
complementary
transaction

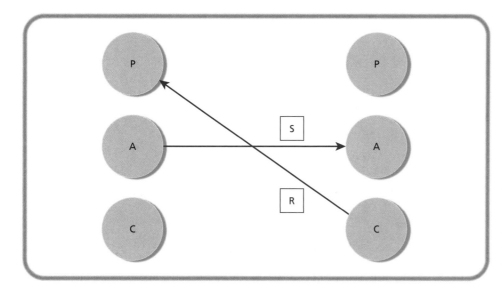

Figure 15.2
Crossed
transaction:
adult-adult,
parent-child

and the child data against the reality of today, accepting it or rejecting it as appropriate, estimating probability in order to devise solutions. Each interaction between two people with one of these ego states is deemed a 'transaction'. Berne's first rule of communications concerns complementary transactions (see Figure 15.1): as long as transactions remain complementary there is nothing to break the stimulus–response process and the exchange can continue indefinitely.

Berne's second rule of communication concerns crossed transactions (see Figure 15.2): when a transaction is crossed, a break in communication occurs and one or both individuals will need to change ego states in order for communication to be re-established.

Berne's third rule of communication concerns ulterior transactions. In ulterior transactions, two messages are conveyed simultaneously: one is an overt, social level message, the other a covert, psychological message. Berne's third rule of communication states that the behavioural outcome of an ulterior transaction is determined at the psychological not the social level. An example he gives is expressed diagrammatically in Figure 15.3, overleaf.

Salesman: This one is better, but you can't afford it.
Customer: That's the one I'll take.

The salesman, as Adult, states two objective facts: 'This one is better' and 'You can't afford it.' At the ostensible, or *social*, level these are directed to the Adult of the customer, whose Adult reply would be: 'You are correct on both counts.' However, the ulterior, or *psychological*, vector is directed by the well-trained and experienced Adult of the salesman to the customer's Child. The correctness of his judgement is demonstrated by the Child's reply, which says in effect: 'Regardless of the financial consequences, I'll show that arrogant fellow I'm as good as any of his customers.' At both levels the transaction is complementary, since the customer's reply is accepted at face value as an Adult purchasing contract.

(Berne 1964: 31)

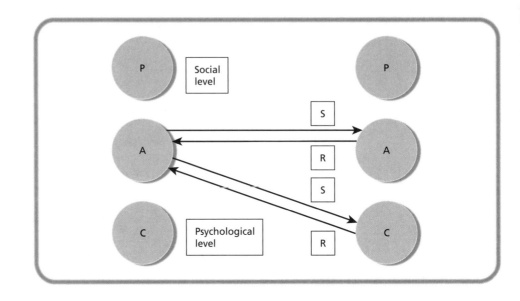

Figure 15.3
An adult
angular
ulterior
transaction

Theory of strokes

The notion of strokes is closely related to Transactional Analysis. Berne (1961) describes as 'stimulus hunger' that arising from the need for physical and mental stimulation. Babies with insufficient stimulation may have physical and emotional difficulties as a result and Berne's choice of the word 'stroke' reflects this infant need for recognition. Amy and Thomas Harrris (1985) argue that not everyone appears to need the same amount of stroking. We all have what they call 'comfort zones' and we function well as long as we stay inside these comfort zones. 'If there is too much (stimulation) – too many people, too much commotion, too many phones ringing, too many demands, even too many compliments – our receiving system shuts down and we long to get away' (1985: 135). However, when we fall below our comfort zone, when we are understimulated, we have a need for physical and emotional stroking. The Harrises point out that our need for strokes can be satisfied by reliving past, often childhood experiences when we re-imagine the praise we experienced from parents for our achievements. Strokes in current relationships and interactions are given and received in a variety of ways, according to the Harrises:

1. Eye contact – or indeed the lack of eye contact – can be used to give a variety of positive and negative strokes. Looking away from someone while in conversation can signal a variety of things, from a lack of interest to a desire to get away: the socially ambitious at an event will be constantly looking over someone's shoulder while talking to them in case someone more useful or important is available to engage with. In our teaching, direct eye contact with a responding student can give them the impression that what they are saying is important; scanning the group can be an inclusive gesture.

2. 'Among the greatest strokes is listening to what someone else is saying' (1985: 145) and ensuring they know you are listening to them. Listening

with care or active listening involves not rushing the conversation, avoiding head motions which urge the speaker to get on with it or interruptions which signal impatience.

3. Ask questions – everyone likes talking about themselves and a question is a stroke expressing interest in them and what they have to say.

4. Use names – a name is a deeply individual part of someone's identity and the (appropriate) use of their name is a positive stroke, an acknowledgement of their individuality. A common mistake of new teachers when taking a new group is to delay learning and using names. Once that is achieved, it takes the relationship of the teacher with individual students and the group as a whole to a higher level.

5. Give yourself away – how many of us have avoided people at social occasions because, although we know we know them, we can't remember their name and how we know them and, worse, we might get ourselves into a position in which we may have to introduce them to someone else! It is easy to spot if someone can't remember you: go over to them and explain who you are and how you may have met.

6. Be a rewarder – no matter how busy you are, make a positive stroke – send an email, a note, a card thanking someone, saying how useful the meeting has been, and do it now, avoiding the paragraph in the future which explains interminably why you haven't been in touch!

7. Don't allow discounting – 'the opposite of discounting is accounting. If you say "hello" to someone and he or she doesn't acknowledge your greeting, persist. Repeat yourself. "Hey, hi!" Maybe he didn't hear you. Maybe he is pretending not to hear you. If that person persists in ignoring you, then it's *his* problem' (1985: 151).

8. Loosen up – 'Humour is the whipped cream of life', it can sweeten situations and laughter can lighten duty, responsibility and difficult challenges.

9. Doers do and triers try – a clear indication of an individual's non-commitment is the word 'try'. I'm going to try to get more people into my life, take charge of my life, be more friendly. 'Substitute "will" for all the "trys" and the prognosis is good. Substitute action for will and the deed is done!'

ACTIVITY

Choose five recent interactions you have had with individual students or groups. They may be negative interactions – asking a student to be quiet, scolding them for lateness, telling them to turn off their mobile – or positive interactions – thanking a student for a presentation, praising written work, commenting on a student spoken response. Considering the communication models/theories above, do any cast light on the nature of the interaction itself?

Features of learning

Important determinants of teaching methods are the different features of learning teachers will be attempting to bring about as part of the 14–19 reforms. Some of the key features of diploma learning are outlined by the Qualifications and Curriculum Authority (QCA 2008). A total of 50% of principal learning must be **applied learning**, which is defined as:

> acquiring and applying knowledge, skills and understanding through tasks set in sector or subject contexts that have many of the characteristics of real work, or are set within the workplace. Most importantly, the purpose of the task in which learners apply their knowledge, skills and understanding must be relevant to the workplace.
>
> *(QCA, 2008: 26)*

Central to applied learning, it is argued, is **experiential learning**. This was considered in Chapter 11 in connection with teachers' learning but the QCA sees the reflection–review planning as central to young people's learning. This process supports the **personalisation** of learning which helps to 'ensure sufficient challenge, pace, rigour and progression for the learner' (QCA 2008: 7). There is an emphasis on the importance of learning through **participation** rather than through **acquisition**:

> 'Learning through participation', rather than 'learning by acquisition', is a social theory of learning (Felstead et al., 2005, drawing on Sfard, 1998). *Situated learning theories* also suggest that roles and relationships affect learning in sites of learning such as the workplace, or other sites of learning, for example 'trainees or new employees learn situation-specific processes and behaviours from more experienced workers and their peers rather than by transference of what they have learnt in the classroom' (Beach, 2003).
>
> *(QCA 2008)*

Finally, learners need to be able to transfer their skills, knowledge and understanding from one situation to another, to achieve what the QCA calls '**connectivity**'. The QCA suggests the following are some of the practical implications for learning of the key features described above.

RESEARCH FOCUS

What is already known about *experiential learning* (Kolb, 1984; Dewey, 1938; Lewin, 1951; Boud et al., 1993; Boud and Miller, 1996; Piaget, 1950; Bruner 1960 and 1996) suggests that learners will benefit from:

- first-hand investigation and active enquiry – learning by doing
- learning which is planned by learners that is relevant to their own interests and concerns, with opportunities for reflection and review

- learning experiences that are tailored to the individual's cognitive and affective development needs, and build upon their existing knowledge and understanding
- use of a wide variety of learning experiences (multi-sensory learning), including use of innovative learning technologies and collaborative work
- assessment for learning which encourages and supports further development

What is already known about situated learning (Lave and Wenger, 1991; Bruner, 1986; Brown et al., 1989) suggests that learners will benefit from:

- access to rich and varied learning environments
- opportunities to participate in expansive learning environments (e.g. to carry out tasks involving access to broader knowledge about organisations), and develop or improve participation through role enhancement and peer support
- learning through authentic tasks, i.e. tasks which have a meaning and a purpose in relation to a socially recognised practice such as work or social enterprise
- learning from a variety of others who occupy (or have experienced) recognised roles within a relevant environment, workplace, trade or profession
- opportunities to learn in different ways in different contexts (e.g. collaborative on-the-job learning, learning by demonstration or modelling), and to take risks when working collaboratively in order to try out strategies, develop independence and be creative.

What is already known about *connecting up learning* (Young, 1998; Griffiths and Guile, 2003; Engerström, 1996; Beach, 1999) suggests that learners will benefit from:

- access to varied learning environments, including appropriate and alternative sites for learning
- opportunities to try out processes, techniques, knowledge and skills developed in one context in contrasting contexts, and bring together concepts and processes from different subjects or practices to address particular problems or tasks (cross-disciplinary learning)
- support from mentors and teachers across contexts, with opportunities to discuss and articulate skills which are 'generic' in relation to a number of different contexts
- opportunities for the learner to shape the programme of learning so that the sequence of learning experiences meets individual needs, and to develop meta-cognitive capabilities (e.g. reflection, synthesis)
- enterprise approaches where the learners initiate, organise and sustain an activity that serves purposes they have chosen and that also functions as a context for learning (e.g. cooperative learning).

(QCA 2008: 11)

WHAT DO YOU THINK?

Consider the features of learning discussed above: applied, experiential, personalised, participatory, situated and connected-up learning. What do you think are the key teaching methods which will be needed to bring about these features of learning?

Teaching style

Although a teacher may use a range of methods and techniques, a teacher's *style* will be expressed in the highly individual way in which they use those methods and techniques. That style can be characterised in a variety of ways. Jarvis (2006) refers to McGregor's (1960) distinction between Theory X and Theory Y, according to which:

> Theory X suggests that managers assume that those with whom they work dislike it so that they have to controlled, coerced and directed in order to achieve the desired outcomes, whereas Theory Y concentrates on the way that managers focus on the human side of their employees and endeavour to develop them as people. Clearly both of these approaches are very relevant to teaching.

(Jarvis 2006: 33)

Jarvis goes on to discuss Lippitt and White's (1958) examination of the leadership styles of youth leaders,

> highlighting a threefold typology: authoritarian, laissez-faire and democratic. They found that:
>
> - authoritarian leaders create a sense of group dependence on the leader, that their presence held the group together and in their absence no work was done;
> - laissez-faire leaders achieved little whether they were present or absent;
> - democratic leaders achieve group cohesion and harmonious working relationships whether they were present or not.

Jarvis goes on to apply the above to teaching styles and consider different approaches to examining teaching style: 'so that teachers are seen as having formal or informal approaches, friendly or distant, humorous or dry, confident or withdrawn and so on' (Jarvis 2006: 34).

A key determinant of our teaching style will be our own educational history. There is some evidence that new teachers will often adopt a teaching style they experienced as learners, in spite of their experience of this style being negative rather than positive! Our view of what our own subject should be about will influence our teaching style: the Art and Design teacher who values draughtsmanship above all in drawing will have a different approach from the teacher who prizes originality. Our own personal philosophy of education, our notion about what constitutes effective learning, will have an effect on the approach we take. Most important, however, are likely to be our own personal attributes. As Jarvis (2006: 35) argues:

> The character of the teacher plays a fundamental role in teaching – teachers themselves are their best teaching aids. Emphasis on teaching methods tends to standardize teaching but emphasis on style highlights the individuality of teachers and allows for the recognition that every teaching session is a unique event with the teachers alone being the common element in the different classes they teach.

IN PRACTICE

What kind of teaching style do you have?

Complete the teaching styles questionnaire at the end of this chapter.

WHAT DO YOU THINK?

Look back at the features of learning above: applied, experiential, personalised, participatory, situated and connected-up learning. How far will the elements of your own teaching style, explored above, enable you to facilitate these kinds of learning?

Teaching roles

The dramatic increase in participation of 14–19-year-olds in education and training over the past decade has led to greater diversity across the student population as well as a wider range of student needs and therefore a requirement that teachers play a more complex set of roles than previously. Such a requirement relates also to an increasing pressure to retain students who may be poorly motivated for funding or education/training targets. The three principal roles a 14–19 teacher may play are as *teacher*, as *tutor* and as *adviser*.

Teacher

We saw in Chapter 6 that the 14–19 teacher is less likely to need be a teacher of a subject but more likely to be a specialist in a particular curriculum area who teaches as part of an integrated programme. We also saw above that as well as this specialism, teachers are going to need increasingly to be adept as facilitators if they are to bring about the applied, experiential, personalised and situated learning which is at the centre of the 14–19 reforms.

Tutor

The nature of the applied, personalised approach to learning will necessitate the teacher's involvement in the emotional and affective dimension of students' learning which is expressed in the role of the tutor. The pastoral role of the teacher is well established in schools but less well developed in further education. In fact Butcher (2005: 122) argues that:

> Too often, the contact with 16–19 students is in brief registration periods when little support for individual learners can be offered. This is low status time in 16–19 education and can often be treated grudgingly, as a necessary chore by students and tutors.

The pastoral role is carried out in different ways in different institutions. Some further education colleges have specialist tutors whose role is to address specifically retention issues by offering, for example, catch-up coaching for late starters, monitoring lateness and attendance.

Adviser

As we shall see in Chapter 19, student transition through the 14–19 phase is already complex, and, as the curriculum is transformed, so the importance of students' access to impartial, informed guidance to navigate such complexity will increase. There is a wide variety of practice across the sector regarding information, advice and guidance provision with a number of personnel playing a role. The individual teacher as adviser is unlikely to have the knowledge and information required to give comprehensive advice, and most FECs will have a specialist student services department and centre.

IN PRACTICE

Below is a set of teaching roles. Select those which apply to your teaching practice. Compare these with others: does any pattern emerge in the relationship between teaching roles and individual teaching contexts?

assessor	teacher
leader	expert
coach	instructor
discipliner	developer of talent
sponsor	guide
protector	guardian
role model	motivator
helper	opener of doors
facilitator	consultant
friend	counsellor
tutor	adviser
mentor	

Source: Pearson Education Ltd. Ian Wedgewood

Photo 15.2
Teachers can play a variety of roles in one session

The key aspects of teaching roles are as follows. How far are they active or passive in nature? A teacher assessing a plumbing student's on-the-job-performance would be taking an active role, while a teacher in a learning centre who suggests students come to him if anything needs explaining would be adopting a relatively passive role. How far they are controlling/directive or non-directive? A teacher going through the instructions for using a piece of machinery and demonstrating its use would be very directive, whereas an art tutor spelling out the ways a landscape might be developed but leaving it to the student to choose how would be non-directive. Finally, roles can concentrate on meeting intellectual/cognitive needs or can be nurturing in as far as they concern themselves with emotional/affective need. The former would be demonstrated by a teacher explaining the structure of Plato's Republic to a group, while the latter would be an instance of a drama tutor helping students to use their own emotional lives in the development of a character.

IN PRACTICE

Place each of the roles in the 'In Practice' box opposite in the appropriate boxes in Figure 15.4 (overleaf) according to what you think their position against the three axes should be.

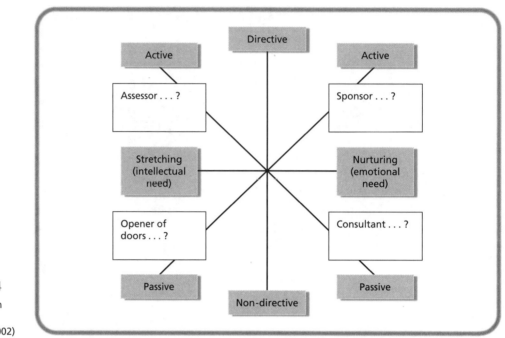

Figure 15.4
(Adapted from Klasen and Clutterbuck 2002)

WHAT DO YOU THINK?

Look back at the features of learning discussed in the Research Focus section on pages 282–3: applied, experiential, personalised, participatory, situated and connected-up learning. Which of the teaching roles described above will, in your view, be the most effective in facilitating each feature of learning?

SUMMARY

This chapter has considered the various dimensions of the teacher's repertoire. The factors which influence the choice of teaching method were examined: central to this choice were the features of learning that teachers were going to need to encourage in their learners – learning which is applied, experiential, personalised, participatory, situated, connected-up. Whereas the same methods may be used by many teachers, the highly individualised way in which they use these marks the teacher's style, determined by such factors as their view of their subject, their own philosophy of education, their view of what effective learning is and their personal attributes. Finally, the increasing diversity of students and their learning needs has meant teachers need to play a wider range of teaching roles.

Find out more

There has been relatively little work done on pedagogy 14–19 compared with that relevant to the primary and secondary phases. However, research and development work available to practitioners is increasingly emerging.

Teaching and Learning Research Programme (2006) 14–19 Education and Training Commentary.
The TLRP is the most extensive education research project ever undertaken in the UK. A number of its projects are directly relevant to the phase. The 2006 Commentary is a summary of the TLRP's work. Section 3 'Teaching and learning in further education and their implications for 14–19 education and training' is most relevant to this chapter. Available at: **www.tlrp.org/ pub/documents/14-19%20Commentary.pdf**.

Harkin, J. (2007) *Excellence in Supporting Applied Learning*, London: LLUK.
Joe Harkin's report for TDA/Lifelong Learning UK surveyed existing provision for those students at which the diplomas would be aimed, identifying good practice and a range of challenging issues which need to be managed if the diplomas were to be successful, implying a strategy for workforce development. The section on learning, pp. 33–48, is of particular interest. Available at: **www.tda.gov.uk/about/publicationslisting/ tda_excell_supp_appliedlearning.aspx**.

Qualifications and Curriculum Authority (2008) *The Diploma and its Pedagogy*, London: QCA.
This report, commissioned by the QCA, concludes that diploma learners would benefit from

- rich and varied learning environments that engage learners in authentic tasks
- different ways of learning, including 'learning by doing', use of new technologies and

- collaborative, problem-based approaches, that meet affective as well as cognitive needs
- playing a central role in planning and reviewing their own learning to meet their interests and needs
- interactions with a variety of others, particularly those with experience of working in relevant sectors or contexts
- assessment for learning and development of meta-cognitive capabilities, such as reflection, that promote deeper learning and the making of connections between contexts and subjects (QCA 2008: 3).

The research and theory which underpins the identification by this report of the key features of diploma learning is indicated on pages 282–3 of this chapter. Available at: **http://www.qcda.gov.uk/ 26029.aspx**.

Coffield, F. (2008) *Just suppose teaching and learning became the first priority . . .* LSN.
Frank Coffield's 2008 pamphlet for the Learning and Skills Network is an inspirational call to create a world-class learning and skills sector by transforming the culture of learning and teaching in sector institutions through the professionalisation of tutors, the increased agency of learners and through improving the relationships between them. Available at: **www.lsnlearning.org.uk/search/ results.aspx?SearchString=coffield**.

Nuffield Review of 14–19 Education and Training.
This was a six-year independent review of the phase completed in 2009. It has contributed valuable and useful publications covering a wide range of issues relevant to those working in the phase. These are available at: **www.nuffield14-19review.org.uk**.

Bibliography

Beach, K. (1999) Consequential transitions: a socio-cultural expedition beyond transfer in education, *Review of Research in Education*, 24: 101–39.

Beach, K. (2003) Consequential transitions: a developmental view of knowledge propagation through social organisations, in Tuomi-Grohn, T. and Engerström, Y. (eds) *Between School and Work: new perspectives on boundary-crossing*, Oxford: Pergamon.

Berne, E. (1961) *Transactional Analysis in Psychotherapy*, New York: Grove Press.

Berne, E. (1964) *Games People Play*, Harmondsworth: Penguin.

Boud, D., Cohen, R. and Walker, D. (eds) (1993) *Using Experience for Learning*, Buckingham: SRHE/Open University Press.

Boud, D. and Miller, N. (eds) (1996) *Working with Experience: animating learning*, London: Routledge.

Brown, J. S., Collins, A. and Duguid, P. (1989) Situated cognition and the culture of learning, *Educational Researcher*, 18: 32–42.

Bruner, J. (1960) *The Process of Education*, Cambridge, MA: Harvard University Press.

Bruner, J. (1986) *Actual Minds, Possible Worlds*, Cambridge, MA: Harvard University Press.

Bruner, J. (1996) *Towards a Theory of Instruction*, Cambridge, MA: Harvard University Press.

Butcher, J. (2005) *Developing Effective 16–19 Teaching Skills*, London: RoutledgeFalmer.

Dewey, J. (1938) *Experiential Education*, New York: Collier Books.

Engerström, Y. (1996) Development as breaking away and opening up: a challenge to Vygotsky and Piaget, *Swiss Journal of Psychology*, 55: 126–32.

Felstead, A., Fuller, A., Unwin, L., Ashton, D., Butler, P. and Lee, T. (2005) Surveying the scene: learning metaphors, survey design and the workplace context, *Journal of Education and Work*, 18(4): 359–88.

Griffiths, T. and Guile, D. A. (2003) Connective model of learning: the implications for work process knowledge, *European Educational Research Journal*, 2(1): 56–73.

Harris, A. B. and Harris, T. A (1985) *Staying OK*, London: Pan Books.

Jarvis, P. (ed.) (2006) *The Theory and Practice of Teaching*, London: Routledge.

Kolb, D. (1984) *Experiential Learning*, Englewood Cliffs, NJ: Prentice Hall.

Lave, J. and Wenger, E. (1991) *Situated Learning: legitimate peripheral participation*, New York: Cambridge University Press.

Lewin, K. (1951) *Field Theory in Social Sciences*, New York: Harper & Rowe.

Piaget, J. (1950) *The Psychology of Intelligence*, Cambridge, MA: Harvard University Press.

Qualifications and Curriculum Authority (2006) *The Diploma: an overview of the qualification*, London: QCA.

Qualifications and Curriculum Authority (2008) *The Diploma and its Pedagogy*, London: QCA.

Quinn, F. M. (2000) *The Principles and Practice of Nurse Education* (4th edn), Cheltenham: Stanley Thornes.

Rogers, A. (2002) *Teaching Adults* (3rd edn), Buckingham: Open University Press.

Schramm, W. S. (1954) How communication works, in *The Process and Effects of Communication*, ed. Schramm, W. S., Urbana, IL: University of Illinois Press.

Sfard, A. (1998) On two metaphors for learning and the dangers of choosing just one, *Educational Researcher*, 27(2): 4–13.

Shannon, Claude E. and Warren Weaver (1948) *A Mathematical Model of Communication*, Urbana, IL: University of Illinois Press.

Young, M. (1998) *The Curriculum of the Future: from the 'New Sociology of Education' to a critical theory of learning*, London: Falmer Press.

Teaching styles questionnaire

Below is a series of statements about teaching. Choose one statement in each row which most closely describes an aspect of your own teaching.

1a My lessons mainly consist of chalk and talk, with some student activity such as group work.	1b Students are engaged in active learning throughout my sessions.	1c My lessons only consist of chalk and talk.	1d Students are mainly active throughout my sessions.
2a Overall, imparting knowledge is important but I do encourage students to find some things out for themselves.	2b The most important outcome of my sessions is students acquiring knowledge from me.	2c Students are engaged in self-supported learning throughout my sessions.	2d Students find things out for themselves for much of the time but there are some things I need to inform them about.
3a Developing students' skills and competencies is a more important outcome of sessions than the knowledge they have gained.	3b The content of what students know is a more important outcome of my lessons than what they are able to do.	3c What students know is the most important outcome of my lessons.	3d The development of skills and competencies is the most important outcome of my lessons.
4a Students work as individuals and small groups for most of the time with occasional large or class group sessions.	4b All student learning is in large or whole class groups led by me.	4c Students work as individuals or in small groups all the time in my sessions.	4d Student learning is in large or whole class groups led by me most of the time with some individual/small group work.
5a I direct all student learning activities.	5b Students often engage in self-directed research project work.	5c Students engage in self-directed research project work at all times in my sessions.	5d Students are directed by me in most activities although there is some room for individual choice of activity.

6a Students either develop their own resources or use those individually customised for them by me.	6b My key resources are whiteboard and PowerPoint.	6c I use whiteboard and PowerPoint a great deal but supplement their use with class handouts and worksheets.	6d Most of the resources students use are either developed by themselves or customised by me but I supplement these with class handouts and worksheets.
7a Teacher talk dominates my sessions but there is question and answer, pair work and small group activities.	7b I talk to students for most of each session.	7c Students are engaged in pair and group work for most of the time and I make only occasional spoken interventions.	7d There is a balance of my talking to students and their interaction with each other.
8a I decide on and direct much student activity.	8b Students make decisions about most of their activities but I decide on some of the things they do.	8c I always decide on what students do.	8d Students have complete choice over what they do.
9a My teaching is mainly inductive: students investigate, experience and problem-solve and out of what they discover I draw theories and general conclusions.	9b My teaching is entirely inductive: students investigate, experience and problem-solve and out of that they draw theories and general conclusions.	9c My teaching is mainly deductive: I give students theories and information and they relate it to their own experience.	9d My teaching is entirely deductive: I give students theories and information and then I relate it to practical examples.
10a Students learn entirely through their own activity and I make them answer their own questions.	10b Students learn mainly by doing and I will guide where necessary.	10c My teaching is mainly via instruction and demonstration but I will also ask students to demonstrate what they have learned.	10d I teach entirely through instruction and demonstration.
11a My question and answer is designed to develop student knowledge and understanding.	11b I use Q and A to assess what students know.	11c I always ask very open questions which invite a wide range of responses.	11d I use Q and A to find out if students understand.
12a I will often rethink the structure of learning activities according to student response.	12b My lesson plans allow for variations in sequence and length of activities.	12c I always follow my lesson plan to the letter.	12d I generally stick to my lesson plan but may vary the length of activities.

13a All my teaching takes place in a classroom.	13b Most of my sessions are classroom-based but some involve external visits, field trips, workplace visits.	13c Most of my sessions are workshop, simulated workplace, lab-based with some classroom-based teaching.	13d All my teaching is in workshops, workplaces, labs.
14a I regard students as chiefly responsible for the construction of their own knowledge and understanding.	14b I regard students as entirely responsible for the construction of their own knowledge and understanding.	14c I regard students as recipients of knowledge and understanding.	14d I regard students as recipients of knowledge and understanding but with responsibility for ordering and making sense of what they learn.
15a I only use peer and self assessment.	15b I assess student work but there is some peer and self assessment.	15c I mainly use peer and self assessment but also assess some work myself.	15d It is only me who assesses student work.
16a Overall, students are passive in my lessons with some active learning.	16b Students are active throughout all of my sessions.	16c Students usually play a passive role in my lessons.	16d Students are mainly active in my sessions.
17a Developing knowledge of subject content is the paramount aim of student learning.	17b Although developing subject knowledge is important, there should also be an understanding of the principles and methods of a subject.	17c The principles and methods of a subject are more important for students to grasp than content.	17d Subjects are simply vehicles for student learning.
18a Overall, I try to encourage intrinsic motivation but sometimes need to drive and direct students.	18b Student activity is driven by student interest alone.	18c I motivate students entirely by extrinsic factors such as exam success, university entrance, work or career achievement.	18d I motivate mainly through extrinsic factors but try to pass on my interest in and passion for the subject.
19a I differentiate consistently taking student learning style into consideration.	19b I always use the same teaching method for the whole class.	19c I use the same teaching method for the whole class but there is some choice of learning activity according to the individual learning styles of students.	19d Each student is encouraged to engage in learning activities which suit them as individuals.
20a I often praise students but some need to be directed to concentrate and stay on task.	20b I use a great deal of praise and encouragement.	20c I spend a lot of my time directing students and getting them to concentrate and stay on task but I try to praise and encourage as much as possible.	20d Most of my time is spent disciplining and directing students to get on with their work.

Now score your responses as indicated below. Add up your score and find the appropriate description of your teaching style.

1. a 3 b 1 c 4 d 2
2. a 3 b 4 c 1 d 2
3. a 2 b 3 c 4 d 1
4. a 2 b 4 c 1 d 3
5. a 4 b 2 c 1 d 3
6. a 1 b 4 c 3 d 2
7. a 3 b 4 c 1 d 2
8. a 3 b 2 c 4 d 1
9. a 2 b 1 c 3 d 4
10. a 1 b 2 c 3 d 4
11. a 2 b 4 c 1 d 3
12. a 1 b 2 c 4 d 3
13. a 4 b 3 c 2 d 1
14. a 2 b 1 c 4 d 3
15. a 1 b 3 c 2 d 4
16. a 3 b 1 c 4 d 2
17. a 4 b 3 c 2 d 1
18. a 2 b 1 c 4 d 3
19. a 2 b 4 c 3 d 1
20. a 2 b 1 c 3 d 4

65–80 You rarely deviate from your lesson plans. You use whole class teaching for most of the time, with whiteboard or PowerPoint as aids. You might use demonstration or instruction. For you, students are recipients of knowledge and expertise and what they know is the key outcome of learning. You decide on student learning activities without reference to the students. Any question and answer will be to assess what students have learned. You assess student work: there is little or no peer or self assessment. You spend a great deal of your time disciplining students and getting them back on task. You motivate them mainly by informing them of what they need to do to gain qualifications and access university or careers.

50–65 Most of your sessions are classroom-based but you do see the value of practical workshops, visits and trips. You usually keep to your lesson plan but may vary the length of activities. You use whole-class teaching for much of your sessions but do use pair and group work. Although you rely heavily on whiteboard and/or PowerPoint as resources, you supplement these with handouts and worksheets. For you, what students know is an important outcome of your teaching but you do encourage them to find out things for themselves. You decide on learning activities but you take student need and interest into consideration in the way they will carry them out. You use question and answer to find out what your students have understood of what you have said. You assess student work but also use peer and self assessment. Although you spend time getting students back on task, you try to use praise and encouragement. You motivate students both by by informing them of what they need to do to gain qualifications and access university or careers and encouraging an interest in the subject through your passion and enthusiasm.

35–50 Many of your sessions will be practical/workshop-based and you value the importance of active student experience to their learning. Your lesson plans are flexible and allow for variations in sequence and length of activities. Students work as individuals and in pairs and small groups most of the time. They are mainly active. You encourage them to find things out for themselves although there are some stages at which you need to make an input. Most of the resources students use are sourced by themselves or customised by you for them. Developing their skills and abilities is more important than the content of what they know. Their learning activities are largely the outcome of their own needs and interests. Your use of question and answer is designed to develop student knowledge and understanding. You use peer and self assessment a great deal but also assess student work yourself. You try to motivate by harnessing student interest although students may need some external motivation.

20–35 All your sessions will be practical/workshop-based and you believe students' experience is the best basis for their learning. For you, a subject is a vehicle for student learning which is all about process rather than product. You will often rethink the structure of your sessions and be prepared to change them entirely according to student response. Students work on an individual, pair or small group basis throughout all sessions using a research/project approach. Developing their skills and abilities is more important than the content of what they know. All resources are found or developed by students themselves. Students have a great deal of choice about their learning activities. Students find and develop all their own resources. Any question and answer will consist of very open questions to which there may be a range of answers. You prize peer and self assessment as the most effective methods of assessment for learning. You use a great deal of praise and encouragement and you believe students are only motivated by their interests.

Pearson Education Ltd./Ken Wilson-Max

PART **4** Learning Futures

This part considers current and future developments in the phase.

- Chapter 16 builds on Chapter 7, Environments for Learning and asks whether learning technology enables us to address the opportunities and threats currently visible in the educational landscape and perhaps those as yet indistinct. Can learning technologies be categorised as somehow distinct from other aspects of teaching and learning without distorting our understanding of their place?

- Chapter 17 builds on Chapter 13 Collaborating to Promote Learning in considering the current and likely future emphasis on partnership working and investigating why partnership and collaboration are excellent in theory but that bringing about the best in the shared delivery of education and training has always been a challenge.

- Chapter 18 considers the international dimensions of 14–19 education both locally in the four nations and globally, focusing on both similar and contrasting features.

- Chapter 19 highlights those aspects of the teacher's role which are likely to be most affected in changing learning institutions: the requirement to personalise learning; the need to understand the features of assessment for learning, in particular the relationship between learning approaches and assessment strategies; a capacity to teach generic skills; an awareness of how information, advice and guidance might be given to students; the need to consider the challenges of working in collaboration and an awareness and understanding of the importance of reflective practice.

- Finally, Chapter 20 recognises that all teaching roles involve both leadership and management and considers the relationship between these two notions, aspects of good practice in management and leadership, the relationship of managerialism to professionalism, the importance of emotional competences and intelligence in working with other people and the importance of effective curriculum management to 14–19 delivery.

 Learning Technologies

In this chapter you will:

- Consider the background to the use of learning technology
- Examine the area of defining learning technologies
- Consider the role of policy in relation to technologies for teaching and learning
- Explore the potential of learning technology for a range of applications with case study examples
- Consider the role of learning technology in assessment and resource provision
- Understand the importance of being aware of e-safety

Pearson Education Ltd./Ken Wilson-Max

Introduction

As a teacher, how important is technology to you? You may use a wide range of mobile and digital devices but are you confident in the classroom to design and support learners in these e-environments for learning? This chapter can only try to outline and direct you to some interesting and important aspects of learning technology which you will already be aware is a rapidly shifting area.

The intention here is to emphasise the importance of teachers being confident as learners; being prepared to learn from and alongside our pupils and students and above all ensuring that the technology serves us and not vice versa.

Learning technologies defined

Learning technology and related areas can seem very complex. They encompass hardware, software, multiple applications and pedagogies. The literature relating to ILT is vast and includes, very naturally, much web-based material. What follows is a very brief representative summary of researcher and practitioner views.

Information technology generally refers to the hardware and commercial software available within systems. ICT extends this to communication elements which include remote and mobile capabilities and personal devices and covers a wide range of tele-communication, global networks, intra and extranet, satellite systems and all kinds of digital audio-visual storage and retrieval. Almost as soon as a new element is identified it is superseded. In this context, the effective application of technology for learning is the focus. E-learning supported by appropriate technologies results from learner-focused planning and design.

The best way to gain an understanding of this world is to follow digital natives and explore so that learning is experiential. But how do we recognise quality and fitness for purpose as we navigate through a wealth of options claiming to support learning or just attracting our learners? Good critical skills are vital in this as in other areas of learning, a requirement that holds good for teachers as well as for learners.

Background and discussion

> To contribute well to our Knowledge Age society we need a new set of skills –
> knowledge work skills. And now, when we apply these skills to our daily work,
> we participate in a vast intricate web . . . We will all need to learn new ways to
> live and work in our highly complex, technological, information rich world.
>
> *(Trilling and Hood 2001)*

The debates surrounding learning technologies are not new. In certain circles, pedagogy and policy issues are intensely argued as an increasing number of schools of thought and practice enter this expanding field. More recently, this world of digital literacies with all its associated terminology has had greater impact on mainstream teaching and learning. Rightly or wrongly, many policy makers and educationalists are attributing technology-based approaches to living and learning with the power and significance to drive forward positive change. Policy and consultation documents dwell upon e-solutions to a plethora of concerns; key stakeholders are informed of best practice and exhorted to follow suit; learners are wooed with the products of an expanding industry and the digitally illiterate tremble at perceived threats to their status quo.

WHAT DO YOU THINK?

As you begin to consider this topic, it may be helpful to ask yourself:

Can learning technology enable us to address the opportunities and threats currently visible in the educational landscape and perhaps those as yet indistinct? How do you feel about your learners teaching you?

Can learning technologies be categorised as somehow distinct from other aspects of teaching and learning without distorting our understanding of their place?

What are the practical implications for learning and teaching of developments in **ILT** (information learning technology) as they relate to the 14–19 phase?

The definition of terms and concepts, the measurement of real value for learning and the establishment of ownership are among the issues debated by specialists within the field. However, for the majority of teachers such concerns can seem irrelevant to their practice. They are more likely to be frustrated by a lack of resources and access to what they call technology – meaning software, equipment and suitable accommodation – or perhaps simply too afraid to experiment and too pressured to spend time on acquiring new skills. However, all teachers will need to become more engaged with technologies, as education and vocational training along with many other areas of social, political and economic activity enter a new phase of development.

Learners in the 14–19 phase in Europe and the USA are active participants in all kinds of technologies. A survey conducted by the Pew Internet and American Life Project (Hitlin and Rainie, 2005) found that

> roughly 21 million youth between the ages of 12 through 17 – approximately 87 percent of the entire age bracket – use the Internet. Of those 21 million online teens, 78 percent (about 16 million students) say they use the Internet at school. This translates into 68 percent of all teenagers, up from 47 percent in 2000. The survey also found that most teens believe that the Internet helps them do better in school (86 percent of teens, 88 percent of online teens).

They tend to display far greater expertise and exhibit less fear of the new, having been born into a highly technological world. Younger teachers and trainees also fall into this category and it can be their trainers and mentors and nature of their training which fails to take full advantage of the possibilities of available technologies.

The following quote from a trainee learning journal illustrates this:

> My mentor seems to believe that learning technology starts and ends with the use of PowerPoint and a bit of clip art. This really contrasts with his students in our vocational centre who are sending each other video clips of their design work by phone . . . I think we are missing out on something.

The extent and speed of innovations is often emphasised as a barrier or a challenge, and yet for a digital generation consisting of many young and an increasing cohort of older participants, facility with new communication channels and technologies supporting social, business and entertainment applications is a given. E-based activity is not a challenge to this generation but a natural and frequently pleasurable part of life, and the constant acquisition of new skills and openings is viewed as a necessary and exciting characteristic. For others less comfortable in these environments, whose e-skills are less developed, whatever level of enthusiasm they may bring to change, the minimum technology literacy requirements for living in the twenty-first century seem to rise by the day. Just as keyboard skills were once the almost exclusive province of secretaries and the ability to set up a website or conduct a business transaction online required a programming expert, now pre-school children are avid users of all kinds of technology, including interactive learning websites, and silver surfers buy, sell and date on the net.

Photo 16.1
Technologies occur in all kinds of areas which stimulate students

Source: Pearson Education Ltd. Ken Wilson-Max

It is vital to consider the rapid expansion of global communication and commerce networks in perspective. They are only a part of a far larger set of shifts, but the technology concerned should not be underestimated in that it does enable radically different approaches to age-old situations and creates whole new areas of possibility and danger. This complex interface of old and new worlds goes some way to explain the often emotional response evident in the debates mentioned. We would do well as reflective professionals to be sensitive to the very different views and profiles of both learners and colleagues with respect to learning technologies.

The 14–19 group of learners have been born into this post-1980s world and with few exceptions are much more at home with all forms of technology than their parents. Their inherent acceptance of this digital world has led to the use of terms like 'digital native' for this generation and 'digital immigrants' for the older less literate. (The US educationalist, writer and speaker on learning and education, Mark Prensky, is best known as the inventor and populariser of the terms 'digital native' and 'digital immigrant'.) These young people do not tend to see any form of technology as a protected space to be inhabited by experts and usually lack the fear of the generations before them.

> Digital Natives are used to receiving information really quickly. They like to parallel process and multi-task. They prefer their graphics *before* their text rather than the opposite. They prefer random and instant access (such as hypertext). They function best when networked. They thrive on instant gratification and frequent rewards. They prefer games to 'serious' work. (Does any of this sound familiar?)
>
> *(Prensky 2001)*

These are our 14–19 learners, and in some cases ourselves.

Policy and learning technologies

If we fail to come to terms with the present and future technological realities, will we be, as Prensky has suggested, 'struggling to teach a population that speaks an entirely new language' (Prensky 2001)? Policy can be seen to engage with such questions at all levels especially as it relates to the learners of 14–19 and below. We now link e-skills to employability and this makes use of the learning technologies so relevant. Use of technology in the classroom and other learning settings models the working world. It can be associated with other elements commonly accepted as desirable in current thinking, including learner-centred approaches, personalisation and re-engagement as well as to standardisation and economies of scale.

The DfES published *Harnessing Technology: transforming learning and children's services* in March 2005 which laid out the direction of its e-strategy. The strands apparent in this continue to dominate the agenda:

- Strategy is aimed at establishing effective use of technology across education and other services
- Interactive and digital technologies should enable personalisation
- A range of stakeholders should be involved – parents, learners, teachers, employers.

Long-term goals are certainly ambitious and the vision is optimistic:

> In ten years, building on the newfound capabilities of our workforces, our newly skilled graduates, and our new appetite for innovation, we could be anywhere – if we have the ambition and the imagination to go there.

The strategy encompasses the following objectives:

- transforming teaching, learning and child development, enabling children and learners of all ages to meet their highest expectations
- connecting with hard-to-reach groups in new ways
- opening up education to partnerships with other organisations
- moving to a new level of efficiency and effectiveness in our delivery.

The e-strategy has six priorities:

- an integrated online information service for all citizens
- integrated online personal support for children and learners
- a collaborative approach to transforming teaching and learning
- a good quality training and support package for practitioners
- a leadership and development package for organisational capability in ICT
- a common digital infrastructure to support transformation and reform.

The overall thrust of this approach demonstrates a clear commitment to linkage across sectors in terms of systems and actions applying to the schools, 14–19 and lifelong learning, HE and children's services sectors.

The Green Paper, *Raising Expectations: staying in education and training post 16*, presents the development of new learning contexts and approaches for a proportion of the 14–19 sector, including the provision of relevant experiences in employment-related contexts for some; opportunities for 'stretch' and early experience of HE for others; and a flexible, attractive and appropriate offer of options for all. Admittedly there are huge challenges involved in implementing many of the new initiatives but the cost of ignoring the needs of learners in this age range is surely higher. Unless there is an infrastructure established for 14–16-year-olds and those about to enter the phase, then there will be no real engagement with these new demands.

Learning technologies have been identified as a key contributing element in the delivery of new modes of learning. *Success for All* (2002) set out reforms for those in FE and beyond involved in lifelong learning to address a range of issues considered central to the sector for the future, including e-learning and employer engagement. There is significant attention throughout current consultation and legislation to demonstrate the continuation of this focus on technology as a means to implement and support change.

Equipping our Teachers for the Future (DfES 2004), identified new areas of training and work, and other developments such as the move towards diplomas, changes in apprenticeships and employer/private sector training provision have all increased the demand for teachers who are trained to deliver in vocational areas to young people 13–19. Many of the staff employed are qualified and experienced in a vocational area but are far from gaining teaching qualifications. While they embark on this journey, there may be a strong professional support network within a school or local college for generic aspects of training but their specialist area may remain unsupported. The

2003 Ofsted survey of FE teacher training, now so relevant to 14–19 teaching and learning quality, identified this aspect as a systemic weakness. The implications of this are widespread but specific aspects of practice can be addressed to some extent through innovative approaches which will be discussed later in the chapter.

Learning technologies can provide valuable shared resources, interactive materials and even advice and support through e-mentoring and joint project working for professionals as well as for young learners. Learners in this phase will be often be accessing study support, seeking samples of work and comparing notes with peers in various ways online, whether these facilities are made available through educational institutions or not. High-quality support for this age phase really does require teacher awareness of issues, like the prevalence of sites which make plagiarism easy (e.g. essay banks) and the needs of many students to air and share problems and pressures.

An emphasis on e-learning for this phase has been emerging over a number of years and has proved to be one of the enduring elements now being embedded in models for the future. Of all the elements proposed in the Tomlinson Report (published 18 October 2004 – concerned primarily with ensuring that 'all young people are equipped with the skills and knowledge they need to succeed and progress in education, employment and adult life') and widely accepted by both education and employment sector, the e-agenda seems destined to survive. The White Paper (2005) deliberately avoids detail and prescription in this area, which it calls 'the ongoing development of technologies that support learning', and concentrates instead on setting out 'the changes in curriculum and qualifications that will improve what is available to young people' (Donovan 2005). E-learning development is being undertaken by the Standards Unit but can be seen in a wide range of more embedded policy initiatives.

RESEARCH FOCUS

As young learners are increasingly directed towards the workplace at an earlier stage in their education, some commentators have criticised the final report of the Leitch Review of Skills (2006) for failing to take account of digital technologies when approaching strategic skills planning issues:

Unfortunately, Leitch's Review misses a crucial and critical dimension. A word search of the document produces an interesting insight into the lack of understanding of the implications of digital technologies either as a discreet component of the global economy or as an essential component of other global economic developments. (With the term 'skills' mentioned 1727 times, 'treasury', 21 and e-learning, digital economy, new technology, social networking and other fairly surprising omissions receiving no mention at all.) *It is difficult to see how this review prepared with an 'Industrial Age' mindset can help deliver world-class skills for the 'Information Age'.*

(Harrison 2007)

This future-focused report does have an impact on the whole area of skills development and while it must be recognised that others, for example the Quality Improvement Agency, have responded far more favourably, there is clearly a lack of consensus across government, education and employment of the wider role of e-skills and their relationship to a digital world of work.

WHAT DO YOU THINK?

Do you believe that you and your learners are being adequately prepared for full participation in the 'Information Age'?

In what ways could the use of learning technologies support this preparation?

A great deal of trust has been placed in the potential for ICT, Information and Communication Technologies, to deliver results across the 14–19 sector. This work is supported by the partners referred to below and by LLUK as it becomes responsible for elements of learning in this area.

> ICT can improve the quality of teaching, learning and management in schools and so help raise standards. That's why ICT is at the heart of the DfES' commitment to improving learning for all children.
>
> *(DfES 2007)*

Using active learning and technology

Learning technology provides tools and approaches to support vocational and academic learning across a wide range of subjects and specialisms and in many settings. It can be integrated successfully into more conventional learning contexts and bring the world of work to the classroom, and equally it can draw wider learning opportunities into the work place for the young as well as for older learners. Where students' more conventional skills may be weak, they can often feel more empowered if they possess higher level e-skills and good knowledge and understanding of digital environments.

ACTIVITY: USE OF CASE STUDIES

In a group let each individual select and examine a different one of the many studies available relating to real school and college experiences with learning technologies. Some starter samples are available below. Try to work with one that presents an aspect of this that is new for you. Then discuss the benefits with other group members, and as continuation decide to engage in further investigation of an area of technology that will benefit your own work with learners.

The very brief clips below show just some of the wide-ranging case studies which are uploaded regularly to the Learning Skills Network site.

Some case study examples from 2010 demonstrate the use of digital media streaming and flip video with NEET students:
www.moletv.org.uk/watch.aspx?v=SRE1W.

City College Plymouth Business Diploma students' radio interview

This first section of an interview relates to students on a 14–19 Diploma in Business Administration and Finance course talking about their development of a business idea. This links to Moleshare and the case study materials available at:
www.moleshare.org.uk/case_studies.asp?ID=86.

Further case study examples from 2010 are available on the web – these demonstrate the use of digital media streaming and flip video with NEET students

Following the success with digital media streaming (video and audio) in phase 1 of the MoLeNET projects, the Learning and Skills Network has introduced MoLeTV which is targeted primarily at colleges in England under the auspices of the Learning and Skills Council.

Dearne Valley College working to re-engage with NEET students

A tutor perspective of how the use of mobile technologies are supporting and engaging the NEET students and their curriculum – this demonstrates the use of technologies to appeal to a range of learners and make re-entering a college more interesting and relevant.

There are many more useful examples on the LSN site:
www.learningtechnologies.ac.uk/.

One of the key advantages of the use of learning technologies, so obvious that it is sometimes under-exploited, is their inherent skills development dimension. When learners are engaged in a variety of e-based activities perhaps by phone, using digital video edit or interacting in a structured way in a VLE (virtual learning environment), they will be extending and practising their e-skills and additional social and learning skills as they teamwork and solve problems together. If they are encouraged to do so in a critical and conscious manner, the wider, cross-subject learning opportunities are further extended. The raising of this kind of learning awareness among individuals and across peer groups contributes to the successful development of learning autonomy.

RESEARCH FOCUS

Liz Keeley Browne provides some useful definitions, evaluative tools for websites and guidance on constructing effective webquests:

Short term WebQuests The goal here is a limited period of time spent searching for new information. It is designed to be completed in one or two sessions and involves using material from the internet, optionally supplemented with video conferencing or commentary, to create a virtual project.

Long term WebQuests These aim to enable a learner to extend and refine their knowledge, analyse some information and create some form of paper-based or electronic presentation to which others can respond.
   The stages involved are as follows:

1. *An introduction sets the stage and provides some background information.*

2. *A task is set. It must be achievable and interesting.*

3. *The learner is provided with a set of information sources needed to complete the task. The sources might include web documents, the contact details of available experts (or a tutor), books, journals. These pointers prevent wasting time searching the web for hours and becoming distracted.*

4. *A description of the process the learners need to engage with, or an activity they need to complete.*

5. *Guidance is given on how to organise the information acquired: produce a mindmap, timeline, quiz, cause and effect diagram.*

6. *Conclusion. The learner is supported in evaluating what they have achieved.*

(Keeley Browne 2007: 88)

IN PRACTICE

Try a WebQuest with your own learners. Use the guidance above to construct your task. Evaluate the finished quest in use – including feedback from your learners. Remember how useful they can be to develop independent learning skills; allow students to work at their own pace and level and yet cooperate and share. Perhaps use one in groups at the end of a topic to encourage criticality and sharing.

Technology is no different from other elements of learning environments in that it cannot and should not be so definitively separated from the world outside education. At their best, the use of technologies for learning is almost invisible in the sense that it should serve rather than dominate the learning experiences.

Learning technologies should be viewed as something for the teacher and the learner to explore together as opportunities evolve and expand. The process of experimentation with innovation can form a part of a very active learning environment without taking great risks. If the drive towards personalised learning is to be more than a virtual exercise, there must be genuine dialogues between teachers and learners and an openness to adapting learning more closely to the lives of individuals. There is a need for reciprocity and increased interaction which can seem very intimidating to those more accustomed to a slower pace of change and to more programmed approaches; but in order for learners and teachers to share their experiences of a rapidly changing world, it is vital that we shift our perspectives. Educators who perceive the opportunities presented by new technologies are already reaping benefits.

IN PRACTICE

Browse the NLN (National Learning Network) site and select one of the resources. Consider how you might use and evaluate it in your own practice. Would you need to adapt the resource for the 14–19 learners?

The National Learning Network consists of a number of major national partners including Becta, JISC, DfES, LSDA, the LSC and others.

Launched in 1999 to serve the post compulsory sector, this network contains nearly 1,000 hours of e-learning materials designed as learning objects (the core concept in an approach to learning content in which content is broken down into 'bite size' chunks) to be fitted into a range of teaching and learning. These resources have been designed to be run through a VLE and can also be incorporated into a school or college intranet.

The NLN emphasise flexibility –

The materials give the learners things to do and a chance to think for themselves – and they are fun. There is plenty of in-built help if learners get stuck, but the materials are very intuitive. Some of the materials include educational games, which enable learning to take place without the student necessarily realising. The materials also support differentiation and the different learning styles of your students.

There are a range of approaches, but each 'learning object' contains some new learning (based on one or two learning objectives), a chance to practise and embed the new information, together with some form of assessment to check that the content has been understood and the learning outcome(s) achieved. The approach makes it easier to produce engaging activities often using game-style elements.

IN PRACTICE *CONTINUED*

In class, materials may be used:

- to visually demonstrate concepts that can be difficult or expensive to teach in the classroom
- to facilitate small-group work using case-study or problem-solving exercises.

For individual study, materials may be used:

- as preparation for a class
- as a refresher or to help students catch up
- as a revision tool.

The materials are free, interactive, multimedia resources which cover many curriculum areas: see Appendix 16.1.

Beyond e-learning resources

Learning technology can increase access, extend and improve conversations and dialogue. With learning technology there is far more involved than the use of some e-based resources.

WHAT DO YOU THINK?

The learning-objects approach described above can become far more active if learners themselves research, plan and create materials for others to use. Consider ways in which your learners might become involved producing multi-media materials.

Where do emerging technologies fit in terms of learner well-being, emotional development and, for those in the 14–19 phase, long-term social growth and the establishment of mature identities? Those expressing concerns often focus on the potentially isolating and even dehumanising effects of technology in learning situations. It is associated with distance learning where the tremendous advantages of technology are countered, perhaps rather inaccurately, by reference to the underlying disadvantages inherent in distance settings. Lack of actual physical proximity and the associated social interactions which can be facilitated around the learning environment are indeed issues for consideration when courses are designed. However, the selection of appropriate elements of learning technology can be employed to overcome barriers to learning created by distance.

It should also be remembered that those who see learning technologies in a rather dated way can fail to recognise the huge social impact of multiple technologies which are effectively distance solutions and innovations in many areas of human interaction. From MySpace to dating online, from texting to the use of digital video, there are tremendous social advantages. Some young learners find real connection with others and a wider world through the internet, music and video or interest networks. The isolated computer geek who gets no exercise can be a false stereotype as evidenced by many young business and sports people whose success has been supported by new technologies. However, we do need to bear in mind the dangers inherent in all activities. Phone bullying and 'happy slapping' are among the shocking examples of abuses of technology.

IN PRACTICE

Select one of the technology-based examples below with a view to incorporating it in your teaching. Evaluate its potential to contribute to learning.

http://podcasts.yahoo.com (Audio recording posted online, much like a short radio show.)

www.youtube.com (YouTube is a popular video-sharing website where users can upload, view and share video clips. Videos can be rated, and the average rating and the number of times a video has been watched are both published.)

www.myspace.com (MySpace is a popular social networking website offering an interactive, user-submitted network of friends, personal profiles, blogs, groups, photos . . .)

WHAT DO YOU THINK?

How might learning technologies support inclusive practice? What safeguards should we put in place to protect learners against misuse of technologies?

Teaching, learning and assessment in a digital world

Some of the most exciting examples of the liberating and imaginative use of technology for learning can be found in creative areas. Technology has great potential to support the transfer of best practice, increase access and to allow fuller exploitation of media.

Creativity has a place in all subjects but it is interesting to see how learning technologies have such a dramatic early impact on arts and media learning. Virtual dance spaces, virtual and actual galleries, shared literature and music production and other overtly creative projects for learning have had success. Equally there are geography, mathematics and engineering learning tools and approaches which are as innovative and stimulating for learners.

Valuable innovations in learning technology are not all generated from within the educational sphere, nor are they fixed to an age range. The exciting aspect of development work in learning is the openness to new ideas. What is of interest to those involved is effective practice rather than some fixed notion of what might be appropriate or currently acceptable. There is huge potential for some very radical changes to learning.

In such circumstances there is the inevitable trepidation and resistance normally associated with rapid change to conventional practice. Teaching and learning, in spite of the myriad texts written and experimental work undertaken within education on curriculum and professional practice development and new pedagogies, as a sector is as risk averse as any other.

IN PRACTICE

One recent example of how the application rather than the technology is central to learning is the idea of interactive homework. This originated as a primary learning system for the 5–7-year-old age group. It is interesting to note how successful the take-up of technologies has been in the primary sector and, in particular, the very creative uses now evident in practice. There seems to be a greater awareness of the need to inject variety, fun and openness into certain aspects of the curriculum. This applies particularly to subjects and courses which suit discovery approaches and multi-platform delivery.

The concept of e-homeworking does not sound new until the element of parental involvement emerges. This is an experimental interactive learning system (HOMEWORK) funded by the Economic and Social Research Council and run by the University of Sussex and London Knowledge Lab which enables parents to monitor the work of their children using tablet PCs. It is used simultaneously in the classroom and the home. The findings to date make this kind of system look interesting. It is claimed that 'Homework':

- Improved the communication between parents, teachers and learners
- Provided continuity between home and school learning
- Made numeracy learning more engaging.

These outcomes sound admirable and would certainly be welcomed by many in the 14+ phase where the difficulties relating to home and learning provider communication can be very challenging. The overt supervisory element of the system is another matter in terms of the age of learners, but the potential for three or more participants provides a model for partnership consideration. In spite of the more sensitive parent and young person issues, there is perhaps more of a need to reassure parents whose older child is moving across different locations and interacting with a range of adults and other older learners that contact and information channels are in place. For the learners themselves, there could be advantages in terms of providing a transparent and easily accessed source of feedback and a sense of control over an education experience split across sites and different institutional cultures.

Select another innovation for yourself and examine the technology or application from various perspectives with real-learning enhancement as the central criterion. Try **www.lsnlearning.org.uk/centre-for-innovation-in-learning/** or do a web search for yourself.

Many existing systems working to track assessment of 14–19-year-olds on vocational programmes are limited to data and reporting components. A more interactive/communicative approach would have potential to support learning.

At its best, learning technology contributes a vital element to the whole learning endeavour. In 2002, Hillier included the use of IT conferencing and other innovations in her discussion of teaching and learning methods and made no special distinctions.

> An extension of learning sets is the use of chatrooms and conferencing. Here learners can discuss their work and how they feel about it asynchronously using e-mail and conferencing facilities. In many distance learning courses, learners are encouraged to communicate with each other through the chatroom, partly to mitigate the fact that they are not meeting to learn together in one place.

The issue of being separated from classmates can just as easily affect the 14–19 learner on placement and they are far more likely as digital natives to be able to use good technological solutions.

> Seminars based on IT conference facilities are similar to traditional seminars, where learners are asked to discuss a set reading or task and to present their own interpretation of it, or general points that can be applied to other aspects of their learning. The difference with IT conferencing is that the discussion can take place asynchronously, giving learners time to think about and read about the issues before responding.

(2002: 160)

This learning-set approach can encourage and enable greater learner autonomy and yet provide supervision. There are some obvious advantages for the 14–19 learner context in such methods in terms of extending the learning autonomy of those involved and it can be very effectively supported through conferencing, VLE and other technologies.

> ### DISCUSSION POINT
>
> Reflect on a possible use of a version of this approach for your own learners. What practical issues may arise? Of timing, negotiating boundaries, clarity of tasks and general comprehension? How might assessment take place in relation to such a context?
>
> What differences would a synchronous version demand?

Chapters 10 and 19 provide a full exploration of assessment, teaching and learning and here the focus is on a consideration of the role of technologies within the wider teaching and learning context. Hillier and Jameson (2003) described the place of ILT within an environment where the definition of education and the role of the teacher are in flux:

> A dualistic view of education as *either* 'instruction by a teacher' *or* 'discovery by the learner' is not particularly helpful, since in the more balanced realities of the classroom, *both* exploration by learners and instruction by teachers is needed . . . Teachers have also increasingly been regarded as 'facilitators' of 'blended learning' strategies enabling knowledge and skills acquisition by learners through a combination of face-to-face teaching and individual on-line learning approaches. This does not replace the role of instruction in transmitting knowledge but complements and transforms it.

The pace and extent of change referred to here has intensified across schools, colleges and other learning contexts in succeeding years. There is no doubt that this is driven by policies linking education to employability, among other factors.

Yet even more radical changes are afoot in 14–19 education, as the classroom is increasingly understood in terms of a work-related place in both a simulated and a real sense. Learning technologies can enable such combinations of virtual and real experience. The whole process of creating, tracking and managing new learner autonomies and generating new environments is increasingly facilitated by technologies as managed learning develops more sophisticated systems approaches.

Learning technologies should be introduced or employed on an informed basis with overall educational aims in mind. They can act as great enablers of study, discovery and research. Such extension of learning can both improve the effectiveness of learning and enhance the ability of the learner to learn more independently. Advocates of these approaches, from primary to higher education, make great claims for the implementation of the right kind of learning technologies. If well supported, appropriately supervised and, in particular, if the management of this process and the modelling of good practice is incorporated into the learning, then critical and analytical skills can be developed.

RESEARCH FOCUS

E-assessment can be used to assess 'new' educational goals. Interactive displays which show changes in variables over time, microworlds and simulations, interfaces that present complex data in ways that are easy to control, all facilitate the assessment of problem-solving and process skills such as understanding and representing problems, controlling variables, generating and testing hypotheses, and finding rules and relationships. ICT facilitates new representations, which can be powerful aids to learning. Little is known about the cognitive implications of these representations; however, it seems likely that complex ideas (notably in reasoning from evidence of various sorts) will be acquired better and earlier than they are at present, and that the standards of performance demanded of students will rise dramatically. Here, we also explore ways to assess important but ill-defined goals such as the development of metacognitive skills, creativity, communication skills, and the ability to work productively in groups.

(Ridgeway, McCusker and Pead 2004)

Futurelab *Report 10* on e-assessment – The purpose of this report is:

- to assert the centrality of assessment in education systems
- to identify 'drivers' of assessment, and their likely impact on assessment, and thence on education systems
- to describe current, radical plans for increased use of high-stakes e-assessment in the UK
- to describe and exemplify current uses of ICT in assessment
- to explore the potential of new technologies for enhancing current assessment (and pedagogic) practices
- to identify opportunities and to suggest ways forward
- to 'drip feed' criteria for good assessment throughout.

DISCUSSION POINT

If the best assessment for learning is about the best formative feedback which engages self, teachers and peers, can learning technology provide new opportunities? (For example, synchronous discussions online or a text consultation with an expert from one workshop to another.)

The DfES supported developments in the area of e-assessment and we can already see significant change in terms of individual learning and reductions in the assessment burden on teachers making use of new technologies.

Barriers and challenges

Chief among the challenges faced by those designing and delivering teaching and learning for the 14–19 phase is the huge weight of expectations and demands placed upon this stage of education. The temptation to reach for e-solutions or to systematise more intensively can be very strong especially when we consider the emphasis on ICT, ILT and new technologies for global contexts. The rigours of meeting quality standards, the sheer quantity of options and entitlements, the shortages of those experienced and qualified to teach and support many of the vocational areas all present problems for 14–19 teaching and learning. Technologies can support but may also undermine good professional practice.

While there are obvious practical factors influencing the development of quite rigid time and phase related structures for 14–19 learners, there is a considerable body of thought opposed to the structuring of learning in very inflexible frameworks which are assessment-driven. This aspect is well covered by Lumby and Foskett (2005) as discussed below:

> The rigidity and archaic nature of the structure has been deplored by many
> commentators (Boyd, 1997; Cuban, 1995; Pring 1990; Stoll and Fink, 1996).
> It both reflects the credentialist agenda and embeds it further. The structure
> has a number of results. Teachers feel driven by the demands of each subject
> and by a perception of lack of time to 'cover' the curriculum. The result is a
> focus on teaching not learning, and a retreat into teacher-centred rather than
> student-centred activities.

The sense of 'lack of time' referred to above can be greatly increased when working with young and sometimes challenging learners in what are for them unfamiliar, applied vocational settings for learning; it is not uncommon for teachers and especially trainees. Learning technologies are often harnessed in the service of piecing together poor-quality responses to the pressures and challenges described above. Unconsidered cutting and pasting for projects; the temptations of plagiarism; unfocused internet browsing and pointless e-based worksheets are all examples of bad practice which can easily proliferate.

WHAT DO YOU THINK?

Think of an inappropriate use of learning technology you have observed or experienced in your institution. Was technology necessary or simply a distraction? How would you have changed the activity?

Linking technology to practice – case studies in Diploma delivery

The case studies below come from Becta's *A guide to e-learning for Diploma delivery*, available at: **schools.becta.org.uk/upload-dir/.../e-learning_diploma_guide.doc**. They provide some useful examples of practical applied e-learning approaches in different contexts.

CASE STUDY

Bassetlaw

Bassetlaw 14–19 Consortium has developed an exciting programme to support the delivery of the engineering Diploma called 'Reach for the Sky' [**www.eastmidlandsnti.co.uk/ CatapultingKidsFurther/Bassetlaw_Area.htm**]. The consortium was keen to develop an e-learning resource that would combine an online interactive experience with real-life contextualised information to meet all of the requirements of the Engineering Diploma.

'Reach for the Sky' is a type of learning platform that was deployed with Diplomas in mind. It enables students to access contextualised learning resources with standard hardware – and without the need to travel between schools, college and workplace providers. An example of the delivery of the module 'hydraulics' within Engineering includes the use of online simulations of a dumper truck, a train and finally visiting an aircraft hanger, all via the learning platform.

CASE STUDY

Derby

Utilising multimedia DVD technology, Derby City Consortium has provided students with virtual experience of the real world of work. It promotes work-related learning applicable to all lines of learning and relies on commitment from 'blue chip' companies. The City approached leading businesses and produced a resource-based DVD that includes 360° tours, interviews with staff, interactive quizzes, templates for paper-based resources and web-linked resources.

A total of 14 DVDs have been produced so far and examples include Rolls Royce, the Post Office and Toyota. The consortium hired a professional to produce each DVD and each one should take a learner up to five hours to complete. The intention in the future is to customise each DVD even further in line with the needs of the Diplomas and Apprenticeship training programme. You can see examples on Derby 14–19 [**http://www.derby14-19.org.uk/ yourlife.html**].

CASE STUDY

Lincolnshire

Lincolnshire local authority is using a proprietary web-based tool to provide students studying a 14–19 Diploma with information on career options and progression. It engages both employers and learners by providing online video content and photographs of different career choices that are relevant to the Diplomas. Students are able to watch 360° presentations about a particular career, providing details on the nature of the job and the skill and knowledge requirements. It currently contains 50 showcases from employers.

The aim was to provide students with easy access to employer information and to increase their understanding of the career opportunities available to them depending on their Diploma choice. This tool also reduces the need for students to travel to workplace providers and enables them to engage with employers that may not necessarily be accessible to them. You can find out more from the Lincolnshire Prospectus [**https://www.14-19.info/CAP/Home.aspx**].

WHAT DO YOU THINK?

Effective use of learning technologies can be part of high-quality learning. Using the links, consider the case studies in more detail and decide if there are any aspects which might transfer to your practice.

Relocating learning

Learning in future as in the past will certainly not be located solely in educational institutions. With rapid advancement in information and communication technologies, the distinctions between formal and informal settings and the actuality of high-speed exchanges continue to erode barriers of distance and access. The boundaries between formal and informal learning are also subject to significant shifts.

Some examples may include the use of podcasts, iPhone posts and blogging associated with residentials and trips and with placement work. It is worth noting that some students undertake this kind of activity, recording and reflecting on their experiences in all kinds of technologically supported ways outside their formal learning. Engagement with technologies is not only an unacknowledged additional learning activity but can be perceived by teachers to compete with set learning tasks at home and in educational settings. Some teachers will automatically label as unproductive what they see as excessive time spent on the construction of personal e-spaces, explorations of music, culture, virtual realities, game playing and diverse peer group engagements through e-space and digital media technologies. Of course there are times where certain activities are inappropriate but there can also be a failure to identify untapped opportunities for enhanced engagement, one of the key government targets for 14–19 education.

Relevance has always been an important concept in analyses of educational success. Contemporary wisdom locates this firmly in terms of vocational education (Higham et al. 2004). Since relevance is widely recognised as a powerful motivator, there is all the more reason to engage with the technologies which hold the interest of learners in the 14–19 range.

Inclusion and learning technology

RESEARCH FOCUS

In the following extract Mike Blamires brings the key issues of e-confidence and real e-pedagogy to the fore.

Towards 'e' confidence

Is there a way of moving forward? The DfES guidance on Transforming Teaching and Learning Through ICT in Schools provided a renewed emphasis on ICTs potential to change educational thinking and practice, where:

- *ICT makes a significant contribution to teaching and learning across all subjects and ages, inside and outside the curriculum;*
- *ICT is used to improve access to learning for pupils with a diverse range of individual needs, including those with SEN and disabilities;*
- *ICT is used as a tool for whole school improvement;*
- *ICT is used as a means of enabling learning to take place more easily beyond the bounds of the formal school organisation and outside the school day; and*
- *ICT capabilities are developed as key skills essential for participation in today's society and economy.*

(DfES 2003)

This indicates a move in policy and practice from the National Grid for Learning initiative that was focused on networking and connectivity towards an emphasis on ICT pedagogy and whole school improvement to develop 'e' confidence among all stakeholders. In the DfES vision 'e' confidence includes high bandwidth technologies, a range of ICT including more mobile devices, readily available whole class displays, managed learning environments incorporating assessment and curriculum content across the school and potentially the community, and creative technologies to manipulate digital content and access technologies with 'intelligent deployment' for learners with communication difficulties and/or disabilities. Implicit throughout the document is a welcome invitation to be creative and inclusive.

Teachers need to be supported in the exploration of different models, theories and practice so that 'e' learning is not merely bolted on but has a shared impact across the school system.

(Blamires 2004)

RESEARCH FOCUS

Jonathan Tummons, like Mike Blamires (see above), draws attention to the value of learning technology in relation to inclusion.

There is something of a chicken and egg argument at work here: has an inclusive approach driven technological change, or has technological change made an inclusive approach possible? Either way, the benefits are tangible:

- *As an assistive technology, ILT can help learners with a variety of disabilities. Visually impaired learners may be able to read from the screen more easily than from paper, as font sizes and images can be easily magnified. Learners with mobility problems might use a trackball instead of a standard mouse. If writing notes is difficult, speech may be recorded instead. Speech recognition software may help with the production of written work.*

(Tummons 2007)

WHAT DO YOU THINK?

Think of an example from your own practice which may provide an opportunity for improving inclusion through the use of learning technology.

Learning spaces – virtual and actual

A key aspect of new learning is new learning spaces. These are often identified as work-related and work-based environments or their simulated equivalents. What should be recognised more fully is the way in which a huge proportion of real economic activity takes place in virtual environments and the impact this actually has on learning through technology. The call-centre worker based far from the customer; the e-trader from the buyer whether they deal in millions of shares and commodities or individual items; the sale of virtual products and services from games to chat and so on into a future with innovations as yet unimagined: all of these provide examples of situations where technology can bring learners much closer to the real world.

For many years, vocational programmes of high quality have employed technologies relevant to the working context. These may be travel-agency booking software and associated packages or electronic motor-vehicle diagnostic hard and software. Training with these technology-based tools forms an essential part of the process of qualifying and preparing for employment. How much of this kind of actual technology use can you find in your institution or among its partners? What could be done to extend the use of this kind of learning opportunity? Are there any drawbacks to be considered?

Some young learners have really benefited from the car and flight simulator type of experience and these can be used at an advanced level of expertise and with beginners, in both instances to good effect. Perhaps more controversially, young offenders have been re-engaged through mixed learning experiences which have included actual racing and virtual gaming and training sessions, with learning technologies playing a key part in the design.

We should not forget overarching educational principles in the rush towards innovation, nor assume that all learning technology is new and specific to educators. New media provides a case in point as channels for communication, net and programming access in addition to learning links via other applications such as GPRS-based tools assume greater importance. Media for learners is as much about production these days as viewing and participation which means that its potential is vastly increased. Learners make and access podcasts both audio and visual and can be very comfortable acting as technical producers, presenters and critics in turn.

Most adults will now use some version of global positioning technology to navigate at some point in their lives, whether directly in cars or through mapping sites and aerial or space viewing. Satellite navigation has been employed imaginatively already on many field trips. Art teachers and students make use of far more than Photoshop and animation software in the best settings. There are huge stocks of art available through virtual galleries, and young people can design and exhibit for themselves as well as creating virtual art.

IN PRACTICE

Choose one of the following and incorporate it into a session that you would normally teach without using technologies:

- an MP3 player
- a satellite navigation device
- a camera phone
- a digital video camera
- a computer game of any kind
- another technology of your own choosing.

In what sense would you argue that the technology became 'technology for learning'? How was this accomplished?

E-safety

This area is of vital importance for children and young people learning in what are exciting but also potentially risky new ways. Common sense and the application of sound professional judgement is the same in this context as elsewhere in teaching and learning. A key aspect is to remain vigilant and up to date. The ideal approaches are whole school and college policies and training with links to national networks providing advice and guidance from expert sources. You can find further information by downloading at the following sites:

- Becta guidance in an electronic version:
  E-safety: Developing whole-school policies to support effective practice (**www.becta.org.uk**).
- *Safeguarding in a digital world: Guidance for learning providers.*
  The four-page leaflet addresses the main considerations regarding e-safety guidance for learning providers. This content will support your duty of care for the safe use of technology (**www.becta.org.uk**).
- 'Safeguard learners online: How are you safeguarding next generation learners?' (**http://publications.becta.org.uk/download.cfm?resID=39134**).
- Childnet provide information including a video, and links to important wider resources and advice on this issue (**www.childnet-int.org/kia/traineeteachers/**).

Technology, training and continual professional development

Newly qualified teachers across the sectors can enter the profession enthusiastic about the use of learning technologies and subsequently become disillusioned if there is insufficient time, support or resource for such approaches. Other disincentives include poor responses from learners which may be put down to the technology rather than to planning, relevance or other more conventional learning design issues. At this stage good mentorship, guidance and access to networks will prove very effective in encouraging perseverance and continued development.

The profiles of those entering teaching for the 14–19 phase differ from those of other teacher trainees. Large numbers are from industry, from FE colleges, public or private sector training as well as from school backgrounds. Many have qualified teacher status gained in service and yet not all have formal degree-level qualifications. They have not generally entered the profession like their counterparts in more traditional primary and secondary roles post-graduation with minimum work experience and are certainly not necessarily younger than their trainers. Some are close to retirement and have received no more than minimal support and no real training. The need for vocational subject experience, industry backgrounds and a wide range of qualifications relevant to work in order to deliver across the new areas in appropriate ways has significantly expanded the profiles of practising teachers, qualified and unqualified, and trainees. Age, background, skills and qualifications do not necessarily follow any kind of predictable pattern and this makes the provision of guidance on learning technologies quite complex.

This mixed profile does not always result in predictable deficiencies in skills and knowledge for learning technology. Technological expertise can be very high in specific areas: for example, engineering, music technologies or CAD (computer aided design) and this in itself becomes a technology for learning.

Lifelong Learning UK have addressed the necessary skills for professionals through ICLT (information communication learning technology) e-learning standards and present the following:

- Encouraging learners to manage their own learning
- Planning to use ILT as part of a learning programme
- Facilitating learning on site using ILT
- Facilitating learning on-line
- Developing and adapting ILT materials
- Assessment and tracking of learner achievements.

(LLUK 2005)

DISCUSSION POINT

Rate your own professional use of learning technology against the standards above. What action could you take to improve your own performance?

Compare this with the Teaching Standards for school and discuss.

Sources of professional support

Networking to extend and improve expertise, connectivity, accessibility and resources is of vital importance in this area as there is no single set of right answers or approaches. Most professionals training or qualified prefer to engage with colleagues or mentors who understand their particular context and can provide real experience.

There is a wide range of web-based specialised support and information available and many sites provide high-quality, up-to-date information and contact with professional networks and expertise.

IN PRACTICE

The examples below provide a small selection of good-quality sources, though there are many more, and new avenues for teachers to access ideas, resources and network opportunities come on stream every day.

- Teachers TV is a channel for education, from heads to NQTs, governors to support staff. It has become widely used and provides access to many resources – e.g. download a recent production of a Shakespeare play at the Globe theatre as an MP3 audio recording, with interviews with the director and actors (**www.teachers.tv**).

- Behaviour 4 Learning – The site contains almost 600,000 documents, including articles; a 'My Profile' facility for users; a 'My IPRN' where users can store their own collections of articles within their 'MyIPRN' page; the usual links to related websites like the Multiverse site on diversity in education, and there are further developments underway (**www.behaviour4learning.ac.uk**).

> **IN PRACTICE** *CONTINUED*
>
> - TTRB – The Teacher Training Resource Bank provides access to the research and evidence base informing teacher education. The materials are quality-assured through a rigorous process of academic scrutiny (**www.ttrb.ac.uk**).
> - Teacher net – a government education site for teachers and school managers (**www.teachernet.gov.uk**).
> - National Learning Network – National partnership programme aiming to increase the uptake of information and learning technology (ILT) across post-16 education in England (**www.nln.ac.uk**).
> - *infed* – This is an informal education site established in 1995. It is constructed as an independent venture by professionals and does not make profit. It is highly participative and heavily used. As well as being commended by Encyclopaedia Britannica, Adult Learning Australia, the Study Web and Schoolzone, the site is now involved in the British Library archiving project and links to UNESCO/NCVER VOCED database, SOSIG (the Social Science Information Gateway) (**www.infed.org**).

How many teacher training programmes devote significant time to learning technologies? Input and practice is often limited to interactive whiteboard use, and beyond this the trainee is reliant upon finding enthusiastic practitioners on placement or among colleagues at work. Specialist training and new ideas can be accessed through dedicated associations, sites, event and conferences, but some have cost implications and all require time without necessarily being able fulfil the additional needs of some professionals for support.

In addition to existing resources available to school teachers working within this phase, new provision will be available through lifelong learning sector developments. The registration database of The Institute for Learning contains a portal for planning and monitoring individual CPD (**www.ifl.ac.uk/cpd_portal/cpd_index**). This provides a suite of tools for supporting teachers in occupational area professional development and is based on tried and evaluated best practice. The intention is to set a benchmark for the sector, accessible for all and perhaps particularly useful for those entering the field with the 14–19 phase developments.

> **IN PRACTICE**
>
> To what extent do you engage with existing and emerging technologies to support and enhance learning? If you are employing such technologies, have you analysed the need, suitability and effectiveness of the chosen approach in each case? Have you accessed professional development opportunities in this area on a formal and sustained basis?

WHAT DO YOU THINK?

Is there a need to relinquish the focus on technology as separate or special? How might this be achieved?

SUMMARY

It is perhaps time to relinquish our tendency to focus on technologies as separate and special additional features and resources. They are so varied and widespread, so much a part of our daily lives whether learning, working or socialising that such distinctions are neither easy nor necessarily useful. An attitude which combines criticality with a creative and open mind seems to produce excellent results, as some of the case studies and your own experience will show. Where might learning technologies take us in the future? Check out the Innovations Workshops area of futurelab.org.uk and continue to experiment and explore.

Find out more

Barnes, S., Timmis, S., Eagle, S., Resmussen, I. and Howard-Jones, P. (2009) *Deep Learning with Technology in 14–19 Learners*, Becta.
Interesting outcomes emerging from a Becta 14–19 deep learning project carried out by the University of Bristol from October 2008 to April 2009. The Bristol group carried out a neuroscience review and conducted case study research in one secondary school and one further education college. This executive summary contains details of the project, key findings and recommendations. The focus of this project was the question: 'What knowledge and skills do learners need in order to be effective deep learners now and in the future?' The aim was to investigate the relationship between ICT and deep learning in authentic, practical settings, looking holistically at the context in which learning takes place, the relationship between the practitioner and the group, the design of the learning and the use of ICT tools, organisational issues, and the relationship between learning and use of ICT in and out of school or college settings.

Sparrowhawk, A. (2007) *Digital resources to support basic skills education for 14–19-year-olds* Futurelab available at www.futurelab.org.uk/ resources/publications-reports-articles/ other-research-reports/Other-Research-Report1103. This report, and the research upon which it is based, was commissioned by Futurelab in response to the Leitch Review of Skills, which identified that significant proportions of the population lacked basic skills by the time they reached adulthood. Three research questions guided the research, which where:

- How are digital technologies being used to support the teaching and learning of basic skills at 14–19?

- To what extent do these approaches fully exploit 14–19-year-olds' use of digital technologies?

- What recommendations should be offered to policy makers, practitioners, researchers and developers in order to improve the development of basic skills at 14–19 through the use of digital technologies?

Bibliography

Armitage, A. et al. (2007) *Teaching and Training in Post-Compulsory Education* (3rd edn), Maidenhead: Open University Press/McGraw-Hill.

Blamires, M. (2004) Virtual learning or real learning, in Hayes, D. (ed.) *The Routledge Falmer Guide to Key Debates in Education*, London and New York: Routledge.

Crockett, L., Jukes, I. and McCain, T. (2010) *Understanding the Digital Generation: teaching and learning in the new digital landscape*, Thousand Oaks, CA: Corwin Press.

Crockett, L., Jukes, I. and McCain, T. (2008) *Teaching the Digital Generation: no more cookie cutter high schools*, Thousand Oaks, CA: Corwin Press.

Davies, C., Haward, G. and Lukman (2005) L. REPORT 13: *14–19 and Digital Technologies: a review of research and projects* available at: **Futurelab.org.uk/research/reviews/10_08.htm** [accessed 30.01.2007].

DCSF (2005) White Paper *14–19 Education and Skills*, HMSO.

DfES (2002) *Success for All: reforming further education and training*, Nottingham: DfES publications.

DfES (2003) *Fulfilling the Potential: transforming teaching and learning through ICT in schools*, available at: **www.dfes.gov.uk**

DfES (2004) *Equipping our Teachers for the Future*, London: DfES.

DfES (2005) *Harnessing Technology: transforming learning and children's service*, Nottingham: DfES publications.

DfES (2006) *Further Education: raising skills, improving life chances*, available at: **www.dfes.gov.uk**

DfES (2007) *Raising Expectations: staying on in education and training post 16*, Nottingham: DfES publication.

Donovan, G. (2005) *Teaching 14–19: everything you need to know about teaching and learning across the phases*, London: David Fulton Publishers.

Harkin, J. (2006) *Excellence in Supporting Applied Learning*, London: LLUK.

Harrison, B. (2007) *Where is the E in L itch? Embedded or Invisible? Leitch Review of Skills: prosperity for all*

in the global economy-world class skills, available at: **http://newsletter.alt.ac.uk/e_article 000728802** [accessed 14.02.07].

Keeley Browne, L. (2007) *Training to Teach in the Learning and Skills Sector*, Harlow: Pearson.

Higham, J., Haynes, G., Wragg, C. and Yeomans, D. (2004) *14–19 Pathfinders*, London: DfES.

Hillier, Y. (2002) *Reflective Teaching in Further and Adult Education*, London: Continuum.

Hillier, Y. and Jameson, J. (2003) *Empowering Researchers in Further Education*, Stoke: Trentham Books.

Hitlin, P. and Rainie, L. (2005) *Teens, Technology and School*, Pew Internet and American Life Project (**www.pewinternet.org**).

Leitch Review of Skills (2006) available at **www.hm-treasury.gov.uk/independent_reviews/leitch_review/review_leitch_index.cfm**

LLUK (2005) **www.lluk.org.uk/s-and-q-for-workforce-electronic-learning-and-leadership-standards.htm**

Lumby, J. and Foskett, N. (2005) *14–19 Education: Policy, Leadership & Learning*, London: Sage.

Ofsted (2003) *The Initial Training of Further Education Teachers: a survey*, London: Ofsted.

Prensky, M. (2001) Digital natives, digital immigrants, in *On the Horizon*, NCB University Press, 9(5) October.

Richardson, W. (2006) *Blogs, wikis, podcasts and other powerful web tools for classrooms*, London: Corwin Press Sage.

Ridgeway, J., McCusker, S. and Pead, D. (2004) *Report 10: literature review of e-assessment*, available at: **www.futurelab.org.uk**

Tomlinson, M. (2004) *14–19 Curriculum and Qualifications Reform*, DfES, available at: **www.14-19reform.gov.uk**

Trilling, B. and Hood, P. (2001) Learning, technology and education reform in the knowledge age or 'We're wired, webbed and windowed, now what?', in Paechter, C., Edwards, R., Harrison, R. and Twining, P. (eds) *Learning, Space and Identity*, London: Sage.

Tummons, J. (2007) *Becoming a Professional Tutor in the Lifelong Learning Sector*, Exeter: Learnng Matters.

Warlick, D. (2006) A Day in the Life of the Web, available at: **www.techlearning.com/shared/ printableArticle.php?articleID=193200296** [accessed 03.04.07].

Websites

Latest news and information and CPD plus materials and ideas from the Learning Skills Network e-learning and technology team:

www.learningtechnologies.ac.uk/

www.futurelab.org.uk/resources/documents/ lit_reviews/Assessment_Review.pdf

Appendix 16.1

- Amenity horticulture Level 2
- Art and design Levels 1 and 2
- Business studies Levels 1 and 2
- Floristry Level 2
- General basic education Level 1
- Generic science Level 1
- Hospitality and catering Level 2
- Health studies Levels 1–3
- Hair and beauty Level 2
- Key skills Levels 1–3
- Mathematics Level 2
- Wider key skills Levels 1–3
- Care, childcare and social care Levels 2 and 3
- Construction crafts Level 2
- Engineering Level 2
- Environmental conservation Level 3
- Health and safety Level 2
- Maths for engineering and computing Levels 1–3
- Performing arts Levels 1–3
- Sport and recreation Levels 2 and 3
- Travel and tourism Levels 1–3
- Basic skills: Literacy Level 1
- Basic skills: Numeracy Level 1 and entry level 3
- Biology with sports science Levels 2 and 3
- Catering Levels 3 and 4
- Construction Levels 2 and 3
- English Level 3 (AS/A2)
- General art and design Levels 1–4
- Geography Level 3 (AS/A2)
- Hair and beauty Levels 2 and 3
- History Level 3 (AS/A2)
- Key skills Level 3
- Maths Level 3 (AS/A2)
- Office administration Levels 1 and 2
- Physics Level 3 (AS/A2)
- Psychology Level 3 (AS/A2)
- Sociology Level 3
- English for speakers of other languages (ESOL) Entry levels 1–3
- ESOL Levels 1 and 2
- Family learning with pre-school children with opportunities for adults to progress to level 2
- Family learning with school age children with opportunities for adults to progress to level 2
- Learning to learn Entry levels 1–3
- Making learning work for you Levels 1 and 2
- Modern foreign languages (generic support) Levels 1 and 2

(The materials are created by commercial developers, in partnership with subject matter experts, with the full involvement of a wide range of colleges. All the materials are fully tested by tutors and students and trialled for accessibility at the Royal National College in Hereford.)

To access the materials or find further information, visit the NLN Materials website: **www.nln.ac.uk/materials**

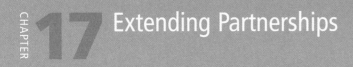

In this chapter you will:

- Consider the policy and background to 14–19 partnership
- Gain an understanding of local partnership working and funding
- Examine the features of effective partnerships and some of the key challenges they face
- Consider the opportunities partnerships offer for teacher's careers and development
- Explore partnerships in action through case study examples

Pearson Education Ltd./Ken Wilson-Max

Introduction

Partnerships across the 14–19 phase have existed for a long time, with many pre-16 learners accessing FE college courses and institutions working productively together to provide post-16 opportunities. As a teacher in this phase you will know or soon discover how the history of partnership working is relevant to work today and illuminating. Partnership is certainly not a new development, nor is it simply a Diploma related initiative.

There are many very successful local and regional relationships that have grown up quite organically in spite of, and sometimes in response to, a competitive environment. Rather than struggling to set up a range of options for a few students, there is a powerful case for formal partnerships to offer the best choice to the majority. While this does present challenges, the potential rewards can be high both for learners and for the teachers who participate in extending their practice into partnership working.

14–19 Partnership can be defined by its strategic role in:

- agreeing the local vision for 14–19 that is consistent with a wider Sustainable Community Strategy
- developing and articulating strategies for the full range of 14–19 priorities
- supporting Diploma consortia so that they are ready to deliver.

Education reform has placed extended partnerships at the heart of a vision for 14–19 education and training. The new national entitlement to diplomas made clear in the 14–19 Implementation Plan requires that every area produces a prospectus setting out the courses and programmes offered in each school, college and other provider, and the advice, guidance and coordination to ensure real access to choice across that area. While it is stated that the key to this kind of joint provision will be a genuine, well-established collaboration, there is a recognition that such arrangements do not exist in all areas. In order to ensure that young learners undertaking the Diplomas receive a full range of choice the government established regional and local partnerships (consortia) for Diploma delivery. Following the election of the coalition government in 2010, there may well be significant changes to policy, but the original requirement was that Diplomas must be a partnership venture and could not be offered like many existing qualifications by single institutions outside a partnership.

Delivery is only now being evaluated and there are many aspects where definitions and operational matters remain unclear. Yet the overall thrust of policy is clear. A good school or college will not be permitted to work in isolation for the exclusive benefit of their own learners, and the financial and inspection structures will ensure compliance with new collaborative arrangements across the board. Partnership should help educational institutions to improve.

14–19 Education and Skills (DfES 2005b) introduced proposals for qualification and curriculum reform in the phase intended to raise achievement, extend equality of opportunity and make education more relevant to success in employment and life. The 14–19 Implementation Plan (see Appendix 17.1) provided the detail of how this would be done and can be linked to the wider policy picture through further proposals in the Green Paper, *Youth Matters* and the White Paper, *Higher Standards, Better Schools for All*. The government focus on improving competitiveness across the workforce and raising skills for employment in this age phase corresponds with priorities for adults.

The implications for partnership are interesting. Some colleges have felt very threatened by the perceived shift in funding away from post-19 work and into the 14–19 phase in support of the new policy initiatives. Others have seen the potential for using existing employer relationships and established work placement and enterprise activity in new collaborative relationships with other providers of 14–19 education.

Personalisation and partnerships

Why have partnerships in the first place? In order to respond to the individual learner, to assess and fulfil needs in a **personalised** way, there must be a system which links the wider contexts in which the learner is placed.

The route to contemporary notions of partnership has been far from smooth and remains provisional. As the pressure to engage in this kind of wider context working has increased and the projects and initiatives have proliferated, the pitfalls have become more evident. In spite of the efforts invested in such pioneering work by many dedicated individuals, the legacy of competition and division is still strongly felt.

Government policy has always been focused on economically viable models of delivery, and partnership is favoured as presenting a means of increasing access to a potentially valuable combination of resources. Examples of the key role always envisaged for the partnership strategy can be seen in the Pathfinder projects and **Increased Flexibility Programmes** in the early years of the century.

The first Pathfinders served to demonstrate some of the fundamental difficulties inherent in partnership working. It was seen to be quite fragile and there were clear, early indications of some predictable difficulties related to negative learner experiences, including operational problems inherent in working across institutions and poor-quality outcomes. In spite of the obstacles encountered, the momentum continued to build and further funding was put in place to support development and progress in the area of partnership working.

> The Increased Flexibility Programme (IFP) began in September 2002 with the aim of launching eight new GCSEs in vocational subjects. In practice it provides school aged pupils with vocational and work-related opportunities in a post-16 environment. A second phase commenced in 2003. The initial round included some 270 partnerships, mostly led by colleges, while the second phase is expected to have 290 partnerships, but with a doubling of the current 40,000 participants to some 80,000. Total funding of £38 million is provided through the Learning Skills Council, with partnerships each receiving £50,000 in support funding. In 2003/4, their local LSCs will receive £100,000 each in discretionary funding.
>
> *(Coles 2004)*

This level of funding and commitment to the idea of partnership as a driving force in future provision of the new vocational education and training was already very clear. Subsequent developments have served to confirm such assumptions.

Post Tomlinson (Report 2004), the new partnerships were a requirement for applications to run diploma qualifications. There is no place in the framework for provision for individual institutions to plough their own furrow and this in itself should establish extended partnership working.

WHAT DO YOU THINK?

Do you believe that these partnerships will serve the 14–19 learners well? Policy has been emphasising the case for greater choice through partnership working across regions. Do you agree that for learners in this age group it is valuable to have choice and wider experience rather than to study more conventionally in one school or college? Is it possible to offer this kind of choice to some if all are not willing to participate?

Local partnership working

At their best, good partnerships will continue the excellent work achieved by many of the participants in recent and longer-term initiatives like the 14–19 Pathfinders. (This 14–19 initiative was developed across 39 areas to give learners a broader curriculum, innovative approaches to teaching and more choice in location of learning.) The Education and Inspections Act (DfES 2006a) puts in place many elements to establish and support joint, cross-sector working from national inspection arrangements across children's services, education and skills to new diplomas which require partnerships for delivery. All the Diploma lines (see Appendix 17.2) have been designed with delivery across partnerships in mind. The advent of a new government in 2010 may well result in a change in this approach, but as things stand at present, the implementation of this legislation will affect schools, colleges, local authorities and others involved in the provision of education and services, including the voluntary sector.

Responsibilities within the Education and Inspections Act (DfES 2006a) require local authorities to ensure that all courses are available in their area in relation to 14–16-year-olds and the Learning and Skills Council to do the same for 16–19-year-olds. It is the responsibility of schools to ensure that all 14–16-year-olds on roll have access to the full entitlement, i.e. a choice from all the learning lines (see Appendix 17.2) as these become nationally available. The new DfE (Department for Education) of the coalition government will certainly make changes to the present qualification offer. As things stand, there are interesting issues here for regional and national partnership working especially in terms of the significant overlap in provision between 14–16 and

16–19. Widespread attempts to remove the old school-leaving point of 16 seem somewhat undermined by the funding arrangements.

Local partnerships of schools and colleges, with their links to employers and other organisations, will have control over certain areas of collaborative work in order to ensure that they can respond in ways most appropriate for their own context. Decisions concerning which institutions deliver which courses within the required joint prospectus; how ICT (Information Communication Technology) is set up to support the partnership; and transport organisation, will all be devolved to local partnerships.

The national picture inevitably receives a huge amount of attention, but with an implementation model which claims to respect the local context, there seems to be a real consensus that policy will succeed or fail through the quality of partnerships. The approaches and solutions currently in place offer some very individual models and there are ambitious plans afoot. Many of the more extended geographical clusters of partners will have to consider the logistical challenges facing their efficient operation for the future.

Collaboration across larger cities or rural areas may appear to have the potential to provide very attractive choice of venues, employer links and resources. Additional shared expertise to fulfil guidance and opportunity requirements may seem accessible in theory, but if the constraints of extensive distances are factored into planning, along with the very real inhibitions and concerns of learners and parents relating to this kind of issue, then successful delivery may not be easily assured across over-extended partnerships.

Even the professionals – teachers, governors, administrators, managers and employers – for whom travel is more acceptable, find that in practical terms the size of partnerships must be carefully considered if long-term relationships, team projects and efficient delivery of learning is to be achieved. Size matters in these local contexts.

The term 'reasonable travelling distance' is used and this is a 'How long is a piece of string?' kind of area. Ten miles need not be a barrier in an area with a cheap or free, one every 15 minute bus service available to young people, as is the case in some metropolitan areas. In a rural location poorly served by public transport, this journey may be completely impracticable without a partnership transport service or timetabling which allows for whole-day delivery slots.

IN PRACTICE

What is the local situation for transportation around existing partnership links for your learners?

What are the attitudes of your learners to travelling for their entitlement and for new opportunties?

Are their aspirations or fears for extended learning contexts well-founded?

How might barriers be overcome?

CASE STUDY

The need for local approaches to meet very different needs can be seen in the lack of generic success factors for transport in the evaluation of Pathfinders. The following table (DfES 2006c) provides an interesting example of rural solutions.

REPLICABLE APPROACHES TO DELIVERING 14–19 EDUCATION AND TRAINING

Practice	Description of practice	Key critical success factors which enabled policy/practice to work
Use of mobile vocational units (Hampshire) 14–16 initiative suitable for sparsely populated rural areas where institutions have limited on-site vocational facilities.	In Hampshire, mobile units equipped with vocational facilities (e.g. a mobile hairdressing salon) gave students in a rural area access to vocational provision. While some travel was required of students, it was not excessive, and could be shared between partner schools – the units were based at different schools at different times. Further details available in the year two national evaluation at **http://www.excellencegateway.org.uk**	Pathfinder response focused on local skills centres as they viewed them as more successful than the mobile units at addressing vocational provision in rural environment.
Local skills centres (Hampshire) 14–19 initiative suitable for sparsely populated rural areas where institutions have limited on-site vocational facilities.	Hampshire established local skills centres to improve vocational provision locally in the two pathfinder partnerships (East and South West Hampshire) and to minimise excessive travelling by young people. In East Hampshire, a catering facility was developed by converting a home economics rooms in one of the partnership schools, with advice on facilities and equipment from an FE college. All schools within the partnership had access to the facility. In the South West partnership, the skills centres were not located in any of the partner institutions, but were managed by a group which included partner representatives. One, located on an industrial estate, provided facilities for courses in construction, hair and beauty and ICT. Another, based at an outdoor activity centre, provided both tourism and education facilities and was also a working farm and thus offered learners opportunities to access a range of learning experiences. The courses were provided in collaboration with local companies and colleges, and were made available to local schools in a prospectus published in January '04. Around 160 students began vocational courses in September '04, with more who started in September '05.	Need a significant amount of start-up funding in order to lease and equip the centres. Appoint a part-time coordinator who has significant entrepreneurial skills. Dedicated time is required to set centres up and should not be an additional task for a member of school or college staff. A critical mass of students and provision of evening courses for adults is needed in order to make the centres viable. All schools need to 'buy-in' and make changes to their timetables to ensure the centres are fully used, e.g. a 4-day timetable for Years 10 and 11 is being developed so as to release both the students and the funding for the centres. Need to involve local employers.

The intention of policy makers has always been to build on the best of existing good practice. In order to work with the configurations already established, some local authorities will certainly develop a number of overlapping partnerships and others will be cooperating to sustain and extend relationships currently in place.

There is also a great deal of scope and encouragement for wider partners to be drawn into collaborative arrangements. These should include the relationships already established within local education areas under different funded initiatives or as a result of historical cooperation and variously termed federations, Increased Flexibility Partnerships, Trusts, clusters and hubs.

Funding for partnerships

Partnerships will certainly face significant change in the funding arrangements following the 2010 change of government and the establishment of the new Department for Education (DfE). While this replaces the DCFS (Department for Children Schools and Families) it still does not cover FE provision as these colleges are the responsibility of BIS (Department for Business Innovation and Skills).

One key aspect of funding which will continue to be relevant for any partnership working relates to the notion of flexible learning space provision.

Flexibility is crucial to create a range of spaces that:

- facilitate personalisation;
- have scope to be adapted for future changes; and
- accommodate groups for different learning purposes.

The table below shows how schools and colleges have accessed capital-funding sources to support 14–19 reform and the delivery of Diplomas.

Funding source	Schools	Colleges
Buildings Schools for the Future (BSF)	Yes	
Devolved Capital Funding	Yes	
Modernisation funding	Yes	
Targeted Capital Fund	Yes	
16–19 Capital Fund	Yes	Yes
Strategy for Change		Yes
LSC support		Yes
Gateway capital funding	Yes	Yes

The following case study provides a valuable example of a very successful city-based response to funding-stream barriers faced by partnerships. As mentioned earlier, from the change of government in 2010 we can expect to see significant adjustments if not radical alterations to funding, structure and delivery of many previous reforms. This would certainly have an impact on the relatively new work on Diplomas.

 **CASE STUDY**

Collaboration with Universities and Specialist Schools to Broaden the Curriculum in an Inner City Area

Wolverhampton 14–19 Pathfinder (Pathfinders – a £46m initiative, funded jointly by DfES and the Learning and Skills Council (LSC), designed to develop collaborative approaches to 14–19 education and training and inform national policy).

What was the issue?

The Pathfinder recognised the need to involve universities and specialist schools to increase the range of provision on offer to 14–19 students.

What were the barriers?

The range of funding streams supporting different types of learning provision challenged the development of a city-wide curriculum. This was because some schools and colleges were inflexible over funding. The Pathfinder developed examples to demonstrate to providers how savings in one area could be used to enhance provision elsewhere. For example, by transferring resources saved by cancelling an unpopular course to pay for transporting learners to other sessions.

What was the solution?

The Pathfinder was led by the City Learning Partnership, an umbrella organisation representing all the key stakeholder organisations. The partnership engaged a cross-section of providers to enhance and expand the curriculum available to learners in the area. Partners included specialist schools, colleges, training providers, and universities. An Executive Group was set up to ensure the strategic development of Pathfinder activities. Operational Working Groups were formed to manage the delivery process. The primary Operational Working Group was known as DepNet. Originally staffed by Deputy Heads, DepNet was extended to include a range of practitioners responsible for delivery. These operational management groups were essential to promote cultural change and facilitate stakeholder collaboration across the Pathfinder. Membership of the group was by elective participation, ensuring that motivated staff drove the agenda. Individual staff fed lessons from collective activity back into their own institutional policies.

The diverse partnership enabled the Pathfinder to develop a city-wide curriculum and enrichment programme in sports, arts and citizenship, and raise attainment levels. Specialist schools in the Partnership hosted a Language Day for Year 11 learners to promote A level and University opportunities. The Partnership constructed a curriculum framework and curriculum models that could be implemented across a range of stakeholder organisations, but also provided flexibility for adaptation to local circumstances.

What was the outcome?

The Pathfinder successfully delivered a city-wide curriculum by working towards a longer planning cycle. Planning for the September 2006 curriculum offer began in May 2005. The Post-16 City-wide Enrichment programme was developed to include over 200 city-wide activities, in addition to 100 activities which partner organisations provided in-house. Over 1,000 students successfully progressed through the accredited programme from Level 2 to Level 3. The Pathfinder also established a series of work placements with renowned organisations such as the Law Society, the Royal Ballet, and the University of Nottingham.

The collaborative model received interest from across the country. Within the West Midlands region, all 14 LEAs (Local Education Authorities) in the Government Office West Midlands region, six LSCs, the Government Office West Midlands, Learning and Skills Development Agency and Networks for Excellence explored how they could develop collaborative working arrangements more effectively in the future. The model was also disseminated nationally at training events for 14–19 providers from Sussex, Essex, Staffordshire, Lincolnshire, Newcastle and Peterborough.

Enrichment activities tied to Gifted and Talented, 'Choose A Real Deal' (CARD) and Aim Higher were closely linked to the development of personalised learning approaches.

(DfES 2005a)

IN PRACTICE

Can you identify aspects of best practice from the case above which would transfer to your own situation?

Which elements would not be appropriate and why?

Opportunities and challenges in partnership

National Diploma line of learning networks

Partners involved in Diploma delivery are supported by networks which are available for each line of learning in every region. The networks provide school and college staff with the chance to get together with colleagues in a local area to develop links, share best practice and resources and maintain communication on more national developments. They are supportive of the more formal partnership arrangements established in Diploma consortia but focus on the teaching and learning support and sharing of practice and experience.

Learning networks have been identified as potentially valuable resources by those involved and by a range of commentators including Hyland and Merrill (2003). They were established to extend the school and FE links as a means to further the efforts of

Diploma Development Partnerships and support workforce development across the new diploma lines. They connect vocational specialist schools with skills academies and with the centres of vocational excellence (CoVEs) where FE college expertise has a strong background in partnership for learning.

Young people are partners too

In what could still be considered a relatively new area of policy and practice, the role and voice of the learners themselves as stakeholders in partnerships is much less prominent. Apart from some very successful exceptions, their position is generally characterised in terms of recipients of services and achievers or non-achievers of outcomes. There is considerable scope for further work to be undertaken in the area of 14–19 partnership from the perspective of the learners themselves.

A recent literature review by the National Foundation for Educational Research (NFER) examined the available evidence on the impact of the voice of this group on policy and practice and on young people themselves.

The main findings of the review are as follows (Halsey et al. 2000).

- There is a growing culture of participation, with insights and ideas from the younger generation recognised as valuable in potentially shaping services and policies which affect their lives and others in the community.

- The engagement of young people in these matters can have diverse impacts on the young people involved. The range of impacts found in the reviewed literature includes those at a personal, school and wider community and societal level.

- There is a relative 'gap' in any routine evaluation and documentation of impact – while the literature review did indeed uncover documentation of impact, the evaluation of that impact was rarely done in a systematic way, nor did it always go far enough.

Photo 17.1 Establishing relationships is the key to partnership at all levels

Source: Pearson Education Ltd. Ian Wedgewood

In spite of a general national lack of extensive consultation with young people, their views are represented in some strategic contexts.

The National Learner Panel

This advises the government on how proposed changes to further education in England will affect learners. It is made up of volunteers taking part in further education – giving young learners voice in shaping learning.

Issues the panel has looked at in the past include:

- how to make sure learners' views are taken into account during college inspections
- how best to introduce reforms to raise the level of skills in the UK
- proposals to raise the minimum age at which young people can leave education or training.

WHAT DO YOU THINK?

- What is your view of the significance of the role or voice of young people themselves in partnership arrangements?
- How else might learners be more engaged in the wider decision-making?

Training and development – careers in partnerships

Real opportunities exist for professional development in terms of working together. As a teacher new to this area or with experience from one of the sectors involved, you will find that your knowledge and expertise are increasingly valued. Many new teachers find that they are promoted to leadership roles very rapidly: e.g. as head of a vocational centre in a school, or leading on Diploma design and partnership in a college.

To support issues arising regarding professional status and development within partnerships, there are a number of initiatives. Both continuing professional development (CPD) and initial teacher education (ITE) are to some extent redefined in the 14–19 phase. The new demand for partnership working draws upon those who have qualified in one sector and gained qualified teacher status (QTS) with perhaps a degree in a subject which can apply to vocational qualification work (e.g. Engineering). As in other professions like health and social work, where individuals may accrue a number of specialisms over the years before entering management or training positions, the new education phases are becoming more flexible and responsive to multi-role, specialism and beyond this to multi-agency working.

Building up a coherent mixed profile is a feature of the new QTLS (Qualified Teacher Learning and Skills) status which recognises those qualified by different routes. The professional standards for the lifelong learning sector now take much greater account of the changing nature of learning phases, environments and reforms. National project work has also ensured that high-quality 14–19 teacher CPD for cross-sector professionals is available. The new structures are still emerging and the aspiration of those involved to provide flexible and coherent professional qualifications which enable partnership working have yet to be tested in practice. The more flexible, credit-based qualification and framework design incorporating mechanisms for transfer, credit accumulation and improved equivalence is a response to training challenges well beyond the 14–19 sector. There is also a database of relevant qualifications for teachers in the sector which provides help for those trying to gain teaching qualifications of the right kind through accreditation of their prior learning and experience (APL and APEL).

Who within the partnership is responsible for the training or does this remain within individual institutions? In terms of new diplomas the bidding process required the matter of workforce training and development to be considered and built into planning and funding models from an early stage by the partnership. It was, quite rightly, recognised as a key component in the successful introduction of new diplomas.

The current differences in teacher qualifications have created serious concerns for the many high-quality institutions from both sectors bearing responsibility for the safety, welfare and progress of diverse learners.

When training, teaching and managing across the area, whether as a new recruit to education or an experienced professional working within an unfamiliar phase or context, the advice must be to ensure that you are well informed. In an ideal world all the support necessary would be provided through structured induction and mentoring both for those in initial training and for professionals in new roles or undertaking CPD. In the reformed 14–19 phase this area which should be a priority is all still under development.

RESEARCH FOCUS

Professional development for the workforce

The DfES asked a range of national partners to develop the capacity of the workforce who will be teaching, supporting or managing delivery of the Diplomas. The TDA (the Training and Development Agency for Schools) worked with Lifelong Learning UK (LLUK) to produce a framework of professional development for the school and college staff planning to deliver Diplomas. In preparation, the TDA and LLUK jointly published the following documents:

Excellence in Supporting Applied Learning – building the evidence base to underpin the development of the new and existing workforce that will deliver specialised Diplomas. This report draws on evidence from the Increased Flexibility and Pathfinder programmes; interviews with senior managers, 14–19 advisers and other key respondents; and literature from the Nuffield Review of 14–19 and other relevant research.

Training and Development Guidance for Teachers of Diplomas. This document details the extent of skills, knowledge and attributes identified as important for teachers of Diplomas, providing a specification against which managers can determine and support the staff development needs of teachers of Diplomas.

Report on Training and Development Guidance for Teachers of Diplomas. This is a report detailing the reasoning behind the contents of the Guidance, and providing further information for each heading.

These documents are available both electronically and in hard copy at the joint TDA/LLUK 14–19 website **www.teach14-19.org**. An online training needs analysis tool has been developed based on these documents, and will be available shortly via **www.teach14-19.org**.

WHAT DO YOU THINK?

Comment on the relevance of the research and guidance findings in relation to your own experience and/or observations within this workforce. If you have worked or been placed in both schools and colleges, what training needs did you notice most? If not, you may want to explore this area further.

Equality and diversity

An area of importance for all partners is the opportunity presented through joint working to share and promote good practice around equality and diversity. It is pleasing to note the positive approach indicated in government communication on the subject. While there is necessary reference to the legal implications, the overall thrust of policy seems to be one of commitment to improvement and change, and evaluation of the work in progress. Chapter 14 contains detail on the progress made through the 2010 Equality Act.

Challenges

How do partners safeguard against serious problems? Or, more positively, how do partners ensure continuous improvement? Government is involved in establishing wider national networks to support the spread of best practice, though there is still a need for evaluation of the many pilots, initiatives and examples of existing practice. Time scales have been so tight that the risks to partners are relatively high unless they have been working collaboratively for years. Many professionals believe that the national policy-driven timetables are far ahead of the respective sectors' ability to deliver.

Clearly it is not possible to avoid all risk, but regular professionally supported assessments conducted across a partnership will cover the partners and their learners and will ultimately prove to be an investment. Other areas where specialised advice might be considered include:

- multiple partnership agreements – potential conflicts of interest
- contractual arrangements, e.g. staff contracts to services and support

- insurances, health and safety
- child protection
- quality systems and external compliance
- tracking, confidentiality and data security
- reporting and discipline
- communication and administration systems
- funding and finance
- joint membership of appropriate networks, CETTs etc.

WHAT DO YOU THINK?

What aspects within your own institution would present particular risks or challenges? What expertise could you or your institution bring to the partnership in relation to any of the above?

The legal, health and safety and learner/child safety aspects do not just impact on schools and colleges who may already have some, if not all, the required expertise. They are of increasing concern to employers who may see such matters as barriers to participation; many take a very informed view of their responsibilities and are not prepared to put children and young people at risk.

Partnership workforce issues

Parity of pay and conditions of service issues cover a highly contentious area for the workforce within partnerships. The concerns of staff and the issues themselves have their roots in the long history of education, work and social change. Attitudes to academic and vocational education, perceptions of the relative status of the different sectors and the impact of this on staff and learners in such settings can still be very divisive. New partnerships may be set up with little attention being paid to serious underlying professional concerns. If this is so, there may well be instabilities and a decline in motivation which proves detrimental to the long-term quality of provision for learning.

These matters as they currently apply to practising teachers are discussed elsewhere (Chapter 19). The fact that institutions within different sectors do not have uniform approaches has always been a factor relevant to some teachers whose part-time work extends across sectors. In cases where collaborative arrangements mean partners need particular staff, then individual arrangements may be agreed. However, this may mean fewer career development opportunities, greater job insecurity and pay differences even for equivalent work, sometimes with the same groups, just because it is carried out in a different institution. In the new climate of partnership working it has become more urgent for those concerned to establish working practices which can be sustained, supported and still attract staff at all levels in what are frequently shortage subjects.

What makes a good 14–19 partnership?

What constitutes an effective partnership? Is there a single model or are there features which can be identified from experience and evaluation of best practice? The DfES (2006b) *14–19 Partnership Guidance* uses evidence from the 14–19 Pathfinders to identify the characteristics common to all successful partnership arrangements. These are:

- a shared sense of ownership
- strategic leadership and vision
- clear objectives and organisation
- recognition of individual strengths
- access to professional advice.

Cross-phase and cross-context working already takes many different forms and the diversity of those involved in 14–19 is great and, as such, presents particular challenges for management. There can be a natural tendency for new partners under pressure from rapid change to look for a quick-fix solution and for government, national and regional bodies to seek security in centralisation. In part, the difficulties of early entrants, the pioneers in this field, can be ascribed to the lack of existing structures, the fragility of current systems in the area, few sources of advice and reference, low levels of reliable research and other issues rooted in the immaturity of this working phase. At the same time, it should be recognised that these very disadvantages also ensure a kind of freedom to operate outside current more restrictive conventions.

For many of those currently working in education, the notion of extension into partnership is already a part of their work. Families are seen to be a key element as are some less obvious partners:

- faith communities
- voluntary groups
- arts providers
- international partners.

WHAT DO YOU THINK?

- Do you think partnership goes beyond formal institutional and operational matters?
- In addition to those included above, what other elements would you identify as significant to a successful partnership?

Sustainability is a key element in successful partnership. Processes for review and development and a real sense of shared vision is vital. Nothing can be future-proof, but in a rapidly changing environment partners must be able to maintain direction yet be capable of responding to contingencies and new openings.

Management is reliant upon high-quality joint systems and an ability to comply with the range of external requirements particular to each sector and phase. For all concerned,

Source: Pearson Education Ltd. Lord and Leverett

Photo 17.2
Good
communication
produces
positive results

the channels of communication and the tolerance and time for relationships across partners will enable learners to obtain the best possible experiences and achievements.

Extending partnerships into HE

Once again partnership is a key element well beyond schools and colleges. Many universities and colleges providing HE courses will have been involved in the design of the new combined academic and vocational qualifications. The opportunity for younger learners to experience HE where appropriate is an innovation emerging from reform. In order to facilitate new relationships and accommodate improved progression and flexibility, partnerships must be established across all institutions.

For the level 3 Diploma to act as a new entry qualification to HE, the partnerships between schools, colleges and universities will need to adjust once more to support a shift in the post compulsory landscape. There are detractors of the changes who believe that vocational qualifications will only contribute to the dilution of quality in HE. Others feel very strongly that the growth in numbers and the expansion of this sector will enhance opportunities for learners and increase national economic advantages.

HE will also be contributing to the effort to extend stretch and differentiation. This will mean bringing HE projects and modules into schools and, in the spirit of Tomlinson (2004), will introduce a more personalised approaches to learning.

The role of FE has already been extensively altered as the national focus has shifted, for better or worse, away from the 19+ work and towards the new 14–19 priority phase. Adult skills may be firmly on the agenda but telling indicators, like funding, give a clear picture of the re-engineering process currently underway in UK education.

For the future, there are significant legislative changes designed to ensure greater participation in HE through the use of existing and new FE-based provision in this area. The boundaries between FE and HE providers have changed over time, with more FE colleges providing degree-level qualifications. As far as government is concerned, it should be possible for the learner to access expertise, facilities and assessment in a very flexible and individualised way in the near future.

Partnerships fulfilling learner entitlements

The national entitlement for every 14–19-year-old to be offered specialised learning lines in every local area was planned to follow the phased introduction and piloting of the specialised diplomas from 2008 to 2010, with pilots complete by 2013. With the advent of the new coalition government in 2010, there is likely to be significant revision of the previous plans.

Delivery is all organised at a local area level by the schools and colleges whose partnership development and management capability has been successfully demon-strated. Many of these lead institutions will have had a previous track record of good practice in the area of innovative partnership working. Some will have participated in such work as 14–19 Pathfinders (initiative designed to help partnerships to widen provision and increase choice; increase participation; raise achievement; improve pro-gression to employment and higher education) and the Increased Flexibility Programme (IFP is a major national programme that allows school learners aged 14–16 to develop practical work related skills outside school).

The Learning Skills Councils, local business and its organisations, individual employers, higher education, local authorities, voluntary sector partners, private train-ing providers and other stakeholders may all contribute to a varied local mix. What issues may arise from the diverse nature of broad partnerships? There are concerns that further pressure will be placed on professionals, though there have been reassurances on this point:

> The Government is committed to reducing pressures on teachers and honouring workload agreements. But teachers, lecturers and trainers will need new skills to extend their teaching range and to work with employers and new delivery partners. A programme to support the development of these skills will be created.
>
> *(DfES 2005a)*

Teachers will need to adjust to working together across and beyond institutions in order to fulfil the requirement to provide new learner entitlements.

In the *14–19 Education and Skills White Paper* (2005b) the DfES set out the national entitlement for the full range of qualifications including the 14 specialised Diplomas. This will be achieved only through partnership across sectors, including all those involved in subject provision and assessment in partnership with the responsible local authority. 'Schools and colleges will lead on local delivery of the entitlement – working with employers, the voluntary sector, local authorities and Learning and Skills Councils. Delivery is to be underpinned by rigorous accountability and timetabling' (DfES 2005b).

What role does partnership have in the 14–19 reforms?

Successful partnerships measure themselves against the aims of the reforms:

- improving stretch and differentiation for learners
- dealing with disengagement
- reducing the assessment burden
- providing a national entitlement to reformed qualifications
- addressing functional skills deficits
- increasing opportunities for training, work and higher education.

The success of these reforms will depend upon the ability of those currently involved in the education and training of children and young people to cooperate in establishing, maintaining and improving access to high-quality learning environments more suited to the proposed new learning.

In pursuit of coordinated and sustainable offers for 14–19 phase learners at a local level, partnerships are charged with producing a prospectus of available provision. The sharing of information and the organisation of practical timetabling solutions to ensure access and choice is a vital component of the extension of available routes.

Consider the following examples of key reform elements:

- Catch up in the basics with curriculum time provided.
- Functional skills – mastery of functional English and Maths by every young person before they leave education.
- New diploma planned for 5 GCSEs including English and Maths.
- Employers and universities with the appropriate sector skills councils are to lead on developing specialised lines of learning (levels 1, 2 and 3 Diplomas) within the 14 broad sector areas.
- New qualifications are intended to motivate and retain the interest and engagement of 14–16-year-olds. The new programme for the most at risk young people will be based around entry to employment. The young people, those who are likely to drop out of education, in this age group are being given access to a wider range of learning environments.

DISCUSSION POINT

Teaching and learning in partnership: will it deliver the desired outcomes for all young people?

- Is partnership the only and/or best way to deliver the reform agenda? What might be lost in the move towards new qualifications and entitlements? Why do you think some schools or colleges prefer to teach without partner institutions?

- What in your view will be gained for learners? What may be lost?

You may work through the questions in a group and compare your own experience with that of others, noting differences and similarities between 14–19 teaching contexts. If possible try to include some focus on the experiences of pupils and students in both schools and colleges.

Learning from partnership experience

CASE STUDY

The case study below provides an example of partnership working by a vocational pathfinder. Gateway bids recently announced were based on finding the most viable partnerships and well-established experience was a factor for many of those bidding. The ability of the partnership to identify and address issues was a key factor in successful bids.

Working with education business links to improve the vocational offer in an urban area

Gateshead 14–19 Pathfinder

What was the issue?

The Pathfinder wanted to develop a Vocational Pathways strand to improve vocational learning and promote vocational career options to Key Stage 4 students throughout the region, particularly in local employment sectors such as health and social care, tourism, engineering and culture. It organised events to market opportunities to young people.

What were the barriers?

There were difficulties in securing staff involvement, and employers were initially reluctant to attend.

What was the solution?

The Pathfinder built on established links with the Education Business Links Service (EBLS) as a vehicle to drive forward improvements in vocational options. A freelance consultant was commissioned to manage and co-ordinate this strand with the EBLS, Connexions, the LEA's 14–19 Manager, employers, schools, Gateshead College, and Northumbria University. Staff were encouraged to attend by tailoring events to curriculum subject areas. The events offered curriculum development opportunities. Teacher networks were established to ensure collaborative development. Area Wide Inspection funding paid for secondments from a school, the College and the work-based learning sector, to promote and facilitate vocational learning opportunities in schools.

Employers were engaged by shorter events that did not require much time away from work. The EBLS helped secure employers' involvement, developed a coherent Vocational Pathways strand, and made links with Pathfinder activity to other EBLS initiatives throughout the borough. It forged links with Connexions to improve personal advisors' understanding of vocational pathways to help with careers guidance. The EBLS reduced the administrative burden for participating schools.

Vocational Pathways events were delivered on the arts, media, health, engineering and tourism sectors, to promote local career opportunities including job diversity in the NHS. Over 330 Year 10–13 students, 30 teachers and 40 employers attended. Attendance encouraged students to develop their generic employability and enterprise skills. Employers played an active role in the Vocational Pathways events, with 32 employers giving talks and running workshops to help students develop vocational

CASE STUDY *CONTINUED*

and career development skills, and increase their understanding of local employment opportunities.

Industry days were also held to develop students' employability skills in the health and leisure and tourism sectors. For instance, employers from two local hotels delivered workshops demonstrating customer service skills to twenty Year 10 students. Teachers attended to ensure the experience could be reinforced in class in the future.

What was the outcome?

The Partnership integrated vocational pathways into the mainstream and longer-term initiatives. It established links with the EBLS, LEA, local college and Connexions (advice on education, careers, housing, money, health and relationships for 13–19 year olds) to facilitate this process. For example, the EBLS is maintaining the employer pool for schools to tap into after the programme. The capacity of the Vocational Pathways Co-ordinator was essential for mainstreaming activities such as linking with the local Centre of Vocational Excellence (CoVE) and a range of FE and Work-Based Learning providers. Discussions with the Gateshead 14–19 Action Plan Manager

and the Aim Higher Co-ordinator developed an exit strategy for the vocational strand by linking in with future funding plans. For example, the 14–19 Action Plan Manager helped transfer funding from the Single Programme to sustain activities.

These continuation activities also supported activities designed to raise the progression aspirations of young people. The selection of the Pathfinder to lead a Young Apprenticeship programme also generated interest in the Vocational Pathways strand, and learning has also been shared with the Stockton Pathfinder.

The Vocational Pathways events were evaluated and positive feedback was consistently gained from students, teachers and employers. Students felt more informed and confident in their career choices, and some had extended their career aspirations as a result of participation. Teachers echoed this view. Employers valued the opportunity to meet young people and help stimulate their career aspirations. All the Vocational Pathways events were oversubscribed. The EBLS will continue Pathfinder approaches in the long term by tailoring the design of activities to meet the vocational needs of individual schools.

(DfES 2005a)

WHAT DO YOU THINK?

Consider this example of partnership working. What could be identified as transferable good practice? What opportunities exist in your own local area for establishing excellent partnership practice or for raising its profile/quality?

The National Foundation for Educational Research have evaluated good practice and provided guidance on this process on behalf of the DfES (2004).

RESEARCH FOCUS

The implications of new partnerships are far-reaching since the most ambitious future visions detach the learner from the individual institution to a much greater extent than is usual at present. It involves the creation of easily accessible and flexible options for all students across the new age phase. In order for this to operate efficiently and really deliver there must be extensive collaboration to enable 'joined up' curriculum planning to take place. The success of these enterprises will certainly depend on the quality of this transition phase. Many education practitioners, commenting throughout the consultation process, have emphasised the significance of Key Stage 3 in the equation. Finally, the options, whether they are more traditional academic exams or vocational qualifications, will need to be supported by good guidance and underpinned with provision of all the necessary elements of student entitlement.

(Donovan 2005)

IN PRACTICE

Partnerships vary in quality and present threats to learners as well as significant opportunities.

What might one of your learners gain from studying in a partnership which extends beyond their own educational institutions and into work places, and what problems might they encounter? Use the headings below and build on the suggestions given.

Opportunities for learners	Threats to learners
• Increased exposure to real work situations • Extended social networks • Development of communication skills in new settings • Exposure to greater diversity in student groups	• Potential for bullying due to decrease in supervision • Isolation in new environments • Exposure to poor practice in work settings

Partnerships and learning for work and life

Partnerships facilitate far more than just mainstream curriculum provision. The value added aspects for 14–19 learning in the widest sense should not be underestimated.

The existing structures for this provision are changing as responsibility shifts from individual agencies and institutions to the local authority and new partnerships. Higham et al. (2004) showed how good relationships between those involved in setting up work-based learning activities in placement could deliver improved motivation, attendance and the extension of vocational learning.

WHAT DO YOU THINK?

Here are some examples of additional initiatives shared across partnerships:

- Work placements organisation
- Mentorship for 14–19
- Subject specialists and coaches in vocational subjects
- Careers events
- 14–19 conferences
- Links with other partnerships
- Access to alternative types of learning support
- Routes into apprenticeship
- Cross-partnership support to improve inclusion.

What opportunities does your local partnership already provide for 14–19 learners to support vocational learning? Are there any areas where opportunities could be added or extended? For example, your own previous work experience or contacts may suggest ideas which could be developed at school or college level and subsequently shared more widely. Many partnerships originally grew as a result of the efforts of active individual teachers.

Working beyond individual institutions

We need to examine the nature of learning environments and experiences into the twenty-first century. Given the thrust towards 'joined up' partnership working which is still designed to encourage regional, local and personal learning approaches and to avoid centralisation, the management of partnership enterprise becomes ever more important.

Key issues for consideration include:

- motivation of young learners across different contexts
- joint workforce training and development
- staff management
- contractual agreements and financial systems
- integration of PSHE
- implementation of consistent policies for SEN, EAL, etc.
- assessment across partnerships
- communication across partner institutions

- emergency, health and safety procedures
- robust tracking systems.

WHAT DO YOU THINK?

Select one of the above issues and examine its implications for the institution(s) in which you work? How might they be addressed?

RESEARCH FOCUS

About the study

Creative Partnerships set out to foster effective, sustainable partnerships between schools and the widest possible range of cultural and creative professionals, in order to deliver high quality cultural and creative opportunities for young people to develop their learning, both across and beyond the formal curriculum.

This study focused on schools involved in Phase One of Creative Partnerships, in an attempt to identify initial indications of impact. It studied all 398 core primary and secondary schools selected by the first 16 Creative Partnerships areas to launch the programme. These schools were located in disadvantaged areas. They received significant investment in projects and programmes, hosted a broad range of projects designed to explore learning needs, capabilities and overall ambitions and in many cases went on to become exemplars and advocates of Creative Partnerships work.

This study was designed to consider the progress in national assessments of young people who had attended Creative Partnerships activities compared with a similar group of young people who did not attend. A statistical technique was used to examine the relationship between attendance at Creative Partnerships activities (or schools) and how much progress young people made in their examinations, taken in summer 2004.

Key findings

- Compared with similar young people nationally, young people who attended Creative Partnerships activities made either similar or slightly better progress in their national curriculum assessments

- Young people known to have attended Creative Partnerships activities out performed those in the same schools (but not known to have attended Creative Partnerships activities) by a small but statistically significant extent at all three key stages.

(Eames et al. 2006)

See: **www.creative-partnerships.com/researchandevaluation**.

The study described above is not one immediately associated with vocational partnerships. In an extended partnerships environment, the early moves have been related to business and employment-related training links using more obvious mechanisms. For the future there should be far greater latitude in the nature and scope of these relationships. The best models are not one-dimensional nor should they be purely self-interested. They represent reciprocity, genuine mutual interest and individual enthusiasm. This commitment and real engagement is of huge value to all involved: learners, education professionals and the wider community.

Successful partnerships overcome the barriers described earlier through the dedication of the individuals concerned and the quality of structures which enable them to concentrate on the relationships and achievements of participants. Each one will be different and should strive to retain their individuality.

The politics of extended partnerships

The terms used for discussion and evaluation of partnership working can easily prevent a real critical engagement with the topic as a whole. Commentators, managers and teachers involved will comfortably argue about practicalities and varying claims to meet and support learning as it is currently defined. Politicians debate the competing roles of stakeholders from parents and employers to local authorities and different sector institutions. What is frequently left unconsidered is the impact these new arrangements may well have upon the education and training itself or the principles behind the endeavour beyond a rather simplistic economic competitiveness position. Yet the territory can certainly be viewed as one that is historically contested, fraught with numerous tensions, conflicting agendas and vested interests.

New configurations of partners require new articulations of central and local control with associated accountabilities and power. It is inevitable that we will see some partners grow at the expense of others and that certain versions of what makes for good education will wither while others thrive.

For some teachers and practitioners, partnerships are an excellent opportunity to involve the wider community and employers in education, while giving the learners a voice or partnership role.

> It is time to build a high trust, democratic education system that respects learners and their experiences, listens closely to their expressions of interest and need, builds partnerships between teachers, learners, parents, the community, and employers so that young adults learn what they wish to learn, and how they wish to learn.
>
> *(Harkin and Dawn 2001: 140)*

For others this is not the kind of education which empowers learners but rather a kind of therapy which listens without changing the real world. Such democratic and shared education experience is for them a vision that

> throws in every social hope that disconnected educators might have in these disconnected times. How real are these hopes? The specific condition of their achievement is that 'we', the educators and educational institutions, should value and accept these new students and their experiences. This is a therapeutic rather than a radical approach.
>
> *(Hayes et al. 2003)*

Partnership is not always about management strategies and institutional agreements on quality and delivery. Support for far deeper and more meaningful professional collaboration is promoted by some commentators:

> [A] greater emphasis on young people becoming emotionally literate focuses on the importance of co-operation. This could become the basis for partnership work between teachers and social educators, integrating all aspects of the current formal curriculum with issue-based work on gender, equality and human rights.
>
> Such a partnership would provide a model which emphasises the crucial nature of social action, developing in young people a realisation that their learning directly informs their behaviour. If young people become more acutely aware that their actions can make a difference to the world they live in, their perspectives on learning will be transformed.
>
> *(Miller 2005)*

DISCUSSION POINT

Working in a group, with the views above as a starting point, consider the following questions and bring examples from your own experience to the discussion.

1. Do you believe that all stakeholders in partnerships can subscribe to a shared vision of what constitutes education for the 14–19 learner?

2. What issues may arise from conflicting views and agendas?

3. Do you think, for example, that employers would subscribe to the idea that young adults 'learn what they wish to learn', and how they wish to learn as readily as many teaching professionals or reach a shared interpretation?

4. Are you as optimistic as Harkin regarding the potential for fundamental change through a transformed 'partnership' education model?

SUMMARY

The educational partnership issues and successes discussed here highlight the need for more considered reflective practice within the education of young people. Policies need to be underpinned by an ongoing re-evaluation of its effectiveness in meeting the needs of successive generations of young people. What is argued here is that more holistic forms of education are required so that improvements in personal and social awareness can enhance more formal elements of the curriculum.

Youth workers operating in schools are in a good position to drive forward such an initiative, yet to succeed it requires the active involvement of teachers. All those engaged in the partnerships need to be committed to a reflective consideration of practice and an openness to the potential learning that engagements with young people provide. Above all, those concerned need to be both convinced and committed to a shared approach in the interests of all young people.

Find out more

Hughes, M. (2000) *Partnerships for skills: investing in training for the 21st century* **https://crm.lsnlearning.org.uk/**
Summary: General background and detail on partnerships and strategic alliances between employers and providers can secure a better match between the skills needed for competitiveness and their development than a purchaser/supplier relationship. This publication considers the rationale for such partnerships, based on theories of partnerships developed in a business context.

The report also provides case studies demonstrating a systematic approach to developing capacity, maximising employee potential and more.

www.blebp.co.uk/staff/home_staff.htm
Education Business Partnership above (EBP) provides a quality innovation and brokerage service to employers, schools, colleges, communities and volunteers who need help, support, advice and guidance. This site contains some interesting case study material.

Bibliography

Armitage, A. et al. (2007) *Teaching and Training in Post-Compulsory Education* (3rd edn), Maidenhead: Open University Press/McGraw-Hill.

Coles, A. (2004) *Teaching in Post-Compulsory Education*, London: David Fulton Publishers.

DfES (2004) *Equipping our Teachers for the Future*, London: DfES.

DfES (2005a) Pathfinder Case Studies, available at: **www.dfes.gov.uk/14-19/dsp_case_study_detail.cfm?csid=62**

DfES (2005b) *14–19 Education and Skills* White Paper, available at: **www.dfes.gov.uk/publications/**

DfES (2005c) *The 14–19 Implementation Plan*, available at: **http://publications.education.gov.uk/default.aspx?PageFunction=productdetails&PageMode=publications&ProductId=DFES-2037-2005**

DfES (2006a) *Education and Inspections Act*, available at: **www.dfes.gov.uk/publications/educationandinspectionsact**

DfES (2006b) *14–19 Partnership Guidance* (**www.dfes.gov.uk/14-19/index.cfm**), available at: **www.dfes.gov.uk/14-19/documents/Partnership%20Guidance.pdf**

DfES (2006c) *Manual of Good Practice*, available at: **www.dfes.gov.uk/14-19/dsp_1419_goodpractice.cfm?**

DfES (2006d) *Race Equality Impact Survey Assessment*, available at: **www.dfes.gov.uk/14-19/index.cfm?sid=31**

DfES (2007a) *Dedicated Schools Grant Guidance*, available at: **www.dfes.gov.uk/14-19/index.cfm**

DfES (2007b) *Guidance for use of Flexible Funding Support 14–19 Partnerships in 06–07 and 07–08*, available at: **www.dfes.gov.uk/14-19/index.cfm**

DfES (2007c) *14–19 Funding and Organisational Pilots*, available at: **www.dfes.gov.uk/14-19/index.cfm**

Donovan, G. (2005) *Teaching 14–19*, London: David Fulton Publishers.

Eames, A., Benton, T., Sharp, C. and Kendall, L. (2006) *The Impact of Creative Partnerships on the Attainment of Young People*, Slough: NFER. Creative Partnerships available at: **www.creative-partnerships.com/researchandevaluation**

Halsey, K. et al. (2000) *The Voice of Young People: an engine for improvement*? Scoping the evidence, NFER for CfBT.

Harkin, J. and Dawn, T. (2001) *Teaching Young Adults*, London: RoutledgeFalmer.

Hayes, D. (2003) Managerialism and professionalism in post-compulsory education, in Lea, J., Hayes, D., Armitage, A., Lomas, L. and Markless, S. (2003) *Working in Post-Compulsory Education*, Maidenhead: Open University Press.

Hayes, D. (2004) The therapeutic turn in teacher education, in Hayes, D. (ed.) *The Routledge Falmer Guide to Key Debates in Education*, London and New York: Routledge.

Higham, J. et al. (2004) *14–19 Pathfinders: an evaluation of the first year*, available at: **www.dfes.gov.uk/14-19_pathfinder_second_year_report_final.doc**

Hyland, T. and Merrill, B. (2003) *The Changing Face of Further Education*, London: RoutledgeFalmer.

Miller, Thoby (2005) Across the great divide: creating partnerships in education, *The encyclopedia of Informal Education*, at: **www.infed.org/biblio/ partnerships_in_education.htm**

Tomlinson, M. (2004) *14–19 Curriculum and Qualifications Reform*, DfES, available at: **www.14-19reform.gov.uk**

Further reading

Case studies featuring joint capital project working, examples of sustainability and efficiency through shared working are available through the following link: **www.dfes.gov.uk/14-19/documents**

The 14–19 Implementation Plan

This document sets out in detail the implementation of 14–19 Education and Skills, and how this will create a system capable of offering a new set of curriculum and qualification opportunities.

The plan focuses on three key areas. The first is the short-term action taken to raise attainment – at level 2 and level 3, as well as how the DfES is increasing apprenticeship rates. The second is: how qualifications and the curriculum for the long term are being reformed – particularly the development of specialised Diplomas, reform to GCSE and A level, the extended project and Key Stage 3 reform.

Finally, it focuses on delivery on the ground – creating the capacity nationally and designing local delivery systems.

The Plan also includes a full timetable for reform and shows how the system will look at various intervals. This should not be seen as a blueprint for all to follow.

At the heart of the reforms is an entitlement for all young people to access high-quality education that is best suited to them, in an appropriate setting. All young people will be able to follow a course in one of 14 new specialised Diploma lines.

Appendix 17.2

Lines of Learning
  Business, Administration and Finance
  Construction and the Built Environment
  Creative and Media
  Engineering
  Environmental and Land-Based Studies
  Hair and Beauty Studies
  Hospitality
  Information Technology
  Manufacturing and Product Design
  Public Services
  Retail Business
  Society, Health and Development
  Sport and Active Leisure
  Travel and Tourism

18 Internationalising Learning: Global and Local

In this chapter you will:

- Explore the continued importance of education, the relationship between the function or purpose of education, and the impact this has on the nature of a country's organised system of education
- Compare the differences and similarities in a range of national systems
- Consider differing data and outcomes
- Explore ideas of a universal entitlement to education for every young person

Pearson Education Ltd./Ken Wilson-Max

Source: Pearson Education Ltd. Phovoir. Imagestate

Photo 18.1
Education is universally valued

Introduction

This chapter begins with an exploration of the relationship between the underpinning philosophy as to the function or purpose of education, its importance and the impact this has on the way in which a society's education systems are formally organised. The impact this has had on the evolution of formal English systems of education provides a basis, which will allow you to compare and explore the differences and similarities of a range of alternative national systems. If a society believes education should be to prepare young people for a world of work, then the curriculum in that system will be work-related and focused. This means vocational qualifications are highly regarded, as is the case in Germany, for example. In Japan, however, a significant number of young people are enrolled in private schools to enhance opportunities for attainment in a society where academic achievement is highly sought after and valued. We will finish by exploring whether there should be a global, or universal, entitlement to education for every young person.

The importance of education

Education can be described as the single most important determining factor in life chances and current and future careers. Educational attainment remains the single most influential **driver** within both the compulsory and the further education (FE) sector. The new Ofsted inspection regime implemented from September 2009 makes clear the focus on attainment, underlining the political importance of outcomes at a personal level, for personal prosperity and health; at a state level in terms of the ability to contribute to the economy; and at an international level in terms of Britain's ability to compete on what is now an international playing field.

The link continues between the successful completion of upper secondary/post secondary training and the increased likelihood of employment in all countries. In the Czech Republic, for example, 'rates of employment for males with an upper secondary level of education are at least 32 percentage points higher than for a male without such attainment' (OECD 2006: 108). More broadly speaking, 'on average, 26% of adults without upper secondary qualifications earn half or less than half the national median earnings' (OECD 2006: 17).

The relationship between educational attainment and life chances remains a key driver in the educational agenda. The increase in the number of young people gaining qualifications has led to a decrease in the inherent value of higher-level qualifications such as degrees. Science degrees have retained their high status: the relative scarcity of young people with science and maths degrees has ensured that the link between these degrees and higher earnings has been retained.

Chart A: Percentage of pupils aged 15 achieving five or more GCSEs or equivalent at grades A* to C, England, 1994/95 to 2007/08

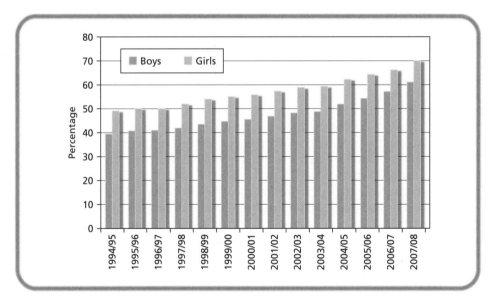

- The percentage of 15 year old pupils achieving five or more GCSEs and equivalent grades A* to C, in all schools in England increased from 43.5 per cent in 1994/95 to 64.8 per cent in 2007/08.
- In 2007/08, 69.4 per cent of girls achieved at least 5 GCSEs or equivalent A* to C grades, compared to 60.4 per cent of boys – increases of 3.9 and 4.0 percentage points respectively on the previous year.
- The percentage of girls achieving 5 or more good GCSEs or equivalent has increased by 21.3 points since 1994/95, while the percentage of boys achieving the same results has increased by 21.4 points.

DCSF 2008: *Trends in Education*

In England, a key performance indicator of success is the number of pupils gaining 5 GCSEs at A*–C by the end of compulsory education. As can be seen from the chart opposite this has increased over the past decade. Ironically this improvement has been ascribed by many to be the result of easier testing as opposed to baseline improvements in pupil learning.

The purpose of education and how it shapes the formal organisation of education

The link between the purpose of education and how that shapes and drives the delivery of formal education systems is important. Many educators work within a system without questioning how that system evolved. It is therefore important to identify the underlying philosophical purpose or function of education within a society, because that underpinning philosophy reflects the formal system of education that is delivered within that society, and within which you as a teacher have to work.

The function of education remains a key political topic and poses many questions – its answers pose many more: what is its purpose, whom should it benefit – society, the economy or the self? What should be taught and how should it be taught? What knowledge should be tested, when, how and how often? The latter question is particularly important when we consider how frequently the children and young people in our society are tested.

WHAT DO YOU THINK?

Consider the following quotes and then

- explain and justify the purpose of education for 14–19-year-olds according to your own values.

    . . . [W]e have come to realise that for most men the right to learn is curtailed by the obligation to attend school.

    Ivan Illich

    When they learn in their own way and for their own reasons, children learn so much more rapidly and effectively than we could possibly teach them, that we can afford to throw away our curricula and our timetables, and set them free, at least most of the time, to learn on their own.

    John Holt

    Education is a weapon whose effects depend on who holds it in his hands and at whom it is aimed.

    Joseph Stalin

WHAT DO YOU THINK? *CONTINUED*

The principal goal of education is to create men who are capable of doing new things, not simply of repeating what other generations have done – men who are creative, inventive and discoverers.

Jean Piaget

It is nothing short of a miracle that the modern methods of instruction have not yet entirely strangled the holy curiosity of inquiry; for this delicate little plant, aside from stimulation, stands mainly in need of freedom; without this it goes to wrack and ruin without fail.

Albert Einstein

I learned most, not from those who taught me but from those who talked with me.

St. Augustine

Education costs money, but then so does ignorance.

Sir Claus Moser

The children who know how to think for themselves spoil the harmony of the collective society that is coming, where everyone would be interdependent.

John Dewey

The relevance of these questions in a chapter focusing on international 14–19 education becomes clear as we try to contextualise the English system and the impact of policy to use as a comparison. No other sector in England is subject to so much change and yet at its core remains the same. This can be illustrated by the controversy surrounding the publication of the Tomlinson Report in 2004. There was (unusually) widespread agreement between employers and education professionals for a new overarching Diploma providing a 'unified framework of qualifications', resulting in a thorough overhaul of the 14–19 examination system. Fundamental recommendations included the replacement of A levels and GCSEs with the Diploma as well as a move from external to internal assessment. These core proposals were rejected and, indeed, on the day of publication the Prime Minister signalled its downfall in a speech stating that A levels and GCSEs would remain. The pupil entitlement to access all diploma lines has been discarded by the coalition government, as was the extended project which was deemed 'superfluous' (Schools Minister, Nick Gibb, 24 June 2010).

It has been argued that this continuous tinkering, or 'policy busyness' (Hayward et al. 2006) implemented in very 'challenging' time limits, has produced more problems than those it has been trying to solve over the past three decades and 'failure to address wholesale reform simply adds to the complexities of the inherent incrementalism' (Jephcote and Abbott 2005: 181).

Nowhere is this seen more clearly than between the ongoing debate in terms of the vocational versus academic divide. Historically, this can be linked to the value and importance of knowledge associated with traditional liberal education. It is only relatively recently (nineteenth century) that mass education has been available and indeed Friedrich Nietzsche (1844–1900), the nineteenth-century German philosopher, argued that 'in large states public education will always be mediocre' (1878). Prior to this, education was for religious purposes or a classical education for a selected few from the upper echelons of society – who were overwhelmingly male. Knowledge was power, and those with power had control. Merchant and craft guilds allowed for the training of apprentices from the twelfth century onwards. Not only was the academic–vocational divide in clear evidence, but this also reproduced educational class inequalities in terms of access and provision, until the 1870 Forster Education Act.

The purpose of education for those from lower socio-economic background remains strikingly similar to reasons cited today in terms of a better educated population providing a more efficient workforce, which improves output and therefore economic return. While in England education is overtly based on a **meritocracy** (access and progression through ability, as opposed to inherited entitlement or through wealth), the numbers of students staying on post-16 in England remains considerably higher for those from higher income backgrounds. 'The level of intergenerational mobility in society is seen by many as a measure of the extent of equality of economic and social opportunity . . . International comparisons indicate that intergenerational mobility in Britain is of the same order of magnitude as in the US, but that these countries are substantially less mobile than Canada and the Nordic countries' (Blanden, Gregg and Machin 2005). The social divisions of education remain evident in England as they have since the inception of mass education. Private schools remain the choice for those who can afford it, arguably grammar schools for those who cannot, secondary for the masses and pupil referral units (PRUs), to be renamed 'short term schools', for what are the most disenfranchised and vulnerable of our young people. Incidentally, PRUs were not included in the general invitation for every secondary school in England to become an academy. A total of 70 per cent of schools which expressed an interest were judged to already be outstanding schools and were from more affluent areas. 'Research, undertaken by Education Data Surveys (EDS), shows that more than twice as many schools in Kent expressed an interest than in the whole of the North East' (*TES* 02/07/2010). This is in direct contrast to one of the fundamental purposes of the academies which was to raise standards and challenge 'cultures of underachievement'. Academies are based on the 'free school' system in Sweden and are also similar to the charter schools in the United States. All are directly funded and are able to offer a differing orientation or focus other than the national curriculum.

The Department for Education website defines academies as 'publicly funded independent schools that provide a first-class education'. Academies can benefit from greater freedoms to aid innovation and raise standards. These freedoms include:

- freedom from local authority control
- ability to set own pay and conditions for staff
- freedom from following the National Curriculum
- ability to change the lengths of terms and school days.

Plans are also being made for further freedoms for academies in the way they engage in local partnerships and deliver 14–19 education (DfE 2010). Critiques of the academy system have raised concerns over increased segregation and increased disadvantage for those from poorer backgrounds.

ACTIVITY

- Identify the range and number of schools and educational establishments within your local authority area. Include all maintained secondary schools, faith schools, independent schools, academies, alternative curriculum, sixth-form schools/centres and colleges of further education.

- How many in total and how many of each type?

- What are the attainment/success rates in each?

- Produce your own LA league table.

National systems

The 14–19 white paper *Education and Skills* (DfES 2005) underlined the growing emphasis on the relationship between education and the economy, and the importance of vocational learning, as well as the acknowledgement of 14–19 education as a distinct phase. It purports to offer 14-year-olds the choice of vocational, academic or a combination of both. The White Paper has at its roots the ongoing concern over low standards – academic and behavioural, the need to up-skill and to provide a competent and able workforce to meet the needs of the economy. Many countries, such as England, Australia, Canada, Ireland and Finland, consider the completion of upper secondary – further education from 16 to 19 – a minimum requirement for entry into the employment market, especially with regard to future opportunities and progression.

It should be remembered that while the White Paper proposes a solution to a wide range of problems, these problems in themselves are not new. Social mobility has provided young people with a choice (albeit a still relatively limited choice) influenced as it is by social background and attitudes, as well as experiences of education. Attitudes towards education within the family, community and nation have a considerable impact. In China, for example, where the importance of education is culturally entrenched, its students spend almost *twice* as much time engaged with educational activities as do their OECD member country peers (OECD 2006, Schleicher and Tremblay 2006).

Instead of wholesale reform, which could tackle the root of these problems as opposed to the secondary factors, the system in England has merely been repackaged and offered as an individual choice of pathways, although still broadly speaking academic or vocational, within one system. The 'Great Debate' (following James Callaghan's speech at Ruskin College 1976), which initiated the process for the implementation of a national curriculum as well as the need for closer links between employers and education, is seen as the key turning point at which this tinkering began. The early 1970s also heralded the need for post compulsory education (post-16) to provide a 'second chance' to adult learners and the school leaving age was raised from

15 to 16 in 1972. The concern over standards and the need for young people to be fully prepared and appropriately trained for the world for work was and remains a key driver for these changes.

The raising of the participation age (RPA) to 17 from 2013 and to 18 from 2015 was set out in a Green Paper (DCSF 2009) by the then Secretary of State Alan Johnson in 2007. This identified the need for this change – the first increase in the compulsory school age for 40 years.

> The RPA is also about our aim for a fairer and more equal society. There is overwhelming evidence of the negative consequences of leaving education or training at the age of only 16. Such young people are disproportionately from poor families and there is a strong correlation between becoming Not in Education, Employment or Training (NEET) and engaging in risky behaviours, having poor health and low income. Outcomes for 16–18-year-olds in a job without formal training are only marginally better than for young people NEET. Education also confers intergenerational benefits for the children of those who participate in education for longer. RPA is a historic opportunity to provide better opportunities for the most vulnerable young people in our society; and to ensure all young people have the same opportunities and expectations of success
>
> *(DCSF 2009: 1–2).*

This will have a particular relevance for the 14–19 phase and bring the UK period of compulsory education in line with many other European and non-European countries. The percentage of NEETs has risen in the UK over the past decade in contrast to Northern Ireland where the percentage of NEETS has declined. The proportion of young people aged 16–18 who are in full time education has increased in both (The Poverty Site: indicator 32).

The group of 14–16-year-olds in further education (FE) is not new but their *visibility* in terms of the increase in numbers is. This has raised concerns in FE in terms of delivery as well as the need for increasingly complex relationships between parents, carers, schools, universities and employers. It also blurred the line between compulsory and post compulsory education. The integration and collaborative schooling of our young people seems likely to increase, especially with the raising of the school leaving age. While this has created considerable media interest, it should be noted that, at the present time, 76.2 per cent of young people aged 16–18 are already in education, employment or training, a figure comparable to most other European countries.

14-19 education internationally

Fears over standards and the numbers of young people leaving education with no qualifications are not confined to the UK. Many states in the United States have raised the legal school leaving age to above 16 at least once over the past three decades (Oreopoulos 2005). In the province of New Brunswick in Canada, the legal school leaving age is 18 which followed the New Brunswick Education Act (1997). Education in the 13 provinces of Canada is regionally managed, provided and funded. While there are similarities, the regional history and culture of each region is in evidence. Broadly speaking, students attend school until grade 11 (16 years) and then go to secondary school (high school or 'école secondaire') to receive their school leaving diploma or certificates. Pre-university courses are generally two or three years in duration. Choice and the availability of differing pathways to match individual interests is a feature of post elementary education in Canada as it is in England, although, crucially, the age at which young people make these decisions which will have an impact on their future careers differs – 14 in England and 16 in Canada and the United States. In Canada, the socio-economic background of the young person has the smallest effect, suggesting more authentic systems of meritocracy.

In Japan, lower secondary schooling (Chûgakkô) provides general education for young people aged 12–15, while the legal school leaving age is at the end of the school year when they reach 15, when future choices are made. They can then apply to attend upper secondary school (Kôtô-gakkô). Entry into upper secondary courses is usually dependent on entrance examinations. Young people have the choice of pathways that last a further three years to gain a certificate of upper secondary education in either general education, specialised (normally vocational) education or integrated courses which offer a combination of both. These are offered in colleges of technology, from which students can progress to university to complete graduate programmes or junior colleges for completion of undergraduate programmes. Part-time pathways and correspondence courses for upper secondary courses are also offered for students who wish to be more flexible with their studies. In 1999 (Chûtô-kyôiku-gakkô) secondary schools were established which provide the required three years of lower and three years of secondary education in one establishment as opposed to clearly delineated and separate places of education. There are other 'miscellaneous' schools that offer those with the lower secondary certificate the opportunity to complete one-year practical vocational courses such as cooking or book-keeping.

In Finland, general education is compulsory from the age of 6 to 16. Students can then choose to go onto a three-year course in general upper secondary education or vocational upper secondary training. Vocational training programmes are much broader than those found within the English system. In addition to the specialist vocational subject which is studied both within the institution and the work place, students are expected to study maths, the mother tongue, the second national language, a foreign language, physical and health education, art and cultural studies, entrepreneurship and workplace studies and social studies. Students are, however, encouraged to learn at their own pace and there is a strong emphasis on the needs of the individual. Completion of the matriculation exam could be achieved from as little as two years or up to four years. A key feature of this system is that students are able to work at their own pace and are not determined by sets arranged into year groups. Completion of the matriculation exam provides pathways for students to apply to polytechnics or universities at age 19. Interestingly, successful completion of the matriculation exam is considered to be the minimum requirement for preparation for employment or higher education. This is reflected in the very small numbers of pupils deciding against immediate continuation of their studies. The focus of education is clearly rooted in equal access and instruction is offered in the students' mother languages – Swedish and Finnish, which are the official languages – or Saami. The Saami are the only remaining indigenous population living in the European Union.

IN PRACTICE

- Identify the support systems for pupils for whom English is not their first language, in your educational organisation.
- Produce a student-centred information leaflet for those pupils/students. N.B. *Remember! English is not their first language.*

Approximately 8,000 Saami reside in the North of Finland (50 per cent of whom have Saami as their mother tongue and 50 per cent Finnish), while there are 2,000 in Russia, 40,000 in Norway and 10,000–25,000 in Sweden. The Finnish education system is considered to be among the best in the world and Finland is one of the few European countries to be able to compete and compare favourably with South and East Asian outcomes, participation and attainment. Learning by 'doing' is a key characteristic of Finnish schools and the pedagogical approach is rooted in the ideology of the French educationalist Célestin Freinet (1896–1966). This pedagogy is rooted in process rather than content and is based on mutual cooperative learning, authenticity, learning through doing, which should be work-related (Pédagogie du travail), employing inductive teaching methods and is child-centred.

The principle of free education is extended to include not only the programme of study but also additional expenditure such as books and other materials. One free meal a day is also supplied for students attending compulsory education. Finland has consistently performed well in international tables. OECD data shows Finland as being the only member country not to have at least '10 per cent of students at Level 1

Source: Alamy Images

Photo 18.2
Pupils enjoying 'hands on' education

and below in mathematics. This is a sizeable percentage of a country's human capital' (OECD 2006: 87). The number of students successfully completing upper secondary and post compulsory education at 90 per cent exceeds the OECD average of 70 per cent. In England, a participation rate of 90 per cent is a target for achievement by 2015.

The German education system differs from that of England and Finland in that it is overt in its stratification and streaming of pupils according to ability. Further, this selection process occurs upon completion of elementary school which children attend from ages of 6 to 9 years. This is followed by two years of orientation between the ages of 10 and 11 (grades 5 and 6) during the first phase of secondary schooling. The educationalist (normally the form tutor) recommends the appropriate pathway for each student, dependent on ability, potential and personal characteristics. There are four main pathways: the Hauptschule is for those with a lower ability. While the same core subjects are studied as those within the other pathways, this is at a lower level in addition to a range of vocational subjects and is therefore limiting in terms of future opportunity and prospects for students. It is on these grounds of reduced opportunities that many parents decide to override teacher recommendations. Some Hauptschule offer a grade-10 year (age 15), but many students will go on to their vocational training, the second phase of secondary education after grade 9 (age 14), which can be full or part time. Successful completion of the programme leads to the award of the Hauptschule Leaving Certificate. The second pathway is that of the Realschule which provides a combination of traditional liberal education and vocational training, although the overarching ideology remains that of traditional education in terms of content and approach. Full-time attendance is compulsory from grades 5 to 10 (age 10–15 years). Upon successful completion, students are awarded the Realschule Leaving Certificate. If this is at a high enough level, students are able to switch pathways to the Gymnasium – schools for students with the highest ability in preparation for university.

For the second phase of secondary education, enrolment into vocational or higher vocational schools (for the professions) follows. This can be completed either full time within the school or the students can be enrolled on to the Duales System (duel system) which combines part-time study and 'on the job training', for which there are 350 professions available. The majority of students (two-thirds) elect this pathway. A key feature of this dual vocational education system is that the employers pay for the work-based training while the Länder (states) are responsible for the school element. Curriculum content is wider than that found within the English system in the vocational schools (Berufsfachschulen) and includes 'German, social studies, mathematics, natural sciences, a foreign language and sport' (Eurydice 2006: 3) in addition to the vocational and specialist subject studies. The successful completion of these programmes leads to certification in a particular trade or field of work by the relevant professional or competent body.

Attendance at the Gymnasium schools is compulsory from grades 5–10 (age 10–16 years) during phase one of secondary education and then at the Gymnasiale Oberstufe for grades 11–13 (age 16–18/19) for the second phase. Its curriculum is clearly focused on that of a traditional liberal education, with preparation for university its main goal. Students must select from each of the following areas: 'languages/literature/the arts; social sciences; and mathematics/natural sciences/technology' (Eurydice 2006: 3). Successful completion leads to the award of Abitur.

A relatively new comprehensive school has been introduced in response to calls for a more democratic system called the Gesamtschule. This enrols all students and, depending on ability, students will either take the Hauptschule leaving certificate at the end of grade 9 or the Realschule leaving certificate at the end of grade 10. Those with higher level Realschule passes have the choice to complete their education at a Gymnasium or within the Gesamtschule if these classes are available. Other students enrol in to the appropriate vocational or higher vocational school for the second phase of their secondary education.

Assessment in all pathways is predominantly teacher-led based on continuous assessment methods. Education is compulsory for all students until the age of 18, although this can be on a part-time basis from the age of 15 or 16 for students not enrolled on a full-time educational pathway. This is the same model being introduced in England with the raising of the compulsory participation age.

The two key differences between the German education system and that of the English are, firstly, that while general education is followed until the minimum age of 14 whereupon more specialist education is delivered be it vocational, liberal or a combination of both, the *selection* process is made much earlier. Initial selection occurs at the end of Grundschule (grade 4, age 9) and informed by the form teacher's assessment. While final choice lies with the parents/carer, the decision is heavily influenced by the teacher. It is possible for change to occur during the two orientation grades (5 and 6 at age 10 and 11) which is closer to age of selection for grammar schools (where these are still available) in England. Selection in England for the grammar stream is via entrance examination and, at age 14, students are able to choose their own pathways from the options available within their school. The second key difference is the overt nature of this stratified system leading to clearly streamed forms of phase two secondary education. This is especially important when considering the relationship between socio-economic background and educational attainment. The inequalities in Germany are larger than in the 'United States, and in both Europe and the United States socio-economic inequalities are larger than in any of the Asian countries' (OECD 2006: 18). Not only are educational opportunities reduced for students from a lower socio-economic background, but also these inequalities are further reinforced by the structural systems. This link is increasingly amplified the earlier this stratification or selection occurs, which is the case with the German education system, where recommendations occur at age 9 for implementation at age 10. This is in contrast to Finland, where selection for specialist pathways occurs at 16. In addition, Finland has one of the smallest relationships between socio-economic background and student achievement within the OECD countries.

Education for students in France is compulsory from ages 6 to 16 years. The secondary system comprises two phases – lower secondary from 11 to 15 (collège) followed by a year in a general and technological lycée or a vocational lycée. Students are typically enrolled in the college or lycée within their geographical area, in contrast to the parental choice offered with the English system. There are three pathways to follow upon the completion of collège. Students enrolling on general or technological studies pathways will need to successfully complete a further three years of study in order to gain the award of the general or technological baccalaureate. The curriculum content for the first two years is common to all students and includes French, Mathematics, Physics and Chemistry, Life and Earth Sciences or Technology of Automated Systems, one modern foreign language, combined History and Geography, Physical Education and Sport. Pupils also have to take two options and can choose to do language lessons, artistic activities or sport. For the third and final year, students elect which baccalaureate they intend to specialise in. There are three general categories – economic and social, scientific or literary and four broad technology courses – tertiary science and technology, industrial science and technology, laboratory science and technology and medical and social sciences, as well as specific technical baccalaureate courses such as hotel management. Students can also choose to opt for a two-year pathway within a lycée professionnel. The focus here is on specific vocational training and, upon successful completion, the student is awarded the Brevet d'Etudes Professionnelles (BEP) or Certificat d'Aptitude Professionnelle (CAP). This pathway tends to lead to direct employment. However, students can elect to continue their education for a further two years in order to gain a vocational baccalaureate in one of 48 specialist fields. The French baccalaureate has been in existence since 1808 and the vocational baccalaureate since 1985.

Students select general pathways at age 14 to begin the following year as in the English system. However, a key difference lies in the final selection of a specialised baccalaureate field for the third and final year of study.

WHAT DO YOU THINK?

- At what age should young people make choices in regards to their future careers?
- How long should general schooling be?
- What are the advantages and disadvantages of a broader curriculum as opposed to a narrowly defined curriculum?
- Should there be clearly distinct educational establishments to provide education for 14–19-year-olds?
- List the key features that would define such a system and the nature of the curriculum offer.

International data set comparisons

Inherent in the systems of the above-mentioned countries are the need for up-skilling, the raising of standards, for skills to meet the needs of the economy and employer demand, and the need to reduce 'dropouts'. The impact of globalisation cannot be ignored here, where international comparisons and competition are key drivers of change.

The OECD (Organisation for Economic and Development) provides statistical information with regard to economic and social issues including that of the educational performance of it member countries. There are 30 member countries: Australia, Austria, Belgium, Canada, the Czech Republic, Denmark, Finland, France, Germany, Greece,

Hungary, Iceland, Ireland, Italy, Japan, Korea, Luxembourg, Mexico, the Netherlands, New Zealand, Norway, Poland, Portugal, the Slovak Republic, Spain, Sweden, Switzerland, Turkey, the United Kingdom and the United States. In addition, the OECD has links with approximately 50 other countries who are observers or participants on at least one working committee (OECD 2006). Their findings have had a significant impact in terms of global competitiveness and act as a driver for those countries who wish to improve their international standing. While competition can lead to a narrow view of education, data also provides information with regard to successful policies and could be used to inform development and change. In 1961, the OECD took over from the Organisation for European Economic Co-operation (OEEC) which operated under the framework for reconstruction drawn up in the Marshall Plan (1947) following the end of the Second World War.

The longevity of the organisation and the cooperation in providing statistical information from its member and voluntary countries has had a significant impact in terms of providing starting points and current positions, allowing for vital tracking information in terms of international progression or decline. Policy makers within the individual countries use the information to inform future policy development and areas for priority. Germany, for instance, has until relatively recently been considered to be one of the most effective providers of education. In particular, it is renowned for its dual system of vocational training. Recent data shows that its position is in decline, which has led to calls for reform and improvement.

Emerging technologies, new skills and the decline of low-skilled work have had a considerable impact on the education systems of OECD countries in terms of the relevance and importance of higher-level skills. This is reflected in the increase in upper secondary participation rates across the OECD countries and further afield. Many current educational systems have failed to consider wholesale reform in order to reflect this change. They were 'adequate at a time when there were plenty of jobs requiring only baseline qualifications, but that no longer works in a world made flat by technology' (OECD 2006: 19). The Green Paper *Raising Expectations: staying in education post 16* (DfES 2007) recognised the need for young people to stay in post compulsory education post 16. It made explicit reference to the change in the employment market and the skills set required, 'we have a duty to prepare all young people for a labour market which will be radically different to the one their parents faced' (Foreword, Alan Johnson). Despite the recognition of these changes, this has still not led to wholesale reform.

Similarly, the dominant values of those with power within a society can act as a means of perpetuating existing inequalities. More females than males graduate at upper secondary/post secondary level in almost all of the OECD countries, with the exception of Turkey and, for vocational courses, employment rates remain higher for men across all countries. Further, female earnings remain less than that of their male counterparts: 'For a given level of educational attainment, they typically earn between 50 and 80 per cent of what males earn' (OECD 2006: 123).

A key area of concern is for those students who leave school with few or no qualifications. Research suggest that the East Asian system of education is much better than that of its European Union counterparts in *not* leaving students behind, as are Canada, Finland and the Netherlands. All countries except Korea and Finland have a sizeable proportion of students (10%) performing at level 1 or below (OECD 2006).

Chart A8.2. Employment rates, by educational attainment (2004)
Percentage of the 25-to-64-year-old population that is employed

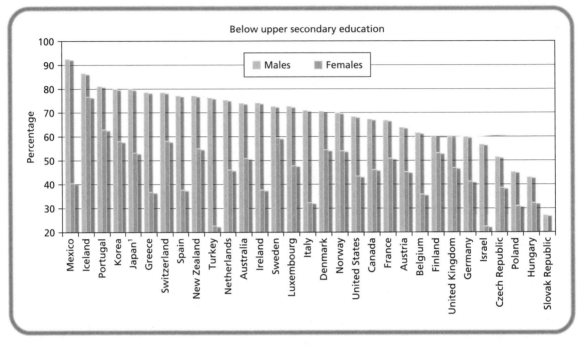

Source: OECD 2006

Again, there is a clear link between poor performance and socio-economic background in most countries. It remains the case that those members of society most needing educational support and advancement figure in the category with the least opportunities to do so.

ACTIVITY

Compare a non-European country's vocational education system with that of your own or a local secondary school in England, Wales, Scotland or Northern Ireland:

- Describe each system, identifying three commonalities and three differences.
- Assess their national standing in international league tables for one or two indicators, for example, participation rates, attainment or pupil well-being.
- Identify one aspect of their system which you would like to see replicated in the English, Welsh, Scottish or Northern Ireland system.

Policy, drivers and reform

Lifelong education is a prominent feature in many countries' underlying philosophies. The following extracts show that, as well as the need for up-skilling and international competitiveness:

- In today's knowledge society, education, training and lifelong learning are the most important prerequisites for an individual's future opportunities in life and employment, as well as for social participation and social integration.

  (Federal Minister, Dr. Annette Schavan Germany)

- The Ministry creates favourable conditions for education, know-how, lifelong learning, creativity, civic participation, and well-being.

  Finland's Ministry of Education

- America's competitiveness and the prosperity of our people in a changing economy depend increasingly on high skill, high wage jobs. Realising our potential will require investing in education and learning for all our people throughout their lifetimes.

  USA Dept of Commerce 1999 in Brown et al. 2001: 1

WHAT DO YOU THINK?

The only education that is purposeful is that which has a direct relevance to the world of work.

- Should education be a lifelong entitlement of every citizen?
- Should all types of education be free to all, or only to those earning below a specified income?
- Is work-related learning the only form of education that can be considered meaningful?
- Should all work-related learning be free to all, or only to those earning below a specified income?

Fears about the decline in standards and a breakdown in traditional values are also common across many countries, as is the need for a core/national curriculum aimed at ensuring all students attain functional skills:

- In Japan the aim of the curriculum is to 'secure improvement of "academic ability" and promotion of "moral education" . . . which aim for the education of children, pupils and students to acquire rudiments and basics firmly as well as the cultivation of a "the zest for living", which means the ability to learn and think independently by and for oneself . . . [this can be achieved through] rooting the rudiments and basics by enriched and elaborate instruction responding to an individual as well as the careful and strict selection of educational content' (MEXT Ministry of Education, Culture, Sports and Science and Technology: Japan).

- In England, 'Never before has it been as important as it is today for every young person to achieve a good level of skill – for young people themselves, for the economy and for society . . . We are developing new functional skills qualifications in English, maths and ICT, defining the elements of these subjects that people need to participate effectively in everyday life, including the workplace' (DfES 2007).

- And in relation to the establishment of the common core (decree 11 July 2006) in France: 'The education system must provide each student with the necessary means to acquire a "common core" of knowledge and skills which are essential in order to do well at school, continue one's studies, build one's personal and professional future and succeed in life and society' (Eurydice 2006: France).

- **Article 29** of the Human Rights states that 'education should develop your personality and abilities to the full. Your education should also teach you to respect your parents, human rights, the environment, and your own and other cultures' (UNICEF).

DISCUSSION POINT

Discuss the quotations above with a colleague – do you think there should be a national curriculum which defines a core learning entitlement? Should education be responsible for delivering academic and vocational knowledge in isolation, or for developing personal skills, socially accepted attitudes in addition to the core academic and vocational entitlement?

N.B. A key Ofsted inspection judgement expressly relates to:

- the spiritual, moral, social and cultural development of the pupils at the school
- the contribution made by the school to the well-being of those pupils (relating to the five *Every Child Matters* outcomes)
- the contribution made by the school to community cohesion.

Key interrelating features are increasing rates of participation and promoting higher levels of attainment and the need to prepare young people for the world of work. Also prominent is the need to offer flexible, individualised programmes of learning, to increase the range of vocational training and closer engagement with employers: for example, the *Reform of the Vocational Training Law*, Germany 2005; the measures set out in *Higher Standards, Better Schools for all* (DfES 2007); and in France *Programmes Personnalisés de Réussite Éducative (PPRE)* (an individualised learning approach) (2005), as well as the implementation of the new national core implemented in Finland in 2005 and in France in 2006. Many of these reforms have been prompted as a result of globalisation, emerging technologies and increased international competition, not only in terms of skills per se but also in a direct response to employment-led needs.

Education for every young person?

Article 28 of the Convention of the Rights of the Child (1989) states that 'primary education should be free and compulsory (required) for all children and that governments should make sure no one is excluded from education because of poverty. Secondary education should also be available to all children'. While primary and secondary education may be in place in developed countries, it is certainly not the pattern for all children and young people. Further, it does not insist on secondary education as a free entitlement or even a requirement.

ACTIVITY

OECD information suggests that higher levels of education beyond that of basic secondary education are key determinants for future employment success. Produce and justify your own 'article/s' for minimum requirements of global education entitlement. Use the full text of article 28/9 (see 'Find out more' at the end of this chapter) and your own research to inform you.

A significant minority of young people are excluded officially or unofficially from school systems despite being legally entitled to an education. While these pupils are legally entitled to education from day 6 of exclusion, their outcomes are significantly lower than for their mainstream-educated counterparts. The ability to engage young people in education continues to be a key subject of debate in terms of how and, among increasing judgmental attitudes, in terms of whether they 'deserve' to be educated.

IN PRACTICE

What are the exclusion rates in your own or your nearest secondary, faith or grammar school or academy?

Compare this to the national exclusion rates in a Nordic country of your choice and either England, Scotland, Wales or Northern Ireland.

SUMMARY

Differences in educational systems relate to underpinning ideologies regarding the purpose and the 'what' of education. This also raises philosophical questions in terms of whether formal state education is the best way to educate our young people. While education may be universally valued politically, young people's access to education can differ considerably. In many developing countries education is patchy and is frequently dependent on charitable organisations. Universally, educational attainment remains a key determinant in one's future life chances; for a significant minority of pupils within the UK formal education is rejected at both a conscious and unconscious level. This rejection of education remains perplexing to many, especially when considering the benefits. Perhaps, these pupils, instead of being seen as difficult, should be seen as courageous citizens, with the moral fibre to exercise their right to challenge existing systems which, after all, continue to promote unequal outcomes.

Find out more

The UNICEF website is a useful source of information and in particular on human rights and the Conventions on the rights of the child: **www.unicef.org**

Convention on the Rights of the Child : Article's 28/29:

Article 28

1. States Parties recognize the right of the child to education, and with a view to achieving this right progressively and on the basis of equal opportunity, they shall, in particular:

(a) Make primary education compulsory and available free to all;

(b) Encourage the development of different forms of secondary education, including general and vocational education, make them available and accessible to every child, and take appropriate measures such as the introduction of free education and offering financial assistance in case of need;

(c) Make higher education accessible to all on the basis of capacity by every appropriate means;

(d) Make educational and vocational information and guidance available and accessible to all children;

(e) Take measures to encourage regular attendance at schools and the reduction of drop-out rates.

2. States Parties shall take all appropriate measures to ensure that school discipline is administered in a manner consistent with the child's human dignity and in conformity with the present Convention.

3. States Parties shall promote and encourage international cooperation in matters relating to education, in particular with a view to contributing to the elimination of ignorance and illiteracy throughout the world and facilitating access to scientific and technical knowledge and modern teaching methods. In this regard, particular account shall be taken of the needs of developing countries.

Article 29

1. States Parties agree that the education of the child shall be directed to:

(a) The development of the child's personality, talents and mental and physical abilities to their fullest potential;

(b) The development of respect for human rights and fundamental freedoms, and for the principles enshrined in the Charter of the United Nations;

(c) The development of respect for the child's parents, his or her own cultural identity, language and values, for the national values of the country in which the child is living, the country from which he or she may originate, and for civilizations different from his or her own;

(d) The preparation of the child for responsible life in a free society, in the spirit of understanding, peace, tolerance, equality of sexes, and friendship among all peoples, ethnic, national and religious groups and persons of indigenous origin;

(e) The development of respect for the natural environment.

2. No part of the present article or article 28 shall be construed so as to interfere with the liberty of individuals and bodies to establish and direct educational institutions, subject always to the observance of the principle set forth in

paragraph 1 of the present article and to the requirements that the education given in such institutions shall conform to such minimum standards as may be laid down by the State.
Conventions on the Rights of the Child (1989)

The Poverty Site in association with the Joseph Rowntree organisation – useful statistics and information on poverty and social exclusion in England, Wales, Scotland, Northern Ireland and the European Union: **www.poverty.org.uk/32/index.shtml**.

The OECD website has a wide range of statistical information including health, education and economic growth (**www.oecd.org**). This also includes PISA (Programme for International Student Assessment) data.

The Ofsted framework for inspection of maintained schools from September 2009 can be found at: **www.ofsted.gov.uk/Ofsted-home/Forms-and-guidance/Browse-all-by/Other/General/Framework-for-the-inspection-of-maintained-schools-in-England-from-September-2009**.

Bibliography

Blanden, J., Gregg, P. and Machin, S. (2005) *Intergenerational Mobility in Europe and North America*. Centre for Economic Performance, available at: **www.onthesite.org/count/LSEreport.dpf**

Brown, P. et al. (2001) *High Skills Globalisation, Competitiveness and Skill Formation*, Oxford: OUP.

Callaghan, J. Speech at Ruskin College 1976. The full text is available at: **http://education.guardian.co.uk/thegreatdebate/story/0,,574645,00.html** [accessed 09.04.06].

Conventions on the Rights of the Child (1989), available at: **www.dcsf.gov.uk/everychild-matters/strategy/strategyandgovernance/uncrc/unitednationsarticles/uncrarticles/** [accessed 12.08.10].

DCSF (2008) *Trends in Education*, available from: **www.dcsf.gov.uk/trends/**.

DCSF (2009) *Raising the Participation Age: supporting local areas to deliver. An Executive Summary*, available at: **http://publications.dcsf.gov.uk/eOrderingDownload/01135-2009-DOM-EN.pdf** [accessed 07.07.10].

DfE (2010) *What are academies?* available at: **www.education.gov.uk/academies/whatareacademies** [accessed 10.07.10].

DfES (2005) *Education and Skills* 14–19. London: HMSO.

DfES (2007) 'Raising Expectations: staying in education post 16', available at: **www.dfes.gov.uk/consultations/downloadableDocs/6965-DfES-Raising%20Expectations%20Green%20Paper.pdf** [accessed 12.04.07].

DfES (2005) *Skills in the UK: the long term challenge* (Leitch Review of Skills), London: HMSO, available at: **www.hm-treasury.gov.uk/media/179/39/leitch_evidencedoc_040405.pdf** [accessed 27.11.06].

Eurydice (2006) *National Summary on Education Systems in Europe and ongoing reforms: Germany/France/Finland* [accessed 10.04.07].

Friedman T. (2005), *The World Is Flat – a brief history of the twenty-first century*. New York: Farrar, Straus & Giroux.

Hayward, G., Hodgson, A., Johnson, J., Oancea, A., Pring, R., Spours, K., Wilde, S. and Wright, S. (2006)

Nuffield *Review of 14–19 Education and Training*. Annual Report 2005–6. University of Oxford. Available at: **www.nuffield14-19review.org.uk** [accessed 27.11.06].

Jephcote, M. And Abbott, I. (2005) Tinkering and tailoring: the reform of 14–19 education in England, *Journal of Vocational Education and Training*, 57(2): 181–202.

Mext. Ministry of Education, Culture, Sports, Science and Technology, available at: **www.mext.go.jp/english/**

Ministry of Education. Finland, available at: **www.minedu.fi/OPM/?lang=en** [accessed 11.04.07].

Nietzsche, F. (1878) *Human All-too-Human*, Penguin Classics.

OECD (2006) *International Education Comparisons*, available at: **www.oecd.org** [accessed 12.04.07].

OECD (2006) *Education at a Glance* (full version) **www.oecd.org**.

Office for Standards in Education (Ofsted) (2004) *Developing New Vocational Pathways, Final Report on the Introduction of New GCSEs*, London: OfSTED.

Oreopoulos, P. (2005) *Stay in School: new lessons on the benefits of raising the legal school leaving age* (The Education Papers), commentary 223, available at: **www.cdhowe.org/pdf/commentary223pdf**

Raffe, D. (2005) *Education and Youth Transitions in England, Wales and Scotland*, ESRC Research Report.

Schleicher, A. and Tremblay, K. (2006) *Education and the Knowledge Economy in Europe and Asia*, European Policy Centre.

Statement of the Federal Minister Dr. Annette Schavan: Federal Ministry of Education and Research. Home page (Germany), available at: **www.bmbf.de/ _search/searchresult.php?URL=http%3A%2F%2F www.bmbf.de%2Fen%2F89.php&QUERY= education+and+structure** [accessed 11.04.07].

TES (2010) Vaughn, R. *Wealthy to Dominate Academies*, 2 July, available online at: **www.tes.co.uk/article.aspx?storycode=6049283** [accessed 08.07.2010].

Wolf, A. (2002) *Does Education Matter?* London: Penguin.

CHAPTER 19

The Role of the Teacher in Changing Learning Institutions

In this chapter, you will:

- be introduced to major current and anticipated changes in practice in the 14+ sector and the implications for teachers
- consider the changing contexts for learning that teachers will work within to deliver the 14–19 reforms
- examine the notion of 'personalised learning'
- understand the features of assessment for learning, in particular the relationship between learning approaches and assessment strategies
- consider delivery models for generic skills
- develop an awareness of how information, advice and guidance might be given to students
- consider the challenges of working in collaboration
- examine the main features and understand the importance of reflective practice

Pearson Education Ltd./Ken Wilson-Max

Introduction

A series of tensions now affects and will continue to affect the professional practice of those teaching 14–19-year-olds and the contexts in which they work. The year 2007 saw, arguably, the most extensive ever reform of the professional training and development of those teaching in the learning and skills sector with the implementation of *Equipping our Teachers for the Future* (DfES 2004), which itself was informed by Ofsted's survey inspection of teacher training in the sector (Ofsted 2003). Continuing professional development will assume equal importance with initial training and must be engaged with to maintain Qualified Teacher Learning and Skills status. However, at the same time as such professionalisation, there has never been more variation in the status, conditions of service and pay of those across the sector. There has been a casualisation of the FE workforce with part-time, agency, fixed-term and permanent staff, lecturers, trainers and instructors teaching alongside one another. There is a marked differential not only in the funding of work between schools and other providers such as FE colleges and work-based learning providers but in the remuneration of staff in these organisations.

Hyland and Merrill (2003) describe the potential for FE colleges to be integrated into learning networks incorporating HE, adult and community learning, schools and work-based learning. It is clear that 14–19 reforms, and specifically the delivery of the Diplomas, will only be successful if organisations collaborate and work in genuine partnerships (Harkin 2006). However, a range of factors make such collaboration problematic, not least the competitive environment in which organisations seek to recruit and retain students and trainees. Although such cross-phase and cross-institution work will form the bedrock of 14–19 provision in the future, initial teacher training, in spite of the proliferation of routes into teaching, remains resolutely phase-related. Although *Equipping our Teachers for the Future* foresaw a set of common standards for school teachers' QTS and QTLS, we nevertheless have two distinct sets of standards and this dichotomy will, it appears, continue.

It is clear that there will be a need for teachers of 14–19-year-olds to develop and use the softer, wider skills which will enable them to establish relationships with learners, to engage and sustain their learning and to successfully carry out the key roles which will be central to delivering the new curriculum such as coach, enabler and facilitator. Not only is the development of such personal skills a challenge for those delivering ITT and CPPD, but also many practitioners work in an environment which puts a premium on the more hard-edged classroom-focused skills which are outcome-oriented and lend themselves much more to performance evaluation. Furthermore, there are those who argue that the development of these softer, wider skills of emotional intelligence on the part of teachers is an insidious development:

> There has been a growing debate as to whether the new work requires a different workforce more orientated around 'emotion work' or 'aesthetic labour' which requires a different sort of training that is shifting towards a concern with 'emotional literacy' and 'emotional intelligence' (Mortiboys 2005). The obsessive concern with young people's self-esteem is well known and there is a growing concern with 'emotional well-being' and even

'happiness' as educational goals. There are sociological explanations as
to why this has happened. The argument is that there is a general loss of
confidence in the possibility of human progress that has led to a downplaying
of the intellectual in favour of the emotional (Furedi 2004, Hayes 2006). In
PCE the humanistic aspect of training is now dominant but has taken on a
specific aspect which ignores the normal content of humanistic approaches,
a liberal education or real skills involving the training of judgement, whether
or not in the distorted form of Competence Based Education and Training,
and concentrates instead on ways of approaching the inner emotional life
(Hayes 2003a; 2003b; 2003c; 2004).

(Armitage et al. 2007)

Teachers' knowledge, skills and attributes

What is the distinctive knowledge, the skills and attributes which are going to be
required of teachers to effectively deliver the new 14–19 curriculum? A report for
Lifelong Learning UK (Tribal Education and Technology 2007) on the evidence base
for a professional development toolkit being developed by LLUK and the Teacher
Development Agency identifies six areas in which teachers will need to be proficient:

- Personalised learning
- Assessment for learning
- Generic learning skills
- Information, advice and guidance
- Working collaboratively
- Developing reflective practice.

Personalised learning

Personalised learning has been at the centre of government reform arising from the
Every Child Matters agenda. It is described by DCSF as having five components:

1. Assessment for learning

   A personalised offer depends on really knowing the strengths and weaknesses
   of individual children and young people. We believe a key means of doing so is
   assessment for learning and the use of evidence and dialogue to identify every
   pupil's learning needs. Whatever the contextual practice, the rationale is always
   the same: clear evidence about how to drive up individual attainment; clear
   feedback for and from pupils so there is clarity on what they need to improve
   and how best they can do so; and a clear link between student learning and
   lesson planning.

2. Effective teaching and learning strategies

   Personalised learning demands teaching and learning strategies that develop
   the competence and confidence of every learner by actively engaging and
   stretching them. For teachers, it means a focus on their repertoire of teaching

skills, their subject specialisms and their management of the learning experience. Personalised learning requires a range of whole class, group and individual teaching, learning and ICT strategies to transmit knowledge, to instil key learning skills and to accommodate different paces of learning.

3. Curriculum entitlement and choice

Personalised learning demands a curriculum entitlement and choice that delivers a breadth of study, personal relevance and flexible learning pathways through the education system. The National Curriculum is a vital foundation for all 5–14-year-olds. New GCSEs in subjects like Engineering, ICT, Health and Social Care broaden the offer. But it is teachers and schools who have the capacity to harness the enquiry and enthusiasm of students. At 14–19 it means schools working together to extend curriculum choice.

4. School organisation

Personalised learning demands that school leaders and teachers think creatively about school organisation, so as to best support high-quality teaching and learning and to ensure that pupil performance and pupil welfare are mutually supportive. Across the country there is a range of innovative responses. At Lynn Grove High School in Norfolk effective use of ICT means that the school's four walls are no longer a constraint to pupil progress. A 'virtual school' provides online materials and support that are used extensively by students outside normal hours. At Ninestiles School in Birmingham there is a clear and consistent policy on 'behaviour for learning' to create an environment in which all students feel safe and secure and can flourish as individuals. The common purpose linking these strategies is a focus on the progress of every pupil. Their shared effect is to ensure pupils receive a consistently good experience of education, with the emphasis both on progress and enjoyment.

5. Strong partnership beyond the school

Personalised learning demands strong partnership beyond the school to drive forward progress in the classroom, to remove barriers to learning and to support pupil well-being. This means a strong partnership with parents and carers, so that they become more closely involved in their child's learning and help improve behaviour and attendance. It means strong partnerships with local institutions to extend the learning opportunities of young people and broaden their horizons. It means using the opportunities of the Green Paper *Every Child Matters* to integrate children's services by bringing family support, social care and health services together with education to help support all children and in particular those with additional needs. Extended schools, such as King's Park Primary in Bournemouth and Dyke House School in Hartlepool, can lead the way by reaching out to the community.

Source: Adapted from DCSF (since changed to Department of Education)
The Five Components of Personalised Learning, available at:
http://nationalstrategies.standards.dcsf.gov.uk/node/83149?uc=force_uj
Crown Copyright material is reproduced under the terms of the Click-Use Licence

WHAT DO YOU THINK?

Consider each of the components of personalised learning described above. To what extent do you, your department/faculty, your organisation promote these components? What is the evidence for your views?

Assessment for learning

Harkin (2006) cites Ecclestone (2006) who describes the varying perspectives on assessment of vocational and academic teachers.

RESEARCH FOCUS

Vocational tutors regarded 'good assessment' as practical, authentic and relevant activities, work-experience and field trips: there was a very strong view amongst vocational teachers that 'these students' do not want or like written assessment, that they are less secure, need more group affinity and to be in a more protected safe environment. In their beliefs about 'comfort zones' and 'protecting' students, vocational teachers saw assessment as integral to a strong ethos of personal development that minimized stress or pressure; assessment to develop subject knowledge did not feature in their espoused goals for students . . . A minority of students doing an AS qualification alongside their vocational course compared the familiar, tight-knit atmosphere and cohesive group of tutors unfavourably with the fragmented, individualised AS groups where students moved between four separate subjects with different cohorts in each . . . Students in academic qualifications practised examination answers that would help them get good grades. Written feedback was more general and open ended than in the vocational course and tutors did not offer direct advice about higher grades. One tutor offered written comments, or comments in class that evaluated the strengths and weaknesses of answers: these comments were strongly critical and occasionally positive . . . In contrast to assessment observed in the vocational courses, this combination of question, answer and feedback was much more robustly focused on eliciting the cognitive skills demanded in the exam.

Ecclestone, K. (2006) Assessment in post-14 education:
the implications of principles, practices and policies for learning and achievement,
Nuffield Review of 14–19 Education and Training Research Report 2

The 14–19 teachers will then have a range of experience of assessment, familiarity with specific assessment strategies and work within a particular culture of assessment. According to Harkin (2006: liv),

> FE teachers are used to designing assessments and carrying out internal verification of assessment; school teachers are less used to such autonomy and may need to learn about the formative and summative assessment of applied learning from more experienced FE colleagues.

The Assessment Reform Group (Assessment Reform Group 2002) define assessment for learning as 'the process of seeking and interpreting evidence for use by learners and their teachers to decide where the learners are in their learning, where they need to go and how best to get there.'

They suggest there are 10 principles of assessment for learning. It should:

1. be part of effective planning of teaching and learning
2. focus on how students learn
3. be recognised as central to classroom practice
4. be regarded as a key professional skill for teachers
5. be sensitive and constructive because any assessment has an emotional impact
6. take account of the importance of learner motivation
7. promote commitment to learning goals and a shared understanding of the criteria by which they are assessed
8. give learners constructive guidance on how to improve
9. develop learners' capacity for self-assessment so that they can become reflective and self-managing
10. recognise the full range of achievements of learners.

Delivery of the specialised diplomas will require personalised learning, as described above, which actively engages and stretches students:

> Applied learning is about active engagement with subjects, teachers, other learners and the world beyond. It is about *doing*, being an *agent of change*, *influencing one's own life and the world*, being a *citizen*, as well as potentially an *employee*. It is about excitement in following one's interests and therefore about some *power* to make informed choices.
>
> *(Harkin 2006: xliv)*

The valid assessment of such learning will require a range of assessment strategies which are fit for this purpose.

IN PRACTICE

In the left-hand column below is a series of active learning approaches and strategies which are likely to be utilised by those teaching on and taking the specialised Diplomas. On the right are listed a number of assessment strategies. Taking individual learning strategies, exemplify specifically how each might be used in your subject/curriculum area. Then select an assessment strategy or strategies which might be validly used in relation to it.

Active learning approaches/strategies	Assessment strategies
Practical workshop activity	Self-assessment
Problem-solving activity	Questioning
Mobile e-learning	Witness testimony
Teamwork	Personal testimony
Self-management	Video/DVD/still photography record
Workplace learning such as customer service, handling and storing resources	Product evaluation
	Interview record
Educational visit (to, for example, an art gallery, museum, site of historical interest, theatrical performance, holiday resort and leisure centre, manufacturing plant, shopping centre, newspaper, broadcaster, sports event, hotel, farm, hospital, police station, fire and rescue station.)	Practical test
	Peer assessment
	Diary/logbook
	Demonstration of skills/routine
Design and make a product	Role-play
Employer-led activity in school/college	Group discussion
Research activity involving individual survey/enquiry, interviews, data presentation and interpretation	Presentation
	Tutor/student discussion
	Display
Use of specialist equipment/technologies	
Understanding of safe working practices	
Developing a budget for a project	
Creative thinking activity	
Personal development activity	

Source: Education Photos Ltd.

Photo 19.1
Educational
visits present
opportunities
for active
learning

Generic learning skills

Generic learning skills within the Diploma include:

- functional skills in English, ICT and Maths at Levels 1, 2 and 3;

- six transferable personal, learning and thinking skills (PLTS) in independent enquiry, creative thinking, reflective learning, teamworking, self-managing and effective participation;

- a Diploma project or extended study involving investigative and project management skills;

- skills gained through work experience.

DCSF defines functional skills as follows:

> They cover large chunks of what's already being taught in English, Maths and ICT. If you think of what is currently taught and assessed (for example by GCSE) as giving pupils a toolkit of techniques, functional skills is about the ability to select the right tools to solve different problems. It's about relating the curriculum to how it should be used in everyday life – for example, in English, understanding written instructions and being able to write intelligible messages to work colleagues.
>
> *(DCSF 2008b)*

QCDA is developing standards for functional skills and examining boards are, at the time of writing, developing approaches to assessment and assessment methods. It is planned for functional skills to replace key skills and skills for life (basic skills). Like key skills, it is intended that functional skills will be available in a variety of contexts, including educational and work-based contexts. Functional skills qualifications will be available as both stand-alone awards and related to other qualifications such as GCSE.

One of the determinants of success in key skills teaching has been the mode of delivery and this is likely to be crucial in the effectiveness of functional skills teaching. Smith and Mannion describe four such models below.

RESEARCH FOCUS

Model 1: The discrete model

Students usually have to move to other teaching and learning areas to 'pick up' their skills where they are taught by the key/core skills 'expert'. Students are then expected to carry these skills and adapt them for use within their vocational areas. For students the main problem that this approach poses is that of relevance. 'What has this got to do with construction or catering?' is the question core skills' staff hear frequently. They develop a view that learning the content of their course and learning the literacy aspects of this course are separate. For vocational staff the problem is one of transfer . . . The question frequently heard here is: 'If they can write an essay for core skills why can't they write a letter for Business Studies?' This approach sees literacy as something which happens within the individual head of the student and decontextualised from the activities in which it is usually found.

Model 2: The contextualised model

This is very similar to the discrete model in that students are taught core/key skills away from the vocational area by a specialist skills teacher. However, the core/key skills teacher makes the content relevant to the students they meet from the various vocational areas . . . Because the teacher is not located in the vocational area, it is more difficult for the teacher to develop a critically sensitive approach; skills remain abstractions as a result and the epistemological position that regards skills as generic and transferable is sustained. This model still works from a premise that learning reading and writing is one form of learning and learning in the vocational area is another. The benefit is that the student may see some relevance but it can lead them to undertaking personal responsibility for 'failing' when they are unable to transfer.

Model 3: The integrated model

Other terms have been used to describe this approach but 'integrated' seems to capture it best. This model works on a continuum. Formal and informal planning between vocational and core skills staff is necessary for integration to occur. At one extreme, integration occurs where the core skills staff and the vocational staff agree on an assessment instrument that could meet the requirements of

▶

RESEARCH FOCUS: *CONTINUED*

both units. They still teach their separate aspects in their separate classrooms but work towards the same assessment goal. The problem with this is that the assessment instrument can become so complex it causes extra challenges for the student. Additionally the student may pass the vocational element and fail the core skills element or vice versa both of which reinforces the view that reading and writing are different from the 'doing' the content of the programme. At the other extreme, the core skills teacher and the vocational teacher work together in partnership usually in the vocational area classroom; sometimes the core/key skills teacher is also a practitioner from the vocational area with a background in the industry themselves.

Model 4: The embedded model

In this model, vocational teachers do not 'teach' core skills. In advance of teaching any course or programme, the teaching team look at the curriculum and decide which elements provide opportunities for students to develop key/core skills. These decisions are validated by both internal and external moderators. Staff are encouraged to make explicit to the students which activities are developing their core skills as well as their vocational skills. At one level then, this model recognises that literacy is part of the vocational area students are studying and so could be said to be a situated view of literacy. However, we argue that literacy can become invisible if not made explicit.

Smith, J. and Mannion, G. (2006) What's 'Key'/'Core' about literacy in FE? Authorising resonance between everyday literacy practices and formal learning. Paper presented at the British Educational Research Association Annual Conference, University of Warwick, 6–9 September 2006

IN PRACTICE

Consider the following questions in relation to how Key/Core Skills is currently delivered in your curriculum area:

Does it conform to one of Smith and Mannion's models above?
What are students' attitudes to developing Key/Core Skills?
Do you regard Key/Core Skills as transferable to your curriculum/vocational area?
How are Key/Core Skills assessed? Is such assessment, in your view, valid and reliable?
Is there a tendency for Communications, Application of Number and ICT to take precedence over the wider Key Skills, Improving Own Learning and Performance, Problem Solving and Working with Others?

Information, advice and guidance

Student transition through the 14–19 phase is already complex and, as the curriculum is transformed, so the importance of students' access to impartial, informed guidance to navigate such complexity will increase. There is a wide variety of practice across the sector regarding IAG provision with a number of personnel playing a role. IAG can be provided by teachers, personal tutors, specialist careers staff, careers advisers, year heads, LEA inspectors/advisers, governors, employers, FE admissions tutors, personal tutors and work-based learning trainers. From April 2008, responsibility for commissioning IAG is being devolved from the Connexions Service to local authorities, working through children's trusts, schools and colleges, whose role in IAG provision will therefore increase. The contexts for IAG provision are numerous. It can be offered discretely as part of a separate enrichment programme, integrated into the curriculum in either academic or vocational qualifications, through extended activity such as work experience or work visits, be part of a tutorial programme or system, be gained through supported self study, accessed online or as a complement to work-based training.

IN PRACTICE

Profile the approach to IAG in your own institution by describing how students/trainees might develop or gain access to the following. In which context would this take place and which personnel would be involved in delivery?

1. Progression opportunities within the organisation.
2. Progression opportunities beyond the organisation – to college, work-based learning, HE.
3. Awareness of own knowledge and skills relating to employment opportunities.
4. Awareness of entry requirements to qualifications.
5. Understanding of the local labour market.
6. Awareness of the variety of career routes in the relevant sector.
7. Work experience and work-related learning.
8. Decision-making skills.
9. Application procedures for qualifications or employment, including the ability to write letters of application, personal statements and construct CVs.
10. Awareness of the role of self-presentation in interview situations.
11. Interview experience.
12. Awareness of employers' requirements.
13. Health and safety issues at work.
14. Changes in career patterns in the relevant sector.
15. Goal setting, review and action planning to support own progress and achievement.
16. Awareness of the influences on their attitudes and values relating to learning and work.
17. Ability to access sources of careers information.

Working collaboratively

The nature of the 14–19 entitlement makes it evident that no school acting alone will be able to meet the needs of all young people on its roll; and that very few colleges will be able to offer the full breadth of curriculum on their own. Consequently, schools, colleges and training providers will need to think together and with local agencies about how to offer more between them than any one could individually.

(DfES 2006)

Partnership working 14–19 was explored fully in Chapter 17 but here we are interested specifically in the features of collaborative working which will impact on teachers' practice. What we know about effective practice in partnership working 14–19 has been gained largely from the outcomes of the Pathfinder Project, designed to explore and trial over a period of three years, ways of managing and delivering 14–19 provision on a partnership basis. Details are given in evaluation reports of the project, specifically DfES (2006), Higham et al. (2004) and Higham and Yeomans (2005).

IN PRACTICE

Find out as much as possible about your institution's current and intended future collaborative activity and consider the extent to which it is intending to attend to the key aspects of practice below:

- the importance of teacher networking across the partnership, including both face-to-face and virtual contact and particularly between subject specialists;
- developing a common cross-partnership approach to assessment and learning;
- having a clear understanding of the institution's role in the partnership and practitioner's own role in relation to this;
- exchange of good practice;
- peer and experienced practitioner observation and feedback;
- cross-partnership mentoring and coaching;
- peer, co- and team teaching;
- enhancement of skills in teaching and learning in vocational subjects, particularly in delivering the applied GCSEs;
- vocational subject up-skilling, including sector work experience;
- using and assessing learning in the workplace;
- enhancement of pedagogical skills in applied learning;
- age-related training in pedagogy or behaviour management, for example;
- curriculum development expertise;
- acquaintance with new software packages.

Source: Pearson Education Ltd. Mind Studio

Photo 19.2
Collaboration
between
institutions
may involve
movement
of students
between them

Developing reflective practice

There is an extensive literature relating to reflective practice, some of which is included in the reading for this chapter. The term is often used broadly to include all staff development which involves some sort of cognition relating to the practice of teaching. Reflective practice was the main focus of Chapter 11. However, views on what reflective practice might comprise are given below.

RESEARCH FOCUS

Dewey described the general features of a reflective experience as

perplexity, confusion, doubt, due to the fact that one is implicated in an incomplete situation whose full character is not yet determined;

- *a conjectural anticipation – a tentative interpretation of the given elements, attributing to them a tendency to effect certain consequences;*

- *a careful survey (examination, inspection, exploration, analysis) of all attainable consideration which will define and clarify the problem in hand;*

▶

RESEARCH FOCUS: *CONTINUED*

- *a consequent elaboration of the tentative hypothesis to make it more precise and more consistent, because squaring with a wider range of facts;*

- *taking one stand upon the projected hypothesis as a plan of action which is applied to the existing state of affairs; doing something overtly to bring about the anticipated result, and thereby testing the hypothesis.*

(Dewey 1933: 177)

Schon distinguishes between reflection-in-action and reflection-on action. The former can be characterised as follows:

When we go about the spontaneous, intuitive performance of the actions of everyday life, we show ourselves to be knowledgeable in a special way. Often we cannot say what it is that we know. When we try to describe it we find ourselves at a loss, or we produce descriptions that are obviously inappropriate. Our knowing is ordinarily tacit, implicit in our patterns of action and in our feel for the stuff with which we are dealing. It seems right to say that our knowing is in our action.

(Schon 1991: 49)

According to **Brookfield**,

– we have available four lenses through which we can view our teaching –

1. Our Autobigraphies as Learners and Teachers   *Consulting our autobiographies as learners puts us in the role of the 'other'. We see our practice from the other side of the mirror, and we become viscerally connected to what our own students are experiencing. Investigating our autobiographies as teachers is often the first step on the critical path. Through personal self-reflection, we become aware of the paradigmatic assumptions and instinctive reasonings that frame how we work. When we know what these are, we can start to test their accuracy and validity through conversations with students, colleagues, and books.*

2. Our Students' Eyes   *Seeing ourselves as students see us makes us aware of those actions and assumptions that either confirm or challenge existing power relationships in the classroom. They also help us check whether students take from our practice the meanings that we intend.*

3. Our Colleagues' Experiences   *By inviting colleagues to watch what we do, or by engaging in critical conversations with them, we can notice aspects of our practice that are normally hidden from us. As they describe their readings of, and responses to, situations that we face, we see our practice in a new light.*

4. Theoretical Literature   *Theoretical literature can provide multiple interpretations of familiar but impenetrable situations. It can help us understand our experience by naming it in different ways, and by illuminating generic aspects of what we thought were idiosyncratic events and processes.*

(Brookfield 1995: 29)

For **Pollard et al.**

– seven key characteristics of reflective practice – are:

1. *Reflective teaching implies an active concern with aims and consequences as well as means and technical efficiency.*

2. *Reflective teaching is applied in a cyclical or spiralling process, in which teachers monitor, evaluate and revise their practice continuously.*

3. *Reflective teaching requires competence in evidence-based classroom enquiry, to support the progressive development of higher standards of teaching.*

4. *Reflective teaching requires open-mindedness, responsibility and wholeheartedness.*

5. *Reflective teaching is based on teacher judgement, informed by evidence-based enquiry and insights from other research.*

(Pollard et al. 2005: 14)

According to **Hillier,**

If we reflect critically, we can begin to formulate propositions from our own personal, informal theories which then become public and testable. We can then begin to advance both our practical and theoretical knowledge, taking into account the important interplay between what is happening in practice and what sense is being made of our practice by others.

(Hillier 2005: 17)

CASE STUDY

Below is an extract from a PGCE student's Individual Development Planner, including her reflective journal. Which of the features of reflective practice described above does she demonstrate?

INDIVIDUAL DEVELOPMENT PLANNER
Week 19 / Beg. 1 January 2009

Monday	Tuesday	Wednesday	Thursday	Friday	Notes
Happy New Year!	Self Study	P	P	Comms + N	

University sessions

Communications
- Communication for teaching your subject specialism
- Comparison and development

Numeracy
- Shapes and angles

Standards focus

Course LOs: Comms 1–4
Skills standards: 1.6, 1.9, 1.10, 1.11, 3.5, 3.7, 4.6
Skills and Attributes

With your mentor, identify areas for reflection and study over the vacation. Record below. (Comment in relation to last week's target. Reflection in your journal will support this target setting and planning.) With your mentor, identify in advance a session for your third STE. Set up a pre-meeting with your mentor, prepare carefully and complete the documentation.

Areas for reflection over the vacation are on how I began to prepare my students for their January exams. What will be the examiner be looking for in their answers and are my students able to match those expectations? Marking the AS Sociology mock papers was very slow; the more they wrote the easier it was to mark. I found myself re-reading answers to reward marks to a few students whose answers were not as structured or complete. I was constantly re-checking the marking grid. I felt I started marking papers too harshly at first. I think that if I had marked more essays from the group in the past, I would have found it an easier process.

In the future, on newer topics, I would set more practice essays as homework or timed essays as I have better knowledge of their strengths and weaknesses. There is also a need for 1:1s with me to improve how I communicate to them about improving their essay writing for the summer exams.

Writing the Scheme of Work for BTEC Business was at first daunting. Then I began to reflect on my own experiences in retail/sales and creative activities and it came quite easily to me. Because I had met them a few times before I had a good idea about their learning styles.

Target and Planning

- Do lesson plan and power point for first BTEC Business lesson on Thursday 7th January.
- Read up on Marketing, the A level Business course for a meeting with Tutor Y next week.
- Prepare for STE pre-meeting on 10th January. The third STE my mentor next Thursday 14th January. It is the BTEC Business course.

Mentor signature:

Reflective journal –

Focus: Communication for Learning

How have the university sessions and associated reading influenced your perspective on communication in a learning environment?

I am surprised about how much new material I have learnt in the sessions. I assumed communication was easy to learn because we do it every day but it's more about how we do it as professional teachers that has grabbed my interest.

There is so much more under the surface. In the classroom you are working hard to communicate; it is not as natural as I thought – it is an acquired teaching skill. There are so many barriers to communication such as verbal (low level chattering) and non verbal noise (builders working outside). The way you speak and present the information (be it written or verbal) needs to keep them engaged. I have had to be flexible in my communication style because some students understand better with diagrams and images rather than a straight lecture. I very often communicate successfully using up-to-date and relevant scenarios/images that they can relate to and make links to the concept taught.

Reading on communication especially about NLP, TNA and 6CIA and the models of Schramm and Shannon and Weaver have helped me to identify where my communication has broken down in my lessons and how I can improve. At the beginning of the course I did not think communication was as important as assessment or curriculum planning but now I see it as more important because I need to develop a good rapport with these students and because of their diverse socio-economic backgrounds/issues it is a key tool for a more student centred learning approach required in FE.

IN PRACTICE

Do you engage in reflective practice as part of your professional role? Is it related to a course of initial or in-service training you are undertaking? Is there a formalised system in your institution which might involve mentoring, peer or advanced practitioner observation? Or is your reflection more informal or tacit, resembling Schon's reflection-in-action? How far does your reflective practice exemplify the features described in the Research Focus box on pages 391–3?

Changing institutions

The capacity to engage in reflection on practice to develop knowledge, skills and understanding is a key feature of the teacher as professional. Other features, referred to by Hughes (2000), include autonomy, a lengthy period of training, knowledge and expertise, a strong community service orientation and adherence to a code of values and ethics. There are those who argue that some of these features are inhibited rather than encouraged in staff by the mission and culture of the institutions they work in. They claim that many FE colleges, for example, have, since incorporation in the early 1990s, become managerialist in nature. Randle and Brady's (2000) chart below sets out what they regard as the main areas for potential conflict between managers and FE professionals.

Professional paradigm	Managerialist paradigm
Goals and values	
• primacy of student learning and the learning process	• primacy of student through-put and income generation
• loyalty to students and colleagues	• loyalty to the organisation
• concern for academic standards	• concern to achieve an acceptable balance between efficiency and effectiveness
Key assumptions	
• lecturers as funds of expertise	• lecturers as flexible facilitators and assessors
• resources deployed on the basis of educational need	• resources deployed on the basis of market-demand and value for taxpayers' money
• quality of provision assessed on the basis of input	• quality assessed on the basis of output/outcomes
Management ethos	
• collegiality/'community of practice'	• control by managers and the market
• professional autonomy/the trust principle/accountability to peers/tacit knowledge	• management by performance indicators and surveillance
• pluralism	• unitarism

IN PRACTICE

Consider the institution you work in. Overall, do you think it fits the professional or managerialist paradigm? Or is there evidence that it exhibits features of both?

The nature of the institution in which teachers work is a key influence on the way in which they practise. However, any difficulty in coming to judgements about the nature of your institution in the reflection above could be connected with your own position within the institution, which will give you a partial and highly subjective point of view. Your role and position in the institution will further be influenced by the organisational culture you are part of. Although a single organisational culture may be common to an institution as a whole, it is more likely that a variety of cultures exist in any institution, which may be common to a faculty, department, or a small group of colleagues. Hargreaves (1994) identifies a number of cultures found in educational institutions.

RESEARCH FOCUS

Individualism

Teaching has a long tradition of individual working. This may result from the architecture of institutions, the classroom-based nature of the job. There may be limited physical space for teachers to associate and work together. Equally, such individual working could be related to the nature of the accountability and responsibility connected with the role. Such a culture may be isolating for the teacher but may equally be sought as a preferred way of working.

Balkanisation

Here, groups of staff operate as city states, their loyalties and identities tied to the group. They will share a view of professional practice, an attitude to the institution and its values. The group operates as a protection against those outside it, whether inside or outside the institution.

Collaborative culture

This culture is underpinned by sharing, trust and support. Collaborative working is central to the teachers' professional practice. Such a family structure may lend itself to paternalistic or maternalistic leadership. This is a culture which values and undertakes continuous improvement.

RESEARCH FOCUS: *CONTINUED*

Contrived collegiality

This does not arise spontaneously as an initiative by teachers but from an attempt institutionally to impose a culture on teachers which requires them to meet and work together, engaging in such activities as collaborative planning, peer coaching and observation, team teaching or staff development sessions.

The moving mosaic

In this culture, groups have blurred boundaries with overlapping membership and values. It is a culture which can enable flexible, dynamic, responsive practice but runs the risk of creating uncertainty and vulnerability for staff.

Source: Adapted from Hargreaves, A. (1994) *Changing Teachers, Changing Times*, London and New York: Continuum

IN PRACTICE

Do you recognise any of the cultures above characterising your own institution or groups of teachers within it?

Look back at the key requirements of teachers to enable them to deliver the 14–19 curriculum in Chapter 19. Do any of the cultures above make it more likely that they will effectively carry this out?

SUMMARY

The chapter asks the question: what are the distinctive knowledge, skills and attributes which are going to be required of teachers to effectively deliver the new 14–19 curriculum? The evidence base for a professional development toolkit being developed by LLUK and the Teacher Development Agency identifies six areas in which teachers will need to be proficient: personalised learning, assessment for learning, generic learning skills, information, advice and guidance, working collaboratively, developing reflective practice. The chapter considers each of these in turn, drawing out the implications for the initial and continuing training and development of teachers. Finally, the changing settings in which teachers are working are examined and a relationship described between the culture and structure of institutions and teachers' professional practice.

Find out more

Shift Happens

'Shift Happens' was originally a Powerpoint presentation by a teacher at an American high school for a staff development session, intended to give his colleagues an idea of the world their students would be growing up in in the twenty-first century. Only months after it had appeared on the Web in 2007, it had been seen by 5 million viewers. It can be seen at: **http://shifthappens.wikispaces.com/**.

House of Commons: Children, Schools and Families Committee (2010) *Training of Teachers: Fourth Report of the Session 2009–10.*
This report (2010: 7) drew attention to the lack of parity between those teaching in schools and further education and made the following recommendations:

37. At the very least, teachers with Qualified Teacher Learning and Skills status should immediately be able to work as a qualified teacher in schools if they are teaching post-16, even post-14, pupils. (Paragraph 184)

38. In the context of the 14–19 reforms, the Department should put in place a mechanism for assessing vocational or professional qualifications as equivalent to degree status. (Paragraph 185)

39. Over the longer term we recommend that the training of early years teachers, school teachers and further education teachers become harmonised through generic standards. Alongside this, we envisage Qualified Teacher Status becoming more specific, clearly denoting the age

ranges and the subjects for which a trainee was qualified to teach. Chartered Teacher Status we would see as becoming similarly specific. (Paragraph 186)

40. Diplomas represent one of the most significant initiatives in our education system for many years, and will be expanded considerably this year. This demands greater fluidity – and shared development opportunities – across the school and further education sectors. (Paragraph 187)

41. In order to enhance collaboration between schools and further education in the development of the 14–19 curriculum, we support the establishment of a centre that would provide joint professional development provision for school and further education teachers in the neglected area of pedagogy and assessment in vocational education. (Paragraph 188)

(Available at: **www.parliament.uk/csf/**)

Futurelab (http://www.futurelab.org.uk/)
Futurelab describes itself as 'an independent not-for-profit organisation that is dedicated to transforming teaching and learning, making it more relevant and engaging to 21st century learners through the use of innovative practice and technology. We have a long track record of researching and demonstrating innovative uses of technology and aim to support systemic change in education – and are uniquely placed to bring together those with an interest in improving education from the policy, industry, research and practice communities to do this.'

Bibliography

Armitage, A. et al. (2007) *Teaching and Training in Post-Compulsory Education* (3rd edn), Maidenhead: Open University Press/McGraw-Hill.

Assessment Reform Group (2002) *Assessment for Learning: 10 principles*, available at: **http://arg.educ.cam.ac.uk/index.html**

Brookfield, S. D. (1995) *Becoming a Critically Reflective Teacher*, San Francisco CA: Jossey-Bass.

DCSF (2008a) *The Five Components of Personalised Learning*, available at: **http://nationalstrategies.standards.dcsf.gov.uk/node/83149?uc=force_uj**

DCSF (2008b) *Generic Definition of Functional Skills*, available at: **www.dcsf.gov.uk/14-19/index.cfm?go=site.home&sid=3&pid=225&lid=188&ctype=Text&ptype=Single**

DfES (2004) *Equipping our Teachers for the Future*, London: DfES.

DfES (2006) *Manual of Good Practice*, London: DfES, available at: **www.dfes.gov.uk/14-19/ dsp_1419_goodpractice.cfm?sid=9&pid=199&_ ctype=None&ptype=Contents**

Dewey, J. (1933) *How We Think: a restatement of the relation of reflective thinking to the educative process*, Chicago: Henry Regnery.

Ecclestone, K. (2006) Assessment in post-14 education: the implications of principles, practices and policies for learning and achievement, *Nuffield Review of 14–19 Education and Training Research Report 2.*

Ecclestone, K. and Hayes, D. (2009) *The Dangerous Rise in Therapeutic Education*, London: Routledge.

Furedi, F. (2004) *Therapy Culture: cultivating vulnerability in an uncertain age*, London and New York: Routledge.

Hargreaves, A. (1994) *Changing Teachers, Changing Times*, London and New York: Continuum.

Harkin, J. (2006) *Excellence in Supporting Applied Learning*, London: LLUK.

Hayes, D. (2003a) New Labour new professionalism, in Satterthwaite, J., Atkinson, E. and Gale, K. (eds) (2003) *Discourse, Power, Resistance: challenging the rhetoric of contemporary education*, Stoke-on-Trent: Trentham.

Hayes, D. (2003b) The changed nexus between education and work, in Lea, J., Hayes, D., Armitage, A., Lomas, L. and Markless, S. (2003) *Working in Post-Compulsory Education*, Maidenhead: Open University Press.

Hayes, D. (2003c) Managerialism and professionalism in post-compulsory education, in Lea, J., Hayes, D., Armitage, A., Lomas, L. and Markless, S. (2003) *Working in Post-Compulsory Education*, Maidenhead: Open University Press.

Hayes, D. (2004) The therapeutic turn in teacher education, in Hayes, D. (ed.) *The Routledge Falmer Guide to Key Debates in Education*, London and New York: Routledge.

Hayes, D. (2006) Rehumanising education, in Cummings, D. (ed.) *Debating Humanism*, Exeter: Imprint Academic/Societas.

Higham, J. et al. (2004) *14–19 Pathfinders: an evaluation of the first year*, available at: **www.dfes.gov.uk/ 14-19_pathfinder_second_year_report_final.doc**

Higham, J. and Yeomans, D. (2005) *Collaborative Approaches to 14–19 provision: an evaluation of the second year*, Leeds: University of Leeds, available at: **www.dfes.gov.uk/14-19/documents/14-19_ pathfinder_second_year_report-final.doc**

Hillier, Y. (2005) *Reflective Teaching in Further and Adult Education*, London: Continuum.

House of Commons: Children, Schools and Families Committee (2010) *Training of Teachers: Fourth Report of the Session 2009–10*, London: The Stationery Office Limited.

Hughes, M. (2000) Professionals and the management of organisations, in Hall, L. and Marsh, K. *Professionals, Policies and Values*, London: Greenwich University Press.

Hyland, T. and Merrill, B. (2003) *The Changing Face of Further Education*, London: RoutledgeFalmer.

Mortiboys, A. (2005) *Teaching with Emotional Intelligence: a step-by-step guide for further and higher education professionals*, London and New York: RoutledgeFalmer.

Ofsted (2003) *The Initial Training of Further Education Teachers: a survey*, London: Ofsted.

Pollard, A., Collins, S., Maddock, M., Simco, N., Swaffield, S., Warin, J. and Warnick, P. (2005) *Reflective Teaching* (2nd edn), London: Continuum.

Randle, K. and Brady, N. (2000) Managerialism and professionalism in the Cinderella service, in Hall, L. and Marsh, K. *Professionals, Policies and Values*, London: Greenwich University Press.

Schon, D. (1991) *The Reflective Practitioner*, Aldershot: Avebury Ashgate Publishing Ltd.

Smith, J. and Mannion, G. (2006) What's 'Key'/'Core' about literacy in FE? Authorising resonance between everyday literacy practices and formal learning. Paper presented at the British Educational Research Association Annual Conference, University of Warwick 6–9 September 2006.

Tribal Education and Technology (2007) *Professional Development Toolkit for Teachers of the 14–19 Diplomas*, Cambridge: Tribal Education and Technology.

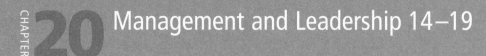

CHAPTER

20 Management and Leadership 14–19

In this chapter, you will:

- consider the relationship between management and leadership
- appreciate aspects of good practice in management and leadership
- understand the strengths and weaknesses of formal and informal models of management and apply them to your own institution
- appreciate the relationship of managerialism to professionalism
- assess your emotional competences in working with other people and consider how they might be developed
- understand the importance of effective curriculum management to 14–19 delivery

Pearson Education Ltd./Ken Wilson-Max

Introduction

Wallace and Gravells (2007: 77) refer to Bennis's (1989) distinction between management and leadership, the former concerned with

> administration, systems, structure, control and maintaining the status quo. In contrast, leadership he sees as being about innovation, development, people, inspiring trust, taking the long view and challenging the accepted way of doing things.

This is not, in the end, they argue, a very helpful distinction since it tends to portray the management role as impersonal and systems-oriented while the leadership role is dynamic and people-oriented. 'It might be more helpful', they continue 'to see these definitions – as complementary parts of a single role at whatever level it is practised' (2007: 78). This suggestion introduces the notion of **distributed leadership and management**, according to which both management and leadership are functions of those working at every level in the organisation. However, although it is recognised that effective distributed management is a key feature of an effective educational institution, as we have seen in Chapters 6 and 19 when considering both teachers' professionalism and the likely demands on them in delivering the 14–19 reforms, the dominance of a managerialist culture in sector institutions over the past 20 years has profoundly affected the capacity of teachers to act as autonomous professionals capable of demonstrating the range of leadership qualities and skills the distributed model requires. Furthermore, in spite of trying a range of flatter organisational models, including matrix models, most FE colleges have adopted a relatively rigid hierarchical structure, with a Principal or Chief Executive and a number of vice, assistant or deputy principals or directors making up the senior management team, who between them will line-manage middle managers who will be curriculum or administrative managers. They in turn will be responsible for departments, schools or sections. Such a structure is not in itself conducive to the effective distribution of leadership and management.

Leadership

Jameson and McNay (2007: 61) present the following features of good leadership practice:

- Prioritisation of student success as the core educational value of the sector
- Communicative clarity and coherence in influencing others
- A strong values-base
- Strategic thinking – big picture
- Capable of motivating others
- Capable of being people-centred/an emotionally intelligent leader
- Capable of authenticity
- Having passion and optimism
- Capable of teamwork
- Capable of building on and using others' perspectives
- Able to engage in self-development.

Photo 20.1
The ability to motivate others is a key feature of an effective leader

Source: Pearson Education Ltd. Tudor Photography

IN PRACTICE

Consider your current professional role. How far is leadership a feature of that role? Which of the qualities above do you demonstrate in your professional role?

Jameson and McNay also refer to Ofsted's 2004 report *Why Colleges Succeed* which highlighted the following features shared by colleges that achieved a Grade 1 'Outstanding' for leadership and management:

- Very good retention and pass rates
- Highly effective teaching
- Extremely successful learning
- Excellent support and guidance for students at all stages in their programme
- An exemplary response to educational and social inclusion
- Outstanding strategic leadership and governance
- Consistently good curriculum management
- Rigorous quality assurance processes which include accurate self-assessment, a detailed and regular focus on classroom practice and effective performance management of staff
- Excellent financial management . . . providers gave excellent value for money

- There is a very 'hands-on' approach of senior managers to the college's core work, which they make it their business to understand fully
- The principal and senior management team are successful in creating a culture where students are at the heart of the college's work . . . [t]here is an unrelenting focus on students and their achievements . . .
- An open and consultative style . . . staff are consulted regularly
- Communication and consultation with staff help to create a culture in which staff morale is high, staff feel valued and share a common purpose with their managers . . . this shared vision is a critical prerequisite for success
- Governors play a significant role in providing strategic direction and monitoring the academic and financial performance of the college
- Governors share the vision for the college with senior managers and staff and are active in pursuing the vision, being both supportive and acting as a 'critical friend'
- Staff have access to accurate and reliable management information
- There is effective teamwork . . . teaching staff meet regularly and good practice is disseminated.

(2007: 76)

IN PRACTICE

From your point of view in the organisation, how many of the above features would you say are characteristic of your institution?

Formal and informal models of educational management

According to Bush (1995: 29) formal models of educational management

> assume that organisations are hierarchical systems in which managers use rational means to pursue agreed goals. Heads possess authority legitimized by their formal positions within the organisation and are accountable to sponsoring bodies for the activities of their institutions.

Bush goes on to describe the key features which formal models have in common. Firstly, they conceive of organisations as systems comprising sub-units which all relate to one another and operate as an integrated whole. These sub-units may be faculties, departments, subject sections. Secondly, there is an emphasis in formal models on the official structure of the organisation, with clear indications of the relationship between those in that structure. These structures will be hierarchical with roles clearly defined in the hierarchy and a rigid vertical authority structure. Thirdly, organisations will be goal-seeking: from their mission statements to the strategic planning which may be at the centre of their governance and management. Fourthly, there is an assumption that management decision-making is rational in nature, with options measured against organisational objectives in a detached intellectual way. Fifthly, the authority of leaders in the organisation comes from their position in the structure, their power regarded as positional. And finally, importance is given to the accountability of the organisation to its sponsoring body.

There are, however, five weaknesses of formal models in their application to educational institutions, according to Bush. Firstly, it may be unrealistic to conceive of schools and colleges as goal-oriented. Official goals are usually vague and generalised and it is the variety of ways in which they might be achieved which make the institution distinctive. There may also be many unofficial or hidden goals pursued by individuals and interest groups in the organisation. Even where goals have been clarified, it is often difficult to ascertain whether they have been achieved. Secondly, the characterisation of decision-making as a rational process is problematic: decisions are often irrational or at least underpinned by non-rational factors. Thirdly, formal models focus on the organisation and assume individuals' behaviour is connected with their role in the organisation rather than their individual qualities and experience. Fourthly, a key assumption of formal models is that top–down management and the acceptance of management decisions is unproblematic. We shall see below how this can result in a conflict between managerialist and professional paradigms. And finally, formal approaches assume that organisations are essentially stable: people come and go but they slot into static roles in the structure. We have considered elsewhere how organisations in the lifelong learning sector are undergoing unprecedented change, structurally, in their relations with the outside world, in their curricula and in the nature and needs of their students. Formal models are not necessarily the most effective in managing that change.

Bush (1995: 52) describes more informal or collegial models as those

> which emphasise that power and decision-making should be shared among some or all members of the organisation. These approaches range from a 'restricted' collegiality where the leader shares power with a limited number of senior colleagues to a 'pure' collegiality where all members have an equal voice in determining policy.

According to Bush, collegial models have the following features in common. Firstly, they are strongly normative in orientation: that is, they hold that management ought to be based on agreement. Secondly, they assume members should be involved widely in the decision-making process. Thirdly, they assume a common set of values among members of the organisation. Fourthly, they assume that all members are formally represented on decision-making bodies. Finally, collegial models assume that decisions are reached by consensus rather than division or conflict.

However, collegial models have the following drawbacks. Decision-making can be slow and cumbersome: management by committee. Secondly, the requirement that decisions are reached by consensus might be frustrated by the views and values of individuals and interest groups within the organisation. Thirdly, there can be a tension between the structural and bureaucratic formal organisation of an institution and the requirements of participative decision-making. Fourthly, there may be a conflict between the organisation management's accountability – to governors, sponsors and other stakeholders – and the views of organisational members on policy. Fifthly, unless members actively support participative decision-making, it will be difficult to implement. Finally, the effective collegial processes are more dependent on the head in a school than on the principal of a college which will have an academic board involving staff in decision-making.

IN PRACTICE

Most institutions are likely to have both formal and collegial aspects of their organisation and operation. Consider your own institution: in what ways does it conform to the formal model of management and in what ways is it collegial in nature? How does each aspect affect your capacity to do your job effectively: for example, is observation of teaching for quality-assurance purposes more or less likely than self or peer evaluation to result in the development of your practice?

Managerialism and professionalism

We saw in Chapter 19 that features of the teacher as professional such as the capacity to engage in reflection on practice, to develop knowledge, skills and understanding and other features including autonomy, a lengthy period of training, a strong community-service orientation and adherence to a code of values and ethics, could all be seen to be inhibited rather than encouraged in staff by the mission and culture of the institutions they work in – many of which, it is thought, since incorporation in the early 1990s, have become managerialist in nature. Randle and Brady (2000) consider the key features of this managerialism to include the primacy of student throughput in terms of retention and achievement which provides the key focus for quality assurance, loyalty to the organisation, lecturers as flexible facilitators and assessors, deployment of resources according to market demand and value for taxpayers' money and management by performance indicators and surveillance.

Perhaps the most significant change and challenge to teachers' professional autonomy in the sector over the past 20 years has been in the increase in and nature of their accountability. The most obvious manifestation of this accountability has been in the form of the public scrutiny of the quality of their teaching by inspection bodies, most notably Ofsted. In considering how inspection has affected everyday work practice, Lea et al. (2003) observe:

> There comes a time when lesson plans and schemes of work lose whatever initial interest they may have had and become a burdensome chore. However, knowing that inspectors will call forces all practitioners to make explicit whatever may have been implicit before, i.e. if it cannot be seen it cannot be inspected. And, to some extent, *saying what you do* now becomes a natural corollary of doing what you do.

The danger here, Lea goes on to argue, is that the most easily measurable aspects of teaching and learning will receive the greatest emphasis in practice: a learning outcome is easier to frame when conceived of as a pre-specified behavioural objective rather than as a complex cognitive process. And the implication could easily be that external inspection regimes make teachers risk averse and deter them from developing the complex repertoire of teaching skills necessary for their delivery of key aspects of the 14–19 reform agenda, such as personalised learning. Even more dangerous, Hayes would want to argue, is the apparent move in inspection frameworks towards more light touch self-evaluation and self-regulation. This is 'more demanding and intrusive as it requires the internalization of the standards of these government bodies and quangos' (Lea et al. 2003: 94).

A further manifestation of the changes to teacher's accountability lies in what is implied in the attempt to bring about a 'social market' philosophy in education:

> [A] sense that what lies at the root of accountability is a desire to see education responding efficiently to consumer demand. One of the effects of this has been an increasing sense that education is a commodity, just like any other, and the sense that the public should get what the public wants. Students thus become customers with needs, and it is the job of the educational organisation to satisfy those needs with appropriate 'products', i.e. courses, programmes and qualifications.
>
> *(Lea et al. 2003: 62)*

IN PRACTICE

Specify the people or bodies you feel accountable to as part of your professional role. Now examine the nature of that accountability: what impact does it have on your professional practice? Do the internal and external quality-assurance processes you experience, for example, affect how you do your job? How do the ways you and your students view their needs and expectations affect your relationship with them?

It may be that the traditional dichotomy between managers and professional teachers is now dated and no longer reflects the current and future roles those working in the sector are adopting. Briggs (2006), for example, talks of a 'New Professionalism' and refers to Simkins and Lumby's (2002) contention that

> managerialism and professionalism represent different understandings of how student needs should be met, and how quality of performance should be measured: in effect they are different interpretations of accountability. They claim that the values and interests of different groups can be shared, and that the 'them and us' distinction between other staff has become blurred.
>
> *(Briggs 2006: 10)*

This new professionalism is often characterised in terms of the importance of team-work and collaborative working. Although Lea admits to the appeal of the postmodern notion of teamwork, 'conjuring up images of democratic collaboration and quick responses to need' (2003: 71), he invokes Sennett's warning that

> most real forms of modern teamwork [are] composed of nothing more than 'demeaning superficiality', a façade that is at the heart of modern communications in work settings. The emphasis on teamwork, on getting things done, on sharing knowledge, hides the extent to which the concept has no depth – no long-term development of relationships, no overriding principles, no meaningful commitments – everything is short term and on the surface.

Jameson and McNay refer to the model of distributed leadership mentioned above and argue that a high level of emotional intelligence will be required of teaching staff if the model is to work effectively in practice. However, as we saw in Chapter 19, there are those who decry the recasting of teachers' roles as emotion workers (Hayes in Lea et al. 2003, Ecclestone and Hayes 2009):

> The trends towards a new ideology of managerialism and professionalism, based upon the therapeutic ethos may ultimately lead to the establishment of the *therapeutic college* . . . The students attending the therapeutic college will be impoverished human beings taught to seek not dangerous things like knowledge and truth but more communication experiences that build up their self-esteem and that of others.
>
> *(Hayes in Lea et al. 2003: 100)*

WHAT DO YOU THINK?

Where do you stand on the issue that post-14 education now concentrates too much on the emotional development of students and the emotional intelligence and competencies of their teachers in a form of 'edutherapy'? Chapters 3 and 4 of Ecclestone and Hayes (2009) will be most useful in addressing this question.

Working with people

In spite of the arguments considered above about the current and future role of teachers as 'edutherapists', many consider the development and use of softer or people skills to be of central importance for those managing and delivering the reformed 14–19 curriculum. And, setting aside the worries about how distributed leadership can operate effectively in hierarchical organisations, there are now more professional roles in the sector which require the demonstration of these soft skills than before. There are roles as coaches, mentors, staff developers, team leaders, section, department and faculty heads, assistant head teachers, course leaders and convenors. And these roles, as well as the inter- and intra-personal skills associated with them, will need to be deployed in increasingly complicated and broader organisational contexts: in consortia of schools and colleges delivering the diploma, in local authority wide subject organisations, for example. The interpersonal skills required in a leadership role are in many cases the same needed by those whose role is to participate in the teams, groups or sections they lead.

IN PRACTICE

In the table below, where 5 is high, self-assess your own emotional competencies as demonstrated in your professional practice

	Self-regulation	1 2 3 4 5
Self-control: Managing disruptive emotions and impulses	**People with this competence:** • Manage their impulsive feelings • Stay composed, positive and unflappable even in trying moments and handle distressing emotions well • Think clearly and stay focused under pressure	
Trustworthiness: Maintaining standards of honesty and integrity	**People with this competence:** • Act ethically and are above reproach • Build trust through their reliability and authenticity • Admit their own mistakes and confront unethical actions in others • Take tough, principled stands even if they are unpopular	
Conscientiousness: Taking responsibility for personal performance	**People with this competence:** • Meet commitments and keep promises • Hold themselves accountable for meeting their objectives • Are organised and careful in their work	
Adaptability: Flexibility in handling change	**People with this competence:** • Smoothly handle multiple demands, shifting priorities and rapid change • Adapt their responses and tactics to fit fluid circumstances • Are flexible in how they see events	

IN PRACTICE *CONTINUED*

	SELF-REGULATION	1 2 3 4 5
Innovativeness: Being comfortable with and open to novel ideas and new information	**People with this competence:** • Seek out fresh ideas from a wide variety of sources • Entertain original solutions to problems • Generate new ideas • Take fresh perspectives and risks in their thinking	

	SELF-MOTIVATION	
Achievement drive: Striving to improve or meet a standard of excellence	**People with this competence:** • Are results-oriented, with a high drive to meet their objectives and standards • Set challenging goals and take calculated risks • Pursue information to reduce uncertainty and find ways to do better • Learn how to improve their performance	
Commitment: Aligning with the goals of the group or organisation	**People with this competence:** • Readily make personal or group sacrifices to meet a larger organisational goal • Find a sense of purpose in the larger mission • Use the group's core values in making decisions and clarifying choices • Actively seek out opportunities to fulfil the group's mission	
Initiative: Readiness to act on opportunities	**People with this competence:** • Are ready to seize opportunities • Pursue goals beyond what's required or expected of them • Cut through red tape and bend the rules when necessary to get the job done • Mobilise others through unusual, enterprising efforts	

SELF-MOTIVATION	1 2 3 4 5

Optimism: Persistence in pursuing goals despite obstacles and setbacks

People with this competence:
- Persist in seeking goals despite obstacles and setbacks
- Operate from hope of success rather than fear of failure
- See setbacks as due to manageable circumstance rather than a personal flaw

SOCIAL AWARENESS	

Empathy: Sensing others' feelings and perspective, and taking an active interest in their concerns

People with this competence:
- Are attentive to emotional cues and listen well
- Show sensitivity and understand others' perspectives
- Help out based on understanding other people's needs and feelings

Service orientation: Anticipating, recognising, and meeting customers' needs

People with this competence:
- Understand customers' needs and match them to services or products
- Seek ways to increase customers' satisfaction and loyalty
- Gladly offer appropriate assistance
- Grasp a customer's perspective, acting as a trusted adviser

Developing others: Sensing what others need in order to develop, and bolstering their abilities

People with this competence:
- Acknowledge and reward people's strengths, accomplishments and development
- Offer useful feedback and identify people's needs for development
- Mentor, give timely coaching, and offer assignments that challenge and grow a person's skills

IN PRACTICE *CONTINUED*

	SOCIAL AWARENESS	1 2 3 4 5
Leveraging diversity: Cultivating opportunities through diverse people	**People with this competence:** • Respect and relate well to people from varied backgrounds • Understand diverse worldviews and are sensitive to group differences • See diversity as opportunity, creating an environment where diverse people can thrive • Challenge bias and intolerance	
Political awareness: Reading a group's emotional currents and power relationships	**People with this competence:** • Accurately read key power relationships • Detect crucial social networks • Understand the forces that shape views and actions of clients, customers or competitors • Accurately read situations and organisational and external realities	
	SOCIAL SKILLS	
Influence: Wielding effective tactics for persuasion	**People with this competence:** • Are skilled at persuasion • Fine-tune presentations to appeal to the listener • Use complex strategies like indirect influence to build consensus and support • Orchestrate dramatic events to effectively make a point	
Communication: Sending clear and convincing messages	**People with this competence:** • Are effective in give-and-take, registering emotional cues in attuning their message • Deal with difficult issues straightforwardly • Listen well, seek mutual understanding, and welcome sharing of information fully • Foster open communication and stay receptive to bad news as well as good	

SOCIAL SKILLS		1 2 3 4 5
Leadership: Inspiring and guiding groups and people	**People with this competence:** • Articulate and arouse enthusiasm for a shared vision and mission • Step forward to lead as needed, regardless of position • Guide the performance of others while holding them accountable • Lead by example	
Change catalyst: Initiating or managing change	**People with this competence:** • Recognise the need for change and remove barriers • Challenge the status quo to acknowledge the need for change • Champion the change and enlist others in its pursuit • Model the change expected of others	
Conflict management: Negotiating and resolving disagreements	**People with this competence:** • Handle difficult people and tense situations with diplomacy and tact • Spot potential conflict, bring disagreements into the open, and help de-escalate • Encourage debate and open discussion • Orchestrate win–win solutions	
Building bonds: Nurturing instrumental relationships	**People with this competence:** • Cultivate and maintain extensive informal networks • Seek out relationships that are mutually beneficial • Build rapport and keep others in the loop • Make and maintain personal friendships among work associates	

IN PRACTICE *CONTINUED*

	SOCIAL SKILLS	1 2 3 4 5
Collaboration and cooperation: Working with others toward shared goals	**People with this competence:** • Balance a focus on task with attention to relationships • Collaborate, sharing plans, information and resources • Promote a friendly, cooperative climate • Spot and nurture opportunities for collaboration	
Team capabilities: Creating group synergy in pursuing collective goals	**People with this competence:** • Model team qualities like respect, helpfulness and cooperation • Draw all members into active and enthusiastic participation • Build team identity, *esprit de corps* and commitment • Protect the group and its reputation; share credit	

(*Source*: adapted from **www.elconsortium.org/reports/emotional_competence_framework.html**)

WHAT DO YOU THINK?

Having assessed your individual emotional competences using the framework above, consider with a colleague which competences are relevant to your roles and which might be less so.

IN PRACTICE

Having identified above which competencies are relevant to your practice, how might you go about developing those competencies you felt less confident about? Mortiboys's *Teaching With Emotional Intelligence* would be helpful here.

Managing the curriculum

For those working to implement the 14–19 reforms, the key challenges in delivering and managing the new curriculum have been, firstly, the requirement for staff and institutions to work collaboratively; secondly, the associated need for common timetabling; thirdly the increased need for the information, advice and guidance and finally, the engagement of employers.

RESEARCH FOCUS

A review of good practice in 14–19 collaborative working identified the following features:

What works: Building on existing partnerships

- Linking with existing initiatives to support and diversify local developments
- Linking with other partnerships to build on existing good practice and promote continuity in local delivery
- Networking with local support services, such as Connexions, to ensure a co-ordinated approach
- Learning from the management arrangements of previous partnerships
- Encouraging established partnerships to support new activity

What works: Building on existing provision

- Conferences, seminars and networking activities initially to establish collaboration and identify existing good practice
- Ensuring the commitment of key local players such as the LEA, LSC, Further Education (FE) college(s) and Local Learning Partnership
- Linking with other initiatives, such as the IFP and the Aim Higher Programme
- Using the outputs of previous partnership work as the starting point for Pathfinder work
- Identifying outputs and actions

What works: Identifying appropriate and relevant partners

- Consulting a variety of sources to identify relevant partners
- Developing provisional aims and objectives that support existing local priorities
- Approaching key local players and fund holders (such as the LEA and EBP) and 'selling' the value of activity
- Gaining buy-in from a cross-section of local providers, including schools, colleges and training providers
- Securing employer interest to help develop the activity focus and finalise aims and objectives

RESEARCH FOCUS: *CONTINUED*

What works: Agreeing the 'right' management structure

- Deciding the scope and size of the partnership. (See the year two national evaluation report for detailed information on management structures. This can be accessed on the good practice section of the 14–19 web site at **www.dfes.gov.uk/14-19**.)
- Determining if working groups should be established within larger partnerships to share responsibility
- Confirming the capacity and interest of each partner to help manage the project
- Agreeing how formal management arrangements should be
- Securing the commitment of local key players to partnership activity

What works: Strategic management

- Commitment from senior individuals from all partner organisations
- Strong local leadership, particularly at the outset to encourage project development
- Agreeing a common 'vision' and purpose for the project
- Identifying outputs and actions
- Allowing sufficient time to develop processes and practice
- Meetings at key milestones
- Establishing health and safety protocols to safeguard learning outside the school environment
- Embracing change management and devolving responsibility to delivery agents as the partnership matures
- Ensuring young people are represented in strategic management decisions

What works: Operational management

- Regular meetings and consistent attendance
- Clear checklists and agreement on responsibilities
- A central co-ordinating role: Pathfinder co-ordinators have been critical as enablers of, and catalysts for, change
- Staff development time
- Identifying outputs and actions
- Capitalising on different organisations' strengths
- Establishing a common curriculum
- Developing transferable materials for use across the Pathfinder to ensure learning quality
- Consulting young people to help design, trial and evaluate activities

(*Manual of Good Practice from 14–19 Pathfinders* (Department for Education and Skills 2005), Crown Copyright material is reproduced under the terms of the Click-Use Licence.)

IN PRACTICE

Carry out an audit of your own institution's collaborative activity, considering the following questions:

What are the strengths of existing practices?
How were partners selected for collaboration?
How is the partnership managed strategically?
How is the partnership managed operationally?
What barriers were there to partnership working? Have they been successfully overcome?

Source: Pearson Education Ltd. Ian Wedgewood

Photo 20.2
Conferences, seminars and workshops are important for developing collaborative activity

One of the most challenging factors for effective consortium working, especially for the delivery of the diploma, is the establishment of common timetabling. Below is a case study of how one consortium managed this task.

CASE STUDY

Stevenage 14–19 Partnership

What was the issue?

The Stevenage 14–19 Partnership consists of the town's six community schools – Barclay, Barnwell, Heathcote, Marriotts, Nobel and Thomas Alleyne, together with North Hertfordshire College (NHC). Increasingly, curriculum links with the town's special schools are also being formed.

It was founded in 2003 out of three previous consortia, each of which consisted of two schools. At the time NHC had a loose link with each consortia with learners able to join their courses, should timetables permit. The six Headteachers and the College Principal held a series of discussions, determined to improve choice for students. In short, although learners were able to access courses across the town, in theory barriers effectively limited both course choice and movement.

What were the barriers?

The principal barriers were organisational arrangements and timetabling. The schools at that time were working to different lesson patterns, some held five lessons each day, some held six; the timings of these lessons varied from 45 minutes to 60 minutes; the length and timing of the midday break was not consistent; and the start and finish times of the schools were also different. Further, the College ran its own timetable with three sessions per day, rather than the two run by the schools.

Additionally, each of the three consortia devised their own offer independently, with final decisions as to what courses would run sometimes being made very late in the summer term.

Finally, although each Headteacher was committed to partnership and left meetings positively, daily organisational tasks took attention away from developing this further.

What was the solution?

The solution was to appoint someone to co-ordinate this activity. Someone who had, by dint of their experience, both the authority and personal attributes to enable the various stakeholders reach the compromises needed if we were going to make progress. We decided to pitch this post at Head level to get the necessary skill set and to ensure they worked directly to the Heads and Principal. We were determined to arrive at a locally determined solution. The six schools and the College jointly committed to funding his salary, and that of a Personal Assistant, for three years. We were, though, successful in applying for 14–19 Pathfinder status and that largely met our costs. Since Pathfinder funding ended in August 2005, we have continued to encourage the Director to undertake other consultancy work and this, too, has provided funding for the Partnership's activities.

The person chosen was, at the time, a Head from one of the six schools. He knew the local scene very well and held the confidence of fellow Heads. Further, he was able to work with senior staff at the College at a common level to seek a common solution. Even then it was not an easy birth. Apart from the Heads and Principal, we had to carry the governors and staff from each participating institution. More importantly, we had to carry the parents and learners with us also. We needed to move from putting institutional interests first, to putting the needs of our learners first. Many months of discussions took place, with evolution being the key process, not revolution. In all, it took us two years to get to where we are now.

What was the outcome?

From 2005–06, each school has run five lessons a week, timetabled on a fortnightly basis; all start within five minutes of each other; and all have four lessons in the morning with one lesson and tutor time in the afternoon. The College has also shifted its curriculum delivery to match this pattern.

The Post-16 timetable is organised across five columns for both Level Two and Level Three courses, each column filling up five hours of teaching a week. An AS course, for example, fits into one column; an Applied AS or BTEC Diploma runs in two columns. All the columns are timetabled at the same time in every centre across the town, including the College. Learners choose from 14 L2 and 45 L3 courses and are able to follow L2, L3, or L2/3 programmes. This gives some 3500 combinations.

Each column takes up a long morning (all schools and colleges running four lessons each morning) and a short afternoon session (i.e. one lesson) on another day, allowing learners to move to another centre without missing any lessons in other subjects. Learners have the same subjects in a morning session and a different one in the afternoon. One of the afternoon sessions is used for enrichment activities, additional short courses and other events in the seven home centres; it is also a time when learners from the different centres can join up for special town-wide sessions and activities. Learners go directly to their first course each day, further reducing travel costs, and make their own way home – irrespective of venue – at the end of the lesson each day.

Timetabling this way means learners only have to move sites during the lunchbreak when transport is laid on for them.

The Partnership is currently running one KS4 common day to allow vocational course delivery across the town. We will also be offering new Diplomas in all five lines of learning from September 2008, and will then run two KS4 common days each week to enable this.

Common reporting formats and timings exist for Post-16 courses, and curriculum-related field visits are jointly planned at senior level. We also co-ordinate our school closures (term start and end dates, half-term dates, training days, etc.) to a large extent, liaising with local primary schools to provide a more coherent pattern for students and families. NHC, too, works as closely to this schedule, although they do not take half-term breaks. Learners thus gain an extra teaching week if they attend this centre.

Finally, from September 2007 we are piloting a common, SIMS-based, attendance and assessment system for learners across the Partnership.

IN PRACTICE

What were the key features of the common timetabling arrangements which enabled effective delivery of teaching and learning for the Stevenage consortium? Investigate any collaborative provision your own institution is involved in or that of institutions in your area. What solutions did it or they adopt in establishing common timetabling?

IN PRACTICE

Below is advice given by DCSF to Gateway 3 diploma applicants (those intending to start in September 2010 and 2011) in relation to the Information, Advice and Guidance arrangements for their consortia. Investigate the IAG arrangements in place for 14–19-year-olds in your institution or area and profile them using the questions to consider below.

EXPECTATION	QUESTIONS TO CONSIDER
A2.1 Ensuring delivery of high quality, comprehensive and impartial IAG	
The consortium has reviewed its provision against the requirements set out in the Quality Standards and has a detailed implementation plan to make good any weaknesses and drive continuous improvement.	What are the strengths and weaknesses of current IAG provision across the consortium area when compared to the requirements of the Quality Standards? Have you a detailed plan for building on these strengths and correcting weaknesses? By what date do you expect fully to meet the Quality Standards? How will performance against the standards be monitored, reviewed and evaluated? How are young people and parents/carers to be involved in this process?
IAG is impartial and learner led.	Impartial IAG on learning and career options may result in young people making decisions that are contrary to the best commercial interests of their school/college. What makes you confident that the learners' needs will take precedence over all institutional interests?
The consortium sets out local plans for innovative activities ensuring the impartial provision of information about careers and learning opportunities across the consortium area that will develop the understanding of both young people and their parents/carers.	Are you confident that all the people in the consortium who are providing IAG about learning and careers options have a good understanding of the full range of progression options available to young people and are able to provide advice on the full range of options? How will you review the IAG provided on learning/careers issues to ensure that it has been truly impartial?

EXPECTATION	QUESTIONS TO CONSIDER
The strength of local collaboration can be demonstrated through active partnership arrangements and evidence of good practice.	How do you demonstrate that all IAG providers understand their roles and responsibilities?
Clear plans are in place for engaging leaders and managers across the consortium to take forward your IAG strategy.	How will you identify strengths, weaknesses and actions for improvement?
	How will you engage leaders and managers in the IAG agenda and ensure it remains high on their list of priorities?
Young people and their parents and carers are involved in the design, delivery and evaluation of IAG services.	How are young people and their parents and carers involved in the design, delivery and evaluation of the service?
	How do you ensure that the young people and their parents and carers who are involved in this process reflect the make-up of their communities?
Details of professionally qualified advisers (who can provide impartial, confidential advice and guidance about careers) are accessible.	Are the advisers easily accessible to young people? • Where are they based? • Are they from a diverse range of backgrounds? • Have they the relevant qualifications?

A2.2 Raising aspirations and demonstrating progression routes, with clear links to local employers and Higher Education (HE)

IAG raises the aspirations of young people.	How does the consortium intend to raise the aspirations of young people?
Young people will be provided with up-to-date IAG on local, regional and national labour markets, in particular around Diplomas, apprenticeships and other learning options.	Where will you get this information from? How will you keep it up-to-date?
	How will you convey it in a way that's meaningful for the young person?

IN PRACTICE *CONTINUED*

EXPECTATION	QUESTIONS TO CONSIDER
Impartial IAG around HE opportunities, especially Diploma routes in, is delivered and understood by young people and their parents.	Are you involved with your local university? Are you familiar with the HE admission procedure and the universities' own admission policies? Are you aware of the financial support available to those wishing to enter HE?
Diplomas are available to all young people in the consortium area.	How will they access provision if it's only available through a limited number of institutions?
IAG will help young people challenge stereotypes, especially around race and gender.	How does the consortium intend to challenge stereotypes? How will this be managed across different cultures? What support is available to the young person to help them manage parental and peer pressure? How will success be measured?
Additional help will be provided to young people with special educational needs.	What form will this additional help take? Is information provided in a variety of formats? Are effective monitoring systems in place to ensure all young people are accessing the service? Do you know who is carrying out S140 assessments* in your consortium area now responsibility has transferred to local authorities?
Consortia will work with parents and carers to help them support their children effectively and engage them in raising their child'(ren)'s aspirations.	How will you engage all parents and carers? How will you ensure they are aware of all the options open to their child? If necessary, how will you raise the parent/carer's aspirations for their child?

EXPECTATION	QUESTIONS TO CONSIDER
Every young person will have access to quality experiential learning and mentoring which challenges low expectations and self-confidence.	Where will the experiential learning take place and where will the mentors be drawn from?
	How will you ensure the mentors are the right people to challenge low expectations and self-confidence?
	What practical actions will be taken to ensure young people widen their horizons and conditions?
	Will these arrangements be applied across the consortium area? How will their success be reviewed?

*Section 140 of the Learning and Skills Act 2000 places statutory responsibility on the Secretary of State (SoS) for the assessment of young people with learning difficulties from the final year of compulsory education up to age 24 years, when they are undertaking or believed likely to undertake post-16 education or training or higher education.

The 14–19 reforms rely heavily on the capacity of providers to engage employers in a variety of ways so that the work-related and work-based applied learning dimension which is at the centre of the reforms can be fully realised. Of course, many schools, colleges and local authorities have extensive relationships with employers already, and consortia have found that a coordinated, well-managed approach to employers is essential to fostering productive links. One consortium offered employers a menu of opportunities:

Diploma delivery requires:

- Visits for students to the company
- Donation of products and resources made in South Yorkshire
- Support of students in school
- Setting projects
- Feeding back on design ideas
- Mentoring
- Work experience placements
- Teacher placements
- Long-term relationship with schools in the area

– and specified that employers valued:

- the opportunity to promote Engineering to young people
- interaction with schools
- recruitment advantages

- the chance to influence which skills young people acquire (directly addressing the complaint that young people are leaving schools without the skills for employment).

http://www.dcsf.gov.uk/14-19/index.cfm?go=site.CaseStudiesDetailConsortia
&sid=53&pid=422&ctype=TEXT&ptype=Single&csid=126

Other elements of employer engagement have been:

- A range of events involving employers such as launches, seminars, conferences
- Establishing a consortium data base of work-experience opportunities
- A consortium approach to work-experience placements with a single point of contact
- A diploma website, allowing employers, teachers parents and students an opportunity to network
- A strategic network of public and private sector employers in one learning line/occupational area
- Student/teacher visits to employers videoed for the benefit of other students/teachers
- Teacher secondments to employers
- Technological projects
- Design competitions
- Recruitment of employer diploma champions
- Involvement of employers in developing learning materials.

IN PRACTICE

Investigate the extent to which your institution is engaged with employers. Which of the elements above are features of your relationship with them?

SUMMARY

Both formal and collegial models of education management have strengths and weaknesses when applied to educational institutions. Many FE colleges have developed as managerialist institutions following incorporation in the early 1990s and this can militate against distributed leadership, particularly if their organisational structure is hierarchical. This can also hinder FE teachers operating as autonomous professionals, as can their increased accountability in the form of public scrutiny by inspection bodies. The development of softer people skills, or emotional intelligence, is considered by many to be central to the current and future role of teachers. For those working to implement the 14–19 reforms, the key challenges in delivering and managing the new curriculum have been, firstly, the requirement for staff and institutions to work collaboratively; secondly, the associated need for common timetabling; thirdly, the increased need for the information, advice and guidance and, finally, the engagement of employers.

Find out more

Continuum's *The Essential FE Toolkit Series* contains a range of titles which will be of interest to all teachers, particularly those with leadership and management responsibilities. They deal with such issues as policy, managing higher education, governance, financial management and race equality. They are available at: **www.continuumbooks.com/authors/details.aspx? AuthorId=152276&BookId=134474&SubjectId= 940&Subject2Id=1204**.

Mortiboys, A. (2005) *Teaching with Emotional Intelligence.*
Mortiboys addresses teachers' relationships with their learners, their need to function in an emotional environment, effective listening, reading and responding to the feelings of individuals and groups, the development of self-awareness, recognising own prejudices and preferences, improving non-verbal communication and acknowledging and handling feelings. For a critical analysis of the increasing role of emotion and feelings in education, as 'edutherapy', see:

Ecclestone, K. and Hayes, D. (2009) *The Dangerous Rise of Therapeutic Education.*
'The principal problem addressed by this book is the difficulty contemporary society has in giving meaning to education. A sense of disorientation about the purpose of education coincides with a confusion about what society ought to expect of its children. The downsizing of children's potential has been one of the outcomes of this confusion. Children are now systematically represented as 'vulnerable' and 'at risk'. Many educators believe that children are so vulnerable that the management of their emotions constitutes one of the principal functions of their school. Although the project of emotional education is well intended, its main outcome is to disempower young people. The therapeutic turn in education also distracts schools from providing a genuine intellectual challenge to young people.'

(2009: vii)

Bibliography

Adair, J. (2003) *Effective Strategic Leadership*, London: Pan Macmillan.

Bennett, N., Crawford, M. and Riches, C. (eds) (1992) *Managing Change in Education*, London: Paul Chapman.

Bennis, W. G. (1989) *On Becoming A Leader*, London: Random House.

Briggs, A. (2006) *Middle Management in FE*, London: Continuum.

Bush, T. (1995) *Theories of Educational Management*, London: Paul Chapman.

Collins, D. (2006) *A Survival Guide for College Managers and Leaders*, London: Continuum.

DfES (2005) *Manual of Good Practice from 14–19 Pathfinders*, London: DfES.

Ecclestone, K. and Hayes, D. (2009) *The Dangerous Rise of Therapeutic Education*, Abingdon: Routledge.

Handy, C. (1976) *Understanding Organisations*, London: Penguin.

Jameson, J. and McNay, I. (2007) *Ultimate FE Leadership and Management*, London: Continuum.

Law, S. and Glover, D. (2000) *Educational Leadership and Learning*, Buckingham: Open University Press.

Lea, J. et al. (2003) *Working in Post-Compulsory Education*, Maidenhead: Open University Press/McGraw-Hill Education.

Mortiboys, A. (2005) *Teaching with Emotional Intelligence*, Abingdon: Routledge.

Randle, K. and Brady, N. (2000) Managerialism and professionalism in the Cinderella service, in Hall, L. and Marsh, K. *Professionals, Policies and Values*, London: Greenwich University Press.

Simkins, T. and Lumby, T. (2002) Researching leadership and management, *Research in Post-Compulsory Education*, 1(1), March 2002.

Wallace, S. and Gravells, J. (2007) *A to Z for Every Manager in FE*, London: Continuum.

Glossary

Academy: a school that is directly funded by central government. It does not come under the control of local government. It has a far greater degree of autonomy and is not bound by the National Curriculum

Accommodators: according to Kolb, those with a learning style which involves intuition, risk-taking and adapting to rapidly changing circumstances

Acquisition: learning through acquisition is to take in knowledge and understanding in a detached way rather than through participation

Action research: form of investigation enabling a self-reflective process

Andragogy: 'The art and science of helping adults learn' (Knowles)

Applied learning: learning through doing in practical or vocational contexts involving interaction with other learners through group work

Apprenticeship: learning scheme enabling learner to learn 'on the job' and gain a qualification

Article: one of a series of obligations in a treaty by those states choosing to be bound under that treaty (sometimes referred to as a provision)

Assessment for learning: 'the process of seeking and interpreting evidence for use by learners and their teachers to decide where the learners are in their learning, where they need to go and how best to get there' (Assessment Reform Group)

Assimilators: Kolb's term for those learners who reason inductively, create theoretical models and assimilate diverse ideas into an integrated explanation

Autonomous: able to make decisions and implement these decisions independently

Cambridge Pre-U: academic alternative to A-level qualification aimed at 16–19-year-old students preparing for higher education entrance

Codify: to organise and sort principles, agreements, expectations or norms into formal systems

Connectivity: the capacity to transfer acquired skills and understanding from one learning situation to another

Connexions: an advisory service for 13–19-year-olds, organised on a local basis, which can give young people information, advice and practical help with a range of issues which might be affecting them at school, college, work or in their personal or family life

Convergers: according to Kolb, those who learn through problem-solving, decision-making and the practical application of ideas

Counselling: support provided by a professional person, which allows you to explore and understand your own problems and feelings in a non-judgmental manner. This process facilitates greater autonomy and confidence, allowing people to make their own choices and change

Deep learning: learning which leads to making sense of or abstracting meaning, interpreting to understand reality and changing as a person

Diagnostic assessment: assessment which aims to determine a learner's potential and likely learning needs

Differentiation: A teaching and learning approach enabling the teacher to adapt specific strategies to individuals or groups to enhance learning. This can be done via learning activities or assessment

Discourse: a lengthy and detailed discussion (verbal or written) of a topic

Discovery methods: teaching methods which encourage the learners to find out for themselves

Distributed leadership and management: the view that both management and leadership are functions of those working at every level in the organisation

Divergers: learners who, according to Kolb, rely on imaginative ability and awareness of meaning and values

Driver: an influential force, something that provides impetus or motivation

Egocentricism: interested in the self, lack of consideration or caring about others

Egotistical: concerned only with oneself

Emotional competence: highly developed skills of self-regulation, self-motivation, social awareness and social skills

Emotive: a topic that has a strong impact on your own emotions, or that of others. Often used to impose views through use of 'tugging at the heart strings'

Entry to employment: learning scheme designed for 16–18-year-old students to progress on to employment

Evaluative methods: teaching methods which encourage students to learn through making judgements about events, objects, created artifacts

Experiential learning: active learning which occurs in real or simulated environments

Extended project: free standing or as part of the Diploma qualification enabling students to research a specific focus of interest

Extrinsic: it is valued because of its consequences, for example a qualification that will further your career

Feedback: a commentary on the learning or progress of a pupil

Focus group: interactive research activity aiming at gathering views and opinion about a specific issue

Formal models of educational management: these assume that organisations are hierarchical systems in which managers use rational means to purse agreed goals (Bush)

Formal operational stage: (Piaget) a stage of an individual's cognitive development as they develop the ability to think about abstract concepts and 'what ifs'

Formative assessment: assessment which aims to give feedback to learners on their progress

Formative: information, gathered from assessment, that is used to shape the future learning programme of a pupil or group of learners

Generic learning skills: functional skills in English, ICT and Maths, six transferable personal, learning and thinking skills (PLTS) in independent enquiry, creative thinking, reflective learning, teamworking, self-managing and effective participation, a Diploma project and skills gained through work experience

Green Paper: A government publication that details specific issues, and possible courses of action in terms of policy

Hegemony: the overt and covert influence and power of the ruling political party, individual or group in contributing to unquestioned or even challenged societal norms

Hermeneutic view of teacher education as a practical science: a view which conceives of the teacher developing their practice through action research as well as reflection

High stakes testing: a test that has important consequences for the person being tested as in progression or entry to employment routes such as a professional qualification, or for a group or organisation, such as the consequences of a school being named and shamed for having lower than average SAT results

Ideology: an organised system of beliefs and ideas which form the basis of a social, economic, or political philosophy or curriculum

Inclusion: ensuring through policy and practice that schools and colleges allow for and celebrate difference in students and pupils rather than demanding uniformity from them

Increased Flexibility Programme: IFP is a major national programme that allows school learners aged 14–16 to develop practical work-related skills outside school

Independent learning: centres upon the move in ownership and responsibility for learning from the teacher to the student or pupil. It covers the learning to learn process and includes motivation, understanding and skills

Individual learning plan: strategy enabling students to consider and review strengths and weaknesses

Infant determinism: the view that early childhood experiences have irreversible, lifelong effects

Informal models of educational management: these emphasise that power and decision-making should be shared among some or all members of the organisation (Bush)

Initial assessment: assessment of a student's ability prior to and following admission to a programme to gauge their suitability for it

International Baccalaureate Diploma Programme: international qualification aiming at 16–19-year-old students preparing for Higher Education entrance

Intrinsic: is valued as good by or in itself

Jesuit: an influential Roman Catholic religious order engaged in missionary and educational work

Judgement: to form an opinion, usually perceived as authorative, stating something believed or asserted

Labelling: how the self-concept and thus behaviour of individuals may be shaped or determined by the labels others apply to them. This can lead to self-fulfilling prophecy. In teaching, evidence shows that pupils in lower ability classes are taught to a low ability and are unlikely to move up as the teachers' expectations of pupils' ability is also shaped by the label and is thus low

Local area agreement: sets out the priorities for a local area agreed between central government, local authority and its key partners

Magnum opus: from the Latin 'great work', normally referring to the best, or most known or influential work of an author, artist or composer

Managerialism: the domination of institutions by a market ethos: managers through regular surveillance monitor whether performance indicators are being met and quality is assessed on the basis of inputs and outcomes

Marshall Plan: officially the European Recovery Programme, a support package offered by the US to European countries following the Second World War between 1947 and 1951

Maturation: naturally occurring changes that are genetically programmed

Meritocracy: a social system which provides opportunities for all according to ability rather than social standing or wealth

Moral judgement: a view of what is right or wrong based on your own feelings or conscience, as opposed to the law, for example. Often emotive

Mores: the customs and habitual practices that a group of people accept and follow, especially as they reflect moral standards, within a society at a given time in the development of that society

Multidirectionality: the theory that some aspects of intelligence increase as others decline in adulthood

Myelination: the increase of fatty white matter which coats the axons of nerve cells and increases the efficiency and accuracy of communication or messages between the brain's circuitry

Narcissism: excessive self-centredness

Neurons: nerve cells that store and send information

Ontogeny: (in this case) the development of behaviour – patterns and responses throughout stages of development

Participatory methods: teaching methods which encourage active involvement on the part of students

Pedagogy: 'The art and science of teaching children' (Knowles)

Peer learning: collaborative learning

Personalised learning: the use of assessment for learning, engaging and stretching learners, providing breadth of study, personal relevance and flexible learning pathways through the education system in institutions which are creatively organised

Plasticity (of the brain): the way the brain is able to change and adapt according to environmental demands and stimuli

Presentation methods: teaching methods which are teacher-centred such as the lecture or demonstration

Professionalism: having the capacity to engage in reflection on practice, to develop knowledge, skills and understanding, working autonomously, having had a lengthy period of training and with a strong community service orientation and adherence to a code of values and ethics

Progression data: data showing students' achievement and progression, e.g. school report or ILP

Protective factors: those factors that help reduce adverse outcomes for young people despite their unfavourable situations or experiences

Pruning: the brain's natural system for disregarding synapses and connections that are unused

Psychosocial: combination of psychological and social factors affecting development (particularly that of mental health) – psychological relating to the mind, and social – the external environment and relationships. The inclusion of 'bio' relates to life as in 'biological' when theories relate to the **Biopsychosocial stage** – a period of development

Qualitative research: method of enquiry aimed at gathering views and perspectives

Quantitative research: methods of enquiry aiming at getting empirical data

Questionnaire: research tool aiming at gathering statistical or opinion information

Rationalist view of teacher education: a view of the teacher as a rational-autonomous professional whose practice is derived from a theoretical understanding of educational values and principles

Record of achievement: document recording progress made and achievement as part of a learning programme

Reflection-in-action: Schön's term for our ability to adjust, change our action or performance on the spot as we go along

School Action: a means of identifying a pupil with SEN who requires additional intervention and support from the school to support a young person who is not making adequate progress despite appropriate differentiation and use of wider school strategies

School Action Plus: additional support from specialist and other professionals is likely to be required when a pupil has been on School Action but has not made adequate progress

Self-efficacy: the belief in oneself to effect change and have an impact

Self-fulfilling prophecy: causing something to happen by believing it to be true, thus unconsciously changing our behaviour or expectations to make it true. For example, if a pupil is labelled 'low ability', they will not try as it is 'too hard'; to compound this the teacher will not set more difficult work and challenge the pupil as they also believe it to be 'too hard'. Also known as the Pygmalion effect

SENCO: special educational needs coordinator – takes responsibility for the onward referral of pupils to the appropriate support such as an educational psychologist

Sentient: able to feel, perceive and be aware

Situated learning: learning which takes place in the context of real-life practice such as in a workplace, trade or profession through authentic, i.e. purposeful and meaningful, tasks

Skype: software application for making free voice calls between Skype users via the internet, instant messaging, file transfer, and videoconferencing.

Social learning theory: learning theory which considers that people learn behaviour through the observation of other people's behaviours

'Social market' view of teacher education: a competency or output model of teacher education

Special educational needs: Children or young people who have learning difficulties or disabilities that make it harder for them to learn than most children of the same age. These children may need extra or different help from that given to other children of the same age

Statement of special educational needs: a statement which sets out a child's needs and the help they should have following assessment by a Local Authority educational psychologist

Streaming: placing students according to ability within a defined year group

Student-centred: the focus is on the whole child

Student/child centred learning: student-centred learning requires students to be active, responsible participants in their own learning and puts their needs first

Subjective: the personal opinions or beliefs of an individual formed through own experiences

Summative assessment: assessment which comes at the end of a course of study, normally as a formal procedure

Surface learning: learning which is based on increasing knowledge, memorising or storing information and acquiring facts

Synapses: a tiny gap between the neurons – chemical messages 'jump' and are transmitted across these gaps

Teacher-researcher: teacher undertaking research – usually focused on own teaching and learning context

The minimum core: in the lifelong learning sector, teachers' knowledge and understanding relating to literacy, language, numeracy and ICT

Tutorial: individual teacher–learner session enabling the discussion of a specific point of learning or issue

Validity: the measure of assessment is justifiable and sound, that is, *valid*

Value: the intrinsic worth of 'something'; this differs from a simple monetary cost

Vocationalism: the stressing of vocational training in education

White Paper: finalised government paper announcing policy to be implemented

Index

Page numbers in *italics* denotes a figure/table